Portraits of Pioneers
in Psychology

VOLUME IV

Portraits of Pioneers
in Psychology

VOLUME IV

Edited by

Gregory A. Kimble

Michael Wertheimer

AMERICAN PSYCHOLOGICAL ASSOCIATION
Washington, DC

LAWRENCE ERLBAUM ASSOCIATES, PUBLISHERS
Mahwah, New Jersey

Published by
American Psychological Association
750 First Street, NE
Washington, DC 20002

Lawrence Erlbaum Associates, Inc., Publishers
10 Industrial Avenue
Mahwah, NJ 07430

Typeset in Times by Matrix Publishing Services, York, PA

Printer: Port City Press, Inc., Baltimore, MD

Project Manager: Debbie K. Hardin, Charlottesville, VA

Library of Congress Cataloging-in-Publication Data

Portraits of pioneers in psychology/ edited by Gregory
  A. Kimble and Michael Wertheimer
    p. cm.
    "Sponsored by the Division of General Psychology,
  American Psychological Association."
    Includes bibliographical references and index.
    ISBN 1-55798-712-2. ISBN 1-55798-713-0 (pbk.)
    1. Psychologists - Biography.   2. Psychology -
  History.   I. Kimble, Gregory A.   II. Wertheimer,
  Michael.   III. American Psychological Association.
  Division of General Psychology.
    BF109.A1P67   1991
    150'.92'2—dc20
  [B]   91-7226
                                             CIP

Portraits of Pioneers in Psychology: Volume IV has been published under the following ISBNs:
    APA: 1-55798-712-2
         1-55798-713-0 (pbk.)
    LEA: 0-8058-3853-8
         0-8058-3854-6 (pbk.)

British Cataloguing-in-Publication Data
A CIP record is available from the British Library.

Printed in the United States of America
First edition

Contents

Preface

The chapters in this book, like those in the previous three volumes in this series, offer glimpses into the personal and scholarly and professional lives of some of the giants in the history of psychology. They will be of interest to psychologists and scholars in related fields in general and to students and teachers in courses in the history of psychology in particular. Taken together, these four volumes contain materials that will help make the pioneers in various subfields of psychology and the other life sciences come alive. The following paragraphs show how the chapters in *Pioneers I, II, III,* and *IV* relate to a number of important topics in these fields. Teachers may wish to assign relevant chapters in the four volumes as supplementary readings. The selection is somewhat arbitrary because every chapter covers more than the indicated subject matter and some materials in other chapters are (less directly) relevant to these topics.

Philosophical, Methodological, and Statistical Foundations: Pioneers I: Galton, Tryon. *Pioneers II:* Fechner, Rhine. *Pioneers III:* Binet, Ebbinghaus, Hickok, Thurstone. *Pioneers IV:* Eysenck, Hathaway, Heider, Koch, Müller, Schneirla, Spearman, Terman, Upham.

Schools and Systems: Pioneers I: Carr, Freud, Heidbreder, Hull, Jung, Köhler, Pavlov, Titchener, Tolman, Watson, Wertheimer. *Pioneers II:* Dewey, Guthrie, Sechenov. *Pioneers III:* Duncker, Hickok, Lewin, Piaget, Rogers, Skinner, Spence, Wundt. *Pioneers IV:* Heider, Horney, Müller, Stumpf, Upham.

Biological/Genetic/Evolutionary/Physiological Psychology: Pioneers I: Galton, Hunter, Lashley, Pavlov, Tryon. *Pioneers II:* Blatz, Burks, Graham, Hebb, Schiller, Yerkes. *Pioneers III:* Darwin, Festinger, Krech, Kuo, McGraw, Nissen. *Pioneers IV:* Beach, Helmholtz, Schneirla, Sperry.

Sensation and Perception: Pioneers I: Köhler, Wertheimer. *Pioneers II:* Fechner, Gibson, Graham, Hebb, Rhine. *Pioneers III:* Duncker, Festinger, Piaget, Wundt. *Pioneers IV:* Heider, Helmholtz, Müller, Sperry, Stumpf.

Animal Behavior: Pioneers I: Hull, Hunter, Köhler, Lashley, Pavlov, Thorndike, Watson. *Pioneers II:* Schiller, Yerkes. *Pioneers III:* Darwin, Kuo, Nissen. *Pioneers IV:* Beach, Schneirla, Sperry.

Learning and Conditioning: Pioneers I: Calkins, Hull, Hunter, Köhler, Lashley, Pavlov, Thorndike, Tolman. *Pioneers II:* Blatz, Guthrie, Hebb, Sechenov. *Pioneers III:* Duncker, Ebbinghaus, Krech, Skinner, Spence, Underwood. *Pioneers IV:* Bartlett, Beach, Hovland, Müller, Schneirla.

Cognitive Psychology: Pioneers I: Calkins, Köhler, Lashley, Tolman, Wertheimer. *Pioneers II:* Dewey, Stern. *Pioneers III:* Duncker, Ebbinghaus, Hickok, Piaget, Underwood, Wundt. *Pioneers IV:* Bartlett, Heider, Müller, Stumpf, Terman.

Motivation and Emotion: Pioneers I: Freud, Hull, James, Jung, Sullivan, Tolman. *Pioneers II:* Milgram, Schiller, Tomkins, Yerkes. *Pioneers III:* Erickson, Festinger, Lewin, Spence. *Pioneers IV:* Beach, Heider, Horney.

Developmental Psychology: Pioneers I: Freud, Leta Hollingworth, Puffer, Watson. *Pioneers II:* Blatz, Doll, Murchison, Witmer. *Pioneers III:* Binet, McGraw, Piaget. *Pioneers IV:* Horney, Schneirla, Terman.

Individual Differences: Pioneers I: Galton, Leta Hollingworth, Pavlov, Tryon. *Pioneers II:* Burks, Doll, Milgram, Stern. *Pioneers III:* Allport, Binet, Thurstone. *Pioneers IV:* Eysenck, Hathaway, Horney, Spearman, Terman.

Personality: Pioneers I: Calkins, Freud, Jung. *Pioneers II:* Tomkins. *Pioneers III:* Erickson, Rogers, Thurstone. *Pioneers IV:* Eysenck, Hathaway, Horney.

Applied Psychology: Pioneers I: Jastrow, Puffer, Titchener, Watson. *Pioneers II:* Dix, Gilbreth, Harry Hollingworth. *Pioneers III:* Skinner, Thurstone. *Pioneers IV:* Bartlett, Hathaway, Münsterberg.

Psychopathology and Clinical Psychology: Pioneers I: Freud, Leta Hollingworth, Jastrow, Jung, Sullivan. *Pioneers II:* Dix, Doll, Tomkins, Witmer. *Pioneers III:* Binet, Duncker, Erickson, Rogers. *Pioneers IV:* Eysenck, Hathaway, Horney.

Social Psychology: Pioneers I: Puffer. *Pioneers II:* Dix, Milgram, Murchison. *Pioneers III:* Allport, Festinger, Krech, Lewin. *Pioneers IV:* Cook, Heider, Hovland.

Psychology and Gender, Politics, Poverty, and Race: Pioneers I: Calkins, Heidbreder, Leta Hollingworth, Puffer. *Pioneers II:* Burks, Dix, Doll, Milgram, Murchison. *Pioneers III:* Allport, Darwin, Krech, Lewin, McGraw. *Pioneers IV:* Hooker, Horney, Münsterberg, Schneirla, Spearman, Sumner, Terman.

All of the books in this series owe their existence to the contributions of many people. Primary among them, of course, are the authors of the chapters, to whom we extend a vote of thanks. We acknowledge the financial support of the Society for General Psychology, Division 1, of the American Psychological Association. The publishers, in the persons of Lawrence Erlbaum and Gary VandenBos, provided sound advice as the manuscript developed. At Duke and Colorado, re-

spectively, Hazel Carpenter and Mary Ann Tucker managed the details involved
in preparing the manuscripts for publication.

Gregory A. Kimble
Michael Wertheimer

Portraits of the Authors and Editors

Helmut E. Adler, author of the chapter on Hermann Ludwig Ferdinand von Helmholtz, was born in Nuremberg, Germany. He emigrated to England in 1935, and five years later came to the United States. After military service with the U.S. Army in the Philippines, he obtained his bachelor's, master's, and doctorate degrees at Columbia University. He then taught at Columbia and at Yeshiva University, where he is currently professor emeritus. Much of his research was carried out at The American Museum of Natural History, where his major interest was the sensory basis of orientation in bird navigation. He published *Orientation: Sensory Basis,* based on a conference at the New York Academy of Sciences. In collaboration with his wife, Dr. Leonore Loeb Adler, he investigated observational learning in dogs and studied the behavior of bottlenose dolphins, beluga whales, and California sea lions at the Mystic Marine Life Aquarium in Mystic, Connecticut. He became interested in Helmholtz when Nicholas Pastore asked him to translate some of Helmholtz's popular lectures. His publications in history include a translation of volume I of Fechner's *Elemente der Psychophysik* and *Aspects of the History of Psychology in America* 1892/1992, coedited with Robert Rieber, to celebrate the 100th anniversary of the founding of the American Psychological Association. He is the author of the chapter on Fechner in *Pioneers II* and of a chapter on Fechner in the second edition of *Psychology: Theoretical–Historical Perspectives.* He was secretary-general of the Section on Comparative Psychology and Animal Behavior of the International Union of Biological Sciences from 1972 to 1986. He served as chair of the Section on Psychology of The New York Academy of Sciences, and he received the Wilhelm Wundt Award of the Academic Division of the New York State Psychological Association.

    Ludy T. Benjamin, Jr., author of the portrait of Hugo Münsterberg, is professor of psychology and educational psychology at Texas A&M University, where he has been on the faculty since 1980. He received his doctorate in experimental psychology from Texas Christian University in 1971. He was a member of the faculty at Nebraska Wesleyan University for eight years and then education director at the American Psychological Association for another two years before joining the faculty at Texas A&M. He has served as president of two APA divisions: Division 26 (History of Psychology) and Division 2 (Teaching of Psychology). He also served as president of the Eastern Psychological Association. He has received several teaching awards from Texas A&M and, in 1986, the Distinguished Teaching in Psychology Award from the American Psychological Foundation. In 1996 he was named University Professor of Teaching Excellence at Texas A&M. His scholarly interests are in the history of psychology, particularly the early history of American applied psychology. His chapter on Münsterberg grows out of a larger interest in the history of psychology in American business.

John C. Brigham, author of the chapter on Stuart W. Cook, grew up in Upper Montclair, New Jersey. He received his bachelor's degree from Duke University, and his master's and doctorate degrees from the University of Colorado in social–personality psychology. At Colorado he worked on studies of racial attitudes under Stuart Cook, and also spent many enjoyable afternoons being trounced by Cook on the tennis court. After receiving his PhD, he took a position in social psychology at Florida State University. He has remained there except for a year teaching at U.S. and NATO military bases in Europe and Turkey, two stints teaching at the Florida State University Study Centre, and a semester as visiting professor at the University of Arizona. His early interest in racial prejudice and stereotypes, stimulated by his work with Cook, evolved into a concern with the effect of race on a broad interest in various psychology and law issues. He is a Fellow of the American Psychological Association and the American Psychological Society. He has served as president, secretary–treasurer, treasurer, and council representative for the American Psychology–Law Society (Division 41) of the APA. He has been on the editorial boards of *Journal of Personality and Social Psychology, Law and Human Behavior,* and *Journal of Applied Social Psychology.* With Walter Stephan, he coedited an issue of *Journal of Social Issues* in "intergroup contact" that was dedicated to Stuart Cook. His current research interests focus on the accuracy of eyewitness identification, especially factors determining the "own-race bias" in face recognition, and other psychology and law issues such as perceptions of and opinions about children as witnesses and the study of racial attitudes and stereotypes.

James N. Butcher, author of the chapter on Starke Rosecrans Hathaway, is a professor of psychology in the department of psychology at the University of Minnesota. He graduated from Guilford College in North Carolina with a bachelor's in psychology in 1960 and received master's in experimental psychology and doctorate in clinical psychology from the University of North Carolina at Chapel Hill. He was awarded an additional doctorate, honoris causa, from the

Free University of Brussels in 1990. He has published 40 books and 170 articles in abnormal psychology, personality assessment, and cross-cultural psychology. He maintains an active research program in those areas (especially assessment), as well as in abnormal psychology and computer-based personality assessment. He is the former editor of *Psychological Assessment* and serves as consulting editor for numerous journals in psychology and psychiatry. He is a member of the University of Minnesota Press's MMPI Consultative Committee and was on the team of psychologists responsible for revising and restandardizing the MMPI. In 1965 he founded the Symposium on Recent Developments in the Use of the MMPI to promote and disseminate research information on the MMPI, and he continues to organize this conference. He founded the International Conference on Personality Assessment, which has sponsored conferences in Australia, Belgium, Denmark, Italy, Israel, Japan, Mexico, the United States, and Norway.

Jennifer Randall Crosby, first author of the chapter on Lewis Terman, graduated from Stanford University with a bachelor's in psychology with honors in 1994. In 1997 she earned her master's in psychology from Yale University, where her research focused on the interactions among racial and gender stereotypes and academic achievement. She is the coauthor, with Jennifer L. Eberhardt, of "The Essential Notion of Race" (*Psychological Science, 8,* 198–203). On completing her master's degree, she worked as the program coordinator at the Institute for Research on Women and Gender at Stanford University. She is currently working at the Research Institute of Comparative Studies in Race and Ethnicity at Stanford, coordinating interdisciplinary research networks and overseeing research dissemination.

Donald A. Dewsbury, author of the chapter on Frank Beach, is a professor of psychology at the University of Florida. Born in Brooklyn, New York, he grew up on Long Island and attended Bucknell University. His doctorate is from the University of Michigan and was followed by postdoctoral work with Frank Beach at the University of California, Berkeley. Through much of his career he has worked as a comparative psychologist, with an emphasis on social and reproductive behavior, but in recent years his work has shifted so that his primary focus is on the history of psychology, with work in comparative psychology remaining as a secondary interest. He is the author or editor of 11 books, including *Comparative Animal Behavior* and *Comparative Psychology in the Twentieth Century.* He edited a series of volumes on the histories of the APA divisions, *Unification Through Division,* published by the American Psychological Association. He also has published more than 300 articles and chapters.

David Finkelman, coauthor of the chapter on Sigmund Koch, grew up in New York City. He received his undergraduate degree from the State University of New York at Buffalo and his doctorate from the University of Minnesota. He began graduate studies at Minnesota with an interest in the psychology of language, and worked with James J. Jenkins. He soon transferred (some would say defected) to the clinical psychology program and completed his dissertation under the direction of Norman Garmezy. Since 1981, he has been a faculty member at St. Mary's College of Maryland, where his course offerings have included abnormal psychology, personality, psychological assessment, and history of psychology. With Frank Kessel, he edited a recently published collection of Koch's papers, *Psychology in Human Context: Essays in Dissidence and Reconstruction.* His current interests include the area of psychology and law, on which he has published several articles and book chapters.

Alfred H. Fuchs, author of the chapter on Thomas Upham, is professor of psychology, emeritus, at Bowdoin College in Brunswick, Maine. Born in New Jersey, he earned his undergraduate degree at Rutgers University, his master's at Ohio University, and his doctorate at The Ohio State University. His dissertation research on motor-skill learning was conducted under the direction of George Briggs, professor of psychology and director of the Aviation Psychology Laboratory at Ohio State. After a postdoctoral year with William C. Howell and a year as a human factors scientist at General Dynamics/Electric Boat, he joined the faculty of Bowdoin College in 1962. His early publications on short-term memory were the result of summers spent with Arthur Melton at the University of Michigan's Human Performance Laboratory. He has taught the history of psychology course since his first year at Bowdoin and has conducted research on various aspects of that history. He was chair of the Bowdoin department of psychology before serving as dean of the faculty there from 1971 to 1991. He was president of the APA's Division 26 (History of Psychology) in 1998 to 1999. Currently he is preparing a book-length biography of Thomas C. Upham.

Linda D. Garnets, coauthor of the chapter on Evelyn Hooker, is a lecturer in psychology and women's studies at UCLA, where she teaches a course that she created 12 years ago, Psychology of the Lesbian Experience. She is also a psychotherapist and organizational consultant in Los Angeles, specializing in work with gay male and lesbian clients and with nonprofit organizations. She has specialized in consultation to local and national gay, lesbian, and AIDS agencies. She coedited an anthology with Douglas Kimmel, *Psychological Perspectives on Lesbian and Gay Male Experiences.* She has written and presented numerous papers on the state of the art in research and practice in gay and lesbian psychology. Topics have focused on gay and lesbian experiences (e.g., identity development, parenting, community building, heterosexism, and victimization of gay men and lesbians) and on providing services to gay and lesbian populations (e.g., social–community interventions and gay–lesbian affirmative psychotherapy). For the past 15 years, she has been actively involved in addressing sexual orientation issues in the APA. She is past chair of the APA Board for the Advancement of Psychology in the Public Interest; past chair of the Committee on Lesbian, Gay, and Bisexual Concerns (CLGBC); past cochair of CLGBC's Task Force on Bias in Psychotherapy With Lesbians and Gay Men; past member of the Executive Committee of APA Division 44 (Society for the Psychological Study of Lesbian, Gay and Bisexual Issues); and past member of the Award Research Review Committee for the American Psychological Foundation's Wayne Placek Fund. She is currently coediting, with L. Anne Peplau, a special issue of the *Journal of Social Issues* on "Women's Sexualities: Perspectives on Sexual Orientation and Gender."

Robert V. Guthrie, author of the chapter on Francis Cecil Sumner, was born in Chicago and grew up in Kentucky. He received his bachelor's degree from Florida A&M University, his master's degree from the University of Kentucky, and his doctorate from the U.S. International University in San Diego. He has been a professor at the University of Pittsburgh, research psychologist at the National Institute of Education, and associate director of Psychological Sciences at the Office of Naval Research. As a supervisory research psychologist, he later retired from the Navy Personnel and Development Center in San Diego. After several years in an independent private practice, he became a professor of applied experimental psychology at Southern Illinois University in Carbondale, retiring from that position in 1996. He is the author or editor of five books, including *Even the Rat Was White: A Historical View of Psychology.* He is currently enjoying retirement in Playas de Rosarito, Mexico. Guthrie is a Fellow of the American Psychological Association and the American Psychological Society.

Albert H. Hastorf, who coauthored the chapter on Lewis Terman, received his bachelor's from Amherst and his master's and doctorate from Princeton. He is professor of psychology, emeritus, at Stanford University. At Stanford since 1961, he has served as head of the Department of Psychology, dean of the School of Humanities and Sciences, director of the Youth Studies Center at Stanford, and as vice president and provost. He held the Benjamin Scott Crocker Professorship in Human Biology. His publications include *Person Perception* (Addison Wesley); *Cognitive Social Psychology* (Elsevier North-Holland); and *Social Stigma: The Psychology of Marked Relationships* (W. H. Freeman). He is a Fellow of the American Psychological Association and the American Academy of Arts and Sciences. He has been a trustee of the Center for Advanced Studies in the Behavioral Sciences and of the Packard Children's Hospital at Stanford. He has been awarded honorary degrees by Dartmouth and Amherst; he is now director of the Terman Study of the Gifted at Stanford University.

William Ickes, coauthor of the chapter on Fritz Heider, is a professor of psychology at the University of Texas at Arlington, where he has taught for the past 18 years. He received his doctorate in experimental social psychology in 1973 from the University of Texas at Austin and has held previous academic positions at the University of Wisconsin—Madison and the University of Missouri—St. Louis. He has held visiting positions at the University of Washington—Seattle and the University of Canterbury, Christchurch, New Zealand. He is the editor of *Empathic Accuracy* and *Compatible and Incompatible Relationships.* He is a coeditor of three volumes of *New Directions in Attribution Research* and two volumes of the *Handbook of Personal Relationships.* He has also coauthored chapters for the *Handbook of Social Psychology* and the *Handbook of Person-*

ality. He has served as an associate editor of the *Journal of Personality and Social Psychology* and continues to serve as a consulting editor to that and other journals in the areas of personality, social psychology, and personal relationships. In 1997 he received the Berscheid/Hatfield Mid-Career Achievement Award from the membership of the International Network of Personal Relationships. His vita includes a long list of books, book chapters, journal articles, commentaries, and reviews.

Arthur R. Jensen, author of the chapters on Hans Eysenck and Charles Spearman, was born in California. He received his undergraduate degree from the University of California, Berkeley, and his doctorate from Columbia. After completing a clinical internship at the University of Maryland's Psychiatric Institute and a postdoctoral fellowship under Eysenck at the University of London's Institute of Psychiatry, he joined the faculty of the University of California, Berkeley, in 1958, as professor of educational psychology and research psychologist in the Institute of Human Learning. After a decade of research on individual differences in human learning, Jensen turned to the nature and causes of individual, cultural, and racial differences in scholastic performance. His 1969 article, "How Much Can We Boost IQ and Scholastic Achievement?" argued that psychometric *g* is the strongest single predictor of scholastic performance and that genetic as well as environmental factors should be considered among the possible causes, not only of individual differences but also social–class and racial differences in cognitive abilities. This suggestion elicited a storm of protest from many educators and social scientists. The hypothesis that both individual and racial differences in cognitive abilities result from essentially the same genetic and environmental causes has come to be termed "Jensenism"—often pejoratively. For the past 20 years Jensen has pursued laboratory investigation of the correlation between *g* and speed of information processing in various elementary cognitive tasks and also various physical correlates of *g*. He has published approximately 400 articles and 7 books on these subjects, including *Educability and Group Differences, Bias in Mental Testing,* and *The g Factor.*

Frank Kessel, coauthor of the chapter on Sigmund Koch, received his undergraduate and early graduate education at the University of Cape Town, where he was introduced to some of Koch's writings by Kurt Danziger and others. He then pursued his interests in cognitive and language development at the University of Minnesota in the late 1960s. After a postdoctoral period at the University of Alberta's Theoretical Psychology Centre, he became involved in international early education efforts, first as research director of the Early Learning Centre in Cape Town and then as scientific associate at the Bernard van Leer Foundation in The Hague. Joining the faculty at the University of Houston in 1976, he helped organize the "Houston Symposium" series. It was at the first Houston Symposium that he met Koch, who participated in a number of those scholarly events. Among the edited volumes resulting from this "impresario" role are *The Child* *and Other Cultural Inventions; The Development of Language and Language Researchers: Essays in Honor of Roger Brown; Contemporary Constructions of the Child: Essays in Honor of William Kessen;* and *Psychology, Science, and Human Affairs: Essays in Honor of William Bevan.* Since 1991, he has been a program director at the Social Science Research Council in New York, primarily responsible for the work of an international, interdisciplinary group of scholars under the rubric of Culture, Health, and Human Development. Most recently, he collaborated with David Finkelman in publishing a collection of Sigmund Koch's writings.

Gregory A. Kimble, senior editor of Volumes I to IV of *Portraits of Pioneers in Psychology,* was born in Iowa and grew up in Minnesota. His bachelor of arts, master's, and doctorate degrees are from Carleton College, Northwestern University, and the University of Iowa, respectively. He also has an honorary degree, Doctor of Humane Letters, from the University of Colorado. His major academic appointments have been at Brown University, Yale University, the University of Colorado, and Duke University. He is currently professor emeritus of psychology at Duke. He served as director of Undergraduate Studies and Graduate Studies at Duke, and as chair of the Department of Psychology at Colorado and Duke. He has been president of APA Divisions 1 (General Psychology) and 3 (Experimental Psychology). He was the last editor of the now-discontinued *Psychological Monographs* and the first editor of *Journal of Experimental Psychology: General.* His books include *Principles of General Psychology* (which appeared in six editions, the last five with Norman Garmezy and Edward Zigler as coauthors), *Hilgard and Marquis' Conditioning and Learning, How to Use (and Misuse) Statistics,* and *Psychology: The Hope of a Science.* He was the 1999 recipient of Division 1's Hilgard Award for Distinguished Career Contributions to General Psychology and the APA award for Distinguished Contributions to Education and Training in Psychology.

In January 1999, **Douglas C. Kimmel,** coauthor of the chapter on Evelyn Hooker, retired from City College, CUNY, where he taught and wrote on adolescence, adulthood, and aging for 28 years. He is now in private practice in Hancock, Maine. He has been involved with gay, lesbian, and bisexual issues in the APA since 1973. He was chair of the Association of Lesbian and Gay Psychologists, the APA Committee on Lesbian, Gay, and Bisexual Concerns, and president of APA Division 44, Society for the Psychological Study of Lesbian, Gay, and Bisexual Issues. Since 1996, he has been on the board of the American Psychological Foundation, where he oversees the Wayne Placek Trust and the Royce Scrivner Fund, which provide support for research on gay, lesbian, and bisexual topics. He is coeditor with Linda Garnets of *Psychological Perspectives on Lesbian and Gay Male Experiences.* He has also written on the historical origins of Western ideas of sexual orientation for Japanese and Chinese medical journals. His current research is on Asian gay men and lesbians; with Clarence Adams he is completing a study of older African American gay men. He is author of *Adulthood and Aging,* which appeared in three editions, and coauthor with Irving Weiner of two editions of *Adolescence.*

D. Brett King, author of the chapter on George Croom Robertson, obtained his doctorate in cognitive psychology from Colorado State University, working with Wayne Viney, author of the chapter on Dorothea Dix in *Pioneers II,* who helped him consolidate his interest in the history of psychology. The original version of the chapter on Robertson was written for a seminar on the history of psychology while King was still a graduate student. King has been a member of the faculty at the University of Colorado at Boulder since 1990, teaching courses on the history of psychology, social psychology, personality, and cognitive psychology, as well as introductory psychology. Author or coauthor of many articles and convention presentations on the history of psychology, he is coauthor with Viney of the second edition of *A History of Psychology: Ideas and Context.* He and Michael Wertheimer are preparing a book-length biography of the Gestalt psychologist Max Wertheimer. The two recently taught a combined undergraduate honors and graduate psychology seminar on Gestalt theory and Wertheimer. Together with his wife Cheri, who also obtained her doctorate in cognitive psychology, he is coarchivist for the Rocky Mountain Psychological Association.

Bertram F. Malle, first author of the chapter on Fritz Heider, was born in Graz, Austria, where Heider himself grew up and received his doctorate. He studied philosophy, linguistics, and psychology at the University of Graz, and after moving to the United States in 1990 he obtained a doctorate in psychology from Stanford University. During graduate school he studied Heider's writings and began to examine the problems that were most central to Heider's thinking: the folk theory of mind and behavior, especially people's conception of intentionality and their explanations of behavior. His dissertation on these topics received the 1995 Dissertation Award from the Society for Experimental Social Psychology, and subsequent research received a National Science Foundation Career Award. Since 1994 he has held a position at the University of Oregon, Eugene, in the psychology department and the Institute of Cognitive and Decision Sciences. With Oregon colleagues Lou Moses and Dare Baldwin he is currently editing an interdisciplinary volume on *Intentionality: A Key to Human Understanding.*

Bernard J. Paris is author of the chapter on Karen Horney and emeritus professor of English at the University of Florida. His books on Horney and the application of her theories to literary criticism areas include *Experiments in Life: George Eliot's Quest for Values; A Psychological Approach to Fiction: Studies in Thackeray, Stendhal, George Eliot, Dostoevsy, and Conrad; Character and Conflict in Jane Austen's Novels: A Psychological Approach; Bargains With Fate: Psychological Crises and Conflicts in Shakespeare and His Plays; Character as a Subversive Force in Shakespeare: The History and Roman Plays;* and *Imagined Human Beings: A Psychological Approach to Character and*

Conflict in Literature. In *Karen Horney: A Psychoanalyst's Search for Self-Understanding,* he examined the evolution of Horney's ideas in relation to her personal experience and her quest for relief from her own personal difficulties. This volume was selected as a Notable Book of the Year by the *New York Times.* He has edited two volumes of Horney's unpublished and uncollected writings: *The Therapeutic Process: Essays and Lectures* and *The Unknown Karen Horney: Essays on Gender, Culture, and Psychoanalysis.* He received his doctorate from The Johns Hopkins University and has taught at Lehigh University and Michigan State. He has been a visiting professor at the Victorian Studies Centre of the University of Leicester. He is an honorary member of the Association for the Advancement of Psychoanalysis, a scientific associate of the American Academy of Psychoanalysis, and a member of the editorial board of the *American Journal of Psychoanalysis.* He is editor of the Karen Horney Series of the Shanghai Literature and Art Publishing House and founder and director of the International Karen Horney Society.

Antonio E. Puente, author of the chapter on Roger W. Sperry, received his undergraduate degree from the University of Florida and his graduate training at the University of Georgia. He has taught anatomy at a medical school, worked as a clinical psychologist at a teaching hospital, and is currently part of the faculty of the University of North Carolina, Wilmington, where he is professor of psychology. He has held visiting appointments at several other universities, including the University of Madrid. He has devoted most of his academic career to neuropsychology and has published several books and numerous scientific articles in that field. He is currently editor for a book series in neuropsychology and is editor-in-chief of the *Neuropsychology Review.* In addition, he has been president of several organizations, including the National Academy of Neuropsychology. He currently serves on the APA Council of Representatives, representing Division 40 (Clinical Neuropsychology).

Henry L. Roediger III, author of the chapter on Sir Frederic Bartlett, is the James S. McDonnell Distinguished University Professor at Washington University in St. Louis. He was educated at Washington & Lee University (bachelor's, 1969) and Yale University (doctorate, 1973). Since leaving Yale he has taught at Purdue University, the University of Toronto, and Rice University. His research interests lie in human learning and memory. He has published widely on many different topics in those domains, particularly on retrieval processes in remembering. He has published approximately 130 articles, chapters, and reviews, as well as three textbooks (with coauthors): *Psychology* (4th ed), *Experimental Psychology: Understanding Psychological Research* (6th ed.) and *Research Methods in Psychology* (6th ed). In addition, he coedited (with Fergus I. M. Craik) *Varieties of Memory and Consciousness: Essays in Honour of Endel Tulving.* He served as editor of the *Journal of Experimental Psychology: Learning, Memory and Cognition* from 1985 to 1989 and was its associate editor from 1981 to 1984. He was founding editor of *Psychonomic Bulletin & Review* and has served as consulting editor of five other journals. He was elected to the Governing Board of the Psychonomic Society (1986–1991) and served as its chair in 1989 to 1990. He is a Fellow of the American Association for the Advancement of Science, the APA, the American Psychological Society (APS), and the Canadian Psychological Association. He has been president of the Midwestern Psychological Association (1992–1993) and serves on the Board of Directors of APS. He is currently president of Division 3 of the APA. He was elected to the Society of Experimental Psychologists in 1994. According to a 1996 study by the Institute of Scientific Information, his papers had the greatest average number of citations in the field of psychology from 1990 to 1994.

Roger N. Shepard, author of the chapter on Carl Iver Hovland, received his Yale doctorate under Hovland in 1955. Later, while at the Bell Telephone Laboratories, Shepard collaborated in studies of concept learning with Hovland at Yale until Hovland's death in 1961. Following his eight years at the Bell Labs, where he developed the first method of nonmetric multidimensional scaling, he was appointed professor of psychology at Harvard and, two years later, at Stanford, where he is now Ray Lyman Wilbur Professor of Social Sciences, Emeritus. He is a member of the American Academy of Arts and Sciences, the American Philosophical Society, and the National Academy of Sciences. He is a recipient of the APA Distinguished Scientific Contribution Award, the Warren Medal of the Society of Experimental Psychologists, and the 1995 National Medal of Science. His books include *Mental Images and Their Transformations* (with Lynn Cooper) and *Mind Sights.* Currently he is working on a book based on the William James Lectures, Mind and World, that he gave at Harvard in 1994.

Helga Sprung, first author of the chapter on Carl Stumpf and coauthor of the chapter on Georg Elias Müller, was born at Hennigsdorf, near Berlin, Germany, in 1939. She studied psychology at the universities of Berlin and Jena, graduating with a major in experimental psychology from Humboldt University in Berlin in 1962; she obtained her doctorate in experimental psychology from Humboldt University in 1971. From 1962 to 1977 she worked as an experimental clinical psychologist in a hospital of the German Academy of Science in Berlin, and from 1977 to 1987 she performed scholarly work independently. She was affiliated with the Department of Philosophy at the Academy of Science of the German Democratic Republic in Berlin from 1987 to 1991, and from 1992 to 1999 she directed a research project on the history of psychology, sponsored by the German Science Foundation, at the Free University in Berlin. During that time she taught in the areas of the history of psychology and women in psychology and performed research and scholarly work in psychophysiology, methodology, psychodiagnosis, history of psychology, theoretical psychology, and women in psychology. She is the editor of *Carl Stumpf: Schriften zur Psychologie, neu Herausgegeben, Eingeleitet und mit Einer Biographischen Einführung Versehen* [Carl Stumpf: Psychological writings, newly edited, introduced, and provided with a biographical introduction] and coauthor, with Lothar Sprung, of *Grund-*

lagen der Methodologie und Methodik der Psychologie [Foundations of methodology and technique in psychology]. She has published more than 130 articles and monographs in German, English, and Spanish. Recently retired, she is working on a biography of Carl Stumpf.

Lothar Sprung, first author of the chapter on Georg Elias Müller and coauthor of the chapter on Carl Stumpf, was born in Berlin in 1934. He studied at the universities of Berlin and Jena, and graduated with a major in experimental psychology from Humboldt University in Berlin in 1962. He obtained his doctorate in experimental psychology in 1970 and his doctor of science degree in 1980, both from Humboldt. As a faculty member at the universities of Jena and Berlin, he taught and did research on cognitive psychology, methodology, psychodiagnosis, experimental psychopathology, the history of psychology, theoretical psychology, and human development, and served in the administration of the psychology department of the University of Berlin. Among his books with Helga Sprung are *Grundlagen der Methodologie und Methodik der Psychologie* [Foundations of methodology and technique in psychology], 2nd ed. (with Friedhart Klix, Hans-Georg Geissler, Werner Krause and Hubert Sydow); *Organismische Informationsverarbeitung* [Organic information processing] (with Georg Eckard); *Advances in Historiography of Psychology* (with Georg Eckardt and Wolfgang Bringmann); *Contributions to a History of Developmental Psychology,* (with Jürgen Guthke and Hans R. Böttcher); two editions of *Psychodiagnostik* [Psychodiagnosis] (with Wolfgang Schönpflug); *Zur Geschichte der Psychologie in Berlin* [On the history of psychology in Berlin]; and (with Siegfried Jaeger, Irmingard Staeuble, and Horst-Peter Brauns) *Psychologie im Soziokulturellen Wandel: Kontinuitäten und Diskontinuitäten* [Psychology in sociocultural change: Continuities and discontinuities]. He has published almost 200 articles in German, English, Spanish, and Polish. Now professor emeritus of psychology at the University of Berlin, he is working on the history of psychology in Germany.

Ethel Tobach, who wrote the chapter on T. C. Schneirla, received her doctorate in comparative and physiological psychology from the Department of Psychology, New York University, in 1957. She worked as a graduate student with T. C. Schneirla in the Department of Animal Behavior at the American Museum of Natural History until it closed in 1981. At that time, she was a curator, and is now curator emerita in the Department of Mammalogy. She is also adjunct professor in the developmental psychology program in the Graduate School of the City University of New York, in the Department of Biology at City College, and in the Biopsychology Program at Hunter College. She has studied behavioral, genetic, and physiological processes in a variety of organisms, including Aplysia, orangutans, and human beings. She has been coeditor of a series of books related to the theories of T. C. Schneirla (T. C. Schneirla Conference Series), coeditor of books and the journal of the International Society for Comparative Psychology, and coeditor of the Genes and Gender Series. She has been president of the Division of Comparative Psychology of the APA and vice president of the Behavioral Sciences Division of the New York Academy Sciences.

Michael Wertheimer, coeditor of this and the preceding three volumes of *Portraits of Pioneers in Psychology,* was born in Germany and came to the United States when he was 6 years old. Educated in the public schools of New Rochelle, New York, and at Fieldston School in New York, he received his bachelor of arts from Swarthmore College, his master's in psychology from The Johns Hopkins University, and his doctorate in experimental psychology from Harvard. After teaching at Wesleyan University for three years, he joined the faculty of the psychology department at the University of Colorado at Boulder in 1955. From 1961 to 1993 he was professor of psychology there, becoming professor emeritus in 1993. Author, coauthor, editor, or coeditor of hundreds of publications, many of them in the history of psychology, he has also served on many boards and committees of the APA and has been on APA's Council of Representatives during more than 20 of the past 30 years. He has been president of several APA divisions, including Division 1 (General Psychology), Division 2 (Teaching of Psychology), Division 24 (Theoretical and Philosophical Psychology), and Division 26 (History of Psychology), and of Psi Chi (the national honor society in psychology) as well as of the Rocky Mountain Psychological Association. Recipient of several awards for teaching and for service, he directed the undergraduate honors program in psychology at the University of Colorado for almost four decades. Among his recent publications are the fourth edition of *A Brief History of Psychology* and (with Stephen F. Davis) an oral history of Psi Chi. Currently he is working (with D. Brett King) on a biography of his father, the Gestalt psychologist Max Wertheimer.

Chapter 1

The Psychology of Thomas Upham

Alfred H. Fuchs

In the first decades of the 19th century, psychology was taught under such titles as "intellectual philosophy" and "mental philosophy" in North American colleges and universities. The first textbook to use the term "psychology" in its title is usually considered to be the book by Rauch (1840; Fay, 1939; Roback, 1952a), although Caleb Henry translated Victor Cousin's (1834) textbook as *Elements of Psychology* (Rieber, 1980). "Psychology" did not, however, become a generally accepted name for the discipline until the last decade of the 19th century. Before that, textbooks in intellectual or mental philosophy were the basis for the study of the mind. The first textbook in intellectual philosophy written specifically for undergraduate students was published in the second decade of the 19th century by Thomas C. Upham (Upham, 1827). Upham's book initiated the era of textbooks in mental philosophy by American academic authors almost three decades before other textbooks appeared (Evans, 1984), and it contained the substance of "a truly indigenous American system of psychology" (Rieber, 1980, p. 104).

Upham and others [Joseph Haven of Amherst College, Laurens Hickok (chap. 1, *Pioneers III*) of Union College, and Francis Wayland of Brown University] who wrote textbooks and taught philosophy in the colleges and universities of the United States in the early decades of the 19th century paved the way for the acceptance and development of the new laboratory psychology of the last quar-

A version of this chapter was presented as the Address of the President of Division 26 (History of Psychology) of the American Psychological Association at the annual convention of the association in August 1999.

*Photograph of Thomas Upham courtesy of the Bowdoin College Library, Archival Photograph Collection, Special Collections and Archives.

1

ter of the century (Fuchs, 2000). This "new psychology" was promoted by its champions as a clear break with the "old psychology" of the mental philosophers and as a new beginning for an old discipline. This view was captured by Hermann Ebbinghaus (chap. 4, *Pioneers III*) in his frequently quoted (translated) statement that "psychology has a long past, yet its real history is short" (Ebbinghaus, 1908, p. 3). Proponents of the new psychology, in characterizing their discipline as new in their rhetoric (Leary, 1987), traced their lineage to the German psychology of the last quarter of the 19th century. For example, in paying tribute to Wilhelm Wundt's (chap. 3, *Pioneers III*) contributions to psychology, an American student wrote, "We psychologists in America, his followers, might say he contributed us and our psychological laboratories" (Weyer, 1921, p. 182).

But psychology in America was not simply Wundtian psychology translated into English. Rather, the character of Wundtian psychology, and German laboratory psychology more broadly, was influenced by its transplantation to the North American environment. Its acceptance and development in college and university curricula depended in part on the preparations provided by mental philosophers of the 19th century who had established mental philosophy as a significant part of the undergraduate curriculum. The study of mind as an independent subject within philosophy was well-established before American scholars returned from German laboratories to proclaim the new psychology.

There are continuities between the old intellectual, or mental, philosophy and the new psychology that rest on the contributions of the mental philosophers. These contributions include (a) securing a place for the study of mind within the curriculum, a place that psychologists were to come to occupy; (b) establishing the study of mind as an empirical science—the later laboratory method became a new and powerful addition to accepted empirical procedures for gathering facts; (c) addressing a wide range of mental processes that became topics for investigation by the new psychology; and (d) treating mental processes as functions of mind and body. Upham's textbook is the first instance of pre-Civil War mental philosophy in which these broad continuities may be found.

BACKGROUND

Thomas Upham was born in Rochester, New Hampshire, in 1799, the oldest son of Nathaniel Upham and Judith Cogswell Upham. Nathaniel Upham was a storekeeper who represented his state in Congress for four terms (1816–1824) as a Jeffersonian Republican. Judith Cogswell loved the poetry of Walter Scott and William Cowper and passed that love to her first-born son. Thomas Upham's first book of poetry (he would publish several more in his lifetime) was published shortly after his graduation from Dartmouth College (Upham, 1819). His poetry celebrated the natural beauty of his native state, the values of the farmer, and the exploits of early settlers and the generation that fought in the Revolutionary War. One copy of that volume was read by a youthful Henry Wadsworth

Longfellow, who imitated one of Upham's poems in a very early poem of his own (Thompson, 1938).

As an undergraduate at Dartmouth, Upham was caught up in one of the many religious revivals that swept college and university campuses; after his graduation in 1818, Upham enrolled in the Andover Theological Seminary to prepare for a career in the ministry. Seminaries provided the only graduate training then available in the United States; colleges and universities appointed professors from among seminary graduates because their advanced education in languages and philosophy prepared them to teach undergraduates a classical curriculum. Moreover, seminary graduates were assumed to possess the character necessary for the *in loco parentis* care of youth. The practice of appointing theologians to professorships of philosophy was not limited to the early part of the 19th century. As late as 1879, Bowdoin College appointed George Trumbull Ladd to a professorship in philosophy from a church in Milwaukee. Coincidentally Ladd, like Upham, was a graduate of the Andover Theological Seminary (Mills, 1969).

When Upham studied at the seminary, Andover was the preeminent institution for Trinitarian congregationalism. Biblical scholarship was undertaken to defend the Puritan heritage in contrast, for example, to the Unitarian views of the Harvard Divinity School (Brown, 1969). Greek, Latin, and Hebrew were necessary for the study of Biblical texts, and German was necessary for the new theological scholarship emanating from the continent. Upham's training in German gave him access to German philosophers, not simply to German biblical scholarship.

More pertinent for future teachers of mental philosophy, however, was study devoted to the philosophy of mind, which Upham found in the books of John Locke (1690/1975) and Dugald Stewart (1808). This study of mind was important to ministers for at least two reasons: (a) understanding the mind was part of the attempt to know the Deity by understanding His creation, and (b) understanding the mind was useful to counsel and influence members of the church. These studies were pursued as empirical and inductive sciences (natural philosophy and natural theology) in tandem with studies of the Bible (revealed religion). Such preparation also provided a basis for teaching in colleges and universities. In that religious context, the study of mind made philosophy compatible with prevailing religious sentiment and therefore acceptable to those who were responsible for undergraduate education.

Moses Stuart, the chief representative of Congregational orthodoxy, an innovative teacher of Hebrew, and a serious student of German, employed Upham at Andover as an assistant in teaching Hebrew and Greek. At Stuart's suggestion, Upham translated *Jahn's Biblical Archaeology* (Upham, 1823) from an abridged Latin edition. He added passages from the original unabridged German version that he translated himself (Upham, 1823). That book, which described the geography of the Holy Land and Jewish culture and traditions, was in keeping with the empirical spirit of collecting facts. Upham also taught at Andover Academy; he wanted to further the study of languages in France after his graduation, perhaps to pursue an academic career. However, a shortage of funds and the offer of a position as assistant pastor led him home to Rochester, where he spent a profitable year building a congregation before accepting the offer of a professorship at Bowdoin College.

Appointed in September of 1824, Upham fulfilled his duties to his Rochester church and prepared himself for his new career as professor of metaphysics and ethics. He began teaching in February of 1825 and married Phebe Lord of Kennebunkport, Maine, in May of that year. Phebe's portrait, painted by Gilbert Stuart just before her marriage, is in the collection of the Bowdoin College Museum of Art. Upham became a much beloved member of the faculty at Bowdoin and was described by a student in the 1840s as "a tall man [who] always walks with his head inclined a little . . . his eyes fixed on the ground, his hands crossed— put a book under his arm, and this is [an accurate] picture of the good man" (Hanscome, 1846, p. 201).[1]

During 43 years at Bowdoin, Upham participated in most of the important social movements of the pre-Civil War period. On the national scene, he was part of the peace movement that arose after the War of 1812 and increased with opposition to the Mexican War of the 1830s. His articles in support of peace were published as a book (Upham, 1842) by the American Peace Society, in which Upham served as vice president from 1843 until his death in 1872. At the time of its publication, this book "was considered by the London Peace Society to be the best manual on the whole subject which had ever been written" (Phelps, 1930, p. 71). At the time of Upham's death it was still "considered the best general book on the subject" (Whitney, 1929, p. 144). Upham served as a vice president of the American Colonization Society, which supported the policy of repatriating slaves to the colony of Liberia on the African coast; he supported, as did Abraham Lincoln, a policy of compensated emancipation for slaves before the Civil War. From 1840 to the time of his death, he published several popular books (e.g., Upham, 1843) that espoused his version of the holiness theology (Salter, 1986).

In Maine, Upham was known as an opponent of capital punishment and he supported temperance movements on campus and in the state. Upham was also instrumental in bringing Calvin Stowe to Bowdoin and Calvin's wife Harriet Beecher Stowe to Brunswick, where she began to write *Uncle Tom's Cabin*. Stowe's experiences in Brunswick with the Uphams provided material for her book (Hedrick, 1994). Characteristics of Uncle Tom were drawn from a description of a freed slave in Brunswick provided by Phebe Upham (Hovet, 1979a) and the structure of the book was influenced by Thomas Upham's holiness theology (Hovet, 1979b). Upham retired from Bowdoin in 1868 as professor of mental and moral philosophy, emeritus (Fuchs, 1999), having raised significant funds

---

[1]Quotation from the *Diary of James William Hanscome* used by permission of Bowdoin College, Brunswick, ME.

for the college and earning a distinguished reputation for his philosophical writing.

INTELLECTUAL PHILOSOPHY

Upham's 1827 *Elements of Intellectual Philosophy* preceded the publication of most other American textbooks of intellectual or mental philosophy by decades. The first half of the textbook had been published for student use in 1826 (Upham, 1826), with a second revised edition in 1828 (Upham, 1828). The subtitle of that book, in those and all subsequent editions, included the phrase "designed as a textbook." This textbook was the first to introduce students to intellectual philosophy by summarizing and interpreting original sources. In this sense, Upham's text, like modern textbooks, was eclectic and depended on the work of previous authors of more specialized books and articles. His goal was to present an impartial view of the discipline and spare the student the perplexity of determining truth from conflicting and contradictory arguments. The task of the author of a textbook and of a teacher consisted, for Upham, of sorting through the mass of fact and argument to arrive at established principles, and the facts on which they rest, to give the student as clear a picture of the state of the discipline as possible. In addition, Upham was mindful that the texts most often used to teach intellectual philosophy, John Locke's *Essay* and Dugald Stewart's *Elements*, were not written with the college undergraduate in mind and, moreover, were becoming scarce and too expensive for students to buy. The addition of the words "for Academies and High Schools" to the title of the abridged third edition made Upham's textbook the first for use in secondary schools (Engle, 1967; Louttit, 1956; Roback, 1952b).

Upham's first chapter on the utility of mental philosophy, like most introductory chapters in contemporary textbooks, described the discipline and made an effort to convince the reader of its scientific nature and usefulness. For Upham, this entailed distinguishing mental philosophy from metaphysics and its association in the public mind with speculations for which there were no answers and no practical utility—for example, whether angels occupy space. Upham argued, rather, that intellectual philosophy is not metaphysics but "is prosecuted on different principles and with different results" (Upham, 1827, p. 11) that would prove useful to educators, parents, and the prevention of mental errors, for example. Psychology as a useful science is still the subject of introductory chapters in contemporary psychology textbooks; for example, "Using Psychological Knowledge to Improve the Quality of People's Lives and Enable Society to Function More Effectively Is the Final Goal of Psychology" (Zimbardo & Gerrig, 1976). Mental and moral philosophy, or ethics, comprised virtually the whole of philosophy taught in the undergraduate curriculum in the early part of the century. Natural philosophy was the province of the natural scientists. The branches of philosophy taught in the early decades of the 19th century were differentiated within the curriculum: "Natural philosophy teaches us the laws of external nature; Intellectual philosophy, the laws of the human mind; Moral philosophy has to do with the laws of human conduct and duty" (Haven, 1859, p. 15).

The scientific method used to determine the laws of nature, mind, or human conduct was empirical and inductive. Science emphasizes collecting and organizing facts (empiricism) and inferring from them (by induction) the general laws or principles that govern them. In accord with Bacon's proscriptions against hypotheses (or *a priori* speculations), the philosophers of nature, mind, and conduct were suspicious of metaphysics, in which answers to questions are approached by deductions from general principles, and whose questions, as Upham noted, are often incapable of being answered.

Upham rejected the past identification of intellectual or mental philosophy with metaphysics and argued for the pursuit of intellectual philosophy as a science of facts. Although in the later decades of the century, science would imply laboratory investigations, in the early part of the century it implied simply fact gathering. Facts of intellectual philosophy came from any source that seemed to provide insight into the operations of mind, with the most important observations being the consciousness of one's own behavior and the behavior of others. Additional observations of human nature came from trusted and sensitive observers, in plays, poems, legal briefs, and medical treatises and cases. For example, in using a medical case history of an individual born deaf and blind as evidence for the importance of external stimulation, Upham wrote, "Such instances as these, however they may first appear, are extremely important. They furnish us with an appeal, not to mere speculations, but to fact. And it is only by checking undue speculation, and by continually recurring to facts, that our progress in this science will become sure, rapid, and delightful" (Upham, 1886, p. 24).

Elements of Intellectual Philosophy contained 33 chapters, most of them with titles that are still found in modern introductory textbooks: perception, consciousness, thought, language, principles of association (learning), attention, memory, reasoning, emotion, instincts, prejudice, testimony, and mental alienation (abnormal psychology, which covered apparitions, by which Upham meant delusions associated with the use of drugs or certain religious experiences). Topics in most modern textbooks that were not addressed by Upham included the physiology underlying psychological processes (although information on the anatomy of the senses was provided), social psychology, individual differences in intelligence and personality, and developmental psychology.

The omission that most sharply differentiates Upham's textbook from modern treatments is the absence of results of laboratory experiments, measurement, and statistical analysis that were to become important in the psychology of the future. Upham also cited literature (prose and poetry) and appealed to conscious experience as evidence for his ideas, rather than using literature and conscious experience as a means of relating scientific results to everyday phenomena, as a modern textbook author might do. Despite these differences in substance, Upham's textbook, and its modern counterparts, all present their subject matter as a science of facts—however different those facts may be—organized in categories of psychological processes that refer to functional attributes of mind or behavior. Beyond that, Upham's and modern textbooks all attempt to arrive at general principles that account for the facts of mind and behavior. Their similarities do not arise because modern textbooks are derived from Upham, but rather because both Upham and contemporary psychologists address the same subject matter, using terms that a common language and a shared understanding provide.

FROM INTELLECTUAL TO MENTAL PHILOSOPHY

In 1832 Upham published the third edition of his textbook under the title, *Elements of Mental Philosophy*. Topics were now organized under two "departments of mind," *intellect* and *sensibilities*. In 1834 Upham added a third "department," the *will*, an addition that eventually led him to revise and complete his system for a three-volume edition of his philosophy. It was not until 1861, however, with the publication of an abridged edition, that the three departments of mind were encompassed in a single volume. The *Elements of Mental Philosophy* in three volumes was reprinted many times; the abridged edition of 1861 was last printed in 1886 and advertised for sale as late as 1892 (Dewey, 1892).

Over the years from 1827 to 1886, Upham changed publishers from William Hyde of Portland, Maine, to Hilliard, Grey and Wells and Lilly, Boston, and, finally, in 1840, to Harper and Brothers of New York. Thus within 13 years from the date of his first edition, Upham had moved from a local publisher, to a larger one in Boston, to the still larger and more prestigious publisher in New York. Upham's textbook was used at the University of Georgia continuously from 1840 until 1870 [(Ziegler, 1949); Ziegler referred to Upham as "Upshaw," but the university catalog of the period identified Upham correctly]. No extensive sales figures or records of college and university adoptions are available, but the shifts in publishers and the long history of the book in print serve as evidence of the popularity and profitability of Upham's mental philosophy as a textbook. As Roback has observed, "It is only the classic textbook which survives the author" (1952a, p. 50).

The change in title (from *Elements of Intellectual Philosophy* to *Elements of Mental Philosophy*) and the organization of the chapters into departments of mind was significant. Mental philosophy constituted a broader representation of all that mind contained, not simply or primarily the cognitive content signified by the earlier title. Those textbooks that continued to use "intellectual" rather than "mental" in their titles concentrated on the rational or cognitive processes of mind, to the relative neglect of the irrational, emotional, and motivational processes and the will (e.g., Porter, 1868; Wayland, 1857). With a more inclusive term to describe the range of mental processes identified in mind, Upham initiated a classification of processes that was in fact a system or theory of mind. His tripartite organization described how the basic mental processes operate and translate into behavior.

The 1861 abridged edition of *Elements of Mental Philosophy* is a succinct statement of Upham's position and is the statement of his system described in this chapter. In the abridgment, the intellect and sensibility sections were the same as the full statements in single volumes, but the section on the will was considerably condensed by omitting or summarizing the arguments surrounding determinism or the freedom of the will.

INTELLECT, SENSIBILITIES, AND WILL

As a classification of mental processes, the intellect and the sensibilities each comprise two subclasses of processes. The intellect consists of separate processes of external origin and internal origin. These subclasses reflect Upham's position in the debate over the origins of mind—the view that there is nothing in mind but that which experience provides, compared to the view that mind exists prior to experience. The processes that Upham categorized as of external origin—dependent on stimulation from the external world—included the experience of sensation and perception, "conceptions" (images or representations that occur in the absence of the stimulus object), ideas and associations among them, and dreaming, which Upham conceived of as prompted by external stimulation during sleep. Processes of internal origin include consciousness itself, suggestion (the mechanism of association, in which one idea "suggests" another), and the origin of ideas that do not depend on external objects, such as the idea of self and the processes of reasoning, memory, and imagination.

Like the intellect, the sensibilities were divided into two categories: natural sensibilities and moral sensibilities (or conscience). The former include the emotions and desires or motives (including instincts, appetites, propensities, and affections). The latter include emotions of moral approval or disapproval and feelings of moral obligation. In making this categorization, Upham balanced the nature of human beings as creatures of the earth, sharing in the nature that is common to humans and other animals, and the special responsibility of human beings, created in God's image, to act with moral responsibility.

Upham's theory of mind was explicit in the relation of the processes of the intellect to those of the sensibilities. "The action of the *Sensibilities* is subsequent in time to that of the *Intellective* nature" (Upham, 1886, p. 261). Any excitement of the processes of the sensibilities depends on activation by some process of the intellect. Emotions and desires, natural or moral, can be activated by perception or memory, focused perhaps by attention or through past association. Whether action results or not, and the nature of such action, depends on the activation of the will, which occurs subsequent to the initiation of the sensibilities.

Upham's treatment of the will was the most philosophical of his accounts of the three "departments" of mind. He did not divide the will into subclasses or processes. Rather, he dealt with the concept in terms of fundamental issues: the nature of the power of the will and whether it is governed by laws or is free. On the latter question, Upham concluded, as a good scientist, that the will is indeed governed by laws, because the uniformities in human behavior imply lawful regulation. At the same time, however, because human beings are confronted with choices, they are free to choose among alternatives—for good or ill, either from the instincts or passions or from motives of moral responsibility. Thus Upham concluded that the will is both free and governed by laws. How could both of these conclusions be true? Upham was content to leave the answer to that question a mystery, perhaps never to be resolved. On the issue of the power of the will, Upham noted that education and parental child-rearing practices provide for the exercise of will in the making of moral choices. On this point his argument is much the same as that which William James described later when he laid out his maxims for strengthening habits (James, 1890, pp. 120ff.).

Eventually habits—and their basis in learning—came to dominate explanations of behavior, and the concept of will gradually disappeared from psychology. More recently, however, contemporary psychology has adopted the position that psychological phenomena "are determined jointly by processes instigated by acts of conscious choice and will" (Bargh & Chartrand, 1999, p. 463). Although for some the debate has shifted to the question of the circumstances under which the environment or the will instigates action, others argue that "the will is not a psychological force that causes action" but "is a conscious experience that may only map rather weakly, or perhaps not at all, onto the actual relationship between the person's cognition and action" (Wegner & Wheatley, 1999, p. 481). This continuing debate suggests that current psychologists wrestle with the old issues but use new methods and new ways of framing the underlying questions.

In summary, Upham categorized the mind into three "departments" whose processes are initiated first in the intellect, either from internal (e.g., memory) or external (e.g., sensory stimulation) sources, then in the sensibilities (e.g., emotions, natural and moral), that may give rise to the need for action, mediated by the will—sometimes functioning freely, sometimes expressing general laws that govern its action—with its power dependent on the frequency and pattern of its past exercise. In this way, Upham described mental processes apparent in consciousness, labeled by common consent in language as used in common discourse, and at the same time he suggested how mental processes could result in action.

Upham's system was influential in his era. The three-part division of mind was adopted by Joseph Haven, who noted that there were "many reasons for such a distinction; they have been well stated by Professor Upham" and "generally adopted by the more recent European writers of note, especially in France and Germany" (Haven, 1857, p. 36). But Upham's textbook was read and adopted because it was comprehensive for its time: It was judged to "furnish a full view of our mental operations in all their parts and complexities; to leave no class of facts unnoticed, no class of laws unexplained" (Smith, 1837, p. 628). Another reviewer noted that Upham "presents the views of others and himself with great good judgement, candor, clearness, and method. . . . The student by the aid of a thorough teacher, may gain a competent systematic view of the leading principles of the science" (Anonymous, 1840, p. 253). In collecting facts of mind, classifying them and providing a systematic view of mind and its processes, Upham provided a model for the legion of introductory textbooks that followed, including those of the 20th and 21st centuries.

IMPERFECT AND DISORDERED MENTAL ACTION

In later editions of his textbook, Upham included one chapter on excited conceptions or apparitions and another on mental alienation. Any discussion of mental alienation in a textbook of intellectual philosophy was unusual for the time and for the tradition in which Upham wrote (Madden & Madden, 1983), but Upham believed that the aberrations of mind could help to illuminate its normal functions. The content of the first chapter dealt with "excited conceptions or apparitions," by which Upham meant seeing things that did not exist—hallucinations of ghosts or other images—that he attributed to the lack of bloodletting or the use of drugs (opium), explanations consonant with the medical understanding of the time. In these examples of, and explanations for, seeing apparitions taken from the medical literature, Upham recognized the reciprocal influences of body and mind. Mental alienations are disorders of mind without a clear (if any) dependence on bodily disorders and reflect the independence of mind as nonmaterial but having a real existence nevertheless. Just as mind is affected by bodily disturbances, so is the body affected by mental disturbance, as in the case of delusional feelings or pain. The second chapter dealt with a variety of mental abnormalities: "idiocy," or diminished intellectual functioning, several forms of hypochondriasis, reasoning in partially insane individuals, insanity of the passions, total insanity or delirium, and moral accountability of insane individuals and the treatment owed to them.

In writing his treatise on the will, Upham included a chapter on the "alienation of the will." One example is that of an individual whose will became a captive of the passions, with resultant violent behavior that led to institutionalization (Upham, 1834, pp. 303–304); another is the powerlessness of the will in melancholia, or depression, when action seems impossible. Similar examples, although from an evolutionary point of view, were used by Ribot (1894) to shed light on the normal functions of will.

In 1840 Upham published *Outlines of Imperfect and Disordered Mental Action* in Harper's Family Library series, addressed to a popular audience. The alienations that Upham addressed in this publication involved mental processes that were related to his triarchic organization of the mind: Disorders of the intellect that are external in origin included sensory disorders, such as apparitions, disordered attention (e.g., an inability to fix attention), and somnambulism. Disorders of the intellect that are of internal origin were identified with such processes as memory (senility) and imagination (delusions).

The sensibilities had their own disorders: of appetites (alcoholism), of affections (hypochondriasis or phobias), or derangements of moral sensibilities (the absence of conscience).

Disorders of the will, in which a person's actions seem to be determined by passions and the absence or subjection of the will, led to the question of moral responsibility for acts committed in the absence of the exercise of will. In these cases, Upham believed that individuals should be regarded as free of responsibility for their actions. At the same time, however, he proposed no criteria for determining when an individual should or should not be held accountable, leaving that to be decided on the basis of particular circumstances. Upham provided no general chapter on treatment for imperfect or disordered mental action but suggested medical remedies having their origins in ills of the body (e.g., bloodletting).

Upham's analysis of disordered mental action introduced his system of the mind to a popular audience, recognizing "that the public mind is but little informed, certainly much less than it should be, in relation to the true doctrines of regular or normal mental action; but it is, undoubtedly, much more ignorant of the philosophy of defective and disordered mental action" (Upham, 1840, iii).

CONCLUSION

The development of a new psychology, in the United States and elsewhere in the world, in the last quarter of the 19th century did not occur in a vacuum. German psychology was not written on a North American *tabula rasa*. Rather, the German psychology was met in the United States by a psychology that had its roots in British philosophical traditions (Blumenthal, 1980). Upham contributed significantly to the acceptance of intellectual and mental philosophy as a science of empiricism and induction. His interest in the facts of mind and their indications of normal and disordered action offered an array of topics that modern psychology eventually came to address. Moreover, Upham helped create an environment in the colleges and universities of the United States that shaped the new psychology and enabled it to flourish.

As psychology matured in the 20th century, it continued to reflect Upham's interest in normal and abnormal states of mind. Eventually, however, advances in psychological knowledge that followed in the wake of the growth of a new psychology replaced Upham's descriptions, both of normal mental processes and their imperfect action. Although Upham's classification of mental disordered action cannot claim modern descendants, he can be credited with recognizing the importance of including this concern within his mental philosophy.

REFERENCES

Anonymous. (1840). Review 21. *New York Review, VI,* 253.

Bargh, J. A., & Chartrand, T. L. (1999). The unbearable automaticity of being. *American Psychologist, 554,* 462–479.

Blumenthal, A. (1980). Wilhelm Wundt and the two traditions in psychology. In R. W. Rieber (Ed.), *Wilhelm Wundt and the making of a scientific psychology* (pp. 117–135). New York and London: Plenum Press.

Brown, J. W. (1969). *The rise of biblical criticism in America, 1800–1870.* Middletown, CT: Wesleyan University Press.

Cousin, V. (1834). *Elements of psychology* (C. Henry, Trans.). Hartford, CT: Cooke.

Dewey, J. (1892). *Psychology.* New York: Harper.

Ebbinghaus, H. (1908) *Psychology* (M. Meyer, Trans.). Boston: Heath. (Original work published 1908)

Engle, T. L. (1967). Teaching psychology at the secondary school level: Past, present, possible future. *Journal of School Psychology, 5,* 168–176.

Evans, R. (1984). The origins of American academic psychology. In J. Brožek (Ed.), *Explorations in the history of psychology in the United States* (pp. 17–60). Lewisburg, PA: Bucknell University Press.

Fay, J. W. (1939). *American psychology before William James.* New Brunswick, NJ: Rutgers University Press.

Fuchs, A. H. (1999). Upham, Thomas Cogswell. In J. A. Garraty & M. C. Carnes (Eds.), *American National Biography* (Vol. 22, pp. 112–114). New York: Oxford University Press.

Fuchs, A. H. (2000). The contributions of American mental philosophers to psychology in the United States. *History of Psychology, 3,* 3–19.

Hanscome, J. (1846, Oct.). *Diary.* Miscellaneous manuscript volumes: Diary of James William Hanscome. Special Collections and Archives, Bowdoin College Library.

Haven, J. (1857). *Mental philosophy.* New York: Sheldon.

Haven, J. (1859). *Moral philosophy.* New York and Chicago: Sheldon.

Hedrick, J. D. (1994). *Harriet Beecher Stowe.* New York: Oxford University Press.

Hovet, T. R. (1979a). Mrs. Thomas C. Upham's "Happy Phebe": A feminine source of Uncle Tom. *American Literature, 51,* 267–270.

Hovet, T. R. (1979b). Principles of the hidden life—Uncle Tom's Cabin and the myth of the inward quest in 19th century American culture. *Journal of American Culture, 2,* 265–270.

James, W. (1890). *Psychology.* New York: Holt.

Leary, D. E. (1987). Telling likely stories: The rhetoric of the new psychology. *Journal of the History of the Behavioral Sciences, 23,* 315–331.

Locke, J. (1975). *Essay concerning human understanding* (P. Niddich, Ed.). Oxford: Clarendon Press. (Original work published 1690)

Louttit, C. M. (1956). Psychology in nineteenth century high schools. *American Psychologist, 11,* 717.

Madden, M. C., & Madden, E. H. (1983). Thomas Upham on relations and alienation. *Transactions of the Charles S. Pierce Society, 19,* 227–253.

Mills, E. S. (1969). *George Trumbull Ladd.* Cleveland, OH: Press of Case Western Reserve University.

Phelps, C. (1930). *The Anglo-American peace movement in the mid-nineteenth century*. New York: Columbia University Press.

Porter, N. (1868). *The human intellect*. New York: Scribner.

Rauch, F. A. (1840) *Psychology; Or, a view of the human soul; Including anthropology* (2nd ed.). New York: Dodd.

Ribot, T. (1894). *The diseases of the will*. Chicago: Open Court.

Rieber, R. W. (1980). The Americanization of psychology before William James. In R. W. Rieber & K. Salzinger (Eds.), *Psychology: Theoretical-historical perspectives* (pp. 104–123). New York: Academic Press.

Roback, A. A. (1952a). *History of American psychology*. New York: Library Publishers.

Roback, A. A. (1952b). Psychology in American secondary schools in the 90's. *American Psychologist, 7*, 44–45.

Salter, D. (1986). *Spirit and intellect: Thomas Upham's holiness theology*. Metuchen, NJ: Scarecrow Press.

Smith, H. B. (1837). Review of Upham's *Mental Philosophy*. *The Literary and Theological Review*, 621–659.

Stewart, D. (1808). *Elements of the philosophy of the human mind*. Brattleborough, VT: William Fessenden.

Thompson, L. (1938). *Young Longfellow, 1807–1843*. New York: Macmillan.

Upham, T. C. (1819). *American sketches*. New York: David Longworth.

Upham, T. C. (1823). *Jahn's Biblical Archaeology*. Andover: Flagg and Gould.

Upham, T. C. (1826). *Elements of intellectual philosophy*. Brunswick, ME: J. Griffin

Upham, T. C. (1827). *Elements of intellectual philosophy*. Portland, ME: Hyde.

Upham, T. C. (1828). *Elements of intellectual philosophy* (2nd ed.). Portland, ME: Shirley and Hyde.

Upham, T. C. (1832). *Elements of mental philosophy*. Boston: Hyde.

Upham, T. C. (1834). *Philosophical and practical treatise on the will*. Portland, ME: Hyde.

Upham, T. C. (1840). *Outlines of imperfect and disordered mental action*. New York: Harper.

Upham, T. C. (1842). *The manual of peace*. Boston: American Peace Society.

Upham, T. C. (1843). *Principles of the interior or hidden life*. Boston: D. S. King.

Upham, T. C. (1861). *Abridgment of elements of mental philosophy, including the three departments of the intellect, sensibilities, and the will*. New York: Harper.

Upham, T. C. (1886). *Abridgment of mental philosophy, including the three departments of the intellect, sensibilities, and the will*. New York: Harper.

Wayland, F. (1857). *The elements of intellectual philosophy*. New York: Sheldon.

Wegner, D. M., & Wheatley, T. (1999). Apparent mental causation: Sources of the experience of will. *American Psychologist, 54*, 480–492.

Weyer, E. M. (1921). In memory of Wilhelm Wundt. *Psychological Review, 28*, 181–183.

Whitney, E. L. (1929). *The American Peace Society: Centennial history* (3rd Rev. ed.). Washington, DC: American Peace Society.

Ziegler, M. (1949). Growth and development of psychology at the University of Georgia. *Journal of Genetic Psychology, 75*, 51–59.

Zimbardo, P. G., & Gerrig, R. J. (1976). *Psychology and life*. (14th ed.). New York: HarperCollins.

Chapter 2

Hermann Ludwig Ferdinand von Helmholtz: Physicist as Psychologist

Helmut E. Adler

In the second half of the 19th century in Germany, mental philosophy, or psychology, transformed itself from a discipline of metaphysical discussion to empirical and especially experimental research. Physiologists, physicists, and physicians all played a role in this movement, following in the footsteps of Gustav Theodor Fechner (chap. 1, *Pioneers II*), the physicist, who founded psychophysics (Fechner, 1966)—in Fechner's view a means of measuring psychological processes (Adler, 1996). Hermann Ludwig Ferdinand von Helmholtz, an individual with wide-ranging interests, was among those who contributed to this change. By inclination he was a physicist, but at various times he also was a physician, a psychologist, a physiologist, an anatomist, a meteorologist, a mathematician, and a chemist. In addition he was deeply involved in promoting empiricism in science and in educational reform. He stressed the teaching of science in the German schools instead of Latin and Greek.

Helmholtz's contributions to psychology centered on the experimental study of acoustics and optics, where his name lives on in the Young–Helmholtz theory of color vision. In other circles he is remembered for his law of the conservation of energy, his measurement of the speed of nerve conduction, his invention of the ophthalmoscope, and his contributions to the understanding of magnetism and electricity. Through his student Heinrich Hertz, Helmholtz's influence can be tied to the invention of radio and television. Carl Stumpf (chap. 4, this volume), professor of psychology in Berlin, in 1895, assessing Helmholtz's influence on psychology, wrote that Helmholtz, above all others, "helped build

---

*Photo of Hermann Ferdinand von Helmholtz courtesy of Helmut E. Adler.

the bridge between physiology and psychology that thousands of workers today go back and forth upon" (Turner, 1982, p. 148).

EARLY YEARS

Helmholtz was born August 31, 1821, in Potsdam near Berlin in Prussia, where his father, Ferdinand, was a professor at the Gymnasium (German high school). His mother, Caroline Penne, was descended from William Penn. Helmholtz's father had enlisted in the Prussian army in 1813 and was promoted to second lieutenant on the battlefield after the battle of Dresden in the Napoleonic wars. After the Peace of Paris, 1814, Helmholtz Sr. returned to his studies at the university. Originally he had studied theology, but he found himself in disagreement with the hyperorthodox religious attitudes prevailing at the time and switched to classical languages. Although he had a teaching position in the Gymnasium, teachers' salaries were so low that the family always had money problems.

Hermann was sickly as a child and did not go to school until age 7. He entered the Gymnasium in 1832, where he became an enthusiastic student of science, less so in history and grammar. Koenigsberger (1965/1906) related that while other students in his class were reading Cicero or Virgil, Helmholtz would often be engaged in working out the passage of rays of light through a telescope under his desk. When he graduated from the Gymnasium, Helmholtz wanted to attend the university to study science, but his family could not afford the expense. As a result, in 1838, he went to the Royal Friedrich-Wilhelm Institute for Medicine and Surgery in Berlin, where education was subsidized in return for eight years of service as an army surgeon.

MEDICAL STUDIES

As a medical student, Helmholtz was allowed to attend courses at the University of Berlin, and he took full advantage of this opportunity. He was particularly interested in Johannes Müller's lectures on physiology and Eilhard Mitcherlich's on zöo-chemistry. After passing his preliminary examinations at the institute, Helmholtz did independent research with Müller, who was the foremost physiologist of the day and was especially famous for his doctrine of specific nerve energies: The type of information relayed by a nerve from sense organs to the central nervous system depends on the sense organ. People "see stars" when they receive a blow to the eye. Müller conjectured that nerve activity was electrical, but it remained for his student, Emil du Bois-Reymond, to establish that fact.

Helmholtz and his friends du Bois-Reymond, Carl Ludwig, and Ernst Brücke agreed on the principle that "No other forces than common physical chemical ones are active within the organism." They banded together as a small private organization that they called the Berlin Physical Society to discuss this mechanistic philosophy (Bolles, 1993). It is interesting to follow the careers of this small group of friends. Du Bois-Reymond eventually succeeded Müller at Berlin; Ludwig went to Leipzig, where Ivan Pavlov was one of his students, and Brücke went to Vienna, where Sigmund Freud studied under him.

Soon after starting work with Müller, Helmholtz bought a small microscope and began work on his thesis. But when he brought his results to his professor, Müller advised him to do some more work and offered him much better instruments that were at Müller's disposal. With this equipment, Helmholtz continued to work on his doctoral thesis, "*De Fabrica Systematis Nervosi Evertebratum*" ("The Structure of the Nervous System in Invertebrates"), which was finally accepted on November 2, 1842. This thesis showed that nerve fibers and nerve cells are connected to one another, a fact that had not been demonstrated previously in invertebrates.

Helmholtz's next contribution grew out of a scientific controversy about the nature of fermentation and decomposition of organic materials. The chemists claimed that these processes could be reduced to purely chemical reactions, such as oxidation and reduction. Working in Müller's laboratory, Helmholtz showed that they were caused by living organisms. Paradoxically, these results, published before Pasteur, were seized by a faction of physiologists known as vitalists as support for their position that all life processes could not be explained by purely physical and chemical reactions. Physicists, on the other hand, regarded Helmholtz's results with suspicion. Gustav Magnus, the professor of physics at Berlin, whom Helmholtz was to succeed many years later, offered him his laboratory "to throw more light on the subject than . . . a young army surgeon living on his pay could afford" (Koenigsberger, 1965/1906). Helmholtz carried out more experiments on this issue but never published further on the subject.

ARMY SURGEON

Earlier, Helmholtz had been appointed house surgeon at Charité Hospital, a position he disliked because of long hours working with patients, most of whom were incurable. He completed his service there with distinction, however, and was appointed assistant surgeon to the Royal Hussars at Potsdam in 1843. In that role the young surgeon's military duties were not onerous and he continued his scientific education. In particular, he studied higher mathematics, in which he had never had instruction as a student. Helmholtz also equipped a small laboratory at his barracks and continued his research.

A burning question at the time was whether the functioning of living organisms could be explained by the same forces that shaped the inorganic world or whether an added vital force (*vis vita*) had to be postulated. The central issue was whether the energy expended by an organism was balanced by the energy provided by food intake and respiration. Helmholtz measured the energy expended by muscle movements in terms of the heat produced by contraction, using frogs' thigh muscles. From the results of his experiments he concluded that the mechanical forces in a response and the electrical and chemical forces energizing that response are equivalent and could be transformed from one another.

Casting the results of his experiments in mathematical form, Helmholtz presented them in a paper "On the Conservation of Energy" read to the Physical Society in Berlin in 1847 (Helmholtz, 1971/1847). This statement aroused much controversy. The older generation of scientists rejected Helmholtz's conclusions. But the military authorities were impressed by the work of their young surgeon and praised his work. A further controversy subsequently developed over priorities because earlier Julius Robert Mayer had established similar equivalencies, but without experiments, and C. P. Joule had measured the mechanical equivalent of heat experimentally. Helmholtz had not been aware of either of these contributions at the time but later he acknowledged their priority.

External circumstances now led to radical changes in Helmholtz's career. His friend Brücke had been instructor of anatomy at the Academy of Arts and assistant at the Museum of Anatomy and Zoology in Berlin. When Brücke was called to Königsberg as professor of physiology and general pathology, Helmholtz was recommended for the vacated position. After a successful trial lecture, he was appointed to the post but only served for one year. Brücke was called from Königsberg to Vienna and Helmholtz was nominated for the Königsberg position. Thus in 1849, at the age of 28, Helmholtz was appointed "extraordinary (associate) professor and director" of the Physiological Institute.

With a salary that matched the level his father had reached after many years, Helmholtz was ready to marry. Olga von Velten, his bride, came from a prominent family who had moved to Potsdam in 1846. Her grandfather had distinguished himself in the battle of Kunersdorf during the Seven Years War. During the Prussian retreat, von Velten had saved the life of King Frederick II ("the Great"). As a result he was ennobled and received the order *pour le mérite*. Olga's father was a surgeon-major and her mother the daughter of a court painter and gallery director.

KÖNIGSBERG (1849–1855)

After settling down in Königsberg, Helmholtz commenced an extremely fertile period of scientific activity. In 1850 he published his first discoveries on the speed of nerve transmission. The accepted view at that time was that the speed of nerve conduction is equal to the speed of light. But stimulating the sciatic nerve of large frogs, Helmholtz found that it took 0.0014–0.0020 seconds for the nerve impulse to reach the calf muscle—a speed of 42.9–25 m/sec. As had happened in the case of his law of the conservation of energy, these data ran into opposition. This time the philosophers objected on the grounds that there could not possibly be a lapse of time between an idea and its resulting action. When they were finally convinced, Müller transmitted the results to the Academy of Science in Berlin, and Alexander von Humboldt had them published in the *Comptes Rendus* of the Académie in Paris, with an explanatory footnote of his own.

Helmholtz followed up the measurement of the speed of nerve conduction with determinations on himself and others. He knew about the problems astronomers experienced with reaction times when they had to report the precise timing of the passage of a star in their telescopes. Now he stimulated himself with an electrical shock and measured the time it took to move his hand. With other research participants he found that stimulating the toe and thigh resulted in different reaction times. These data seemed to establish the rate of transmission of both motor and sensory nerves at 50 to 60 meters per second, slower than the speed of sound. As Helmholtz mentioned in a lecture, "A whale probably feels a wound near its tail in about a second, and requires another second to send back orders to the tail to defend itself" (Koenigsberger, 1965/1906, p. 72).

Although still engaged with these measurements, Helmholtz began to construct an apparatus with which one could observe the interior of the eye. "It was so obvious, requiring, moreover, no knowledge beyond the optics I learned in the Gymnasium, that it seems almost ludicrous that I and others should have been so slow as not to see it" (quoted in Koenigsberger, 1965/1906, p. 74). By means of an arrangement of mirrors and lenses, Helmholtz constructed the first ophthalmoscope. Light reflected from a mirror was introduced into the eye via the pupil and reflected by the retina. The lens magnified the view and the blood vessels in the eye, and the exit of the optic nerve (blind spot) was easily seen through the transparent interior of the eye.

After publishing this discovery in 1851, it took some time for it to be accepted by the medical profession. One distinguished surgeon told Helmholtz that he would never use the instrument—it would be too dangerous to admit the naked light into a diseased eye. Another physician was of the opinion that the mirror might be of some service to oculists with defective eyesight—but he himself had good eyes and wanted none of it (Koenigsberger, 1965/1906). On the recommendation of the medical faculty, however, the Prussian ministry of education acknowledged Helmholtz's invention of the ophthalmoscope, along with his other contributions, and promoted him to Ordinary (Full) Professor on December 17, 1851. Helmholtz's reputation was now established.

That year Helmholtz used his summer vacation to inspect various other physiological laboratories and, on a visit to Heidelberg University, he first heard the suggestion that he might be offered the professorship there. He wrote to his wife that "Heidelberg would not be a bad place to work in." Crossing the Rhine to Strasbourg in France, he was amused that *"liberté, fraternité,* and *égalité"* were flaunted everywhere; "property of the nation" was posted on all public buildings;

and many private houses displayed "frightfully" democratic devices reminiscent of the revolution (Koenigsberger, 1965/1906, pp. 80–83).

For Helmholtz these opinions seem to indicate a change of heart; his earlier ideas had been quite liberal. In 1848 he was caught up in events in Frankfurt, where an attempt to launch a unified, liberal, constitutional monarchy for all of Germany had failed. His sister-in-law wrote that, after that, he had visited her and pinned a black, red, and gold (the colors of the reformists and later the Weimar republic and post-World-War-II Germany) cockade on her child's head.

Helmholtz's promotion required an inaugural lecture. His, titled "On the Nature of Human Sense-Perceptions," marked a turning of his attention to the physiology of vision. Later on, he presented for his habilitation thesis a dissertation "On the Theory of Compound Colors," the first effort to examine the laws of color mixture for pigments as well as lights. Sir Isaac Newton, who had discovered that white light is made up of a mixture of colors, had assumed that the laws of color mixture are the same for pigments as for colored lights. Helmholtz discovered, however, that these mixtures are quite different. The disparity is most marked in the combination of blue and yellow, which yield green when pigments are mixed but white with the mixture of spectral lights. Helmholtz's explanation was that pigments reflect only the color that an observer sees and absorb all others. Thus blue pigments reflect green, blue, and violet, whereas yellow substances reflect green, red, and yellow. Only green is common to both and thus green is seen by the observer.

Helmholtz also stressed the important role of the sense organ in the origin of sensations. Although visible light and heat rays are part of the same spectrum, the eye is sensitive only to the visible rays and only the skin to heat. It is not the nature of the object but the functioning of sensory mechanisms that determines the sensation. This idea, of course, goes back to the concept of specific energies of nerves, endorsed by Helmholtz's teacher Johannes Müller. Helmholtz now extended this idea to color vision. Color is not inherent in the object but depends solely on the stimulation of appropriate receptors. As Helmholtz put it, "Sensations of light and color are only the symbols for relations of reality. They have as much and as little connection or relation with it, as the name of a man, or the letters in his name, have to do with the man himself" (Koenigsberger, 1965/1906, p. 99).

This theory clashed with the ideas of Goethe, the German poet and natural scientist, who was held in very high regard. Goethe had attacked Newton's prism experiments with unparalleled animosity. Helmholtz praised Goethe for his work in osteology and botany, but then pointed out that Goethe had been ignorant of the most elementary principles of optics when he presented his criticism of Newton. "With Goethe," he said, "the phenomenal is the immediate of the ideal . . . and he therefore appreciates experiments that can be carried out in clear sunshine, under the open heavens, in contrast to Newton's slits and glasses" (Koenigsberger, 1965/1906, p. 105). This clash between phenomenalism and empiricism would continue to haunt Helmholtz in his later work on color perception.

In the fall of 1853 Helmholtz visited England to attend a meeting of the British Association in Hull. He passed through London, at that time the largest city in the world, and was much impressed. "Berlin, both in size and civilization, is a village compared to London," he wrote to his wife (Koenigsberger, 1965/1906, p. 109). His lecture was "On the Mixture of Homogeneous Colors." In addition to the 850 members in attendance, there were 236 women. "English ladies are well up in their science," he remarked. "Some come to be seen, some from curiosity, or to listen to the discussions. Still, on the whole, they are attentive, and don't go to sleep, even under provocation" (Koenigsberger, 1965/1906, p. 113).

On February 27, 1855, Helmholtz gave a popular scientific lecture, "On Human Vision," in connection with a Kant memorial. In this talk, he tried to relate his theories to the ideas of Immanuel Kant, who had lived and taught in Königsberg all his life. Helmholtz wanted to reconcile philosophy and science and in the process to provide a basis for a psychological approach to the problems of visual perception. He was not satisfied with the treatment given by psychologists. "Unfortunately we get no help from the psychologists," he remarked, "because introspection has been the only means of acquiring knowledge for psychology, whereas we are concerned here with mental activities about which introspection cannot give us any information. Rather we can infer their existence only from the physiological examination of sense organs" (Helmholtz, 1855).

This 1855 lecture contained the first mention of Helmholtz's controversial theory of unconscious inference. According to Helmholtz, the bridge between sense–organ physiology and phenomenal experience is a hypothetical process of unconscious inference, where brain or mental activities make an interpretation of reality. "These acts occur without our knowledge and therefore cannot be changed voluntarily or according to our better judgment" (Helmholtz, 1855). For example, in the case of visual illusions, we know that our sense impressions are incorrect, but the illusions still persist.

The involuntary associations responsible for such experiences can be established by repetition. Visual-distance judgment, for example, is a result of learning. "I myself still recall clearly the moment when the laws of perspective became clear to me, so that I realized that distant objects appear small. I was walking past a high tower on which people were on the topmost gallery and innocently asked my mother to hand me the cute little dolls, as I was convinced . . . that if she would stretch out her arm she would be able to grasp the tower's gallery. Later I have often looked up to the gallery of that tower, when people were standing up there, but they no longer became little dolls for the practiced eye" (Helmholtz, 1855).

There is some question as to the extent that Helmholtz accepted a nativistic approach, of the sort put forth by Johannes Müller. Certainly at the time he followed the Kantian views (Pastore, 1974). Later on, however, he expanded his empiricist approach into an examination of the basis of geometry. In this instance he directly clashed with Kant, who had proclaimed the foundation of geometry to be intuitive and *a priori*. Without giving up unconscious inference, Helmholtz dissented, hypothesizing that the axioms of geometry are *a posteriori*, abstracted from experience. Boring (1950) compared Helmholtz's unconscious inferences to conscious inferences from analogy, and therefore inductive processes.

Helmholtz's wife's health was deteriorating. Doctors recommended a change from the cold climate of Königsberg. At the time the chair of physiology at Bonn fell vacant and Helmholtz decided to apply for it. Bonn, located in the Rhineland, had a much more temperate climate than East Prussia. On von Humboldt's recommendation Helmholtz was appointed professor of physiology and anatomy at the University of Bonn in 1855.

BONN (1855–1858)

Arriving at his new post, Helmholtz found little equipment for his laboratory and the anatomical museum had been "frightfully neglected," as he writes to his father (Koenigsberger, 1965/1906, p. 148). Moreover he had to prepare new lectures in anatomy, and things did not go well with them. Complaints were filed with the Minister of Education that his lectures in anatomy were inadequate. "I was told that people said I brought a good deal of physiology and chemistry into my anatomy, which restricted the amount of anatomy proper, and they made jokes at the introduction of a cosine in physiological optics. But I received many indications of interest and appreciation from the older students, and from my colleagues" (quoted in Koenigsberger, 1965/1906, p. 149).

At this time, Helmholtz was completing Volume I of his great *Handbook of Physiological Optics*, which appeared in stages, starting in 1856. Now he also turned to the study of acoustics, hoping to establish for the sense of hearing an analysis of its physical, physiological, and psychological basis that would be similar to what he had done for vision. In studying combination tones, for example, he determined that beats arose not only for the difference between two tones closely adjacent on the scale but also for the sum of the frequencies of two different tones. He also received a grant from the King of Bavaria to construct an acoustic instrument that controlled the vibrations of tuning forks by an electromagnet.

Helmholtz had hardly settled in Bonn when he was approached with an offer of a professorship in physiology at the University of Heidelberg. Acceptance would mean that he would have to move from the kingdom of Prussia to the duchy of the Grand Duke of Baden—in those days, Germany was still a mosaic of independent states. But the Baden ministry offered him more money, at the same time that the Prussian ministry kept postponing the building of a promised new institute at Bonn. In 1858, Helmholtz accepted the invitation to

Heidelberg and handed his resignation to the ministry in Berlin. Kirchhoff at Heidelberg wrote to him: "All Heidelberg is rejoicing at your decision, and I hope you will find a congenial atmosphere there" (Koenigsberger, 1965/1906, p. 165).

Even before he had actually moved to his new residence, Helmholtz visited Karlsruhe, the capital of Baden, to deliver two papers at the *Naturforscher Versammlung* (Naturalists' Convention) at that city. One was on after-images. It confirmed some of Fechner's findings and also showed that by means of observing bright spectral light in a field of complementary color, the after-image appeared more saturated in color than even pure prismatic light. The second paper dealt with harmony and dissonance. Helmholtz demonstrated that musical chords were perceived as consonant or dissonant, depending on the ratios of their overtones. In this lecture, he also compared the basilar membrane of the cochlea with the strings on a piano, so that the fundamental and the overtones would be set in vibration simultaneously. This theory, known as the "piano theory" of pitch, was one of Helmholtz's major contributions.

HEIDELBERG (1858–1871)

When Helmholtz arrived at Heidelberg to take over the department of physiology, he was assigned an assistant to handle the required laboratory course. This assistant was Wilhelm Wundt (chap. 3, *Pioneers III*), who was already engaged in research on perception. Wundt apparently was not very happy in this role, and in 1865, when promoted to extraordinary (associate) professor, he was glad to give up his assistantship. Nothing is known of the relationship between Wundt and Helmholtz, but it probably was not close. In any case, when Helmholtz left for Berlin in 1871, Wundt was passed over as his successor, contrary to what might have been expected.

Helmholtz's wife's health continued to deteriorate. After her death in 1859, Helmholtz was incapacitated by migraine, inability to sleep, and fainting fits. In 1861 he met and married Anna von Mohl, much younger than himself, well-educated, and from a socially prominent family. Her father was an important official, her uncle—a naturalized French citizen—professor of Persian at the Collège de France in Paris.

On the occasion of his election as pro-rector (head) of Heidelberg University, Helmholtz used the platform to analyze the relationship of natural science and mental science. He called for improved scientific attacks on the problems of the human mind. For this reason, he favored scientists' giving popular lectures. As he put it somewhat later: "A great gulf still divides the philosophical and historical interests . . . from those of natural science and mathematics; the two worlds hardly understand each other's aims in thought and work" (Koenigsberger, 1965/1906, p. 212).

In 1863 Helmholtz (1954/1863) brought out his major work on the sensations of tone. Part I treated the structure of the ear, as well as overtones, timbre, and pitch. It also contained a description of his resonance ("piano") theory of pitch (see Herrnstein and Boring, 1965, pp. 44 ff.). Part II dealt with harmony, combination tones and beats, and consonance and dissonance, all based on his own experiments. Part III covered musical matters, including the aesthetics of musical composition. Helmholtz had had a lively interest in music all his life. Even when still a student he had brought a piano along to his room at the military institute. Later, he studied Persian and Arabic scales in comparison to Western music.

Helmholtz traveled frequently during these years. In 1864 he spent four weeks in England. He delivered six popular lectures in London, as well as the distinguished Croonian lecture to the Royal Society on "Normal Motions of the Human Eye in Relation to Binocular Vision." In his research he related the motion of the eyes to the horopter, the point in space where the image of both eyes is fused into a single view, whereas closer and further points in space have a doubled representation. Of course, the individual is not consciously aware of the double images (Southall, 1937), a fact that Helmholtz attributed to unconscious inference.

On this trip, Helmholtz admired Oxford University for its well-preserved buildings and trim grass lawns but criticized its educational system for not including much science. He met most of the famous English scientists, Tyndall, Faraday, Huxley ("who is just now the chief partisan of rationalism against the biblical view of science"), William Thomson (later Lord Kelvin, who became a very close friend), and Mr. Gladstone (the prime minister). He also traveled to Manchester, where he met James Prescott Joule, a brewer and "the chief discoverer of the conservation of energy" (Koenigsberger, 1965/1906, p. 224).

In 1866 Helmholtz's *Handbook of Physiological Optics,* which had been published in separate parts, was finally completed (Helmholtz, 1962/1856–1866). Part I summarized the physical and physiological aspects of vision, Part II dealt with visual sensations and included Helmholtz's theory of color vision (see Herrnstein & Boring, 1965, pp. 40 ff.), and Part III covered space perception.

A series of lectures delivered in 1868 provided a more popular exposition of these same topics (Helmholtz, 1868; Pastore, 1973). The eye, Helmholtz said, can be considered a camera obscura, although unlike the camera it has no corners; it is not made of wood but of the stiff white sclera. It differs further in that the eyeball is not empty but is filled with transparent watery fluid. The outer fixed lens of the cornea and the adjustable crystalline lens inside the eye focus an image on the plane of the eye's rear surface. The eye's chromatic and spherical aberrations are considerable and it has another peculiarity, the blind spot, where an image cannot register. "If an optical store would want to sell me an instrument that had all these defects," he wrote, "I would feel completely justified . . . to return the instrument." Despite its flaws, however, Helmholtz concluded that the eye is well-adapted to its function and, under normal conditions, such deficiencies are never noticed.

In the second lecture Helmholtz took up visual sensations. After discussing the nature of light sensitivity and the appearance of colors, he described his theory of color vision, which held that red-, green-, and violet-sensitive nerve fibers can account for all possible perceived colors (see Herrnstein & Boring, 1965, pp. 40–44), and rejected the objections to that theory. In this lecture Helmholtz gave Thomas Young the credit he deserved for developing the essentials of three-color theory. He noted that color vision had been a puzzle for a long time but that

> the solution had been found . . . and made available, by the same Thomas Young, who had been the first to decypher the puzzle of the Egyptian hieroglyphics. He was one of the most acute of men who ever lived, but he had the bad luck to be far superior to his contemporaries in intellect. Thus a mass of his most important thoughts remains buried in the great folios of the Royal Society of London and forgotten. (Helmholtz, 1868)

In his third lecture, after discussing brightness and contrast phenomena, Helmholtz covered space perception, a topic on which there was controversy between the nativist and empiricistic points of view. The nativist position assumed that space perception is a result of an innate (unlearned) ability to interpret stimulation of corresponding points on the retina of each eye in terms of depth and distance. Helmholtz's approach was empiricistic:

> We learn to interpret the local signs. All space perception is based on experience . . . the local signs of our visual sensations, as well as their qualities, are nothing more than signs whose meanings we have learned to interpret by experience. . . . We are led by these investigations . . . into an area of psychic processes, in which so far there has been little scientific research activity, because it is so difficult to express them in words. (Helmholtz, 1868)

In such expressions Helmholtz laid the foundations of an objective psychology, but he did not pursue it further.

Helmholtz's empiricism was not without opposition—much of it by Ewald Hering, professor of physiology at Prague and later at Leipzig. In 1871 Hering wrote,

> There is in contemporary physiology a fatal prejudice in a similar way as was previously in physiology in general. Just as at one time, what one was unable to, or did not want to, investigate physiologically, was explained in terms of a vital force, so now on every third page of a physiological optics, there appears the "soul" or the "mind," the "judgment" or [unconscious] "inference" . . . in order to help eliminate all difficulties." (quoted in Pastore, 1974, p. 380)

Hering also rejected Helmholtz's trichromatic theory of color vision. He proposed instead a system of opponent colors, with four paired primaries, red-green and yellow-blue.

When Gustav Magnus, the chair of physics at the university of Berlin, passed away in 1870, it was natural that Helmholtz's name was put forward as his successor. Helmholtz, of course, was eager to take up this position in the "premier" university of Prussia. But he set certain conditions: a personal salary of 4000 thalers; the promise of a new physical institute, with the necessary equipment for instruction of students as well as the private research of the director; and an official residence in the institute. Until the institute was ready, he requested an allowance for renting a home and rooms in the vicinity for him and his students to carry on his work in physics. Finally, he wanted reimbursement for his moving expenses.

Because the university had only 2000 thalers in its budget, the remaining 2000 were furnished by the Academy of Science. Rooms were found for the institute, but the construction of Helmholtz's own building had to be postponed, because war had broken out between Prussia and France. Helmholtz's son Richard, age 17, enlisted in the mounted division of the Baden field artillery. He was wounded, but not severely. The war ended quickly, resulting not only in the defeat of France but the unification of Germany under Prussian leadership. Kaiser Wilhelm I, who had just been proclaimed emperor, signed Helmholtz's appointment in Versailles on February 13, 1871.

BERLIN (1871–1894)

At Berlin, Helmholtz devoted himself mainly to work in physics, particularly in electrodynamics. He declined a professorship at Cambridge University that was offered in a letter from Sir William Thomson. He also declined an invitation to give a series of public lectures in the United States because he felt that "he still had many things that he wanted to do for science" and he did not want to lose too much time. "Indeed, I begin to think that I shall never see America in this life," he wrote in reply. But he did visit America 20 years later.

In addition to research problems in the fields of electricity and magnetism, the issues that interested Helmholtz were the guidance of hot air balloons, the limits of microscope efficiency, and the meteorology of whirlwinds and thunderstorms. Long before the dawn of the computer age and chaos theory, he predicted that, by rapid and precise calculations, we could understand the "wildest caprices" of a storm, if we had the exact knowledge of the preceding conditions.

In 1877 Helmholtz was also appointed professor in the Friedrich Wilhelm Institute for Medicine and Surgery, the same institution in which he had received his own education. In the same year he gave an address as the newly elected rector of Berlin University on academic freedom in the German universities. In this talk, and later ones, he stressed his ideas of the conditions that made the German university system the best in the world at that time. A nation, he emphasized, should not depend on money, warships, and cannons for power; what matters is education, a democratic government of laws, and a legitimate vote for the working class. There has to be freedom of speech without the interference of authorities. The untrammeled freedom of the German student, which amazes all foreigners, Helmholtz continued, is a treasure that must be guarded.

In the German empire of today, the most extreme consequences of materialistic metaphysics, the boldest speculations on the basis of Darwin's evolutionary theory, can be promulgated as freely as the extreme deification of papal infallibility. (Koenigsberger, 1965/1906, p. 309)

Because the German system stressed science education, based on laboratory research, German science at the time led the rest of the world. He urged students to pursue science for its own sake. In the first half of his own life, he added, when he was still an official of the state, the sense of duty, together with scientific curiosity, played the deciding role in his work. But later, when he was no longer obliged to work for a living, when most workers who have no inward impulse toward science may cease to work, those who continue do so to contribute to the progress of humanity.

In 1881 Helmholtz traveled to London once again to give the Faraday lecture (in English) on recent developments of Faraday's ideas on electricity, which showed, for the first time, the relationship between electrical and chemical forces. After delivering the lecture, he went to Cambridge, where he received the honorary degree of doctor of laws. Then he traveled to Glasgow to stay with his friend Sir William Thomson (later Lord Kelvin). That September he was a delegate to the Electrical Congress in Paris. Speaking in French, he helped decide the standard definitions of electrical units of measurement.

The next year Helmholtz was elevated to the hereditary nobility and was entitled to add "von" to his name. Thus he became von Helmholtz, as he is known in the history books. Other honors followed, such as being made vice chancellor of the "Peace" class of the order *"pour le mérite,"* and granted the title of *"Geheimrat"* (privy counselor). In 1886 he traveled back to Heidelberg to attend the 500th anniversary of the university. He spoke at a banquet in honor of the occasion in the presence of the Crown Prince of Germany, later Kaiser Friedrich III, the Grand Duke of Baden, and the rector of the university. Later he received the Graefe medal of the Ophthalmological Society.

As early as 1872, leading academicians had made proposals to found an institute for the study of science and technology by promising investigators, who would have no academic responsibilities and would be free to pursue their studies without teaching duties. But typical wrangling by academics, government officials, and the finance ministry delayed the founding of the institute until 1888.

In 1884 Helmholtz's daughter Ellen had married Arnold Wilhelm von Siemens, eldest son of Werner von Siemens, founder of a highly technical (and highly successful) enterprise in the electrical industry. It was Werner von Siemans who finally made the institute possible by donating the land in Charlottenburg, a Berlin suburb, and half a million marks. Helmholtz was formally invited to become president of the new physico-technical institute, known as the Reichsanstalt. Although Helmholtz should have given up his teaching position, the faculty of Berlin University petitioned to allow him to continue his connection with the university. When the request was granted, Helmholtz agreed to give a public lecture each term "provided he were relieved from the duty of taking part in the executive work of the faculty and the examinations" (Koenigsberger, 1965/1906, p. 374).

Helmholtz's former student, Heinrich Hertz, had been appointed full professor at Karlsruhe in 1885. When he was offered the chair of physics at either Bonn or Berlin, through Helmholtz's influence he chose Bonn. Helmholtz wrote to him:

> I am personally sorry that you are not coming to Berlin, but . . . I believe it is for your own best interest to go to Bonn. . . . At the end of one's life, when it is more a question of utilizing the points of view one has arrived at, for the education of the coming generation and the administration of the state, the case is different. (Koenigsberger, 1965/1906, p. 383)

Helmholtz admired Fechner, even though he did not always agree with him. In the second volume of the *Optics*, published in 1860, the same year that Fechner's *Elemente der Psychophysik* was published, Helmholtz proposed a generalized Fechner's law and sent a copy to Fechner: "You will find the same subjects in this second part, that you have dealt with lately in your own work," he noted. "I had written the chapter on intensity of light, in all essentials, before I received your treatise on it. I therefore introduced some modifications afterwards" (Koenigsberger, 1965/1906, p. 192).

Helmholtz returned to psychophysics again in the late 1880s. He had joined the editorial board of the *Zeitschrift für Psychologie und Physiologie der Sinnesorgane* (*Journal of Psychology and Physiology of the Sense Organs*), founded by Hermann Ebbinghaus (chap. 4, *Pioneers III*), a psychologist, and Arthur König, a physiologist and a former student of Helmholtz's. Helmholtz contributed four major articles to that journal, generalizing and defending Fechner's law.

The first article (1890) proposed a modification of Fechner's logarithmic equation to take into account the intrinsic light of the retina (the pattern of light flashes that appears when the eyes are closed in the dark) to explain the deviations from Fechner's law at low luminosities.

The second article (1891a) attempted to extend Fechner's law to color vision. He offered a mathematical equation, which treated complex colors as mixtures of three properly chosen primaries and applied Fechner's law to each dimension, contributing to the fused total sensation.

The third article (1891b) attempted to define the three primaries of the Young–Helmholtz theory by mathematical means.

The fourth article (1894) dealt with the origins of sense impressions. In this paper, Helmholtz restated the same opinions as in his 1855 lecture in Königsberg. He called for empiricism in the interpretation of sensory phenomena, without closing the door completely to nativistic interpretations. He was still a resolute opponent of all metaphysical speculation. Unconscious inference accounted for the derivation of our concepts.

In 1893 Helmholtz was again invited to visit the United States. This time the occasion was the World's Columbian Exposition in Chicago. At first he turned the invitation down. But when he was appointed the official German delegate to the Electrical Congress in Chicago, he assented, provided the ministry agreed to increase his allowance so his wife could accompany him. He wrote to his old friend Knapp, who had originally invited him: "I am convinced that America represents the future of civilized humanity . . . while in Europe we have only chaos or the supremacy of Russia to look forward to" (Koenigsberger, 1965/1906, p. 411).

An interesting sidelight of his stay in Chicago was related by Hilgard (1987). At the concluding banquet of the Chicago Exposition, Helmholtz was seated at the dais among the honored guests. He saw Thomas A. Edison, the inventor, seated at a table in the audience and stepped down from the platform to shake Edison's hand. Helmholtz had met Edison before, when the latter had visited him and his friend and benefactor Werner von Siemens in Berlin, following the Paris exposition of 1889. When the audience noted Helmholtz's greeting Edison, they called for Edison to stand up to be recognized with shouts of Edison! Edison!

On this visit to the United States, Helmholtz toured the country. He was impressed by Niagara Falls and he liked Boston but he also had negative observations. "We traveled last night from Chicago to St. Louis," he wrote to his daughter. "On the previous evening, the night express on the same line was held up by a band of twenty robbers, as it was known that there were large sums of money on board. Besides these tales of murder, the newspapers contain excited declamations about the gold or silver currency, over which they have gone quite mad, and about which I was interviewed in St. Louis by a nocturnal reporter, although I assured the man that I had never studied questions of political economy" (Koenigsberger, 1965/1906, p. 416).

Helmholtz's party also visited Denver and Colorado Springs "which, as a matter of fact, possesses no springs, but has a good hotel." The ride from Chicago to Denver was one of "unbroken monotony." There were "endless stretches of corn fields . . . here and there a wooden village, with a wooden lunch room or saloon . . . and a hotel, more fit . . . for fowl than for man" (Koenigsberger, 1965/1906, pp. 414–415).

On the voyage back to Germany, Helmholtz had an accidental fall down a staircase. He was found bleeding from cuts on his forehead and nose, but he was not badly injured. He was helped to his cabin and treated by the ship's doctor. Although the wounds healed well, Helmholtz felt a general lack of energy. He complained that it took him twice as much time as before to complete any piece of work. The next year he suffered a cerebral hemorrhage, and after lingering for some months, he died on September 8, 1894.

REFERENCES

Adler, H. E. (1996). Gustav Theodor Fechner: A German *Gelehrter*. In G. A. Kimble, C. A. Boneau, & M. Wertheimer (Eds.), *Portraits of pioneers in psychology* (Vol. II, pp. 1–13). Washington, DC: American Psychological Association.

Bolles, R. C. (1993). *The story of psychology: A thematic history*. Pacific Grove, CA: Brooks/Cole.

Boring, E. G. (1950). *A history of experimental psychology* (2nd ed.). New York: Appleton-Century-Crofts.

Fechner, G. T. (1966). Elements of psychophysics (H. E. Adler, trans.). New York: Holt, Rinehart, and Winston. (Original work published 1860)

Helmholtz, H. von (1855). On human vision. In *Vorträge und Reden* (5th ed.) (H. E. Adler, Trans.). Braunschweig, Germany: Vieweg & Sohn.

Helmholtz H. von (1868). Recent advances in the theory of vision. In *Vorträge und Reden* (5th ed.). (H. E. Adler, Trans.). Braunschweig, Germany: Vieweg & Sohn.

Helmholtz, H. von (1890). Die Störung der Wahrnehmung kleinster Helligkeitsunterschiede durch das Eigenlicht der Netzhaut [Disturbance of the perception of very small differences in brightness by the intrinsic light of the retina]. *Zeitschrift für Psychologie und Physiologie der Sinnesorgane, 1*, 5–17.

Helmholtz, H. von (1891a). Versuch einer erweiterten Anwendung des Fechnerschen Gesetzes im Farbensystem [An attempt to extend the application of Fechner's law to the color system]. *Zeitschrift für Psychologie und Physiologie der Sinnesorgane, 2*, 1–31.

Helmholtz, H. von (1891b). Versuch, das psychophysische Gesetz auf Farbenunterschiede trichromatischer Augen anzuwenden [An attempt to apply the psychophysical law to color discrimination of trichromatic eyes]. *Zeitschrift für Psychologie und Physiologie der Sinnesorgane, 3*, 1–20.

Helmholtz, H. von (1894). Über den Ursprung der richtigen Deutung unserer Sinneseindrücke [On the origin of the correct interpretation of our sense perceptions]. *Zeitschrift für Psychologie und Physiologie der Sinnesorgane, 7*, 81–96.

Helmholtz, H. von (1954). *On the sensations of tone* (4th ed.) (A. J. Ellis, Trans.). New York: Dover. (Original work published 1863)

Helmholtz, H. von (1962). *Handbook of physiological optics* (J. C. P. Southall, Trans.). New York: Dover. (Original work published 1856–1866)

Helmholtz, H. von (1971). The conservation of force: A physical memoir. In R. Kraft (Ed.), *Selected writings of Hermann von Helmholtz*. Middletown, CT: Wesleyan University Press. (Original work published, 1847)

Herrnstein, R. J., & Boring, E. G. (Eds.). (1965). *A source book in the history of psychology*. Cambridge, MA: Harvard University Press.

Hilgard, E. R. (1987) *Psychology in America: A historical survey*. San Diego: Harcourt Brace Jovanovich.

Koenigsberger, L. (1965). *Hermann von Helmholtz* (F. A. Welby, Trans.). New York: Dover. (Original work published 1906)

Pastore, N. (1973). Helmholtz's popular lectures on vision. *Journal of the History of the Behavioral Sciences, 9,* 190–202.

Pastore, N. (1974). Reevaluation of Boring on Kantian influence, nineteenth century nativism, Gestalt psychology and Helmholtz. *Journal of the History of the Behavioral Sciences, 10,* 375–390.

Southall, J. C. P. (1937). *Introduction to physiological optics.* New York: Oxford.

Turner, R. S. (1982). Helmholtz, sensory physiology and the disciplinary development of German psychology. In W. R. Woodward & M. G. Ash (Eds.), *The problematic science: Psychology in nineteenth-century thought.* New York: Praeger.

Chapter 3

George Croom Robertson and *Mind*: The Story of Psychology's First Editor

D. Brett King

The Victorian skeptic and novelist Samuel Butler (1901/1920) once remarked "that though God cannot alter the past, historians can; it is perhaps because they can be useful to Him in this respect that He tolerates their existence" (p. 151). Butler's sardonic observation emphasizes the historian's selectivity. Inevitably, for reasons that are purely practical, the historian will omit certain facts. One unfortunate by-product of this pragmatic fact is that some omissions, though seemingly innocent, result in a failure to appreciate the contributions of certain people. In the history of the behavioral sciences, George Croom Robertson is such an important but neglected individual.

A protégé of Alexander Bain, Robertson served as the original editor of *Mind*, the first journal of psychology. Despite his editorial contributions, however, Robertson remains a stranger to most accounts of the history of psychology. This chapter explores Robertson's life, his contribution as editor of *Mind*, and the pivotal arguments he advanced for a scientific psychology with a pluralistic subject matter.

ROBERTSON'S LIFE

Born in Aberdeen, Scotland, on March 10, 1842, Robertson exhibited signs of marked intellectual ability at an early age. At age 6, he enrolled in an incorporated trade school and later transferred to a grammar school. During this time, he used his middle name on school reports and was known for the rest of his life

---

*Photo of George Croom Robertson from Bain & Whittaker (1894).

as Croom Robertson. In November 1857, he attended Marischal College and the University of Aberdeen. His studies concentrated on philosophy, Greek, Latin, mathematics, and history. He studied with several distinguished scholars, including the British physicist James Clerk Maxwell and the prominent geologist James Nicol.

In 1860 a major reform occurred in the organization of the Aberdeen institutions of higher learning. Marischal and other individual colleges were incorporated into a larger institution named the United University of Aberdeen (Bain, 1893). This pedagogical reform produced Aberdeen's first chair of logic, which Alexander Bain accepted during the winter session of 1860–1861. Robertson enrolled in Bain's course as a student of moral philosophy and "took a high place in the examinations" (Bain, 1893, p. 3). He was described as Bain's "brilliant student" (Boring, 1950, p. 236; Sully, 1918, p. 184). The harmonious relationship between Bain and Robertson would prove advantageous in many later ventures.

In April 1861, Robertson received his MA degree with highest honors in classics and philosophy. Following extensive preparation with Bain, he was awarded the Ferguson Scholarship in Mental Philosophy in October 1861 (which carried a stipend of £100 a year for two years). The scholarship provided Robertson with the means to pursue an education both in England and abroad.

In winter of 1861–1862 Robertson was in London studying English literature, Greek, and chemistry at University College. In July 1862, he traveled to Heidelberg, Germany, where he studied German for eight weeks. In September of the same year he arrived at the University of Berlin and took courses on Kant, Hegel, and Aristotelian metaphysics. During this period he also studied physiology with Emil DuBois-Reymond.

In April 1863, Robertson arrived in Göttingen, Germany, to study metaphysics with Hermann Lotze and physiology with Rudolf Wagner. Two months later, he journeyed to Paris. Wagner had written a letter of introduction to Paul Broca on behalf of Robertson. Unfortunately, the details of this exchange are lost (Bain, 1893).

ROBERTSON'S CAREER

In September 1863 Robertson returned to Aberdeen in hopes of obtaining a newly vacant position in philosophy. After being rejected for the position, he began a rigorous program of philosophical study. His efforts resulted in a publication on Kant and Swedenborg and on German philosophy (Bain, 1893). During this period, Robertson was appointed teaching assistant for Greek courses at the University of Aberdeen (Bain, 1893). He continued in this capacity from 1864 to 1866 at a stipend of £100 a year.

Robertson had made several unsuccessful campaigns for a chair of philosophy at British and Scottish institutions, but in the summer of 1866, he successfully applied for the chair of the Mental Philosophy and Logic Department at University College, London. He received support from George Grote, then vice chancellor of the University of London, and was appointed to the position in December 1866. He began his appointment in January 1867 and taught a variety of courses, including logic, ancient and modern history of philosophy, and systematic psychology.

Robertson was an effective communicator of the new discipline of psychology. His lectures conveyed revolutionary findings in physiology and perception grounded in a broad philosophical base (see Robertson, 1896a, 1896b). His teaching style, as described by student Caroline A. Foley, was unique but compelling:

> It was not often indeed that he looked other than jaded and "driven" when he entered his class-room, promptly closed the window next him, or else drew on with swift dexterity his black silk skullcap, and took his seat. . . . He never laughed, he could not really be said to smile . . . but touches of humour, like rays of frosty sunshine, not seldom lit up the less crucial phases. . . . His expositions were so artistically disposed that it was comparatively easy to set down in notes without much pressure, not only the substance of what he said but often the form as well. There was an entire absence of verbiage or "padding." The lecture never broke down into a talk; the sentences were terse, pithy, polished. . . . What remained of the Scotch accent, which in his earlier London days he had been at much pains to smooth down, only served with its varied pitch, incisive accents and rhythmic cadences to throw his emphases into higher relief. (1893, pp. 275–277)

After Grote died in 1871, a chair of philosophy was established in his honor at University College, London, and Robertson was named its first recipient. Aside from his teaching responsibilities, Robertson examined candidates for degrees in philosophy. From 1868 until 1873 and again in 1883 until 1888 he served as examiner for the University of London. He also acted as examiner for the University of Aberdeen from 1869 until 1872 and again from 1878 to 1881. In 1877 Robertson was designated Tripos Examiner of Moral Science for Cambridge University and Victoria University, Manchester.

In addition to his professional accomplishments, Robertson's personal life was also flourishing. On December 14, 1872, he married Caroline Anna Crompton, daughter of the prominent Justice Charles Crompton. Caroline Robertson was an inexhaustible source of support for her husband. Bain claimed that "she was in every sense a helpmeet, having the same views on the higher questions of life, and being an earnest labourer in the public questions that he also had at heart" (1893, p. 7). The women's rights movement was one of "the public questions" of interest to the Robertsons. Croom Robertson was an active member of the London Committee for Woman's Suffrage begun by John Stuart Mill, among others (Mineka & Lindley,

1972). He was also an early proponent of admitting women into University College, London, and the general educational system (Bain, 1893).

RELATIONSHIP WITH BAIN

One hallmark of Robertson's professional and personal life was his relationship with Bain. Bain and Robertson engaged in prolific correspondence for more than three decades (1861–1892) and collaborated on several scholarly projects (Bain, 1893). George Grote's will requested that Bain and Robertson be named as editors of the deceased scholar's monumental work on Aristotle. During the autumn and winter of 1871 the two men managed to fashion the manuscript into a book that was published the next year (Bain & Robertson, 1872).

In 1874, Bain consulted Robertson about creating a quarterly journal of psychology and philosophy. From the journal's inception, Bain had decided on Robertson as editor. According to Bain:

> It was at first thought that it might be brought out in the course of the following year, 1875; but as it could not be ready in the beginning of the year, it was finally arranged that the first number should appear in January, 1876. Robertson bore the brunt of the requisite preparations from the start. . . . It was his happy inspiration that gave the title, which commended itself at once to everyone. (1893, p. 9)

Robertson flourished in his capacity of editor, until the appearance of a fatal malady.

ROBERTSON'S ILLNESS

Robertson discovered in 1880 that he was stricken with an incurable disease, which Bain (1893, p. 8) termed "calculus in the kidney," a concentration of mineral and organic deposits formed in the kidney. This ailment was common in Europe and had afflicted such historical figures as Michelangelo, Oliver Cromwell, Thomas More, and Samuel Pepys (Rose, 1982). Despite the lack of an effective treatment, kidney deposits were widely studied during Robertson's life. Although bladder-stone research dominated the 19th-century medical literature, researchers had not discovered an effective treatment for kidney deposits (Asper & Schmucki, 1984).

Sir Leslie Stephens, a close friend and famed literary critic, wrote that Robertson was "seldom free from actual pain, or, at least, discomfort, and never free from harrowing anxiety as to future suffering, he struggled on, doing his duty with the old conscientious thoroughness" (quoted in Bain, 1893, p. 12). Despite the trauma and numerous surgeries caused by the illness, Robertson continued to edit and to teach, although he required the aid of substitute instructors beginning with the 1883–1884 academic session. During the spring of 1892, James Sully substituted when the ailing Robertson was unable to teach. Sully (1918) remembered that "Robertson was a strikingly original and popular teacher. I had sometimes to go down to Gower Street in the afternoon to find on student faces the gloom of disappointment added to that of a foggy London; and I needed all my pluck to confront them" (p. 229).

Although his illness restricted Robertson from scholarly pursuits outside of *Mind*, it did not appear to dampen his personality. William James (1893; chap. 2, *Pioneers I*), impressed by Robertson's demeanor, testified that "for ten years he fought a losing battle against an intensely painful disease, yet never put on a plaintive tone, nor spoke tragically (however he may have felt) about the ruin of his professional career" (p. 255).

ROBERTSON'S FINAL YEARS

Robertson was able to produce two scholarly projects during his health-stricken editorial years. The first was a masterful treatise on Thomas Hobbes (Robertson, 1886). Although fewer than 250 pages, the book was an attempt to fuse biographical data with a coherent overview of Hobbes's system of philosophy. The 10 chapters explored Hobbes's life, from his youth to his later influence on philosophy and psychology.

Robertson began research on the Hobbes project during his first year at University College, London. However, his illness combined with his meticulous nature forced continued interruptions of the project. He finally managed a brief biography of Hobbes for the 1880 *Encyclopedia Britannica* and, after 19 years of preparation, published the book. Bain observed

> Although this work was not executed on the scale originally projected, it preserved the most important part of his labours, and is duly appreciated by students of philosophy. His enlarged purpose would have included more copious reference to the great contemporaries and precursors of Hobbes, to whom he might have done justice in other forms had he been longer spared. (1893, p. 5)

Quinton claimed that nearly a century after its publication, the book "remains to this day the standard and most detailed account of Hobbes' life" (1976, p. 12).

Robertson's second major work was a collaboration with James Sully (Sully & Robertson, 1888) titled *Æsthetics, Dreams; and the Association of Ideas*. Sully was a close friend and successor to Robertson for the Grote professorship in Mental Science and Logic at University College, London. In an effort to work on other scholarly projects, Robertson resolved to leave his editorial labors.

The October 1891 volume of *Mind* was Robertson's 16th and final volume as editor and also marked the end of the "old series" of the journal. George Frederick Stout, a fellow of St. John's College, Cambridge, inherited the editorship of *Mind* and began the "new series" with the January 1892 volume. In addition to resigning from *Mind*, Robertson relinquished his teaching responsibilities.

On May 7, 1892, Robertson retired from University College, London, after nearly 25 years of outstanding contribution. Although weakened by years of poor health, he was now free from academic and editorial demands to pursue scholarly activities at leisure. Not long after this retirement, on May 29, 1892, his wife Caroline Anna Robertson succumbed to illness and died.

Despite the shock of his wife's death, Robertson persevered with his work. His last article was an insightful report on Helen Keller, which appeared in the first volume of the new series (Robertson, 1892) and served as a follow-up from an earlier paper on Keller (Robertson, 1889). However, he was unable to finish a third paper on Keller and the report was later completed by W. J. Greenstreet (Greenstreet, 1893). Stephens noted that despite the loss of his wife,

> He did not . . . abandon his intellectual aspirations. . . . I heard from him not long ago that he intended, upon returning to London, to get to work upon Leibnitz, in whose philosophy he had long taken a special interest. But his constitution was more shattered than he knew. There was to be no more work for him. A slight chill brought on an illness which was too much for his remnant of strength. He died peacefully and painlessly on the 20th September, within four months of his wife. (quoted in Bain, 1893, p. 13)

Robertson's death produced several lamentations from friends and then mostly silence. Perry (1954, p. 155) aptly described him as "one of those men who are fated to be enshrined in the hearts of their friends rather than in monuments of their own making."

ROBERTSON'S LEGACY

Robertson left a subtle and rich legacy for later generations of psychologists. His most significant contribution was his brilliantly edited volumes of *Mind*. His guiding vision for the journal shaped the appearance of the new psychology for a generation of readers. In addition, Robertson advanced definite ideas about the content and scientific status of psychology. An obvious starting point for Robertson's contribution is his editorship of *Mind*.

Editorial Contributions

From his prefatory words in the first volume of *Mind* (Robertson, 1876a) to his valedictory in the final issue of the old series (Robertson, 1891), Robertson edited 16 volumes of *Mind*. The lead article in the first issue featured Herbert Spencer's

(1876) "The Comparative Psychology of Man" and served to establish an emphasis on evolutionary mental science. A host of the greatest 19th-century philosophers and scientists expressed their ideas and research in the pages of *Mind*. A sample of the distinguished contributors during Robertson's tenure as editor includes Alexander Bain, James Mark Baldwin, Alfred Binet (chap. 5, *Pioneers* III), F. H. Bradley, James McKeen Cattell, Stanton Coit, Charles Darwin (chap. 2, *Pioneers* III), John Dewey (chap. 4, *Pioneers* II), Francis Galton (chap. 1, *Pioneers* I), Edmund Gurney, G. Stanley Hall, Herman von Helmholtz (chap. 2, this volume), Leonard Trelawney Hobhouse, William James (chap. 2 *Pioneers* I), Joseph Jastrow (chap. 6, *Pioneers* I), Henry Maudsley, C. Lloyd Morgan, Charles Sanders Peirce, Theodore Ribot, George John Romanes, Josiah Royce, George Santayana, Edward Wheeler Scripture, Henry Sidgwick, George F. Stout, James Sully, Edward Bradford Titchener, John Venn, James Ward, and Wilhelm Wundt (chap. 3, *Pioneers* III). The prestige of these scholars and the quality of their articles surely contributed to the success of *Mind*. Robertson's editorial talent further provided the journal with a necessary structure and cohesiveness.

Perhaps more than any other factor, Robertson's subtle yet strong presence accounted for the prosperity of *Mind*. Bain "regarded him as, in every point of view, a model editor" (1893, p. 10). Stephens also praised Robertson's editorial proficiency:

> As editor of *Mind* he expended an amount of thought and labour upon the revision of articles which surprised any one accustomed to more rough-and-ready methods of editing. . . . Contributors were sometimes surprised to find that their work was thought deserving of such elaborate examination; and it often seemed to me that he could have written a new article with less trouble than it took him to put into satisfactory shape one already written. (quoted in Bain, 1893, p. 11)

William James was one beneficiary of Robertson's editorial skills. James's principal biographer wrote that "it was to Robertson that James . . . owed the revision and publication of several of his earliest philosophical and psychological articles in 1879, when his professorship was at stake" (Perry, 1954, p. 155). James introduced a variety of ideas in *Mind* before elaborating on them in his 1890 classic, *The Principles of Psychology*. James and Robertson were of the same age, shared similar philosophies about life and psychology, and belonged to the "Scratch Eight," a British society devoted to broad philosophic ideas (Perry, 1954). On hearing of Robertson's demise, James wrote from Italy that

> with his convictions, his scholarship, and his energy, he would surely have influenced his generation in other ways than by editing *Mind*, had strength been left him. As it was he clung to that drudgery almost to the end; and those fourteen admirably edited volumes are now, inadequately enough, almost his only monument. The perfume which his manliness leaves is, however, his truer monument. (1893, p. 255)

Robertson managed to review books in addition to contributing and editing articles, notes, and discussions. Each volume of *Mind* contained a large number of book reviews, which acquainted the reader with revolutionary findings and ideas in mental science. After 1884, Thomas Whittaker was primarily in charge of reviewing new books for *Mind* (Robertson, 1891). Whittaker later helped Bain in editing a posthumous collection of Robertson's major writings (Bain & Whittaker, 1894).

The topics of Robertson's book reviews varied from physiological research to logic and metaphysics, with such authors as John Dewey, David Ferrier, T. H. Huxley, Pierre Janet, and Henry Maudsley. Robertson exercised his traditional rigorous standards in this process and "never reviewed a book without thoroughly making himself master of its contents" (Stephens, quoted in Bain, 1893, p. 11).

Robertson never allowed a volume of *Mind* to appear late, despite his conscientious editing and poor health. His editorial judgment granted coverage to a broad cross-section of ideas. According to Robertson, the diversity of topics to be covered in *Mind* could include

> physiological investigation of the Nervous System in man and animals; . . . objective study of all natural expressions or products of mind like Language, and all abnormal or morbid phases up to Insanity; comparative study, again objective, of the manners and customs of Human Races as giving evidence of their mental characteristics, also of mind as exhibited by the lower Animals—such are some of the more obvious heads of inquiry which the psychologist must keep in view. No such statement, however, can come near to exhausting the matter of psychology. (1876a, pp. 3–4)

This prefatory note reflects both his belief in an objective psychology and his optimism about the diversity of the new discipline. As testimony to his editorial plurality, Stephens observed that Robertson

> had some very definite opinions upon disputed questions and belonged decidedly to what is roughly called the empirical school. But, whatever his views, he was always anxious to know and to consider fairly anything that could be said against them . . . . [T]he last accusation that could ever have been brought against him would have been that of hasty dogmatism. He might have failed to appreciate the opposite view; but the failure would not have been due to any want of desire to understand it thoroughly. He was always anxious that *Mind* should contain a full expression of all shades of opinion. Whether he succeeded in this is another question. An editor can open his doors, but he cannot compel everyone to enter. (quoted in Bain, 1893, pp. 11–12)

Robertson did manage to encourage, if not "compel," a great many psychologists and philosophers to contribute to the journal but was never able to establish experimental psychological research in England. Although Robertson and

Bain had christened *Mind* as a "quarterly review of psychology and philosophy," the articles remained loosely empirical rather than strictly experimental.

Robertson's Advocacy for "Scientific Psychology"

Robertson expressed optimism for a scientific psychology in his introduction to the first volume of *Mind*:

> Philosophical thought in England has for the most part been based on psychology, when not wholly merged in it; and psychology, pursued as a positive science, ought to yield a continuous harvest of results, coherent among themselves and standing in relation with other results garnered in the scientific field. . . . Few, however, of its cultivators will deny that it has been far from as fruitful as could be wished, and even the most ardent must admit that it has by no means won the rank of an assured science in the common esteem. Now if there were a journal that set itself to record all advances in psychology, and gave encouragement to special researches by its readiness to publish them, the uncertainty hanging over the subject could hardly fail to be dispelled. . . . Nothing less, in fact, is aimed at in the publication of *Mind* than to procure a decision of this question as to the scientific standing of psychology. (1876a, p. 3)

Robertson's struggle to promote a scientific study of mind in England remained largely futile and, by the eighth volume, he vented his frustration at the absence of scientific articles in the journal. He prefaced an article on the relation between psychology and philosophy with the following expression of concern:

> I will not conceal my own feeling of disappointment that there has not been more of positive contribution to psychological science in [the journal's] pages. If they have faithfully reflected the amount of psychological activity in this country, it can not be said that this has been appreciably increased in the last seven years, because of the opportunity here afforded to any psychologist of bringing the results of his inquiry under the notice of other students. The Journal has not yet succeeded in fostering—if it might have been expected to foster—such habits of specialized investigation in psychology as are characteristic of the workers in other departments of science. There is little sign in our midst of the disposition (or, perhaps, the ability) to work on such special lines of psychological research as other countries give evidence of. . . . For all the name it has made in the world, English psychology has never been remarkable for its elaboration in detail. (1883, pp. 1–2)

Robertson's wish for more experimentation in psychology was reflected by an alteration in the format of the journal. In the first eight volumes of *Mind*, the order of contents consisted of articles, notes and discussion, critical notices, new books, and correspondence. But in the volume following the editorial just quoted, the section titled "notes and discussion" was converted into "research and discussion." By volume 10 "research" was divorced from "discussion" and given a separate section. But did this editorial maneuver inspire an increase in British research articles in *Mind*?

Unfortunately, the answer appears to be no, and Robertson mourned the absence of psychological experimentation in the journal, especially by British authors. In his final address as editor, Robertson wondered if England was

> at last going to take its fair share in the experimental work which, for the present at least, is the most promising of all lines of psychological advance? The later volumes of *Mind*, since the time (1883) when a similar note of interrogation was made, have included a good proportion of experimental research; but it can hardly have escaped attention that it has been contributed mostly from without, by American hands—the same hands that have been or are now organizing psychological laboratories over all the breadth of their own land. The interrogatory note is, therefore, still in place. (1891, p. 559)

The 19th-century British academic system was not conducive to experimental research in psychology. In contrast to German and American institutions, British schools were slow to establish laboratories and chairs in psychology (Bartlett, 1937; Hicks, 1928; Robertson, 1876b). However, Robertson firmly believed that experimental psychology could flourish in England, despite the lack of support from the academic sector. Robertson's self-appointed advocacy of experimental psychology placed him in a unique position. According to Quinton (1976, p. 9), "He was perhaps the first to draw explicit attention to the unprofessional character of English philosophy. (A Scotsman himself, he said that 'by English is here meant in the broadest sense British, inclusive of Irish and Scotch')." Regrettably, Robertson died before the growth of British psychology in the 20th century.

The British Psychological Society was founded in 1902 and two years later the *British Journal of Psychology* was founded by James Ward, W. H. R. Rivers, and Charles S. Myers. Boring commented that "British psychology was becoming self-conscious, twenty years after Germany, fifteen after the United States" (1950, p. 492). The *British Journal of Psychology* was clearly more successful in eliciting articles on experimental psychology than *Mind* had been (Passmore, 1976)—or ever would be. By 1974, nearly a century after its founding, the editorial decision was made to exclude the term "psychology" from the subtitle of *Mind* (see Hamlyn, 1976).

Although Robertson was disappointed with the impact the journal had on experimental research, he was able to inspire many contributors and readers to explore the new discipline. As evidence of this, 74 *Mind* contributors presented Robertson with a gold watch with Albert chain and seal and a signed testimony on the occasion of his retirement. The letter testified to the contributors' gratitude for the great value of the services you have rendered to the study of psychology and philosophy by the steadfastness of your endeavors to maintain the high standard of excellence . . . as well as by your exemplary fairness towards all philosophical opinions, however diverse, that sought for reasoned statement in your pages. (Stout, 1892, p. 452)

Apart from his editorial policies, Robertson had definite ideas about psychology. Although denied the opportunity to develop these concepts into a systematic volume, his writings (especially a posthumous introductory book on psychology culled from his lecture notes) revealed a scientific conception of the discipline.

Robertson (1896a, p. 2) defined psychology as the "Science of Mind—just as Biology is the Science of Life"—and claimed that psychology merits admission as a natural science:

All science properly is natural, else it is not science. *"Natural" nowadays rather indicates method than matter.* Psychology, then, is just as much a natural science as physics; and as such it calls equally for rigid scientific procedure (Robertson, 1896a, p. 10).

The primary distinction between psychology and other sciences centers on the subject. For Robertson psychology was a

positive phenomenal science—positive as to its method, phenomenal as to its subject matter. Its method does not differ from that of other positive sciences, like biology or chemistry, except as the method of any science is modified by the peculiarity of its subject. As phenomenal science, it is occupied with a particular class of facts, taken just as they present themselves. (1883, p. 9)

Although Robertson was eager to adopt an objective method, he recognized that subjectivity is implicit in the study of psychology. Specifically, the individual's subjective experience, or Ego, may not be wholly amenable to objective analysis. Noting this peculiar circumstance, he observed that

our science is double-faced in a way different from any purely objective science. . . . It is only a very shallow examination of mind which includes that it can be studied just like any other object. Let mind be studied through the nervous system and external manifestations by all means, but let it be borne in mind that we have something "not without" far more important to study. (Robertson, 1896a, p. 9)

However, a diverse, objective psychology could yield some insight into shared characteristics of the mind. In his 1866 introductory lecture as professor of Philosophy of Mind and Logic at University College, London, Robertson expounded his pluralistic vision of the content of psychology:

Physiology in particular, among the objective aids to introspection, gives real psychological insight. . . . To take account of the objective states that run parallel with subjective states is not speculative materialism. Nor does all the difference between the common and the advanced psychology consist in talking about nerves and muscles. . . . [I]t could be shown that important aid is to be got from many other sources; from comparative psychology, statistics, history. . . . (1894, pp. 4–5)

Robertson's pluralistic account of psychology was consistent with an empiricist orientation. He espoused the associationism of Bain and J. S. Mill and also accepted Bain's conception of the mind as consisting of feeling, intellect, and volition. Robertson also adopted Bain's dualistic solution to the mind–body issue. He wrote that "it is impossible to study mind without backward reference to bodily phenomena; we are else acting like ostriches" (Robertson, 1896a, p. 33). Robertson modified Bain's parallelism by arguing for "con-comitance," to demonstrate that a parallel can only exist between physical events and not between physical and psychical events. Robertson agreed that

the word Parallelism is used synonymously with concomitance, but it carries us too far if it suggests that when there is a nerve-process there is a fact of mental experience. The parallelism does not hold both ways. . . . The psychical process is not in the least accounted for or explained by the physical process. Mark me here—I protest against such careless phrases as "brain thinks"! It is stark nonsense! As a material organ, it is the seat of a process expressible in terms of motion. (1896a, p. 44)

Robertson's choice of "con-comitance" exemplified his displeasure with the nomenclature of his predecessors. In an animated lecture on the divergent usage of the term "feeling," Robertson (1896a, p. 21) remarked, "see here how notable and deplorable is the state of psychological language!" He objected to Bain's terms "intellect" and "volition" and proposed substituting instead "intellection" and "conation," respectively. Robertson explained his preference for the latter term by noting that

Professor Bain and most psychologists use Will (or Volition). I follow Hamilton in this term Conation (from *Conor*, I try), which presents a parallel to the German use of *Streben, Bestrebung*, as distinct from *Wollen, Wille*. Will (or Volition) is too special a term for something so generic as a phase of mind. It is one thing "to desire," another "to will." But both are covered by the more elementary term Conation, or "tending to act." (1896a, p. 23)

In 1873, Robertson lectured to the Metaphysical Society of London on a clarification of the terminology used in the volition–determinism issue. Bain heralded the speech as "one of the best handlings of the Free Will question on the basis of a critical examination of the verbal improprieties that obscure the issue"

(1893, p. 7). In his lecture, Robertson (1882b, p. 570) urged that clear terminology is essential if psychology is to establish its autonomy from traditional philosophy: "If mental philosophy must use a language devised for purposes other than philosophical, it cannot be too careful about the inferences it founds upon the words." Thus with the proper use of broad descriptors, Robertson envisioned an objective psychology with a generous content area. He believed that physiological psychology should occupy a dominant place in the content of psychology.

Robertson was a vigorous advocate of physiological psychology, a reflection of his early study with Broca and DuBois-Reymond. He devoted numerous articles, book reviews, and course lectures to the physiological foundations of mind. Robertson (1896a) proclaimed that "our psychology should be as physiological as we can make it" (p. 33). He endeavored to fulfill this resolve as both educator and editor.

Indeed, Robertson's 1870–1892 lectures reveal a sophisticated discussion of neuroanatomy and the neural impulse. From the pages of *Mind*, he informed readers of the revolutionary research on such physiological topics as clinical research on neurology (Robertson, 1876c), neurological functioning and localization (Robertson, 1877a, 1877b, 1880b, 1882a) and the physiological basis of mind (Robertson, 1878, 1880a). He supplemented his discussion of physiological psychology with research on sensation and perception, especially visual and tactile perception and muscular sense (Robertson, 1876d, 1896a). Robertson (1894, 1896a) optimistically held that physiological research would eventually formulate a tenable study of the unconscious.

But Robertson did not believe that physiological psychology offers the sole basis for an analysis of mind. He argued that scientific psychology should assume a more holistic approach: "It is not only in connexion with the functions of the nervous system that mind can be objectively considered. The whole frame of things, the sum of natural processes, has been thought a manifestation of mind" (Robertson, 1896a, p. 29).

Another way of objectively studying the mind is to consider its development. In a chapter titled "Growth of the Mind," Robertson noted the import of physiological influences on mental development:

> It is thus quite possible to speak of mental development and growth from the strictly psychological point of view; but the view is rendered much more definite when there is coupled with it a reference to the bodily conditions of mental life. (1896a, p. 50)

For Robertson, physiological development is enhanced through active growth produced by experience. He rejected purely nativistic explanations of growth in favor of a consciousness based on experiential stages:

Some philosophers say we come into the world with a mind containing "innate ideas." This hardly suffices for a psychological explanation, and our only way out of the difficulty is this. There are two stages in the development of our intellectual experience. . . . Our first consciousness is just a vague, confused, chaotic mass, which we have to clear. (Robertson, 1896a, p. 174)

Robertson's dual-stage theory of consciousness allowed a progression from the chaos of infancy to "adult consciousness [which] is more manifold and complex than infant consciousness" (Robertson, 1896a, p. 52). Experience is especially dominant in language acquisition and in the formation of volition. Robertson (1896a) believed that the former proceeds by imitation (p. 238), the latter by early experience with reward and punishment (p. 240).

Although he concentrated on physiology and development, Robertson took cognizance of other areas of psychology. He (1896a) mentioned the promise of *Völkerpsychologie* in revealing cultural manifestations of mind and accepted the importance of data derived from case studies (Robertson, 1889, 1892).

Robertson did not believe that research with human beings provides the only useful insights into the functioning of the mind. Although his writings contain only sparse reference to animal research, he applauded the advances of comparative psychology. Perhaps the best evidence of his interest in animal research can be found in two letters to the editor of *Nature* on perception in dogs (Robertson, 1873). He was joined in this popular topic by Alfred Russell Wallace, Charles Darwin, and George John Romanes, among others.

Robertson advocated scholarship in the history of psychology (Robertson, 1883, 1894). In an enthusiastic review of Hermann Siebeck's 1880 and 1884 books on the history of psychology, he declared that

psychology has now reached a critical stage in its course, when future progress depends not least upon a true understanding of the path, or paths, it has hitherto traversed. . . . its past history cannot be too closely scanned in or out of any relation to general philosophy. (Robertson, 1885, p. 289)

CONCLUSION

Robertson encouraged psychologists to examine the physiological, developmental, and perceptual phenomena of mind. His broad perspective included insights from group, individual, phylogenetic, and historical sources. He embraced this pluralism in his careful editing of *Mind*. His visionary model served to shape a diverse portrait of the new science for his contemporaries. In this sense, Robertson had a profound impact on the evolution of modern psychology.

On hearing of Robertson's retirement and the loss of his wife soon thereafter, William James wrote to James Sully "Poor G. C. R.! Was there ever such a case of a strong man grappling with adversity! He will have a monument in the hearts of his friends, if nowhere else" (Sully, 1918, p. 318). James's remark about the lack of a historical tribute to Robertson was prophetic. However, Robertson's contributions were substantial and his legacy is worthy of acknowledgment. His steadfast advocacy for a scientific psychology, in his lectures, his writings, and especially in his editorial work on the first journal in psychology, make him deserving of much more recognition in the history of psychology than he has received so far.

REFERENCES

Asper, R., & Schmucki, O. (1984). Socio-economic aspects of urinary stone disease in Eurasia in the 19th and 20th century. In R. L. Ryall, J. G. Brockis, V. R. Marshall, & B. Finlayson (Eds.), *Urinary stones: Proceedings of the second international urinary stone conference, Singapore, 1983* (pp. 18–23). New York: Churchill Livingstone.

Bain, A. (1893). George Croom Robertson. *Mind (New Series), 2,* 1–14.

Bain, A., & Robertson, G. C. (Eds.). *Aristotle.* London: John Murray.

Bain, A., & Whittaker, T. (Eds.). (1894). *Philosophical remains of George Croom Robertson.* London and Edinburgh: Williams & Norgate.

Bartlett, F. C. (1937). Cambridge, England, 1887–1937. *American Journal of Psychology, 50,* 97–110.

Boring, E. G. (1950). *A history of experimental psychology* (2nd ed.). New York: Appleton-Century-Crofts.

Butler, S. (1920). *Erewhon revisited twenty years later, both by the original discoverer of the country and by his son.* London: G. Richards. (Original work published 1901)

Foley, C. A. (1893). George Croom Robertson as teacher. *Mind (New Series), 2,* 275–280.

Greenstreet, W. J. (1893). Helen Keller. *Mind (New Series), 2,* 280–284.

Hamlyn, D. W. (1976). A hundred years of *Mind. Mind (New Series), 85,* 1–5.

Hicks, G. D. (1928). A century of philosophy at University College, London. *Journal of Philosophical Studies, 3,* 468–482.

James, W. (1890). *The principles of psychology.* New York: Henry Holt.

James, W. (1893). Letter on the death of George Croom Robertson. *Philosophical Review, 2,* 255.

Mineka, F. E., & Lindley, D. N. (Eds.). (1972). *The later letters of John Stuart Mill, 1849–1873* (Vol. 17). Toronto: University of Toronto Press.

Quinton, A. (1976). George Croom Robertson: Editor 1876–1891. *Mind (New Series), 85,* 6–16.

Passmore, J. A. (1976). G. F. Stout's editorship of *Mind* (1892–1920). *Mind (New Series), 85,* 17–36.

Perry, R. B. (1954). *The thought and character of William James: Briefer version.* New York: George Braziller.

Robertson, G. C. (1873). External perception in dogs. *Nature, 7,* 322–323, 409–410.

Robertson, G. C. (1876a). Prefatory words. *Mind (Old Series), 1,* 1–6.

Robertson, G. C. (1876b). Philosophy in London. *Mind (Old Series), 1,* 531–544.

Robertson, G. C. (1876c). Hughling Jackson's clinical and physiological researches on the nervous system. *Mind (Old Series), 1,* 125–127.

Robertson, G. C. (1876d). Sense of doubleness with crossed fingers. *Mind (Old Series), 1,* 97–104.

Robertson, G. C. (1877a). Ferrier's functions of the brain. *Mind (Old Series), 2,* 92–98.

Robertson, G. C. (1877b). Maudsley's physiology of mind. *Mind (Old Series), 2,* 235–239.

Robertson, G. C. (1878). Physical basis of mind. *Mind (Old Series), 3,* 24–43.

Robertson, G. C. (1880a). *The brain as organ of mind* by H. C. Bastian. *Mind (Old Series), 5,* 120–131.

Robertson, G. C. (1880b). The functions of the cerebrum. *Mind (Old Series), 5,* 254–259.

Robertson, G. C. (1882a). Localization of brain functions. *Mind (Old Series)*, *7*, 299–302.

Robertson, G. C. (1882b). Action of so-called motives. *Mind (Old Series)*, *7*, 567–570.

Robertson, G. C. (1883). Psychology and philosophy. *Mind (Old Series)*, *8*, 1–21.

Robertson, G. C. (1885). *Geschichte der Psychologie* by Hermann Siebeck. *Mind (Old Series)*, *10*, 287–297.

Robertson, G. C. (1886). *Hobbes*. Edinburgh: W. Blackwood & Sons.

Robertson, G. C. (1889). Helen Keller. *Mind (Old Series)*, *14*, 305–309.

Robertson, G. C. (1891). Valedictory. *Mind (Old Series)*, *16*, 557–560.

Robertson, G. C. (1892). Helen Keller. *Mind (New Series)*, *1*, 574–580.

Robertson, G. C. (1894). Psychology in philosophical teaching. In A. Bain & T. Whittaker (Eds.), *Philosophical remains of George Croom Robertson* (pp. 1–5). London: Williams & Norgate.

Robertson, G. C. (1896a). *Elements of psychology*. London: John Murray.

Robertson, G. C. (1896b). *Elements of general philosophy*. London: John Murray.

Rose, G. A. (1982). *Urinary stones: Clinical and laboratory aspects*. Baltimore: University Park Press.

Spencer, H. (1876). The comparative psychology of man. *Mind (Old Series)*, *1*, 7–21.

Stout, G. F. (1892). Croom Robertson testimonial. *Mind (New Series)*, *1*, 452.

Sully, J. (1918). *My life and friends*. New York: T. F. Unwin.

Sully, J., & Robertson, G. C. (1888). *Æsthetics, dreams; and the association of ideas*. New York: J. Fitzgerald.

Chapter 4

Carl Stumpf: Experimenter, Theoretician, Musicologist, and Promoter

Helga Sprung and Lothar Sprung

Carl Stumpf (pronounced "Shtoompf"), whose last name can be translated into English as "dull" or "blunt," was neither. Instead, he was a prominent and effective advocate of the new experimental psychology of the late 19th and early 20th centuries. In particular he supported the objectivity and precision of experimental psychology. Stumpf has received less recognition in English-language histories of psychology than he deserves. He was an ingenious experimenter, a pioneer in the psychology of hearing, a perceptive theoretician, the founder of a major institute of psychology in Berlin (the most prestigious German university of the time), the individual behind the establishment of one of the most influential ethnomusicological collections in the world, and a significant forerunner, promoter, and critic of Gestalt theory.

LIFE HISTORY

On July 13, 1893, the prominent philosopher–psychologist Wilhelm Dilthey wrote to the Royal Prussian Ministry of Religious, Educational and Medical Affairs in Berlin, saying, "We need a man who is at home in . . . experimental psychology" (quoted by Bosse in Hirschfeld, 1893, pp. 194–195). A different letter identified such an individual:

> So we recommend Stumpf to Your Excellencies to be first in line for the new professor's chair. He alone among today's philosophers approaches in natural

Thanks are owed Andrea Lerner, MA (Berlin) and Michael Wertheimer (Boulder, CO) for help on the English version of this chapter, and Wolfgang G. Bringmann (Mobile, AL) for letters from Stumpf to James.

*Photo of Carl Stumpf courtesy of C. A. Stumpf.

psychological talents the great psychologists of recent times—Fechner and Lotze here in Germany, Bain and James abroad. (Hirschfeld, 1893, pp. 200–201)

Five months later, Stumpf received word from the ministry that he had been appointed to Berlin with the obligation "to assume direction of the department of experimental psychology that is to be established" and to "represent this science in lectures and practical courses together with other professors in the field" (Bosse, 1893, p. 129).

Stumpf began his lectures in the summer semester of 1894 at the age of 46, and concluded them 37 years later at the age of 82. He died in Berlin on Christmas Day 1936, 43 years after he had been called to that city. He was buried in the old Lichterfelde Park Cemetery, where many well-known persons—such as flight pioneer Gustav Lilienthal, writer and philosopher Bruno Wille, and Kurt von Schleicher, general and chancellor of the Weimar Republic—are laid to rest. Today his grave is one of the honored burial plots maintained by the city of Berlin.

Early Life

Stumpf was born Friedrich Karl Stumpf on April 21, 1848, in Wiesentheid, Germany, the third of seven children of district court physician Eugen Stumpf and his wife Marie née Adelmann. Wiesentheid, set in a landscape of gently rolling hills in Lower Franconia, is still dominated by the castle of the Count of Schönborn, by its large baroque church designed by Balthasar Neumann, and by its old city hall on the market square. Stumpf lived his first 10 years in this cultural setting, rich in tradition. Stumpf's involvement with music began at a very early age, and his family cultivated a rich musical tradition. He played the violin from the age of 7, and later mastered five additional musical instruments. He also composed music and even considered the idea of a career in music.

A sickly child, Stumpf was tutored during his first few school years by his grandfather Adelmann, and later described that man's influence on his intellectual development in a letter to his cousin Wilhelm Scherer: "Certainly I do not err in tracing back to him the seed of everything that followed, the urge toward truth and philosophical discrimination" (Stumpf, 1873a, p. 1). And his mother's letter to Adolf Merkel, July 8, 1873, asked, "How many years . . . have gone by . . . since Carl was a sweet, industrious little boy, and his grandfather's pride?" (M. Stumpf, 1873, p. 137). Carl attended Latin school in Kitzingen and secondary schools in Bamberg and Aschaffenburg. His father's letter of May 11, 1873, to Adolf Merkel described his scholarly achievements: "He has always been first in each school; here he [was] second or third in the senior class" (E. Stumpf, 1873, p. 134). Stumpf went on to study in Würzburg, where he met Franz Brentano. In 1919, two years after Brentano's death, Stumpf characterized his relationship with Brentano in these words: "My whole conception of philosophy, of true and false methods of philosophizing, the essential theories in logic and epistemology, psychology, ethics and metaphysics that I still advance today are his teachings" (Stumpf, 1919, p. 144). Stumpf earned his doctorate at Göttingen on August 13, 1868, under Rudolph Hermann Lotze with a philosophical treatise on the "relation of the Platonist God to the Idea of the Good." After his degree, he returned to Würzburg and again attended Brentano's lectures on philosophy and some classes in theology as well.

In autumn 1869, Stumpf entered the Catholic seminary in Würzburg. But less than a year later, in July 1870 and after great inner struggle, he left. Discussions (especially with Brentano) about the dogma of papal infallibility, which had been promulgated at the first Vatican Council in 1870, played the decisive role. That the Pope be granted the right to pronounce incontrovertible truths was incompatible with Stumpf's scientific understanding (Baumgartner & Burkard, 1990; Baumgartner, Burkard, & Wiedemann, 1997). In crisis, Stumpf gratefully accepted Lotze's offer to supervise his postdoctoral work in Göttingen and, during the summer of 1870, wrote his mathematical philosophical postdoctoral dissertation, "On the Fundamentals of Mathematics," encouraged both by Lotze and by Göttingen's mathematician Felix Christian Klein. He qualified as a university lecturer in October 1870.

Stumpf also gained experience with experimental techniques at Göttingen, with physiologist Georg Meissner and physicists Wilhelm Weber and Friedrich Kohlrausch. In 1895, looking back on his years of study in Würzburg and Göttingen, he wrote,

> My student years came at the end of the sixties when, after the collapse of the great artificial systems, German philosophy came more and more to value an empirical orientation. Franz Brentano showed me the way down this path that, informed by Aristotle's keenness of perception, gave me a decisive impetus, and provided seeds of the most diverse sort; whereas Lotze's later influence especially promoted my interest in psychological subjects and accustomed me to a broad foundation. (Stumpf, 1895, p. 735)

Stumpf's Career

Before Stumpf's appointment at Berlin he had held five other posts and made several unsuccessful additional attempts to secure others. In 1870, he began lecturing at Göttingen. There he quickly integrated himself into the academic world and actively participated in social and musical life; he played cello in a quartet that performed in private settings. In Göttingen, he learned firsthand about psychophysics from Ernst Heinrich Weber and Gustav Theodor Fechner (chap. 1, *Pioneers II*), who were staying with Weber's brother, Wilhelm, for an extended visit. He was a participant in Fechner's experiments on the "golden section," the most attractive ratio of height to width of a rectangle.

His experiences in Göttingen and the personalities of Weber and Fechner had a lasting effect on Stumpf, determining the direction of his later research on the psychology of music and his commitment to a scientifically oriented experimental psychology. After three years, Stumpf left Göttingen and went to Würzburg, where he lectured on the history of philosophy, logic, metaphysics, and occasionally psychology. At Würzburg, he also began his investigations into tone psychology.

Stumpf's marriage to Hermine Biedermann may have prompted him to look for a better paying position than the one he had at Würzburg. In 1879 Stumpf moved to Prague. Hermine was musically educated and had been a music teacher. Carl played violin and she piano for their home concerts. The couple had two sons and a daughter, Elisabeth, who took up the cello. At Prague Stumpf lectured on philosophy, especially legal philosophy, dealing in this context with emotion and the problem of the will. He continued his investigations into tone psychology and published the results in his extensive work *Tone Psychology*, the first volume of which was published in 1883.

Stumpf lived in Prague during a time of intense conflict between the German and Czech populations. The Czechs were striving for separation in the academic realm and Stumpf looked again for a new position in which he could pursue his academic research in peace. Thus he was pleased to be appointed to a position in Halle and moved there in 1884. Just five years later, he moved again, this time to Munich, where he thought he saw a good situation for research in experimental psychology and the possibility of establishing a research institute. Before Stumpf, Wilhelm Wundt (chap. 3, *Pioneers III*) had been offered the position, and with very favorable conditions, but he turned it down. In the second round, the job went to Stumpf, but with much less favorable conditions. And, as it turned out, Stumpf's efforts to establish an institute were unsuccessful. Later on, Berlin's university made use of this unhappy fact to attract Stumpf there.

WILHELM SCHERER: COUSIN AND SUPPORTER

Stumpf's career was helped along by many people, including Brentano and Lotze, but until 1886 there was only one influential supporter, his cousin Wilhelm Scherer, who was a professor of German studies in Strasbourg at the time. Scherer had tried since the 1870s to smooth the way for his cousin's career. Although many of his efforts came to nothing, Scherer had a distant hand in Stumpf's appointment to Berlin. Toward the end of his years as a lecturer at Göttingen, on July 19, 1873, Stumpf received a letter from Scherer that raised the possibility of an appointment in Vienna. Scherer knew Vienna because he had been a professor there from 1868 to 1872. He wrote,

I've just now realized what small universities or universities in small cities really are like. I regard it as especially fortunate that I reached the age of 30 having lived nowhere else but in Vienna and Berlin. You too would have benefited, I think, from the big city. And I don't wish to give up the thought of seeing you in Vienna. When you receive your appointment . . . it will probably say none other than that you shall take up your position next summer. (Scherer, 1873)

On July 29, 1873, Stumpf replied,

I well understand what you're saying about Vienna. . . . Especially these last few years, I've so often and avidly longed to live in a big city that I could only consider it most fortunate for my further education to go there. . . . Should you be in Vienna and be asked about my readiness to accept an appointment, please answer as I have indicated. (Stumpf, 1873b)

But nothing ever came of Vienna.

In 1882 Scherer tried to have his cousin called to Berlin from Prague. He wrote Stumpf from Berlin on November 3, 1882,

The following is strictly confidential! Dilthey asked me to tell you not to delay with the publication of your tone psychology. They are thinking, presently only in the inner circles, of establishing a third chair in philosophy with the same agenda: scientific education! natural scientific orientation! And Dilthey for his part has you in mind, should your book fulfill his expectations. (Scherer, 1882)

Two days later, on November 5, 1882, Stumpf answered from Prague,

Dear Wilhelm! Again you've tossed a great (but pleasant) bomb on my desk. Things stand as follows. . . . The entire work will be ready by the end of '83. . . . I'm most grateful for Dilthey's favorable opinion and hope that he won't be disappointed. (Stumpf, 1882a)

But nothing came of this either.

Scherer's attempts to have Stumpf appointed at Halle, however, did succeed. From Stumpf's letter to Scherer on July 29, 1884:

Yesterday the letter of appointment from Halle reached me. . . . Please accept my thanks for your efforts to this end and also convey the news to Dilthey with my thanks; he seems to have put in a great deal of effort on my behalf. (Stumpf, 1884)

Scherer died in 1886, so Stumpf made his way to Berlin without his cousin's direct assistance. This time, Dilthey was the man in the background. Dilthey, backed by Helmholtz (chap. 2, this volume), decided in favor of Stumpf over Hermann Ebbinghaus (chap. 4, *Pioneers III*) for the third professorial chair in the summer of 1893. But all this happened later. We must still cover the years between 1889 and 1993, which Stumpf spent in Munich.

FROM BAVARIA TO PRUSSIA

Stumpf was only partially successful in Munich. He became a member of the Royal Bavarian Academy of Sciences, but failed in all his efforts to establish a psychological institute. The University in Berlin took advantage of Stumpf's dissatisfaction in 1893. That institution was looking for a philosopher who would be able to teach the "new psychology" as an experimental discipline yet would also be open to traditional philosophical psychology. The authorities were dissatisfied with their long-time associate professor Hermann Ebbinghaus, who gave them the impression of accepting psychology only as an experimental discipline (Sprung & Sprung, 1987).

As Berlin began to look definite, Stumpf hesitated. He was ambivalent about moving from the Bavarian metropolis to the Prussian capital. Finally, however, he did decide to go to Berlin, and was appointed to the third chair in philosophy at Berlin's Friedrich-Wilhelms-University on December 18, 1893. The statement founding Stumpf's chair designated it as being for "psychology, as well as for all philosophy based on natural sciences, especially for experimental psychology" (Hirschfeld, 1893, p. 200). Stumpf's appointment to Berlin established the independence of psychology within the university.

THE BERLIN YEARS

Stumpf's beginnings in Berlin were modest. When he assumed the directorship of the psychology department at Berlin, the department occupied three rooms, behind the university's main building, two of which Ebbinghaus had used (Stumpf 1910a, p. 203). For a long time Stumpf shared this space with Friedrich Schumann, his only assistant. About the aims of his department, Stumpf wrote, "[our] main focus lies in the strictest exactitude in interpretation of observations, formation of concepts and testing of hypotheses" (Stumpf, 1910a, p. 206).

When the department became a "psychological institute" in 1900 and moved to a nearby building with ten rooms (Stumpf 1910a, p. 204), its influence expanded. From then on, more and more students and colleagues came to Berlin, some of whom would later become more famous than their teacher. Among them were Kurt Koffka, Wolfgang Köhler (chap. 17, *Pioneers I*), Kurt Lewin (chap. 7, *Pioneers III*), and Max Wertheimer (chap. 13, *Pioneers I*).

At Berlin, Stumpf worked in the fields of psychology, philosophy, and musicology. Within psychology, his work and influence as a general psychologist, as a theoretician of science, methodologist, as a forerunner of Gestalt psychology, and as an academic politician must be emphasized. As an experimental psychologist, Stumpf was most interested in the problem of acoustic perception. As a theoretical psychologist, he was concerned mainly with questions of emotional and perceptual psychology, scientific theory, research methodology, and the theory of evolution.

It was important to Stumpf to make the scholarly community aware of the intimate relationship between psychological and philosophical problems (Stumpf, 1910a, p. 206). In Berlin he gave lectures on logic, epistemology, and the general history of philosophy, and conducted practical demonstrations related to "tonal and color sensations and their related activities, temporal and spatial perceptions, associational and volitional processes, involuntary movements, child and animal psychology and musical ethnology" (Stumpf, 1910a, p. 206).

Stumpf repeatedly took stands on the persistent problems in psychology. A central issue for him was the relationship between philosophy and psychology. In 1917, he had a warning for both disciplines: "Anxious gardeners (in philosophy) want to cut off the branches (psychology) with the freshest green shoots. If that separation happens, the internal connections must remain or philosophy will turn into a field of abstractions alien to life, and psychology into a mere practical discipline" (Stumpf, 1917, p. 25).

As the director of the department (later the institute) of psychology, Stumpf was active in academic policy making from 1894 to 1921. In 1895 he was elected to the Royal Prussian Academy of Sciences. As a member of the academy, he promoted the primate research center on Tenerife. Stumpf was behind the appointment of Wolfgang Köhler as the director of that facility, where he performed the famous experiments on intelligent behavior in apes (Heinecke & Jaeger, 1993). During the 1920s, Stumpf was first a member and later the director of the academy committee that prepared the collected works of Kant and Leibniz for publication. During the 1930s, he worked in the same capacity on the publication of the writings of Dilthey and Friedrich Schleiermacher.

Even after his official retirement in 1921, Stumpf continued to lecture until the end of the decade. He retired to Berlin-Lichterfelde only when he was more than 80 years old and continued to work as a theoretical psychologist. In 1927 he began his "Epistemology," a summation of his philosophical, psychological and methodological findings, but did not live to see it published. With advice from Max Planck, his son Felix, a physicist, saw it through to publication (Stumpf, 1939, 1940). Stumpf died in 1936 at the age of 88, before World War II was unleashed from Berlin. Thus he was spared the sight of the destruction of his residence by bombs and the downfall of his city (H. Sprung, 1997).

FROM TONE PSYCHOLOGY TO PSYCHOACOUSTICS

Empirical investigations of acoustic perception were the chief focus of Stumpf's experimental psychological research throughout his life. Before going to Berlin, he had already published his earliest results in the two-volume work, *Tone Psychology* (Stumpf, 1883, 1890). In the first volume, he indicated that he did not want the area to be understood as only a psychology of acoustic perception but as "general psychology," a "theory of discrimination" that was a continuation of "psychophysics" as developed by Fechner.

Stumpf was especially interested in the problem of discrimination, and used the comparison of successive tones as an investigative paradigm; he emphasized how distant his approach was from that of Helmholtz. In contrast to Helmholtz, who focused on the physics of auditory stimuli and their physiological effects, he wanted to investigate psychological factors in acoustic perception. He demonstrated how discrimination depends on psychological factors such as practice, fatigue, and attention. He devoted great attention to the reliability of discrimination. In volume 2, he examined the discrimination of tones sounded at the same time, thereby taking up the problem of consonance and dissonance (Stumpf, 1890). Stumpf discussed "fusion," both physiological and psychological, as a basic mechanism of consonance—making him a precursor of Gestalt psychological thought.

Today Stumpf is seen as having laid the groundwork for the psychology of music. Helga de la Motte-Haber, for instance, wrote in 1972,

> The short history of the psychology of music actually begins with Carl Stumpf, whose two volume work (1883/90) is essentially psychological. Although there is some basis to the claim that Hermann von Helmholtz's "Theory of Tonal Sensations" (1863) should receive first mention . . . still Helmholtz is more concerned with the description of physical and physiological processes than with psychological ones, whereas Stumpf investigates psychological discrimination. (1972, pp. 10–11)

Stumpf continued his experiments on tone psychology at Berlin, turning to the problem of concordance or harmony (effects of the simultaneous combination of two or more tones), and extending his investigations into psychoacoustics.

Stumpf's psychoacoustical research took three general directions: phonetics, auditory pathology, and comparative musicology. His research on phonetics chiefly involved the analysis of vocalization. He wrote about his aim in investigating the sounds of speech "with regard to the tonal and rhythmic relationships of spoken language, where recording dying-out dialects and primitive languages can be useful" (Stumpf 1910a, p. 207). His research on auditory pathology contributed to the development of audiometry and to methods for diagnosing disturbances in language comprehension. This research had consequences for otolaryngology. Shortly after he arrived in Berlin, Stumpf began to work with physicians. One result was the so-called "tone tables," compiled on the basis of frequency determinations of the tones of different octaves (Stumpf & Schaefer, 1901). His research in comparative musicology involved the establishment of an ethnomusicological collection of phonograph records, which Stumpf accomplished in 1904 with the help of Felix von Luschan, director of the Ethnological Museum in Berlin (Stumpf, 1908). In 1910 he explained,

> This enterprise belongs to the border zones of psychology, ethnology, musicology and aesthetics. It serves psychology by way of the comparative research method that no less than the experimental method and in conjunction with it . . . has justifiably gained in significance. It is a matter of complementing the investigations . . . that have been based on European cultures with the study of the cultural conditions and achievements of exotic cultures and indigenous peoples. (Stumpf 1910a, p. 207)

STUMPF, THE THEORETICIAN

Sifting through Stumpf's publications and the archives of his academic activities, it is evident that he worked more theoretically than experimentally during his 43 years at Berlin. His chief areas of concern were the definition of the subject matter of psychology and the development of appropriate taxonomies (e.g., for emotion), a persistent problem in psychology and epistemology.

The Subject Matter of Psychology

Between 1899 and 1928, Stumpf published a series of papers that dealt with the definition of the subject matter of psychology and a taxonomy of the sciences (Stumpf, 1928a; H. Sprung, 1997). Two of them appeared in 1906. In "Phenomena and Psychological Functions," Stumpf introduced his understanding of the subject matter of psychology (Stumpf, 1906a; H. Sprung, 1997). Psychological phenomena consist of sensory perceptions and their memory images or mental representations. The psychological functions, in contrast, involve "noticing phenomena and their relations, the combination of phenomena into complexes, the formation of concepts, apperception and discrimination, affect, desire and will" (Stumpf, 1906a, pp. 4–5). Although phenomena are the point of departure for the natural sciences, such as physics or physiology, and although physics is the fundamental discipline for the natural sciences, psychological functions are the real subject matter of psychology, which constitutes the fundamental discipline for the humanities.

Psychology's Place in the Taxonomy of the Sciences

In his work "On Classifying the Sciences," Stumpf (1906b) treated psychology as "the science of the elementary psychological functions" (Stumpf, 1906b, p. 26). In another paper, "Trends and Contrasts in Today's Psychology," Stumpf (1907) treated psychology as a pluralistic enterprise. He classified the various psychologies into *observational, experimental, subjective, objective, descriptive,* and *genetic (explanatory).* He also differentiated *pure* and *applied* psychologies according to their general aims. Stumpf saw no contradiction in this pluralistic view. For him, all psychologies are aspects of a unified topic. His stated credo:

> Actually, seldom is a path of research pursued by knowledgeable and wise men totally erroneous, the errors usually develop out of one-sidedness and exaggeration. ... But, in the interest of progress, these biases must be presented as precisely as possible and their differences must not be mixed up. (Stumpf, 1907, pp. 903–904)

THE PSYCHOLOGY OF SENSATION, PERCEPTION, AND EMOTION

In his paper "Sensation and Representation," Stumpf presented his theoretical analysis of two basic concepts of psychology (Stumpf, 1918). For him, the distinction between sensations and representations was not qualitative but quantitative. For example, he demonstrated that mental representations—such as images of perceptions—are weaker in intensity than sensations. Beyond this, representations are not as rich in features as sensations; they are more fleeting than sensations and as a rule have weaker emotional effects.

The studies on the psychology of emotion, in which Stumpf devised a system for classifying emotions, have had the most lasting influence. Borrowing from Brentano, Stumpf first introduced a fundamental distinction between *passive feelings,* those generally understood to be emotions in psychology, and *active feelings,* which consist of *drives* and *will.*

Within passive feelings, Stumpf distinguished between *elementary feelings* and *affects.* Elementary feelings are related to perceptions, palpable presentations, and psychological activities, and are further divided into *sensory feelings* and *functional feelings.* Although *sensory feelings* are tied in with sensations or sensory phenomena such as pain, *functional feelings* are bound up with psychological activities—for example, pleasurable or unpleasurable activities. *Affects* are related to contents such as sorrow over a lost friend; they presuppose a higher level of conceptual activity. Within the active feelings, Stumpf differentiated between the *drives* and *will.* With its meshing of emotion and cognition, Stumpf's treatment of emotion represents an early approach within today's cognitive–evaluative psychology of emotions (Reisenzein & Schönpflug, 1992).

Persistent Problems of Psychology

During the course of his long career, Stumpf dealt with several basic problems in psychology, in terms that have a distinctly contemporary ring.

The Mind–Body Problem. New findings in psychophysics, the psychology of perception, neuroanatomy, and neurophysiology led Stumpf to consider the old problem of mind and body in a new way (Stumpf, 1910b; see also H. Sprung, 1997). After discussing various points of view, he concluded,

> We must ask whether the consequence of natural scientific research, especially the theory of evolution, . . . is not to compel us to comprehend the world in all its aspects as a causally interconnected whole, in which each existent does its part, and none is excluded from the general reciprocity. (Stumpf, 1910b, pp. 78–79)

Psychological functions in this context were

> originally only regulatory mechanisms for the organism . . . even when their current significance for higher organisms no longer is taken up with this function. I would also have no serious difficulty with the assumption that psychological life (soul) was, in certain stages of its development, generated by organic processes (organic matter), and still is so generated in the developmental process of each individual. (Stumpf, 1910b, p. 89)

Stumpf finally concluded that

> the philosophical analysis of the concepts of substance and causality, the discovery of the law of energy, the development of psychophysics, the triumphant pervasiveness of evolutionary theory, progress in the anatomy and physiology of the central organs, especially in research on localizing mental activities: all of these have allowed us to break up one question that was presented lock, stock and barrel into many more sharply articulated ones. (Stumpf, 1910b, pp. 92–93)

Evolution and Psychology. The controversy that flared during the 1890s between proponents and opponents of Darwin's theory of evolution (chap. 2, *Pioneers III*) was the background for Stumpf's paper, "Evolutionary Thought in Contemporary Philosophy" (Stumpf, 1899a; see also H. Sprung, 1997). It took up the issue of how broadly evolutionary ideas could be generalized. Stumpf was most interested in the impact of evolutionary theory on an understanding of psychological evolution. He believed that comparative studies are especially useful in fields involving the direct connection between living things and their environments, such as the field of learning, which studies the adaptation of the creature to its circumstances (Stumpf, 1899a, p. 12). Stumpf also saw explanatory use for evolutionary ideas in the psychology of will. In that connection he wrote, "We have been enlightened through the theory of descent better than before about those early stages of actual willed behaviors" (Stumpf, 1899a, p. 14). Concluding his assessment, Stumpf compared the scope of Darwin's concept of evolution with the significance of the Copernican theories that changed the perception of the world centuries earlier (Stumpf, 1899a, p. 32; see also Eckardt, Bringmann, & Sprung, 1985).

Methodology. In "On a Methodology of Child Psychology," Stumpf considered the observational methods used to obtain data and the statistical methods used to analyze them (Stumpf, 1910b). He discussed the advantages, disadvantages, and sources of error in the various perspectives on children's mental development—for example, the perspectives of parents, physicians, and teachers. He treated sampling methods, discussing both single-case analyses such as those used to study so-called child prodigies and group investigations. Finally, Stumpf discussed the significance of statistics, demonstrating that, at the turn of the 20th century, he had already recognized that statistics are an indispensable tool for data analysis in empirical investigations.

Stumpf's article, "Number and Measure in Psychology," was a popular treatment of epistemology that took up the possibilities and limits of measurement and counting in psychology (Stumpf, 1921; see also H. Sprung, 1997). Stumpf argued for an "exact psychology on the model of the natural sciences." He argued that the "sensory phenomena that lie at the basis of all mental activities and the products that proceed from them" are measurable and countable (Stumpf, 1921, p. 121). A psychologist can measure and enumerate psychological phenomena—just as a physicist does physical ones—but does so "to draw not physical but psychological conclusions, namely about the precision of sensory perceptions and the comparisons and discriminations that are based on them, as well as about the effects of concomitant psychological factors, such as attention and memory" (Stumpf, 1921, p. 121). In conclusion, Stumpf addressed the limits of quantifiable methods in psychology:

> Finally, however, we must not forget that . . . the mysterious realm of truth, beauty, and the good is not dealt with by these research methods. . . . Never will one be able to distinguish between truth and falsehood, beauty and ugliness, good and bad through a counting out process or majority rule. (Stumpf, 1921, p. 121)

In his final years, Stumpf recounted the credo of his life's work in "Epistemology" (Stumpf, 1939, 1940). In the words of his son Felix, Stumpf wanted "to give a complete presentation . . . of the views that he had formed in the course of a long lifetime of experiences" (Stumpf, 1939, p. v). Stumpf's epistemology was a philosophy based on empiricism, primarily on the findings of modern psychology and the natural sciences. Clearly Stumpf is rightfully counted among the predecessors of today's psychological methodology when one considers his brief characterizations of three central methodological concepts of the "new" empirical psychology of his time, observation, measurement, and experiment: "Observation differs from mere perception in that specific features of the perceived are recorded, analyzed, and compared over a period of time and subsumed under certain concepts" (Stumpf, 1939, p. 305). "Observation becomes measurement when the observed is taken apart into a certain number of quantitative parts of known size. These parts are units of an arbitrarily established but absolute and virtually unchangeable system of measurement that is independent of momentary sensory phenomena" (Stumpf, 1939, p. 308). "An observation becomes an experiment when, within a given situation, a certain circumstance is arbitrarily altered in order to observe the subsequent effects. . . . Of course, every experiment . . . must be based on some theory or hypothesis derived from an idea that can be discussed scientifically" (Stumpf, 1939, pp. 309–310).

STUMPF AS A FORERUNNER AND CRITIC OF GESTALT PSYCHOLOGY

Stumpf, the student of Brentano and Lotze, is acknowledged as an exponent of holistic thought (Ash, 1995). He was a pathfinder and an inspiration for Gestalt psychology, especially in Berlin. His scientific writings contain phrases later included in the canon of Gestalt psychology, such as "the primacy of holistic thinking," "the primacy of an analysis of phenomena over the analysis of stimuli," and "the principle of psychophysical isomorphism" (Sprung & Sprung, 1995, 1996). Yet Berlin's later Gestalt psychologists seldom referred to this pioneer in Gestalt theory, their teacher and supporter, explicitly or extensively.

Stumpf expressed his opinion on the Gestalt school of psychology toward the end of his life. In the section on Gestalt perception in "Epistemology," he warned of the tendency of all schools to promote their theoretical positions and to ignore competing points of view. For example, he says, "Gestalten and Gestalt qualities represent the solution for an energetic and successful progressive trend in contemporary psychology. Undoubtedly, too little attention was paid earlier to the principles of Gestalt perception. . . . But as happens so often in these cases, one bias has given way to the other. Often the discussions of Gestalt theorists give the impression that our sensory perceptions have no colors or tones, but are nothing but Gestalten" (Stumpf, 1939, p. 242).

Although Stumpf remained a critic of Gestalt theory his ideas touch that theory in many different ways. He practiced holistic thinking from the beginning of his scientific work. His research from the 1880s and 1890s already refers to processes of "fusion" (Stumpf, 1883, p. 101) and "sensory wholes" (Stumpf, 1890, p. 346), concepts that may be seen as precursors of Gestalt ideas. In *Tone Psychology*, he noted that "all sensory qualities, when they go from being successive to simultaneous, enter not only into this state of simultaneity but also into another, that . . . of a sensory whole" (Stumpf, 1890, p. 64). And on "fusion,"

"We called fusion that relation between two contents . . . that forms not a mere sum but a whole" (Stumpf, 1890, p. 128). The Examples abound, and it is safe to assume that Stumpf's students early in the 20th century did not receive their Gestalt psychological impulses solely from the writings of Christian von Ehrenfels, whom they more commonly cite.

But Stumpf was cautious when it came to generalizing his scientific ideas. In this respect, he was not the type to found a school or to claim that his views applied to all or almost all psychological subject areas, as did his Gestalt psychology students and successors at Berlin University. In his own words,

> The author sees himself . . . called upon to take a stand opposing worthy young like-minded researchers on major points. He cannot . . . refrain from objecting to the idea [of the earlier psychologists that psychological life is] merely "summational," "atomistic" [a conglomerate] made up of isolated sensations." (Stumpf, 1939, p. 243)

Becoming still more pointed in his critique of Gestalt psychology, he added, "Has a psychologist or anyone else ever defined a melody as merely the sum total of a succession of notes, connected by 'and'? I am fairly well-acquainted with both psychological and musicological literature, but never have I come across such asinine statements" (Stumpf, 1939, p. 243). And finally he pointed out, "Aristotle's now often-cited phrase 'the whole comes before the parts' was indubitably part of his teleological world view. . . . it means that in works of reason, each part . . . is determined by the idea of the whole" (Stumpf, 1939, p. 244).

To avoid being carried away by our discussion of Stumpf as a critic, we must emphasize that he also praised the work of the Gestalt psychologists: "The author is . . . far from underestimating the great contributions that the Gestalt psychologists have made, both in their demands for recognition of the . . . Gestalt problem as well as by their many . . . inquiries and . . . observations" (Stumpf, 1939, pp. 253–254). Gestalt psychological thought and work were well under way when the Berlin Gestalt psychologists arrived in the city at the beginning of the 20th century (Pastor, Sprung, & Sprung, 1997; Sprung & Schönpflug, 1992; Sprung & Sprung, 1996).

CARL STUMPF AND WILLIAM JAMES

A special aspect in Stumpf's life concerns his friendship with William James (chap. 2, *Pioneers I*; Dazzi, 1995; James, 1920). The two met on two occasions, once in Prague (1882), and once in Munich (1892), and they liked each other immediately (Stumpf, 1928b). James and Stumpf were brothers in spirit. They worked together in academic policy making, and their conceptions of psychology coincided in many points.

In his autobiography Stumpf wrote, "In 1882 I had a visit from William James. He was pleased about my book on space perception. It was a pleasure and the beginning of our long-standing friendship and correspondence" (Stumpf, 1924,

p. 216). Stumpf wrote James on December 8, 1882, soon after their first encounter, "Dear James! I was pleased about your familiar form of address. I had after our short meeting the deep impression that we agree not only in our scientific opinions in so many points. I had the deep impression, too, that it was the beginning of a lifelong friendship" (Stumpf, 1882b). James later wrote about the friendship in a letter dated April 24, 1893, "I am sorry that [because of our ages] those days, those not easily forgotten days that I spent in dear old Munich, are likely to be the last ones of our seeing each other for a long time to come" (Perry, 1935, p. 183). And on May 26, 1893, returning to the point about his age, James wrote Stumpf, "Older I am indeed, . . . but I speak sincerely when I say that during my last visit I felt more intimately and closely the charm of your character and our intellectual kinship than when we were together ten years ago in Prague" (Perry, 1935, p. 183).

The reciprocal relationship between James and Stumpf may very well have contributed to the establishment of psychology as an independent science in Germany and in the United States. James brought Stumpf to the editorial board of the *Psychological Review*, writing him on September 12, 1893, that

> a new Journal is to be started. . . . The *Psychological Review* with Baldwin and Cattell as chief editors, and all the Professors of Psychology in the American universities except Jastrow and Hull [chaps. 6 and 14, *Pioneers I*] as cooperating editors. Such names as Ladd, Münsterberg, Donaldson, James, Scripture. . . . The Editorial Committee now request you (through my hand) to permit your name to be placed on the title page as cooperating editor. Binet [chap. 5, *Pioneers III*] has already allowed his name to be so used for France. (quoted in Perry, 1935, p. 186)

Conversely, with Stumpf's support, James became a member of the Prussian Academy of Sciences in Berlin in 1900. Stumpf wrote the following opinion about James, dated November 30, 1899:

> William James, professor of philosophy at Harvard University in New Cambridge, stands in the first rank of psychologists in the world today. His is the best philosophical mind which the new world has produced. His *Principles of Psychology*, published in 1890 in two large volumes, displays a high level of acquaintance with physiological and psychological knowledge around the world, many original ideas, and an independent point of view. (Stumpf, 1899b, p. 149)

Stumpf and James agreed in their opinion of Wilhelm Wundt and the kind of psychology that he had established and developed so successfully at Leipzig. On February 6, 1887, James wrote to Stumpf, concerning Wundt,

> He aims at being a sort of Napoleon of the intellectual world. Unfortunately he will never have a Waterloo; he is a Napoleon without genius and with no central idea which, if defeated, brings down the whole fabric in ruin. . . . He isn't a genius, he is a professor—a being whose duty is to know everything, and have his own opinion about everything, connected with his [discipline]. (Perry, 1935, pp. 68–69)

Previously, Stumpf had written to James on September 8, 1886, that Wundt

> says to students and many other people that he, Wundt, started a new experimen-
> tal psychology with his experiments on reaction time. Look in his papers, look in
> the papers of his pupils. He has only scorn and mockery for the old psychology.
> In my opinion, reaction time is empty without information about the inner process,
> researched via introspection or self-observation. Wundt is a bad model for his pupils.
> His concepts are unclear and his style of thinking is blurred. (quoted in Perry, 1935,
> pp. 738–739)

Although James and Stumpf were brothers in spirit in many respects, Stumpf
had a lifelong problem with understanding James's philosophical position of prag-
matism (Dazzi, 1995). Stumpf could not accept a utilitarian criterion of truth.
Utility was for Stumpf a nonphilosophical category; he was too much connected
with the long-standing German philosophical tradition of idealism. On May 8,
1907, Stumpf wrote in a letter to James,

> In our philosophical ideas, my dear friend, I observe more and more differences.
> Pragmatism and humanism are strange for me. In this philosophical position we
> have grown apart. I agree much more with the earlier James in this direction, but
> the man, James, . . . is as close a friend to me as before. The basic nature of our
> relationship remains unchanged. (quoted in Perry, 1935, p. 744)

James and Stumpf also agreed on many other points. One was that experimental psychology and its mother-science philosophy need one another, and a
dissolution of the basic connection would come to nothing. They agreed, too,
that the institutionalization of experimental psychology is an important step, but
could also be a dangerous step. The danger or risk lies in the disintegration of
psychology in contemporary terms: the danger of the "miniaturization" of psychology. In this point, we can learn today from the historical conceptions of
Stumpf and James.

CONCLUSION

At a sensitive phase in the creation of the discipline of modern psychology as
empirical psychology, Stumpf produced a significant body of work, which includes treatises on experimental and theoretical psychology (Viney & King, 1998;
Wertheimer, 2000). Of still greater consequence were his achievements as an
academic statesperson in his field, particularly during his tenure in Berlin. He
built up a Psychological Institute, set up a phonograph record archive as an ethnomusicological collection, was instrumental in making the primate research center on Tenerife a center for research in evolutionary psychology, and advanced
national and international scientific discourse. Stumpf's interdisciplinary orien-

tation makes it not a simple task to reconstruct his body of work. What makes his writings so stimulating are their high theoretical level and their thorough analysis of the subject. What makes Stumpf as a person so admirable are his intellectual honesty, courtesy, and tolerance with regard to the trends and contrasts in psychology and philosophy. The history of the science would have been very different without his work and influence (Bringmann, Lück, Miller & Early, 1997; Carpintero, 1996; Gondra, 1997; H. Sprung, 1997; Sprung & Sprung, 1999; Tortosa, 1998; Trommsdorff & Sprung, 2000).

REFERENCES

Ash, M. G. (1995). *Gestalt psychology in German culture, 1890–1967. Holism and the quest for objectivity* (Cambridge Studies in the History of Psychology). Cambridge: University Press.

Baumgartner, W., & Burkard F.-P. (1990). Franz Brentano: Eine Skizze seines Lebens und seiner Werke [Franz Brentano: A sketch of his life and work]. In *Internationale Bibliographie zur Österreichischen Philosophie* (Vol. 4, pp. 6–53). Amsterdam: Rodopi.

Baumgartner, W., Burkard, F.-P., & Wiedemann, F. (Eds.). (1997). *Brentano Studien 7. Zur Entwicklung und Bedeutung der Würzburger Schulen* [Brentano Studies 7. Development and significance of the Würzburg School]. Internationale interdisziplinäre Fachtagung aus Anlass der Berufung Oswald Külpes nach Würzburg anno 1894. Dettelbach: Röll.

Bosse, M. (1893). Schreiben an die Philosophische Fakultät der Berliner Universität, vom 18 December 1893. Universitätsarchiv der Humboldt-Universität zu Berlin, Dekanat der Philosophischen Universität, Akte Nr. 1462, Blatt 129 [Letter to the Philosophical Faculty of the University at Berlin, December 18, 1893, Office of the Dean, Folder 1462, p. 129].

Bringmann, W. G., Lück, H. E., Miller, R., & Early, C. E. (Eds.). (1997). *A pictorial history of psychology*. Chicago: Quintessence.

Carpintero, H. (1996). *Historia de las ideas psicológicas* [History of psychological ideas]. Madrid: Pirámide.

Dazzi, N. (1995). James and Stumpf. Similarities and differences. *Psychologie und Geschichte, 6*(3–4), 244–257.

De la Motte-Haber, H. (1972). *Musikpsychologie: Eine Einführung* [Music psychology: An introduction]. Cologne: Musikverlag Hans Gering.

Eckardt, G., Bringmann, W. G., & Sprung, L. (Eds.). (1985). *Contributions to a history of developmental psychology*. Berlin: Mouton.

Gondra, J. M. (1997). *Historia de la psicología. Introducción al pensamiento psicológico moderno. Vol. 1: Nacimiento de la psicología científica* [History of psychology: Introduction to modern psychological thought. Vol. I: The birth of psychology]. Madrid: Editorial Sintesis.

Heinecke, H., & Jaeger, S. (1993). Entstehung von Anthropoiden-Stationen zu Beginn des 20. Jahrhunderts [Origins of primate research centers at the beginning of the 20th century]. *Biologisches Zentralblatt, 112*(2), 215–223.

Hirschfeld, D. (1893). Berufungsvorschläge der philosophischen Fakultät der Berliner Universität vom 13 Juli 1893. Zentrales Staatsarchiv Merseburg, Rep. 76 Va., Sekt. 2, Tit. IV, No. 61, Band VI, 193–208 [Nominations for candidates by the philosophical faculty at the University of Berlin, July 13, 1893. Central State Archive Merseburg, Rep. 76 VA, Sec. 2, tit. IV, no. 61, Vol. VI, pp. 193–208].

James, H. (1920). (Ed.). *The letters of William James*. London: Longmans.

Pastor, J. C., Sprung, L., & Sprung, H. (1997). La escuela berlinesa de psicología gestalt: Aspectos relacionados con su origen y desarrollo [The Berlin school of Gestalt psychology: Aspects of its origin and development]. *Revista de Historia de la Psicología, 18*(1–2), 245–256.

Perry, R. B. (1935). *The thought and character of William James. As revealed in unpublished correspondence and notes, together with his published writings.* London: Humphrey Milford, Oxford University Press.

Reisenzein, R., & Schönpflug, W. (1992). Stumpf's cognitive-evaluative theory of emotion. *American Psychologist, 47,* 34–45.

Scherer, W. (1873). Letter of Wilhelm Scherer, July 19, 1873, to Carl Stumpf. Family Archives Stumpf, Stuttgart-Bad Cannstatt.

Scherer, W. (1882). Letter of Wilhelm Scherers, November 3, 1882, to Carl Stumpf. Family Archives Stumpf, Stuttgart-Bad Cannstatt.

Sprung, H. (Ed.). (1997). *Carl Stumpf: Schriften zur Psychologie. Neu herausgegeben, eingeleitet und mit einer biographischen Einführung versehen* [Carl Stumpf: Psychological writings, newly edited, introduced, and provided with a biographical introduction]. Frankfurt am Main: Lang.

Sprung, H., & Sprung, L. (1995). Carl Stumpf (1848–1936) und die Anfänge der Gestaltpsychologie an der Berliner Universität [Carl Stumpf 1848–1936) and the beginnings of Gestalt psychology at the University of Berlin]. In S. Jaeger, I. Staeuble, L. Sprung, & H.-P. Brauns (Eds.), *Psychologie im soziokulturellen Wandel: Kontinuitäten und Diskontinuitäten* (pp. 259–268). Frankfurt am Main: Lang.

Sprung, H., & Sprung, L. (1996). Carl Stumpf (1848–1936), a general psychologist and methodologist, and a case study of a cross-cultural scientific transition process. In W. Battmann & S. Dutke (Eds.), *Processes of the molar regulation of behavior* (pp. 327–342). Lengerich: Pabst.

Sprung, L., & Schönpflug, W. (Eds.). (1992). *Zur Geschichte der Psychologie in Berlin [On the history of psychology in Berlin].* Frankfurt am Main: Lang.

Sprung, L., & Sprung, H. (1987). Ebbinghaus an der Berliner Universität: Ein akademisches Schicksal eines zu früh Geborenen? [Ebbinghaus at the University of Berlin: An academic fate of someone born too soon.] In W. Traxel (Ed.), *Ebbinghaus—Studien 2. Passauer Schriften zur Psychologiegeschichte* (Vol. 5, pp. 89–106). Passau: Passavia.

Sprung, L., & Sprung, H. (1999). Rückblicke auf ein schwieriges Jahrhundert: Zur Geschichte der Psychologie im 20. Jahrhundert in Deutschland [A retrospective review of a difficult century: On the history of psychology in twentieth-century Germany]. In W. Hacker & M. Rinck (Eds.), *Zukunft gestalten. Bericht über den 41. Kongress der Deutschen Gesellschaft für Psychologie in Dresden 1998* (pp. 23–143). Lengerich: Pabst.

Stumpf, C. (1873a). Letter of Carl Stumpf, May 15, 1873, to Wilhelm Scherer. Zentrales Akademie-Archiv der Berlin-Brandenburgischen Akademie der Wissenschaften, Nachlass Scherer 671.

Stumpf, C. (1873b). Letter of Carl Stumpf, July 29, 1873, to Wilhelm Scherer. Zentrales Akademie-Archiv der Berlin-Brandenburgischen Akademie der Wissenschaften, Nachlass Scherer 671.

Stumpf, C. (1882a). Letter of Carl Stumpf, November 5, 1882, to Wilhelm Scherer. Zentrales Akademie-Archiv der Berlin-Brandenburgischen Akademie der Wissenschaften. Nachlass Scherer 671, Ergänzungen.

Stumpf, C. (1882b). Letter of Carl Stumpf, December 8, 1882, to William James. Received from Wolfgang G. Bringmann, University of South Alabama, Mobile, Alabama (USA) in 1991.

Stumpf, C. (1883). *Tonpsychologie* [Tone psychology] (Vol. 1). Leipzig: Hirzel.

Stumpf, C. (1884). Letter of Carl Stumpf, July 29, 1884, to Wilhelm Scherer. Zentrales Akademie-Archiv der Berlin-Brandenburgischen Akademie der Wissenschaften. Nachlass Scherer 671.

Stumpf, C. (1890). *Tonpsychologie* [Tone psychology]. (Vol. 2). Leipzig: Hirzel.

Stumpf, C. (1895). Antrittsrede des Hrn. Stumpf und Antwort des Hrn. Mommsen [Inaugural speech by Mr. Stumpf and reply by Mr. Mommsen]. *Sitzungsberichte der Königlich Preussischen Akademie der Wissenschaften. 2. Halbband* (pp. 735–739). Berlin: Reimer.

Stumpf, C. (1899a). Der Entwicklungsgedanke in der gegenwärtigen Philosophie [Evolutionary thought in contemporary philosophy]. Festrede, gehalten am Stiftungstage der Kaiser Wilhelms-Akademie für das militärärztliche Bildungswesen, December 2, 1899 (pp. 5–32). Berlin: Lange.

Stumpf, C. (1899b). Gutachten Carl Stumpfs über William James. Zentrales Akademie-Archiv der Berlin-Brandenburgischen Akademie der Wissenschaften, Historische Abteilung II–III, 130, p. 149

[Opinion of Carl Stumpf about William James, Central Archives of the Berlin-Brandënburg Academy of Sciences, Historical Department II–III, 130, p. 149].

Stumpf, C. (1906a). Erscheinungen und psychische Funktionen [Phenomena and psychological functions]. *Abhandlungen der Königlich Preussischen Akademie der Wissenschaften. Philosophisch-historische Abhandlungen* IV (pp. 1–40). Berlin: Reimer.

Stumpf, C. (1906b). Zur Einteilung der Wissenschaften [On classifying the sciences]. *Abhandlungen der Königlich Preussischen Akademie der Wissenschaften. Philosophisch-historische Abhandlungen* V (pp. 1–94). Berlin: Reimer.

Stumpf, C. (1907). Richtungen und Gegensätze in der heutigen Psychologie [Trends and contrasts in today's psychology]. *Internationale Wochenschrift für Wissenschaft Kunst und Technik. Beilage der "Münchner Allgemeine Zeitung,"* October 19, 1907, pp. 903–914. Berlin: August Scherl.

Stumpf, C. (1908). Das Berliner Phonogrammarchiv [The Berlin collection of phonograph records]. *Internationale Wochenschrift für Wissenschaft Kunst und Technik. Beilage der "Münchner Allgemeine Zeitung,"* Feb. 22, 1908. Berlin: August Scherl, 225–246.

Stumpf, C. (1910a). Das psychologische Institut [The psychological institute]. In M. Lenz (Ed.), *Geschichte der Königlichen Friedrich-Wilhelms-Universität zu Berlin* (Vol. 3, pp. 202–207). Halle: Waisenhaus.

Stumpf, C. (1910b). *Philosophische Reden und Vorträge* [Philosophical addresses and speeches]. Leipzig: Barth.

Stumpf, C. (1917). Zum Gedächtnis Lotzes [In memory of Lotzes]. *Kantstudien, 22*(1–2), 1–26.

Stumpf, C. (1918). Empfindung und Vorstellung [Sensation and representation]. *Abhandlungen der Königlich Preussischen Akademie der Wissenschaften. Philosophisch-historische Klasse* 1 (pp. 3–116). Berlin: Reimer.

Stumpf, C. (1919). Erinnerungen an Franz Brentano [Recollections of Franz Brentano]. In O. Kraus (Ed.), *Franz Brentano: Zur Kenntnis seines Lebens und seiner Lehre* (pp. 87–149). Munich: Beck.

Stumpf, C. (1921). Zahl und Mass im Geistigen [Number and measure in psychology]. *Vossische Zeitung Berlin. Berlinische Zeitung von Staats-und gelehrten Sachen,* May 27, 1921. Abend-Ausgabe 245–B, p. 121.

Stumpf, C. (1924). Carl Stumpf. In R. Schmidt (Ed.), *Die Philosophie der Gegenwart in Selbst-darstellungen* (Vol. 5, pp. 204–265). Leipzig: Meiner.

Stumpf, C. (1928a). *Gefühl und Gefühlsempfindung* [Feeling and sensations of feelings]. Leipzig: Barth.

Stumpf, C. (1928b). *William James nach seinen Briefen. Leben-Charakter–Lehre* [William James: Life, personality, and theory, based on his letters]. Berlin: Pan (Heise).

Stumpf, C. (1939). *Erkenntnislehre* [Epistemology] (Vol. 1). Leipzig: Barth.

Stumpf, C. (1940). *Erkenntnislehre* [Epistemology] (Vol. 2). Leipzig: Barth.

Stumpf, C., & Schaefer, K. L. (1901). Tontabellen [Tone tables]. *Beiträge zur Akustik und Musik-wissenschaft, 3,* 139–146, tabs. I–IX.

Stumpf, E. (1873). Letter from Carl Stumpf's father, Eugen Stumpf, May 11, 1873, to Adolph Merkel. Zentrales Akademie-Archiv der Berlin-Brandenburgischen Akademie der Wissenschaften. Nachlass Scherer 671.

Stumpf, M. (1873). Letter from Carl Stumpf's mother, Marie Stumpf, July 8, 1873, to Adolf Merkel. Zentrales Akademie-Archiv der Berlin-Brandenburgischen Akademie der Wissenschaften. Nachlass Scherer 671.

Tortosa, F. (Ed.). (1998). *Una historia de la psicología moderna* [A history of modern psychology]. Madrid: McGraw Hill/Interamericana.

Trommsdorff, G., & Sprung, L. (in press). Psychology in Germany. *Encyclopedia of Psychology.* Washington, DC: American Psychological Association.

Viney, W., & King, D. (1998). *A history of psychology. Ideas and context* (2nd ed.). Boston: Allyn and Bacon.

Wertheimer, M. (2000). *A brief history of psychology* (4th ed.). Ft. Worth, TX: Harcourt, Brace.

Chapter 5

Georg Elias Müller and the Beginnings of Modern Psychology

Lothar Sprung and Helga Sprung

G. E. Müller should be counted among the founders of modern empirical psychology, and one of its best-remembered pioneers, but he is less well-known today than many of his predecessors, contemporaries, and successors. One purpose of this chapter is to give this giant in the history of psychology the credit he deserves.

FAMILY BACKGROUND AND EARLY EDUCATION

Georg Elias Müller was born July 20, 1850, in Grimma, Saxony, six months before Hermann Ebbinghaus (chap. 4, *Pioneers III*), whose heir he was to become in the psychology of memory. Müller came from a Protestant family headed by a member of the clergy, as did many of the other German pioneers of modern psychology—Gustav Theodor Fechner (chap. 1, *Pioneers II*) and Wundt Wilhelm (chap. 3, *Pioneers III*), for example. At the time of Georg's birth, Müller's father was professor of religion and German in Grimma at the Fürstenschule, a renowned school providing a broad humanistic education. For Müller, the dearth of natural science courses at the Fürstenschule was a major shortcoming. But even at this early age, he had developed the habits of a self-reliant lifelong learner, and the lack of scientific courses spurred him on to additional independent stud-

Kroh 1935 quotations used by permission of Verlag GMBH & Co., Göttingen, Germany.

Thanks are owed to Andrea Lerner, MA (Berlin) and Michael Wertheimer (Boulder, CO) for help on the English version of this chapter and Dr. Horst-Peter Brauns (Berlin) for the reference to the Gutberlet (1905) report.

*Photo of Georg Müller courtesy of Niedersächsische Staats und Universitäts Bibliothek Göttingen.

ies. Even as a full professor at Göttingen, Müller regularly attended lectures in physics, chemistry, and medicine when he needed such information for his research.

In 1868, Müller's father became the parson in Zwenkau, a town near Leipzig, and sent his son to the Nikolaigymnasium in that city. Müller graduated in that same year. Adolf von Harnack, who spent a good deal of time at the parsonage in Zwenkau while teaching at Leipzig, described Müller's father as the "very model of an evangelical priest, wise and plainspoken, firm and decisive, forbearing with others, always lively, never scattered" (Misch, 1935, p. 46). It was typical of Müller's father's zeal for education and learning that, after he retired at the age of 78, he began traveling regularly to Leipzig to attend Wundt's lectures. In an unfinished autobiography that Müller began writing at the age of 80, he stated,

> From my father, I inherited my indignation about that which is illogical or unclear; my tendencies to be thorough and repeatedly to correct what I had written . . . and a memory that is almost always ready to receive impressions. My father also was an outstanding analyzer of the spiritual qualities of the people around him. My need to penetrate the psychology of my fellow human beings may well have been an inheritance from my father, too. (quoted in Misch, 1935, p. 46)

Müller's mother came from an old Leipzig theological family. In his autobiography, Müller reported that she loved ancient languages, French, and literature, and that she wrote poetry until her death at the age of 81. Müller believed that he had inherited his lifelong love of the French language and the French lifestyle from her. Müller also traced back to his mother his temperament, which he describes as "not averse to quick and powerful reactions" (Misch, 1935, pp. 46–47). From her, he also inherited his "critical stance towards other people, a measured evaluation of outer honors or dignitaries." But he especially owed to her his "great love of poetry" that made him an "amateur at learning poems by heart" throughout his entire life. He noted that this came "a little bit into play as I later became so intensely involved with the investigation of memory" (Misch, 1935, p. 47).

UNIVERSITY EDUCATION

Müller began his university studies at Leipzig in October 1868, at first taking courses in philosophy and history. He was especially interested in history. He remained in Leipzig for one year with the goal of becoming a teacher, like his father. In a letter to E. G. Boring in 1928 (cited by Boring, 1935), he summarized his professional ambitions: "[Being a teacher] was to have been my bread-and-butter [work], to help me sometime to get an appointment to a Gymnasium or something of the sort" (Boring, 1935, p. 345). At Leipzig, Müller was especially impressed by Moritz Wilhelm Drobisch's lectures on Herbart's philosophy and psychology. Later he acknowledged that Herbart's teachings had steered him early in the direction of natural scientific psychology. But his major subject was history, and to study history better he went to Berlin university in October 1869. There he attended history lectures and became involved with art history, studying it mainly in museums, not the lecture halls.

At Berlin, Müller attended philosophy lectures on Aristotle by Friedrich Adolf Trendelenburg that considerably broadened his scientific horizons, and he became acquainted with Lotze's writings (Lotze, 1846, 1852). These studies led him to add courses in the philosophy of nature to his study of history, and set him on the path that took him to the philosophy of nature and natural sciences as his major fields of study. History became his minor. Looking back on that shift in interests, Müller wrote to Boring in 1928,

> Although history was a favorite subject of mine, I felt from the time of my first semester as a student, in which I had become acquainted with the writings of Lotze, that, in order really to progress in philosophy, which was my chief and best loved field, I should have to combine with the study of philosophy not the study of history, but the study of natural science and mathematics. However, my historical knowledge was too great; I could not decide wholly to surrender this mental capital, so important for my progress in life. The conflict between these two projects, to keep on with history or to go over to natural science, troubled me greatly at the time—indeed far into my nights. (quoted in Boring, 1935, p. 345)

Then an outside event unexpectedly made the decision for him. The Franco-Prussian War broke out and Müller (as did Ebbinghaus) enlisted as a volunteer. In August 1870 he went to war as a soldier in Berlin's Kaiser Alexander guard regiment. Although his vision had been impaired since the age of 17 as the result of an operation to correct strabismus, he was promoted to the rank of officer. After the victory over France and the establishment of the Second German Reich, Müller and his regiment entered Berlin through the Brandenburg Gate in June 1871. He was proud of that day for the rest of his life. More important for this history, the war had transformed him. In the often-cited letter to Boring, he said, "When, at the end of my military service—the finest year of my life as I recall that glorious time—I tested my historical knowledge. I found that this same mental capital had shrunk badly and no longer deserved consideration" (Boring, 1935, p. 345). From then on, only the experimental sciences appealed to him.

In October 1871, Müller returned to Leipzig to study natural science. In that area he had been especially impressed by Lotze's treatise on medical psychology (Lotze, 1852), Fechner's works on psychophysics (Fechner, 1860) and Helmholtz's studies on physiological optics (Helmholtz, 1867; chap. 2, this volume). Around Easter 1872, he transferred from Leipzig to Göttingen to attend Lotze's lectures and to work with him.

In his letter to Boring, Müller described Lotze's influence this way:

Lotze had a great influence on me to the extent that his writings were for me . . . a study in critical thinking, and that they aroused in me the conviction that a thorough grounding in the natural sciences is requisite for a fruitful pursuit of philosophy. In accordance with my critical frame of mind, I shared Lotze's philosophical views only to a limited extent. He is the one, though, who kept me in a scientific career and helped my progress. I can think of him only with the deepest gratitude. (Boring, 1935, p. 346)

In 1935, Georg Misch also described Müller's relation to Lotze:

What he retained from his teacher—aside from the general principle of logical and methodical exactness—was the scientific orientation that . . . psychology [must be] conducted in the spirit of the natural sciences. . . . Lotze, the brilliant author of "Medical Psychology" . . . put psychology into the hands of natural science, in that he identified the fundamental conceptual task of philosophy as causal explanatory theory, but the search for meaning and significance came above that. Müller . . . was an experimental scientist and wanted to be or appear none other. (Misch, 1935, p. 48)

In March 1873, Müller received his doctorate under Lotze with a thesis "On the Theory of Sensory Attention." But then his "bread-and-butter work" caught up with him. He became a private tutor in Rötha near Leipzig and later on in Berlin. At one point, he returned to his parents' house for a long period because of illness. During his recovery, he began to work on his postdoctoral dissertation, "On the Foundations of Psychophysics." It was submitted to the department of philosophy at Göttingen in the summer of 1876, and in August he was authorized to teach at the university.

CAREER

In 1880, Müller received his first academic appointment as associate professor of philosophy at Czernowitz in Bukowina—in the easternmost outpost of the Habsburg empire and what is now Ukraine. There he gave lectures on general philosophy and the history of Greek philosophy. Unfortunately, the topics of his deepest interests, the philosophy of nature and psychology as a natural science, were not in demand. Partly for that reason, Czernowitz remained alien to him. More important, however, Müller's working habits and his way of life, guided by Prussian virtues and a need for order, made it impossible for him to feel at home in Czernowitz. In 1935, Oswald Kroh recounted talks he had with Müller, noting that

Müller, the critical observer and ethical rigorist, detested the easygoing way of life he encountered in the Austrian crown country, which departed so strangely from the severe, correct Prussian nature of Berlin and Göttingen, so that even in later years, when he recalled his time in Czernowitz and some of his experiences in collegial circles there, he was unsparing with his critical judgment. (Kroh, 1935, p. 162)

In 1881, after just one year in Czernowitz, Müller returned to Göttingen as a professor, becoming Lotze's successor, occupying a chair that Johann Herbart had once held and that Rudolph Lotze had occupied immediately before him. This was an extraordinary feat for a 31-year-old at this time. Later, he would point to three great strokes of good luck in his life. The first was to have been appointed a professor at an early age; the second was to have married an intelligent woman; the third was to have had poor health and a temperament that did not permit him to become overconfident. He gave health and temperament as the reasons he never became a politician, although he took public affairs seriously.

It was a combination of luck and tragedy that led to Müller's obtaining the professorship at Göttingen. After his wife's death in 1879, Lotze had accepted an appointment at Friedrich-Wilhelms-University in Berlin and left Göttingen for that position on November 30, 1880. In 1881, at Lotze's behest, Müller was called from Czernowitz to Göttingen, where he directed the institute of psychology for 40 years, building it into an important center for experimental psychology.

Müller had come to Lotze's attention early on. As a student at Leipzig in the early 1870s, Müller had sent Lotze a critique of his local sign theory, which impressed Lotze as both relevant and constructive. At about the same time, Müller, who was also attending Fechner's lectures, had given Fechner a critique of his psychophysics. Fechner, too, liked the factual, constructive, and self-confident critical capability Müller displayed. Later on, at Göttingen, Müller expanded the critique of psychophysics, leading in part to Fechner publishing a revision of his psychophysics (Fechner, 1882).

Müller's relation to Fechner was ambivalent. He respected Fechner as a methodologist but not as a philosopher. Fechner's pan-psychism was especially unconvincing to him (Sprung & Sprung, 1988). Misch summarized the reasons:

> In founding psychophysics and in [promoting] Weber's law by using it as the basis for an entire field of research, Fechner actually had one intention: he was in favor of the pantheistic vision. . . . Müller dropped all the [pan-psychic] trimmings. He took Fechner's discovery as the first real . . . natural law in the mental realm, as the independent point of departure for experiments that first had to be conducted before attempting to answer the old philosophical question as to the relation between body and mind. (Misch, 1935, pp. 48–49)

Müller also mentioned the nature of his relationship to Fechner in his 1928 letter to Boring: "In those years [1870s] I was also intimate with Fechner, whose lectures I had already heard as a student. For a while we carried on an extensive scientific correspondence, even though it had a rather belligerent character" (Boring, 1935, p. 346). Previously, in 1893, he had written (with no belligerence) about his relationship to Fechner in a letter thanking the faculty of medicine at Leipzig University for awarding him an honorary doctorate:

> At this university, I was introduced to science in three semesters, and was first steered toward the problems of the relationship between body and mind, which form the main subject of my scientific efforts, during the two semesters of Fechner's lectures. Even later, in continuing the efforts proceeding from E. H. Weber, Fechner and Volkmann and under Lotze's influence, I have always retained a certain inner connection to the Leipzig tradition. (Misch, 1935, pp. 49–50)

THE GÖTTINGEN SCHOOL AND MÜLLER AS THE METHODOLOGICAL CONSCIENCE OF PSYCHOLOGY

Müller's critiques of Lotze's and Fechner's work demonstrate his early leanings toward methodology and research methods. The exercise of his expertise in these areas at Göttingen was what would later make him the "methodological conscience" of psychology, as his student David Katz called him (1936, p. 235).

A "Göttingen school" of psychology is less frequently referred to than the schools of Leipzig, Würzburg, and Berlin. Yet the foundation on which Müller built the school was outlined in a commemorative speech by Wilhelm Hische on December 27, 1934:

> What assured the far-reaching results of his scientific research was to a great extent his exemplary scientific methodological stance. It is characterized by . . . rigor and simplicity, its cleanness and reliability and likewise limitation in its interpretation of the results obtained. (Hische, 1935, p. 146)

Although Müller never liked the label "Göttingen School," many of his contemporaries agreed that high methodological standards were what distinguished psychology at Göttingen. Katz expressed it in these words:

> The emphasis on methodological questions was the sole force behind the building of a school that operated with the cleanest of working practices, without imposing any other preconceived beliefs. . . . To honor Müller's lifework is to celebrate his efforts to apply natural scientific observation techniques and natural scientific method to the area of psychology. (Katz, 1936, p. 234–235)

When Katz wrote those words, Müller was already dead, but the Göttingen tradition lived on. With few resources, Müller had built up a leading institute, which became the center of his wide-ranging influence. By the end of Müller's 40 years there, Göttingen was the third largest institute of psychology in the German-language area, following Leipzig and Berlin.

Göttingen Collegial Relationships

One rule of method in the Göttingen school was that Müller himself was a participant observer for every new experimental investigation. Katz later reported, "The doctoral students became accustomed to the most careful working methods, not least because Müller himself served as a subject in each experiment—often over a long period of time" (Katz, 1936, p. 237). And Müller's pupil Oswald Kroh emphasized in 1935,

> So the desire for scrupulous accuracy in method has become the . . . unifying bond that holds the "Göttingen school" together. Müller was never content just generally to review the methodological adequacy of work coming out of his institute. In every series of experiments . . . he himself was a participant, so he could supervise the conditions from the situation of the examinee. (Kroh, 1935, pp. 177–178)

Müller typically attended lectures by colleagues when he thought their contents were relevant to his own work. His student and first (informal) assistant, Friedrich Schumann, for instance, recalled that Müller heard several semesters of lectures on physical chemistry by Walter Nernst while he was studying perceptual processes. And his retirement years found him attending lectures on photochemistry while he was working on problems of color perception—in the 1920s, when he was more than 70 years old (Kroh, 1935, p. 158).

The Primacy of Scientific Rigor

The consequence of Müller's rigorous methodological stance was that students and colleagues were initially accorded little freedom in selecting topics for research. Kroh described his style of academic advising:

> The doctoral candidate was given a precisely defined subject at the outset. Almost all questions prepared for doctoral dissertations served the purpose of contributing to decisions relating to existing controversies or assumed alternatives. Therefore, most experimentation carried out at Göttingen had something of the decisive function of the experimentum crucis [crucial experiment]. (1935, p. 178)

Müller proceeded especially rigorously when it came to documenting scientific work. Kroh reported,

> [A] test, known as "purgatory" at the Göttingen Institute, usually took place in the evening at the Müller residence. There, intensive effort was devoted to going through the work sentence by sentence, table by table . . . talking it out and correcting it. . . . Beauty of expression was not a convincing category for him, and too much fluency easily awoke his suspicion of superficiality and of a malleability that was disagreeable in the extreme to his pithy, gruff nature. (1935, p. 179)

Katz added a note about the moral aspects of this stance: "He could find hard words for [students] whom he didn't quite trust scientifically, because he knew how much scientific achievement was, apart from talent, a sheer matter of character" (1936, p. 239). But Müller's strict manner was tempered by a helpful quality: He could listen. Katz recalled, "When you reported to him about new experimental efforts, you would have his undivided, well-intentioned, benevolent interest. This skillful listening was, to my knowledge, a great encouragement to many colleagues who visited him" (1936, p. 239).

Müller's contemporaries repeatedly stressed that he did not like it when clear statements were "concealed by conventional forms of outer politeness" (Katz, 1936, p. 238). Müller's critique of some of the work of Hugo Münsterberg (chap. 7, this volume) from the late 1880s was an example:

> I saw only that, if the style of thoughtless addiction to production that reigned in those articles were to gain the upper hand in experimental psychology, the latter would be the object of ridicule for all who possess any inkling at all about precision and scientific conscientiousness. That is why I decided to make the sacrifices of my time and good mood necessary to deal thoroughly with those articles. (quoted in Kroh, 1935, p. 170)

Despite all his methodological rigor, Müller possessed a strong tendency to speculate (although he knew how to control it). To those noticing this tendency for the first time, it stood in sharp contrast to his otherwise stringent methodology. Kroh wrote,

> Müller only seldom allowed those who came close to him personally a deeper view into the speculative side of his disposition. . . . With an ease that one hardly expected, he could build up entire theoretical structures from hypothetical starting-points. . . . And it must have necessitated the most ruthless discipline of will, to which he submitted everywhere, to elude the dangers threatening his work from this side of his talent. (Kroh, 1935, pp. 168–169)

Against such a background, Kroh continued, "one can also understand his keenness in weeding-out thoughtless scientific writing. . . . So much is certain at any rate: what Müller set before the scientific world in his treatises was [only that for which] he believed he could take responsibility" for (Kroh, 1935, pp. 168–169). Kroh concluded, "Müller differed significantly from his contemporaries W. Wundt and C. Stumpf in his conscious suppression of all broadly speculative approaches" (Kroh, 1935, p. 169). Boring later described how Müller, Wundt, and Stumpf related to philosophical speculation: "Müller was purely a psychologist. Stumpf claimed always to be a philosopher who psychologized in the interests of philosophy. Wundt claimed to be a psychologist, but we have seen that the philosopher's mind dominated him" (Boring, in Kroh, 1935, p. 169; cf. H. Sprung & L. Sprung, 1996a; L. Sprung & H. Sprung, 1999).

A Society for Experimental Psychology

At Göttingen, early in the 20th century, Müller assembled a group of colleagues who planned a convention and formed a "Society for Experimental Psychology," apparently modeled on the American "Society of Experimental Psychologists." Slightly paraphrased, a contemporary report stated that the initiative for a meeting of representatives of experimental psychology came from Müller and the most renowned experimenters, Ebbinghaus, Külpe, Meumann, Sommer, and Schumann, joined Müller in a committee to plan for the initiative and to issue invitations to attend the initial convention (Gutberlet, 1905, pp. 648–649).

The invitation to participate in the meeting of the Society for Experimental Psychology merits citation as a historical document:

> Although experimental psychology has been cultivated in Germany for more than two decades, and indeed first started on its way in Germany, in our psychological endeavors we still lack a regular convention that would be the equivalent of the special conferences of all other [German] natural scientific disciplines . . . or the one American psychologists already have in their annual convention. However, this kind of a unifying meeting is no less a necessity for psychology than for other scientific disciplines. Because given the variety of specialized research institutions that already have sprung up, and the increasing number of tasks and questions that are posed to psychology from the most diverse areas of human knowledge, activity, and feeling, it is urgently advisable that those who work in the field of psychology be given opportunities more easily and completely to gain a view of prevailing lines of thought and newly-won insights through scientific meetings and personal exchange, and to support and promote each other through the exchange of experiences and thoughts with regard to their methods and the goals of their research. (Gutberlet, 1905, p. 648)

The invitation

> met with a resounding echo in even the most far-flung circles, and men and women not only from Germany and Austria but also from Switzerland, Italy, France, Holland, Sweden, Russia, even Canada and Japan registered to lecture or participate. And so the convention took place last year in Giessen from April 18th to April 21st. . . . Following the conference, a "Society for Experimental Psychology" was [formally] organized, whose board consists of . . . G. E. Müller, R. Sommer, H. Ebbinghaus, S. Exner, O. Külpe, E. Meumann, F. Schumann (as secretary). A telegram of greeting was sent to . . . the [founder] of experimental psychology, the venerable Herr Wundt, and the next convention was set for Easter vacation, 1906 in Würzburg. (Gutberlet, 1905, p. 649)

Müller headed the Society for 23 years, from 1904 to 1927 (Lüer, 1993).

Students and Colleagues

In the 1890s, the Göttingen Institute had a reputation that transcended national borders as a place to study psychology as an experimental science. There was an influx of young men and women, all of whom wanted to be introduced to experimental psychology under Müller's direction. Students and colleagues who came to Göttingen found opportunities to learn clean research methods; they also found in Müller a relentless critic but, in the end, a staunch supporter of their studies. Kroh recalled, "No expression could better convey the value of methodological stringency for that generation of psychologists than the fact that the young scholars who thought to dedicate themselves to psychology sought out the master's rigorous school at Göttingen" (1935, p. 173). Among Müller's students and colleagues were the following:

- *Friedrich Schumann, who was active at Göttingen from 1881 to 1894.* One of Müller's first students, and later his first assistant, Schumann completed postdoctoral work with Müller in 1892 and went to Berlin in 1894 to teach under Stumpf.
- *Oswald Külpe came to Göttingen in 1883 for three semesters.* Like Müller, Külpe had studied history at Leipzig and Berlin. Külpe conducted his research on the "Theory of Sensory-Based Emotions" in Göttingen and received his doctorate for this work under Wundt at Leipzig in 1887. After completing his postdoctoral dissertation (1888) and a period as Wundt's assistant (1887–1894), Külpe made important contributions to cognitive psychology and founded psychological institutes at Würzburg (1896) and Munich (1913).
- *Alfons Pilzecker came to Göttingen in the 1880s to work with Müller.* In 1889, Pilzecker published "The Theory of Sensory Attention," based on his dissertation under Müller. Another monograph, authored with Müller and based on their extensive joint research on the psychology of memory, was "Experimental Contributions on the Theory of Memory" (Müller & Pilzecker, 1900), which is today considered one of the early classics in the experimental psychology of memory.
- *Adolph Jost came to Göttingen in the 1890s.* Under Müller, he investigated how the strengths of associations depend on the distribution of repetitions. His findings, known since then as Jost's laws, were cited in connection with Müller's formulations of 1924.
- *Alfred Binet's pupil Victor Henri exported Müller's thorough research methods to psychology abroad* (Kroh, 1935, p. 174). Henri's treatise "Spatial Perceptions of Tactile Sensations" appeared in 1898. It is "a classic work about the error of localization and the tactual two-point threshold" (Zusne, 1984, p. 183). The methodology had a later influence on his

work in the field of psychophysics and on Henri's studies—together with Binet—about individual differences and the constructing of tests.

• *Lillian J. Martin, from the United States, worked with Müller from 1894–1898* (Boring, 1935, p. 347). In 1899, Martin's findings reported in "On the Analysis of Differential Thresholds" were published jointly with Müller (Martin & Müller, 1899). Martin applied Fechner's scaling method of "right and wrong cases" systematically to the determination of differential sensitivity. The proof that this method made it possible to scale sensory thresholds with great precision led her to give it the name "method of constant differences." Martin was also the third woman, after Kate Gordon (United States) and Marie Borst (Switzerland), to give a lecture at a German psychological convention, the Fourth Conference on Experimental Psychology at Innsbruck (H. Sprung & L. Sprung, 1996b).

Other students at Göttingen include Eleanor McGamble (United States), who worked with Müller from 1906 to 1907 on the method of reconstruction (Kroh, 1935, p. 175); Edgar Rubin, who worked on figure–ground relationships and contour perception and later taught at Copenhagen University; and Géza Révész, who worked in Göttingen before World War I and later was active in Budapest and Amsterdam.

MÜLLER AS AN EXPERIMENTAL PSYCHOLOGIST

For Müller, the key problem of psychology as a natural science was the body–mind issue. Unlike Fechner, he only wanted to study aspects that could be investigated experimentally. Only what could be observed and measured interested him. His aim was not, philosophically, to determine "the nature of the mind," but to investigate "the life of the mind" scientifically. As he stated in 1924,

> One cannot indeed do justice to the significant differences between psychological states and physical processes when observing as a substrate an entity of mind that differs especially from body, . . . but [only] when one assumes in the monistic sense (Spinoza) that the physical and the psychological . . . are only two different . . . attributes of one and the same fundamental nature. . . . so one must define . . . psychology . . . not as a science of the soul but only as the science of the phenomena of consciousness. (Müller, 1924a, p. 1)

With this understanding, he turned to three main areas of work: psychophysics, visual perception—especially color perception—and memory. Beyond this, especially in later years, he also expressed his views on the new psychological developments of the time (e. g., Müller, 1923).

Psychophysics

Psychophysics was the first area Müller examined, the subject of his postdoctoral thesis "On the Foundations of Psychophysics" (1878), whose contents caused Fechner to publish a "Revision of the Main Points of Psychophysics" in 1882, five years before his death (Fechner, 1877, 1882; Müller, 1878). Articles that Boring considered classical monographs on psychophysics included such publications as "On the Psychological Basis for the Comparison of Lifted Weights" (Müller & Schumann, 1889), "On the Psychophysics of Visual Sensations" (Müller, 1897), "On the Analysis of Differential Thresholds" (Martin & Müller, 1899), and "Points of View and the Facts of Psychophysical Methodology" (Müller, 1903; also see Boring, 1935).

Perception

According to Katz, perception was Müller's favorite field, the one to which he had the strongest emotional ties. He especially valued color perception, dealing with it primarily in the 1920s, after he retired. In studying color perception, he did research in a field where he himself was handicapped—he suffered from a color perceptual disorder (Müller, 1924b). His theoretical aim was to link the theories of Helmholtz and Hering. To work on color perception, he decided to break off the autobiography he began writing at the urging of his students after he retired. It remained unfinished. In 1930, his 648-page book "On Sensations of Color. Psychophysical Investigations," was published, and four years later the volume "Brief Contributions to the Psychophysics of Color Sensations" appeared (Müller, 1930, 1934).

Ideational Activity and Memory

Ebbinghaus stimulated Müller to go into the fields of ideational activity and memory. Müller summed up their place in his understanding of psychology 10 years before he died:

> Among the most important tasks of psychology is to establish laws whereby earlier perceptions are reproduced, that is, how they arise again in our consciousness as mental images. The laws of reproduction of images possess a still more general significance in as much as they also function correspondingly in the reproduction of earlier fantasy and dream images, judgments, and other psychological states. (Müller, 1924a, p. 18)

In the analysis of representations, he was concerned with "determining the laws of their arising, changing, and disappearance" (Müller, 1924a, p. 1). His more distant goal was an "ideational mechanics," a "dynamics of mental representation" in which powers of association would play a central role. His research findings were described in publications such as "Experimental Contributions to Research on Memory" (Müller & Schumann, 1894), which introduced significant methodological improvements to Ebbinghaus's procedures, "Experimental Contributions on the Theory of Memory" (Müller & Pilzecker, 1900), in which interference effects such as retroactive and proactive inhibition were presented, and "On Analyzing Memory Activity and the Flow of Mental Images" (Müller, 1911, 1913a, 1917), which provided an extensive presentation of his psychology of memory. The studies of memory that Müller conducted between 1906 and 1913 using the mathematician and mathematical genius Rudolf Rückle to test the learning and reproduction of long number series (Müller, 1913b) also deserve mention.

In 1924 Müller summarized the state of research on memory. In his review, two "laws of reproduction" are differentiated: the "law of contiguity" *(Gesetz der Koexistenz)* and the "law of succession" *(Gesetz der Sukzession).* According to the law of contiguity, "mental images that were in consciousness at the same time have . . . a tendency to reproduce each other." The law of succession states, "If image a is followed by image b, when image a reappears, there is the tendency to reproduce b" (Müller, 1924a, p. 18). On other findings, he wrote,

> Among the propositions established at this time that relate to the strength . . . of associations are the following: 1) Under otherwise identical circumstances, the more frequently elements are simultaneously or successively presented, the stronger the association. 2) The higher the degree of attention concentrated on things presented at the same time or successively, the stronger the association generated. 3) The strength of associations created . . . decreases over time at a decelerating rate of speed. (Müller, 1924a, p. 20)

In addition, Müller offered Jost's two laws to account for the effects of their ages on associations. Jost's first law was that "a new repetition will strengthen an earlier association more than a more recent one." His second law was that "when two associations are of equal strength, but different ages, the older association is forgotten more slowly over time" (Müller, 1924a, pp. 20–21; also see Klix & Hagendorf, 1986; Lüer & Lass, 1997; Traxel, 1987; Wertheimer, 1986).

Toward a Psychology of Memory and Its Elaboration

When Ebbinghaus's 1885 book, *Über das Gedächtnis (On Memory),* appeared, Müller was impressed by the idea of constructing nonsense learning materials to study the laws of learning and memory, and was astonished when Ebbinghaus lost interest in his newly won territory and left it soon thereafter, abandoning the psychology of memory after the first 6 of his 29 years of scientific activity (L. Sprung & H. Sprung, 1986, 1987). Müller seized the opportunity to fill the void left by Ebbinghaus's departure.

Immediately after the appearance of *On Memory*, Müller assigned his student Schumann the task of testing Ebbinghaus's findings (Kroh, 1935, p. 165). Schumann confirmed the results, and Müller decided to begin his own systematic investigations. Schumann later wrote about the beginnings:

> At first we borrowed a kymograph from the physiological institute, which we used to conduct preliminary research on memory. After the ministry approved a small sum, the institute of plant physiology took us in and gave us two rooms. We also acquired a few pieces of equipment. Then an old building was purchased for the university council's offices and there was some extra room, so we got three rooms of our own. . . . More space was later approved by the council, albeit in a building that needed renovation. Financial resources remained extremely limited. It was only a large donation from a wealthy student that enabled us to purchase a small collection of apparatus and storage for it. The ministry, however, still did not want to consider enlarging the institute. (quoted in Kroh, 1935, p. 166)

In the battles for better working conditions, Müller held himself to strict self-imposed moral rules. Katz later reported, "He was not willing to make any concessions to the higher-ups. A proud sense of independence prevented him from visiting a ministry to get funding for his laboratory; rather he made personal sacrifices for his institute, which he occasionally described in jest as the last sanctuary of Prussian thrift" (Katz, 1936, p. 238).

After a thorough study of Ebbinghaus's work, it was clear to Müller that research methods in the psychology of memory had to be improved. Comparing the contributions of Ebbinghaus and Müller, Boring noted that

> it was in 1885 that Ebbinghaus brought the problem of memory within the range of the experimental method. It would seem that Müller must have thought that here was a chance to extend a rigorous methodology to the higher processes. At any rate, Ebbinghaus had more originality than persistence, and Müller took over from him the field of the experimental psychology of memory. . . . Ebbinghaus was careless of systematic matters; Müller brought mnemonic experimentation into the introspective school, and dealt, in characteristically thorough manner, as much with memorial consciousness as with performance in reproduction. (Boring, 1935, p. 347)[1]

The most important improvements in research methods that Müller and Schumann made (Müller & Schumann, 1894) include the following:

---

[1]Ebbinghaus designed 2300 nonsensical syllables. Each syllable was of the type consonant/vowel/consonant—for example, tuk, mod, fal, pus, dep, rip. He constructed a series of nonsensical syllables with a length of 12, 16, 24, or 36, and learned the series under standard conditions. The criterion of learning was two correct recalls for each series in succession. Later he reproduced the series every day and measured the retention. Examples of methods and criteria of learning and retention were the learning method, saving method, and the retained members method.

1. Whereas Ebbinghaus had carried out his experiments on himself, in Müller's work the examiner and the research participant were separated. This separation made possible the use of random sampling of participants and the varying of examiners.
2. The syllables were presented successively rather than simultaneously. The standardized presentation of single syllables allowed for more exact testing of the forward and backward associations that hypothetically developed in the series of syllables presented. Ebbinghaus seems to have been strongly influenced in his method of presentation by the experience of learning poems—he had previously used poems by Lord Byron as the learning materials in his experiments.
3. Syllables were presented by a specially constructed control apparatus, the Müller–Schumann memory apparatus, which came to be called the "memory drum." This allowed the establishment of a standard presentation time for each syllable.
4. Müller and Schumann made Ebbinghaus's nonsense syllables more nearly meaningless by using stricter rules of construction (Rupp, 1909).[2]

MÜLLER AND THE DEVELOPMENT OF PSYCHOLOGY

Some of the major landmarks in the development of psychology since the beginning of the 19th century are the following; Müller's achievements must be viewed in this context:

1. The identification of the subject matter and the creation of the methods of psychology.
2. The establishment of psychological laboratories and institutes attached to universities and colleges.
3. The fragmentation of psychology, first into major schools and then into more limited theories.
4. The development of several fields of applied psychology and practice outside academic institutions.
5. The professionalization of psychology, with the issuing of formal credentials such as licenses for practice, beginning in German-speaking areas in 1941 with state-regulated examinations and standards for diplomas. This

---

[2]Ebbinghaus used nonsense syllable series. All series were meaningless but not all syllables were. Ebbinghaus had linguistic competence in five languages—German, English, French, Latin, and Greek—and many other test participants in this time had the same competence. With this background many syllables were meaningful. According to Wolfgang Bringmann, Ebbinghaus used only 60% meaningless syllables (personal communication). Müller and Schumann corrected this error and standardized the experimental design for memory research.

development spread throughout the world and gained force after World War II. (L. Sprung & H. Sprung, 1999, in press; Trommsdorff & Sprung, 2000)

The Emergence of Applied–Professional Psychology

In German-speaking areas during the 19th century, psychology's growth as a discipline was determined mainly by developments in experimental psychology, a discipline with the scientific orientation and the methods of more established sciences: first experimental physics, later experimental physiology. Therefore it is not surprising that the majority of the founding figures of modern psychology—Weber, Fechner, Helmholtz, Lotze, and Wundt—were originally physicists, medical doctors or, most often, physiologists.

During the second half of the 19th century scientific psychology entered a second developmental phase in which more or less standardized, quasi-experimental methods found a niche alongside experimental methods. The most important of these new methods were the psychometric methods (testing), which grew out of the study of individual differences and a concern with diagnostic procedures.

Müller's Place in History

As is evident from his relationships to Fechner the psychophysicist, Lotze the medical doctor, and Helmholtz the physiologist and physicist, Müller's work was grounded in the experimentally dominated stage. But at Göttingen Müller also promoted applied psychology. Examples included the "Institutes for Applied Psychology and Joint Psychological Research" in Berlin, and in Neubabelsberg near Berlin, directed respectively by Otto Lipmann and William Stern (chap. 6, *Pioneers II*), (Sprung & Brandt, 1992; see also Rüegsegger, 1986; Schönpflug, 1992).

Müller's involvement in applied psychology, where findings obtained with other methods were acceptable, may be seen as recognition of these other modes of empirical psychology, when they were in accordance with a science of experience grounded in the natural sciences (Behrens, 1997; Bringmann, Lück, Miller & Early, 1997; Bringmann & Tweney, 1980; Carpintero, 1996; Gondra, 1997; Tortosa, 1998; Viney & King, 1998).

Müller's acceptance of applied psychology was just one aspect of a liberal outlook on psychology. For a German professor of his time and generation, Müller was unusual in his openness to women as scientists and colleagues. He was an advocate of women in academia when most German-language universities remained closed to them. A more detailed assessment of his achievement in this regard within its historical framework is provided in a separate paper (H. Sprung & L. Sprung, 1996b).

SELF-ASSESSMENT

In 1921 a new Weimar Republic law relieved Müller of his lecturing responsibilities at the age of 71. At first he resisted being forced into retirement, but a few years later he was pleased to have more time to do science. There remained to him 13 productive years as professor emeritus, though these were marked by ever-increasing health problems.

Looking back, Müller wrote to Boring in 1928,

> Perhaps it will interest you to learn how simply and clearly mapped out was the way, in the seventies, for a university student who intended to specialize in psychology as a Dozent [instructor]. He had to be versed in the Herbartian psychology, in the writings of Lotze and Fechner, in Helmholtz's works on physiological acoustics and optics, and he must also have some knowledge of British associationism—of Alexander Bain, for instance. He had, of course, read Wundt's *Vorlesungen über die Menschen–und Tierseele* [Lectures on the Human and Animal Mind], considered a popular book, but nevertheless instructive. After 1877 an acquaintance with Kussmaul's book on the disturbances of speech was assumed; and from about that same time on, Hering's works gained interest. H. Steinthal's *Einleitung in die Psychologie der Sprachwissenschaft* [Introduction to the Psychology of Language Study] was considered to be a leading psychological work through which one could not labor without difficulty. (Boring, 1935, p. 346)

Certain statements in Müller's 1928 letter to Boring, about what he taught within the Leipzig framework, provide the sense that Müller saw some aspects of philosophy as fundamental to scientific psychology, although he regarded the history of philosophy as irrelevant:

> My lectures embraced logic, epistemology, natural philosophy and psychology. As for the history of philosophy, I have given lectures on it only once—in Czernowitz—and they were lectures on the history of Greek philosophers. Outside of that I treated occasionally of Locke or Berkeley or Hume in lectures and conferences during the first two decades of my teaching in Göttingen. (Boring, 1935, p. 346)

On the foundations of education in psychology, he wrote,

> I am of the opinion that students can get a true mastery of psychology only if they receive besides the lectures in general psychology a series of special lectures and recitation courses, in which they are made more familiar with psychological thinking and experiment. The special lectures which I gave from two to four hours a week touched on the following subjects: (1) psychophysical methods, (2) psychophysics and color sensations, (3) memory, (4) the phenomena of volition, (5) the reaction experiments, the time sense, etc. In the last instance, emphasis was . . . on the introduction to experimentation. (Boring, 1935, p. 346)

CONCLUSION

In 1924 Müller put forth his program for scientific psychology: Psychology must "set itself three tasks . . . as the science of the phenomena of consciousness: 1) to describe and classify relevant phenomena with a certain degree of completeness, 2) to ascertain the laws by which such phenomena arise, change and disappear, and 3) to investigate the deeper reasons for the existence of these laws" (Müller, 1924a, p. 1). Methodologically, psychology must rely "only on observation, experiment and mathematical linking of facts" (Müller, 1924a, pp. 3–4). And, as a caution to psychologists, he added, "Psychological thinking is not best taught by treating all psychological questions with the same superficiality" (Müller, 1924a, p. 1). These statements constitute the maxims of the "Göttingen School," and today are part of the canon of research methods in experimental psychology (L. Sprung & H. Sprung, 1984, 1996). Müller died in Göttingen in 1934, the day before Christmas Eve, at the age of 85 (Hische, 1935; Jaensch, 1935; Katz, 1935, 1936), but his contributions remain with us.

REFERENCES

Behrens, P. J. (1997). G. E. Müller: The third pillar of experimental psychology. In W. G. Bringmann, H. E. Lück, & C. E. Early (Eds.), *A pictorial history of psychology* (pp. 171–176). Chicago: Quintessence.

Boring, E. G. (1935). Georg Elias Müller: 1850–1934. *American Journal of Psychology, 47,* 344–348.

Bringmann, W. G., Lück, H. E., Miller, R., & Early, C. E. (Eds.). (1997). *A pictorial history of psychology.* Chicago: Quintessence.

Bringmann, W. G., & Tweney, R. D. (Eds.). (1980). *Wundt studies.* Toronto: Hogrefe.

Carpintero, H. (1996). *Historia de las ideas psicológicas* [History of psychological ideas]. Madrid: Pirámide.

Ebbinghaus, H. (1885). *Über das Gedächtnis. Untersuchungen zur experimentellen Psychologie* [On memory. Investigations in experimental psychology]. Leipzig: Duncker and Humblot.

Fechner, G. T. (1860). *Elemente der Psychophysik* [Elements of psychophysics] (2 vols.). Leipzig: Breitkopf & Härtel.

Fechner, G. (1877). *In Sachen der Psychophysik* [In the matter of psycophysics]. Leipzig: Breitkopf & Härtel.

Fechner, G. T. (1882). *Revision der Hauptpuncte der Psychophysik* [Revision of the main points of psychophysics]. Leipzig: Breitkopf & Härtel.

Gondra, J. M. (1997). *Historia de la Psicología. Introdución al pensamiento psicológico moderno. Vol. 1: Nacimiento de la psicología científica* [History of psychology: Introduction to modern psychological thought. Vol. 1: The birth of scientific psychology]. Madrid: Editorial Sintesis.

Gutberlet, H. (1905). *Psychophysik. Historisch-kritische Studien über experimentelle Psychologie* [Psychophysics. Historical and critical studies on experimental psychology]. Mainz: Kirchheim.

Helmholtz, H. (1867). Handbuch der physiologischen Optik. In *Allgemeine Encyklopädie der Physik* [Treatise on physiological optics.] (Vol. 9). Leipzig: Voss.

Hische, W. (1935). Gedenkrede, gehalten am Sarge von Georg Elias Müller, in Göttingen, am 27.

Dezember 1934. Ein letztes Wort des letzten Schülers für seine Schüler und Fachgenossen [Commemoration speech at the casket of Georg Ellias Müller, at Göttingen, December 27, 1934. Last words from the last pupil for his pupils and colleagues]. *Zeitschrift für Psychologie, 134,* 145–149.

Jaensch, E. R. (1935). Was wird aus dem Werk? Betrachtungen aus dem Gesichtspunkt der Kulturwende über G. E. Müllers Wesen und Werk und das Schicksal der Psychologie [What will become of this work? Observations from the perspective of the cultural change about G. E. Müller's essence and work and the fate of psychology]. *Zeitschrift für Psychologie, 134,* Gedenkheft Georg Elias Müller. 191–218.

Katz, D. (1935). Georg Elias Müller. *Psychological Bulletin, 63,* 377–380.

Katz, D. (1936). Georg Elias Müller. *Acta Psychologica, 1,* 234–240.

Klix, F., & Hagendorf, H. (Eds.). (1986). *Human memory and cognitive capabilities. Mechanism and Performances* (2 vols.). Amsterdam: Elsevier, North Holland.

Kroh, O. (1935). Georg Elias Müller. Ein Nachruf [Georg Ellias Müller, An obituary]. *Zeitschrift für Psychologie, 134,* Gedenkheft Georg Elias Müller, 150–190.

Lotze, R. H. (1846). Seele und Seelenleben. [Soul and mental life] In R. Wagner (Ed.). *Handwörterbuch der Physiologie* (pp. 142–264). Reprinted in R. Pester (Ed.). (1989), Lotze, R. H. *Kleine Schriften zur Psychologie* (pp. 112–234). Berlin: VEB Deutscher Verlag der Wissenschaften.

Lotze, R. H. (1852). *Medicinische Psychologie oder Physiologie der Seele* [Medical psychology or physiology of the soul]. Leipzig: Weidemann.

Lüer, G. (1993). Die Deutsche Gesellschaft für Psychologie e. V. (DGPs) [The German Society of Psychology]. In H. E. Lück & R. Miller (Eds.), *Illustrierte Geschichte der Psychologie* (pp. 238–241). Munich: Quintessenz.

Lüer, G., & Lass, U. (Eds.). (1997). *Erinnern und Behalten. Wege zur Erforschung des menschlichen Gedächtnisses* [Recollection and retention. Paths of research in human memory]. Göttingen: Vandenhoeck & Ruprecht.

Martin, L. J., & Müller, G. E. (1899). *Zur Analyse der Unterschiedsempfindlichkeit. Experimentelle Beiträge* [On the analysis of differential thresholds. Experimental contributions]. Leipzig: Barth.

Misch, G. (1935). Georg Elias Müller. In *Nachrichten der Gesellschaft der Wissenschaften Göttingen. Aus dem Jahresbericht über das Geschäftsjahr 1934/35* (pp. 45–59). Berlin: Weidemann.

Müller, G. E. (1878). *Zur Grundlegung der Psychophysik* [On the foundations of psychophysics]. Kritische Beiträge. Bibliothek für Wissenschaft und Literatur. 23 vols. Philosophische Abtheilung. Vol. 4. Berlin: Grieben.

Müller, G. E. (1897). Zur Psychophysik der Gesichtsempfindungen [On the psychophyics of visual sensations]. *Zeitschrift für Psychologie, 14,* H. 1. 1–76 and 161–193.

Müller, G. E. (1903). Die Gesichtspunkte und die Tatsachen der psychophysischen Methodik [Points of view and the facts of psychophysical methodology]. In L. Asher & K. Spiro (Eds.), *Ergebnisse der Physiologie. 2. Jahrgang. II. Abteilung. Biophysik und Psychophysik* (pp. 267–516). Wiesbaden: Bergmann.

Müller, G. E. (1911). Zur Analyse der Gedächtnistätigkeit und des Vorstellungsverlaufs [On analyzing memory activity and the flow of mental images]. I. Teil. *Zeitschrift für Psychologie,* Ergänzungsband 5. Leipzig: Barth.

Müller, G. E. (1913a). Zur Analyse der Gedächtnistätigkeit und des Vorstellungsverlaufs [Analysis of memory activity and imaginative process]. III. Teil. *Zeitschrift für Psychologie,* Ergänzungsband 8. Leipzig: Barth.

Müller, G. E. (1913b). Neue Versuche mit Rückle [New experiments with Rückle]. *Zeitschrift für Psychologie, 67,* 193–213.

Müller, G. E. (1917). Zur Analyse der Gedächtnistätigkeit und des Vorstellungsverlaufs [Analysis of memory activity and imaginative process]. II. Teil. *Zeitschrift für Psychologie,* Ergänzungsband 9. Leipzig: Barth.

Müller, G. E. (1923). *Komplextheorie und Gestalttheorie. Ein Beitrag zur Wahrnehmungspsychologie* [Complex theory and Gestalt theory. A contribution to the psychology of perception]. Göttingen: Vandenhoeck & Ruprecht.

Müller, G. E. (1924a). *Abriss der Psychologie* [Outline of psychology]. Göttingen: Vandenhoeck & Ruprecht.

Müller, G. E. (1924b). *Darstellung und Erklärung der verschiedenen Typen der Farbenblindheit* [Description and explanation of the different types of color blindness]. Göttingen: Vandenhoeck & Ruprecht.

Müller, G. E. (1930). Über die Farbenempfindungen. Psychophysische Untersuchungen. Band 1 und 2 [On sensations of color. Psychophysical investigations]. *Zeitschrift für Psychologie*, Ergänzungsband 17 and 18. Leipzig: Barth.

Müller, G. E. (1934). *Kleine Beiträge zur Psychophysik der Farbempfindungen* [Brief contributions to the psychophysics of color sensations]. Leipzig: Barth.

Müller, G. E., & Pilzecker, A. (1900). Experimentelle Beiträge zur Lehre vom Gedächtnis [Experimental contributions on the theory of memory]. *Zeitschrift für Psychologie*, Ergänzungsband 1. Leipzig: Barth.

Müller, G. E., & Schumann, F. (1889). Über die psychologischen Grundlagen der Vergleichung gehobener Gewichte [On the psychological basis for the comparison of lifted weights]. *Pflügers Archiv für die gesammte Physiologie des Menschen und der Thiere*, 45, 37–112.

Müller, G. E. & Schumann, F. (1894). Experimentelle Beiträge zur Untersuchung des Gedächtnisses [Experimental contributions to research on memory]. *Zeitschrift für Psychologie*, 6, 81–190, 257–339.

Rüegsegger, R. (1986). *Geschichte der angewandten Psychologie 1900–1940* [History of applied psychology 1900–1940]. Bern: Huber.

Rupp, H. (1909). *Silbenreihen für Gedächtnisversuche nach Müller-Schumann* [Series of syllables for memory research constructed by Müller–Schumann]. Naumburg a. S.: Lippert.

Schönpflug, W. (1992). Applied psychology: Newcomer with a long tradition. *Applied Psychology: An International Review*, 42, 5–66.

Sprung, H., & Sprung, L. (1988). Gustav Theodor Fechner als experimenteller Ästhetiker: Zur Entwicklung der Methodologie und Methodik einer Psychophysik höherer kognitiver Prozesse [Gustav Theodor Fechner as experimental aesthetician: On methodology and techniques of psychophysics of higher cognitive processes]. In J. Brožek & H. Gundlach (Eds.), *G. T. Fechner and psychology* (pp. 217–227). Passau: Passavia.

Sprung, H., & Sprung, L. (1996a). Carl Stumpf (1848–1936): A general psychologist and methodologist, and a case study of a cross-cultural scientific transition process. In W. Battmann & S. Dutke (Eds.), *Processes of the molar regulation of behavior* (pp. 327–342). Lengerich: Pabst.

Sprung, H., & Sprung, L. (1996b). Frauen in der Geschichte der Psychologie: Integrationsformen in die Psychologie und Vortragsaktivitäten von Frauen auf deutschen Psychologiekongressen 1904–1978 [Women in the history of psychology: Forms of integration in psychology and women's lecturing activities at German psychology congresses 1904–1978]. In H. Gundlach (Ed.), *Untersuchungen zur Geschichte der Psychologie und der Psychotechnik* (Vol. 11, pp. 205–222). Munich: Profil.

Sprung, L. & Brandt, R. (1992). Otto Lipmann (1880–1933) und die Anfänge der angewandten Psychologie in Berlin [Otto Lipmann (1880–1933) and the beginnings of applied psychology in Berlin]. In L. Sprung & W. Schönpflug (Eds.), *Zur Geschichte der Psychologie in Berlin* (pp. 139–159). Frankfurt am Main: Lang.

Sprung, L., & Sprung, H. (1984). *Grundlagen der Methodologie und Methodik der Psychologie. Eine Einführung in die Forschungs-und Diagnosemethodik für empirisch arbeitende Humanwissenschaftler* [Foundations of methodology and techniques in psychology. An introduction to research and diagnostics methods for empirical working scientists in human sciences]. Berlin: VEB Deutscher Verlag der Wissenschaften. (2nd rev. ed. 1987).

Sprung, L., & Sprung, H. (1986). Hermann Ebbinghaus: Life, work and impact in the history of psychology. In F. Klix & H. Hagendorf (Eds.), *Human memory and cognitive capabilities. Mecha-*

nisms and performances. Symposium in memoriam Hermann Ebbinghaus. Berlin Humboldt University 1985 (Vol. 1, pp. 23–34). Amsterdam: Elsevier.

Sprung, L., & Sprung, H. (1987). Ebbinghaus an der Berliner Universität: Ein akademisches Schicksal eines zu früh Geborenen? [Ebbinghaus at the University of Berlin: An academic fate of someone born too soon] In W. Traxel (Ed.), *Ebbinghaus–Studien 2* (Vol. 5, pp. 89–106). Passau: Passavia.

Sprung, L., & Sprung, H. (1996). Foundations of the history of methodology and of a system of methodology of modern psychology. In W. Battmann & S. Dutke (Eds.), *Processes of the molar regulation of behavior.* (pp. 291–307). Lengerich: Pabst.

Sprung, L., & Sprung, H. (1999). Rückblicke auf ein schwieriges Jahrhundert: Zur Geschichte der Psychologie im 20. Jahrhundert in Deutschland [A retrospective review of a difficult century: The history of psychology in twentieth-century Germany]. In W. Hacker & M. Rinck (Eds.), Zukunft gestalten: *Bericht über den 41. Kongre· der Deutschen Gesellschaft für Psychologie in Dresden 1998* (Vol. 1, pp. 123–143). Lengerich: Pabst.

Sprung, L., & Sprung, H. (in press). "Ein Zeitalter wird besichtigt": Psychologie in Deutschland im 20. Jahrhundert [A look over an age—Psychology in Germany in the twentieth century]. *Psychologie und Geschichte.*

Tortosa, G. F. (Coord.). (1998). *Una história de la psicología moderna* [A history of modern psychology]. Madrid: McGraw–Hill/Interamericana.

Traxel, W. (Ed.). (1987). *Ebbinghaus–Studien 2.* Internationales Hermann-Ebbinghaus-Symposium 1985 [Ebbinghaus—Studies 2]. International Hermann Ebbinghaus Symposium 1985 (No. 5). Passau: Passavia.

Trommsdorff, G., & Sprung, L. (2000). Psychology in Germany. *Encyclopedia of Psychology,* Washington, DC: American Psychological Association.

Viney, W., & King, D. B. (1998). *A history of psychology. Ideas and context* (2nd ed.). Boston: Allyn and Bacon.

Wertheimer, M. (1986). The annals of the house that Ebbinghaus built. In F. Klix & H. Hagendorf (Eds.), *Human memory and cognitive capabilities. Mechanism and performances* (pp. 35–43). Amsterdam: Elsevier.

Zusne, L. (1984). *Biographical dictionary of psychology.* Westport, CT: Greenwood Press.

Chapter 6

Charles E. Spearman: The Discoverer of *g*

Arthur R. Jensen

A person who wants to become a psychologist but, for whatever reason, must begin study for a degree later than most PhD candidates can take heart from the career of Charles Edward Spearman (1863–1945). Spearman began his formal study of psychology when he was 34 years old and did not complete his PhD until 10 years later. As this chapter will attest, one reason for his delayed entry into the field seems to be inherent in the history of Spearman's intellectual development. Another was the happenstance of war, which interrupted his graduate study. His late start seems in no way to have hindered his brilliant career, however. He went on to become the most influential figure in British psychology in the 20th century and was one of the great originators in psychology, especially in the fields of differential psychology (the study of individual differences) and psychometrics (the measurement of mental traits). The history of these specialties could not be written without recognition of Spearman's creative achievements. After Sir Francis Galton (chap. 1, *Pioneers I*) founded these fields in the second half of the 19th century, Spearman, in the first half of the 20th was their chief engineer, architect, and developer.

Spearman once described his career as "one long fight" (1930a, p. 330). Although he held one of the most prestigious professorships in Britain and earned many honors, including election as fellow of the Royal Society and membership in America's National Academy of Sciences, his contributions were by no means universally esteemed. In particular, many experimental psychologists were antagonistic toward Spearman's legacy. A few years after Spearman's death, Zangwill, the professor of psychology at Cambridge University, historically Britain's

---

*Photo of Charles E. Spearman reprinted courtesy of the Archives of the History of American Psychology—The University of Akron.

bastion of classical experimental psychology, wrote a popular textbook in which he made the following prophecy on the future acceptance of Spearman's major contribution:

> We may submit, with due humility, that factorial analysis, despite its impressive mathematical procedures will strike the future historian of psychology as a brilliant but misguided departure from the central path of empirical psychology. The Spearman factors will take their not unworthy place in the limbo of the discarded elements of the mind. (1951, p. 205)

It is clear today that Zangwill's dismal forecast has been massively contradicted, if the *Science Citation Index* (SCI) and the *Social Science Citation Index* (SSCI) over the 50 years since Spearman's death are indicators of the scientific impact and scholarly interest in his work. Typically, the citation rate of even very prominent psychologists drops to near-zero within the first decade after their death. After that, the cumulative count of their citations shows a marked negative acceleration. Then it levels off, with virtually zero increments in subsequent years. The trend for Spearman is just the opposite. For the 50 years following his death, the curve recording his cumulative citations listed in the SCI and SSCI for every five-year interval is positively accelerated, as shown in Figure 6.1. This is an exceptional phenomenon. Except for E. L. Thorndike (chap. 10, *Pioneers I*), Spearman's notable contemporaries are virtually never cited in the present-day literature except in publications dealing with the history of psychology.

These citations show that most of this continuing interest involves Spearman's discovery and theory of the *general factor* in all mental abilities, which he called the *g* factor. Although his strictly statistical contributions are still valuable, they are now so well-known that they are usually used without attribution. His specific method of doing factor analysis has long been defunct; it is not described in detail in modern textbooks. Neither of these could have added much to the frequency of his present-day citations.

Spearman's career also serves to validate a bit of academic folk wisdom that I have encountered on committees selecting someone for a faculty position from a pool of applicants for an assistant professorship, most of whom are new PhDs. One bit of evidence that usually weighs heavily in these evaluations is the notion that a new PhD who has published at least one research paper in a peer-reviewed journal is more promising than a candidate who published nothing as a graduate student. I doubt that the validity of this hunch has ever been formally tested, but Spearman was a positive example.

Two of Spearman's most frequently cited articles (Spearman, 1904a, 1904b) were published in the prestigious *American Journal of Psychology* in 1904, three years before he received his PhD. And both are still being cited in the current literature nearly a century after their publication. They are generally recognized as exceptionally original and important contributions. The second article, "Gen-

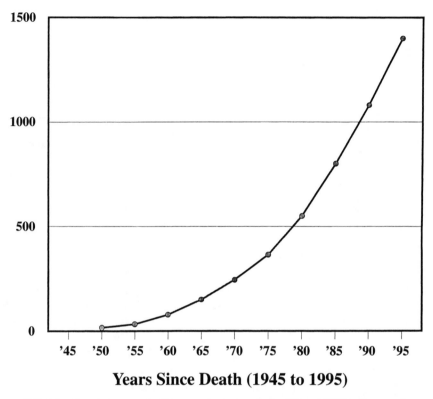

Years Since Death (1945 to 1995)

FIG. 6.1. Cumulative record of Spearman's citations in the SCI and SSCI in five-year intervals over 50 years, from the date of his death (1945) to 1995.

eral Intelligence, Objectively Determined and Measured," is a classic in the history of differential psychology and psychometrics. Moreover, this was not a doctoral thesis done under a mentor's supervision. It was not remotely related to his
PhD thesis, and was even antithetical to the interests and sympathies of his mentor, Wilhelm Wundt (chap. 3, *Pioneers III*), the founder of the first laboratory
of experimental psychology. Despite Spearman's late beginning in psychology,
his self-initiated research as a graduate student not only auspiciously presaged
his later eminence but was even the main feature of it.

BIOGRAPHY

My study of Spearman has led me to believe it would be virtually impossible for
anyone to write a full-scale personal and professional biography of the man. As

for his personality, nearly all we have to go on is a short and overly modest autobiography, which Carl Murchison (chap. 11, *Pioneers II*), the editor of *A History of Psychology in Autobiography* (1930a), persuaded him to contribute to the first volume in that series. It is obvious that Spearman was an exceedingly private person. He abhorred revealing himself in any personal way. He was reticent regarding even his purely intellectual side, as he made clear in his autobiography, stating, "One's own history, even on its intellectual side, involves much that is very intimate. To publish this abroad seems not only egoistic but even of dubious propriety" (Spearman, 1930a, p. 299). Among the many autobiographies I have read, Spearman's anchors one extreme on the scale going from personal self-concealment to self-revelation; the autobiography of another famous British psychologist, Havelock Ellis (1859–1939), anchors the opposite extreme. Although both were great men, such is the difference between a mathematically minded factor analyst and a literary minded sexologist.

Spearman's last doctoral student was the eminent psychologist Raymond B. Cattell (1905–1998), who described Spearman as possessing "remarkable charm and a capacity to stimulate and reassure [students]" (Cattell, 1978, p. 1038). Besides Cattell, the only psychologists I have met who had any personal acquaintance with Spearman were Cyril Burt, Hans Eysenck (chap. 20, this volume), and Philip E. Vernon. Their answers to my questions about Spearman the man were all variations on the theme that he was a reserved and rather austere yet kindly man of high ethical, moral, and intellectual integrity, who seldom hesitated to express his own views strongly and was forthrightly critical of whatever he disagreed with. He was also described as unstintingly helpful to his students and colleagues.

The main reason for the obscurity of Spearman's professional life is that he died just a few months after the end of World War II, when England was in such turmoil that no one took up the task of writing his biography. Because he died at 82, only a few of the relatives, who might have contributed knowledge of the man, outlasted him. And all of the professional contemporaries who knew Spearman personally are now deceased. Some of his correspondence with other psychologists, particularly with Burt, Spearman's successor as professor at University College, London, survives (see Lovie & Lovie, 1993), but it deals only with highly technical aspects of factor analysis.

From Philosophy to Psychology

Born in London on September 10, 1863, Spearman's background has been described as that of "an English family of established status and some eminence" (Cattell, 1978, p. 1038). As a boy he showed strong academic ability and interests. By age 10 he was already concerned with philosophical issues. About his early schooling he wrote that there was "nothing worth chronicling except a secret devotion to philosophy. . . . My deepest urge was to probe further into the nature of existence, knowledge, and goodness" (1930a, p. 299). His strong subject in school and college was mathematics, and he considered becoming a mathematician. Conceding to practicality, however, he abandoned this course to prepare for a career with better prospects for employment, and graduated with a degree in civil engineering.

Philosophy still dominated Spearman's interest, however, and in the course of his self-study in that realm, he became fascinated by the philosophies of India. As a graduate engineer without a job and with a burning desire to study Indian philosophy, he joined the British Army's Royal Corps of Engineers, in hope that he might be stationed in India. Instead of India, however, he was sent to Burma to take part in a military campaign in the Burmese Wars. There his work as an army engineer won him a medal for distinguished service and promotion to the rank of major.

Eventually Spearman's studies led him to dissatisfaction with philosophy because, unlike the empirical sciences, he could find no means to prove its theories. He wondered if the study of psychology might lead him to the solution of this problem. Spearman began reading the psychological literature, speculative and empirically limited though it was, in the early 1890s. His study revealed that the only laboratory of experimental psychology and the only professor of psychology—in fact, the only university in the world that granted a doctoral degree in psychology—were in Leipzig, Germany, where the leading light was Wundt, now considered the father of experimental psychology. So Major Spearman, then 34, resigned his commission in the army and took off for Leipzig to study psychology under Wundt. Concerning his 14 years of army service, Spearman later wrote that "it was the greatest mistake of my life . . . [based on] the youthful delusion that life is long. . . . For these almost wasted years, I have since mourned as bitterly as ever Tiberius did for his lost legions" (1930a, p. 300).

Unfortunately, Spearman was not yet completely free of his army career. His study in Leipzig was interrupted by the outbreak of the Boer War in South Africa (1900–1902). He was recalled to military duty for two years as a staff officer. After completing his service in the war, Spearman returned to Leipzig to resume his study under Wundt. He also visited many other universities and became acquainted with the leading German psychologists of that time—Külpe, Müller (chap. 5, this volume), Husserl, Stumpf (chap. 4, this volume), and Stern (chap. 6, *Pioneers II*). Wundt, however, was the major German influence on Spearman's career. In his autobiography he acknowledged his feeling of gratitude for Wundt's personal kindness toward him, saying that it became "one of the dominant sentiments" of his life.

From Wundt to Galton

An intellectually more important influence during Spearman's student years was another illustrious figure whom he never knew personally, the English polymath

Sir Francis Galton. Because Wundt and Galton were the two major influences in Spearman's career, it may be of interest to compare the characteristics of these two giants in the history of psychological science, as viewed by psychology historian Edwin G. Boring:

> Wundt was erudite where Galton was original; Wundt overcame massive obstacles by the weight of his attack; Galton dispatched a difficulty by a thrust of insight. Wundt was forever armored by his system; Galton had no system. Wundt was methodical; Galton was versatile. Wundt's science was interpenetrated by his philosophy; Galton's science was discursive and unstructured. Wundt was interminably arguing; Galton was forever observing. Wundt had a school, a formal self-conscious school; Galton had friends, influence and effects only. . . . Wundt was personally intolerant and controversial, whereas Galton was tolerant and ready to be convicted of error. (Boring, 1950, pp. 461–462)

It was Galton's book *Inquiries Into Human Faculty and Its Development* (1883), the first important work on differential psychology, that first attracted Spearman. In this book Galton described an odd assortment of "brass instrument" devices and techniques for measuring sensory, motor, and mental capacities. He also introduced the idea of behavioral genetics, suggesting the use of identical and fraternal twins for estimating the relative contributions of heredity and environment to behavioral traits. He offered anecdotal evidence on the remarkable behavioral similarity between identical twins as examples of the influence of heredity. But Spearman was even more intrigued by an idea in Galton's most famous work, *Hereditary Genius* (1869). Galton believed that persons differ widely in a general trait that can be characterized as innate cognitive ability. Besides this *general* ability Galton also recognized a number of *special* abilities or talents, such as linguistic, mathematical, musical, artistic, and memorial. It was the notion of general cognitive ability that especially captured Spearman's interest, however, as well as the idea of measuring individual differences in this general ability with simple tests of sensory discrimination and reaction times to visual and auditory stimuli.

The influences of Wundt, the founder of experimental and nomothetic psychology, and of Galton, the originator of differential psychology and psychometrics, are blended in Spearman's own career. This is evident in his formulation of general laws of cognition and in his empirical analysis of human mental abilities into a general ability that enters into every kind of cognitive activity and special abilities peculiar to various cognitive skills as manifested in different tests, tasks, or talents.

Although it is evident in Spearman's writings that he was as much a hereditarian as Galton was, he himself had no research interest in the genetics of individual differences. He did no original research on it, but he did write one expository article on heredity and ability (1914–1915) and took a cursory glance at the subject in his major work, *The Abilities of Man* (1927). Although Spearman was a Fellow of The Eugenics Society (founded by Galton in 1904, later renamed The Galton Institute), he expressed more hard-boiled opinions on eugenics than Galton ever did, writing, "One can conceive the establishment of a minimum index [of g, or general intelligence] to qualify for parliamentary vote, and above all, for the right to have offspring" (Hart & Spearman, 1912, p. 79). In 1912, this bold statement probably did not violate the operating standards of political correctness as it would today.

PREDOCTORAL RESEARCH ACTIVITY AND
THE BEGINNINGS OF FACTOR ANALYSIS

As a predoctoral student, Spearman's most important research activity was wholly unrelated to his mentor's interest or even to his own doctoral dissertation on optical illusions. Quite aside from his doctoral work, and completely on his own initiative, Spearman investigated the Galtonian notion of a general intellectual ability common to all cognitive tasks. He performed two little experiments, based on groups of 24 and 22 pupils in a "village school" and in a boys' "preparatory school." No psychology student today would be allowed to base even a master's thesis on such small samples and such unimpressive data: teachers' rankings of the pupils on "school cleverness," "common sense," "native intelligence," and standings on examinations in several school subjects. (A halo effect in such data could have spuriously inflated nearly all of the positive correlations among the teachers' ratings and class grades.)

But Spearman's data as such were of little importance. What proved to be momentous were his original ideas and the mathematical formulations for which the data merely served as a vehicle (Spearman, 1904a, 1904b). Spearman evidently had to do all the heavy calculations by hand or perhaps he paid a student to do them for him. In any case, some of the extensive computational work was faulty, though in trivial ways. The errors were later discovered, because Spearman published all of his raw data, which have been re-analyzed by modern computers (Fancher, 1985). Such numerical imperfections have also been pointed out in the works of Galileo, Newton, and Mendel, of course, without diminishing the import of their scientific contributions. A British statistician writing on the origin of factor analysis aptly commented on Spearman's pioneer effort:

> Factor analysis is a highly sophisticated multivariate statistical method which was born before its time. In 1904 the older strands of descriptive statistics and probability had only just begun to coalesce to form modern mathematical statistics. The Biometric Laboratory at University College, London, under Karl Pearson was only just under way and Fisher and all his works lay 20 years in the future. The ideas of correlation developed by Pearson and Yule were virtually the only tools to hand and even they were not widely known and used. What is remarkable is not that Spearman's first attempts were so crude but rather that he was able to give ex-

pression to such a deep and potentially fruitful idea at all. (Bartholomew, 1995, p. 216)

Classical Test Theory

What Spearman accomplished in his two 1904 papers was to lay the foundation for classical test theory and to invent a method later to be known as *factor analysis*, by means of which he achieved the first empirical test of Galton's theory of general mental ability, or *g*. But the broader and more fundamental innovation was that this work opened the door conceptually to what we now know as *latent trait theory*. Spearman provided the first demonstration of the idea that the relationships (correlations) among a number of *manifest* or observed variables could be explained by some smaller number of unobservable *latent* variables, of which the manifest variables are a function. Spearman's *g* factor was the first objectively determined and measured *latent variable* in the history of psychology.

What Spearman showed in 1904 with his meager data was that the matrix of correlations among all the diverse measures in his study could be "explained" by a single factor, *g*. All of the correlations between the different tests were positive, suggesting that they all measure something in common. By means of the mathematical algorithm he invented, Spearman was able to determine, with some margin of error, the degree to which each of the observed measures was saturated (or loaded) with the source of variance common to all of the other measures in his analysis. In other words, he invented a method for determining the correlation of each of the manifest variables with the single latent factor, *g*. The important empirical finding was that, in accord with Galton's original conjecture, all of the measures, including the tests of sensory discrimination, had *g* loadings, although some of them were more highly *g*-loaded than others. Spearman gave the name *specificity* to the non-*g* part of each variable, the variance that it does not have in common with any of the other variables in the analysis and thus is unique to it.

This formulation that every mental test measures a *general factor* (*g*) and a *specific factor* (*s*) became known as the *two-factor theory*. Because Spearman did not precisely reveal the thought processes that led to this formulation, a number of highly detailed and quite technical articles have tried to explain exactly what Spearman did during this most creative period while he was still a mere graduate student and how he did it (Bartholomew, 1995; Burt, 1949; Fancher, 1985; Lovie & Lovie, 1993; Thomson, 1947).

The two-factor theory was not very long lived, however. Within a decade following Spearman's original formulation other psychologists, most notably Cyril Burt, obtained data on much larger samples with a greater number of mental tests, and found evidence for other factors besides *g*. Also, Spearman's particular method of factor analysis was not suited to analyzing a correlation matrix with multiple factors. His method was really conceived as what today is called a *con-*

firmatory factor analysis, intended to test only one specific hypothesis—in Spearman's case, his two-factor theory. Hence the method was too limited to serve as an *exploratory factor analysis* in which, with no initial hypothesis about the number and nature of the factors required to "explain" all the correlations, the investigator analyzes a correlation matrix to estimate these values. Therefore, more complex methods, devised by the mathematical statisticians Karl Pearson and H. Hotelling (principal components), and the computationally simpler adaptations of principal components by Burt (simple summation) and L. L. Thurstone (chap. 6, *Pioneers III*) (multiple-factor analysis) became the preferred methods for analyzing correlation matrices that could not be adequately modeled in terms of a single common factor, as in Spearman's analyses.

Besides the general factor common to all tests of mental ability, these multiple factor methods also revealed factors that are common only to certain groups of tests; hence they were termed *group factors*. Group factors emerge clearly only when data from three or more tests of three or more abilities (e.g., verbal, numerical, and spatial)—hence at least nine tests—enter into the analysis. Spearman's two-factor theory ($g + s$) holds up only when each of the tests in the analysis is clearly distinct from all of the others. Such tests can have only g in common. Spearman reluctantly and even grudgingly acknowledged the existence of group factors, but never conceded them much importance. They detracted from the nice simplicity and singular dominance of g in terms of the proportion of variance in a battery of tests accounted for by g. But the demonstration of multiple factors in no way eliminated the ubiquitous g factor, which is present in virtually every imaginable kind of mental ability test. No one has yet succeeded in creating any mental ability test that is without some loading on g, whatever else the test might measure.

Spearman's early formulation (1904a, 1904b) was instigated by a consequential study performed in James McKeen Cattell's psychological laboratory at Columbia University. Cattell (1860–1944) obtained his PhD under Wundt a few years before Spearman and then spent some time with Galton in London. Like Spearman, Cattell was less influenced by Wundt than by Galton. In 1901, Cattell and his student Clark Wissler tested Galton's theory of general ability and the idea that sensory discrimination and reaction time are correlated with such commonsense indicators of mental ability as scholastic performance. Their research participants were 325 students in Columbia College and the measures of intelligence were average grades in classics and mathematics. Also a number of Galton's tests of sensory discrimination and reaction time were administered. The correlations among the scores on Galton's tests and between these scores and class grades were pathetically small. This led to the conclusion that Galton was wrong on two counts: (1) there is no general factor in diverse mental abilities and (2) simple sensory tests do not measure "intelligence" as this word is commonly understood. So prestigious and influential was the reputation of Cattell and Columbia's psychological laboratory that this study cast a pall over Galtonian thinking in psychometrics for more than a half a century—an indictment that was aided and abetted by the practical success of the intelligence test invented by Alfred Binet (chap. 5, *Pioneers III*).

In hindsight it seems incredible that the faults of the Cattell–Wissler study were not obvious to everyone. But there still was no psychometric science in 1902, and psychometric naiveté prevailed. The idea that measurement error and restriction of the "range-of-talent" can drastically reduce the size of the correlation coefficient and hence underestimate the true correlation in the general population seems not to have occurred to any psychologist before Spearman. Recall that Karl Pearson invented his correlation coefficient (r) only in 1896, and it was scarcely used in psychology before the development of psychometric theory, initiated by Spearman and soon developed further by others, mainly Burt, Thomson, Thorndike, and Thurstone. Examining the Cattell–Wissler study, Spearman put his finger on its chief fault—measurement error probably constituted a large proportion of the total variance in test scores. That is, the manifest variables were exceedingly weak indexes of the latent trait g. Galton's studies, too, had been vitiated by measurement error. But at that time no one knew precisely how to quantify measurement error. That, too, was one of Spearman's contributions.

To make a historically long and complicated story short and simple, Spearman conceived mental test theory in terms of the simple formulation $X = t + e$, where X is an observed measurement, such as a test score, t is a hypothetical *true score* (a latent variable), and e is a random error of measurement. From this simple model many important psychometric formulations were derived. The total variance V_X of a distribution of test scores or measurements of any kind is composed of the *variance* of t plus the variance of e—that is, $V_X = V_t + V_e$. From this, the *reliability* (r_{XX}) of the test can be defined as $r_{XX} = V_t/(V_t + V_e)$. The traditional measure of r_{XX} is the Pearson correlation between scores on the same test given on two different occasions or the correlation between equivalent forms of the test. From this, Spearman deduced the means for correcting an obtained correlation (r_{XY}) between the scores on two different tests, X and Y, yielding the correlation between the true scores on each test. This procedure is termed *correction for attenuation*. The corrected (or *disattenuated*) correlation (cr_{XY}) is $cr_{XY} = r_{XY}/(r_{XX})(r_{YY})$. Many other statistical and psychometric formulations followed. Although Spearman had no formal training in statistics, for his time he was a remarkably able statistician.

ACADEMIC CAREER

In 1907, after Spearman received his PhD in Leipzig, he returned to London, where he succeeded the noted psychologist William McDougall as reader in the Department of Experimental Psychology at University College, London, an unusually distinguished position for a beginner. Later he was promoted to Grote professor of Mind and Logic and then professor (and head) of Psychology. More important than the titles of his posts, as Thomson (1947) pointed out in his superb obituary of Spearman for the Royal Society, was that from the beginning of his tenure until long after his retirement in 1931, Spearman founded and built up "a new school of psychology, with a new outlook, the experimental and statistical. . . ." (p. 373). Rooted essentially in the Darwinian and Galtonian tradition emphasizing a biological view of human nature and armed by Spearman with methods developed in psychometrics, statistics, and experimental psychology, this approach to behavioral science later became known as the London School. Its best-known exponents were Cyril Burt, Hans J. Eysenck, and Raymond B. Cattell (no relation to J. McK. Cattell). Nowadays the essential viewpoint and methodology of the London School has been largely assimilated in the fields of psychometrics, behavioral genetics, and cognitive neuroscience. Spearman devoted the rest of his life to examining his theory of mental ability, particularly the *g* factor and its relationship to educational and social variables, and made interesting discoveries along the way. The main thrust of his work is summarized in his two most frequently cited books, *The Nature of "Intelligence" and the Principles of Cognition* (1923) and *The Abilities of Man* (1927). (For a review of these books, see Carroll, 1991.) In *Creative Mind* (1930b) Spearman explained creativity in terms of his principles of cognition. After his retirement in 1931, he wrote a large two-volume work on the history of psychology, *Psychology Down the Ages* (1937), a fascinating but peculiarly skewed history that devotes much space to demolishing "faculty psychology" and most prominently features Spearman's own theoretical views and contributions. It was his final major effort to extricate psychology from speculative philosophy and move it into the domain of natural science. His last book, published posthumously in collaboration with Wynn-Jones, summarizes and updates his theory and empirical research on *g* and the few group factors that had been established at that time (Spearman & Jones, 1950).

Shortly after his retirement in 1931, Spearman went to the United States as a consultant on a large factor analytic study of abilities conducted by his former student Karl J. Holzinger, then a professor at the University of Chicago. This work, which promoted what came to be known as the Spearman–Holzinger Unitary Trait Study (1933–36), has figured prominently in most textbooks on factor analysis. The presence of several group factors was inescapable, but all together they accounted for less of the total variance in all the tests than did the *g* factor alone—a finding that has since been confirmed in factor analyses of countless other test batteries (Carroll, 1993).

In his 83rd year, on September 17, 1945, as a patient in the University of London Hospital, in poor health and suffering the infirmities of old age, Spearman dramatically ended his life by leaping from a top-story window of the hospital. I once asked Raymond Cattell, a former student and friend of Spearman's, if he had any specific explanation for Spearman's action. He did not and could only surmise, knowing Spearman, that it was probably a rational decision.

MAJOR THEORETICAL CONTRIBUTIONS

Spearman never regarded himself as a methodologist. He invented his methodological and statistical contributions only as tools for the investigation of his
main substantive interest, the nature of cognition. Of his five books, he always
considered his first one, *The Nature of "Intelligence" and the Principles of Cognition* (1923), the most important. On this point, however, history has clearly
second-guessed him. *The Abilities of Man: Their Nature and Measurement*
(1927) is now generally regarded as his magnum opus. It is by far the most
frequently cited. Note that Spearman put "intelligence" in quotation marks in
the title of his first book. He continued to do so in nearly all his subsequent
writing, in part to distinguish it from *g* but also as an implication of his belief
that intelligence is a poorly defined and muddled concept: "'Intelligence' has
become a mere vocal sound with so many meanings that finally it has none"
(1927, p. 14).

Principles of Cognition

Spearman postulated three *noegenetic* "laws" as the fundamental "axioms" of
cognition, regarding them as inherent and self-evident properties of the human
mind, or the brain. The term *noegenesis* refers to the induction or deduction of
new knowledge or mental content, derived from sensory experience acted on by
his three noegenetic principles.

The first noegenetic law, the *apprehension of experience*, is the immediate
awareness of the attributes of whatever has one's focus of attention. The raw elements of apprehension are called *fundaments*.

The second law is the *eduction of relations*, the tendency for the perception
of any two or more fundaments to evoke mentally a relation between them. For
example:

Good − Bad ? Opposite

The third law is the *eduction of correlates*, a *fundament* presented together
with a *relation* evokes a knowing of its correlated character. For example,

Good − Opposite ? Bad

To these three laws were added five quantitative principles of cognition that
affect the quality of noegenesis as manifested in an individual's cognitive activity: *mental energy* (the basis of *g* conceived of as the "eduction of relations and
correlates"); *retentivity* (the basis of conditioning, learning, and memory); *fatigue*
(a refractory period following a cognitive event that produces a tendency opposing its immediate re-occurrence); *conative control* (the effect of drive or motivation on cognition); and *primordial potencies* (individual differences in each
of these quantitative principles).

The Nature of *g*

Spearman's concept of *g* has endured several decades of misunderstanding and controversy, but now is generally accepted as a central construct in the science of human mental ability (Neisser et al., 1996). Spearman understood the problem of talking about *g* in purely verbal terms when it is actually a nonverbal formulation arrived at by mathematical means and can be strictly defined only in those terms. Yet he also believed that *g* represents something more than just the mathematical algorithms that define it. The *g* factor must have underpinnings that are independent of the test scores and mathematical manipulations that identify it, because *g* is not a necessary consequence of either psychometrics or factor analysis. No general factor has been found, for example, in the domain of personality inventories, which yield only uncorrelated group factors. We can note which mental tests reflect *g* more (or less) than other tests, but this tells us little or nothing, because tests of highly dissimilar appearance can have the same *g* loadings. Hence their visible characteristics, their content, their difficulty, or even their apparent cognitive complexity afford few if any clues to the essential nature of *g*. Spearman stated the problem:

> Notice must be taken that this general factor, *g*, like all measurements anywhere, is primarily not any concrete thing but only a value or magnitude. Further, that which this magnitude measures has not been defined by declaring what it is like, but only by pointing out where it can be found. It consists in just that constituent— whatever it may be—which is common to all abilities interconnected by the tetrad equation [i.e., the central mathematical formulation in Spearman's demonstration of *g*]. This way of indicating what *g* means is just as definite as when one indicates a card by staking on the back of it without looking at its face. . . . Such a defining of *g* by site rather than by nature is just what is meant originally when its determination was said to be only "objective." Eventually, we may or may not find reason to conclude that *g* measures something than can appropriately be called "intelligence." Such a conclusion, however, would still never be a definition of *g*, but only a "statement about" it. (1927, pp. 75–76)

Spearman's "theorem" of the *indifference of the indicator* means that *g* is reflected in any and all tests that involve any degree of "eduction" (i.e., inductive or deductive reasoning) regardless of their form or content, provided the *fundaments* composing the test items are familiar to those who take the test. A corollary of this "theorem" is that when a number of different test batteries, each composed of a large number of diverse cognitive tests, are factor analyzed, they should all yield approximately the same *g* factor. This has been borne out empirically (reviewed in Jensen, 1998, pp. 86–87). Spearman discovered that all tests are more highly *g* loaded in samples drawn from the lower half of the population distribution of IQ than in samples from the upper half of the distribution. In other words, for persons with higher IQs, less of the total variance is attributable to *g* and more is attributed to the various group factors and specificity, as compared with persons with lower IQs. Mental abilities of high-g persons are more clearly differentiated than in low-g persons. This phenomenon, which Spearman dubbed the *law of diminishing returns*, has been further substantiated in modern studies (reviewed in Jensen, 1998, pp. 585–588). Spearman (1927, pp. 388–391) also discovered the now well-established sex difference in spatial visualization ability, by noticing that spatial tests are much more highly g loaded for females than for males. Spatial tests have relatively small g loadings for males and have larger loadings on the group factor of spatial ability. Spearman found no evidence of a sex difference in g itself, and this, too, has been substantiated in recent analyses. When sex is included as a variable in factor analyses of a variety of mental tests, it shows a near-zero loading on the g factor, although sex has significant loadings on certain group factors (Jensen, 1998, pp. 531–543).

Spearman disliked describing g in purely verbal terms, but he did state that g appears in all mental activities that involve "the eduction of relations and correlates." Also he noted that the property of "abstractness" increases a task's g loading. Yet even sensory-motor tasks that hardly seem "cognitive," such as pitch discrimination, weight discrimination, perceptual speed, and choice reaction time, have some g loading, although it is much smaller than, for example, verbal and figural analogies, number series, and arithmetic reasoning, which are all highly g-loaded.

g and the Metaphor of Mental Energy

The verbal analogy or metaphor that Spearman most often used to "explain" the hypothetical basis of g was *mental energy*. At times he also spoke of "power," "force," and "neural energy." The complete metaphor invokes a factory (i.e., a person's brain) with various machines that perform different functions (group factors). All of the machines are driven by their connection with a gear that is powered by a single motor with a constant energy supply (g). The energy supplies to different factories (various individuals' brains) have different amounts of "horsepower." Now if we measured the output rates of each of the various machines in a number of different factories, we would find all of the different machines' output rates to be correlated with one another, and a factor analysis of the correlations would reveal a large general factor—call it a "horsepower factor"—that accounts for the differences between the various factories' productivity. But this, of course, would not reveal the actual source of this "horsepower factor"—it could be steam, or gas, or electricity, or nuclear power. To find out, we would have to get inside the factories to inspect their working parts.

Spearman remained theoretically agnostic about the physical basis of this metaphorical "mental energy." He knew that factor analysis, as a purely mathematical technique, could not prove the existence of g or explain its nature. Such understanding depends on finding that g has significant correlations with physical variables, perhaps in brain physiology. He suggested such physiological causes as the richness of the capillaries supplying blood to the brain and the efficiency of the brain's metabolic processes. Although some physiologists speculated about the brain processes involved in g, brain physiology in Spearman's day was too primitive to afford any real help. As Spearman wrote in his autobiography, "The physiologists who had claimed to assist psychology were . . . drawing heavy drafts on the future" (p. 304).

It is also important to show that individual differences in g factor scores have predictive validity for real-life outcomes, such as scholastic performance, occupational level, income, and other personally and socially important variables. Spearman's greater interest, however, was the physical basis of g rather than its social correlates. He wrote, "The final understanding of g must come from the most profound and detailed direct study of the human brain in its purely physical and chemical aspects" (1927, p. 403).

PRESENT g THEORY AND RESEARCH

During the 30 years between Spearman's death and the middle of the 1970s, g theory was in the doldrums, more because it seemed incompatible with the political zeitgeist than for any scientific reason. The transitory debate between Spearman and Thurstone over representing the factor structure of mental abilities in Spearman's fashion, as a unitary general factor (plus specificities for each test), versus Thurstonian fashion, as a number of independent group factors but no general factor, had long since been completely resolved. Thurstone showed that the various group factors could be correlated with one another and that a factor analysis of these factor correlations would yield a higher order factor, which is g. Also, a substantial part of the total test variance remains in the group factors after they are residualized from g. Hence a hierarchical structure like that in Figure 6.2 can represent within a single model both Spearman's g and Thurstone's group factors. (Thurstone called the first-order factors *primary mental abilities*, a term never used by Spearman.) Factor analyses performed on hundreds of psychometric data sets show that such a hierarchical structure, with g at the apex, best accounts for the correlations among virtually all of the presently known psychometric variables in the domain of human cognitive abilities (Carroll, 1993).

CONCLUSION

Empirical research on g has flourished in recent years. Virtually all of it has been referenced and reviewed in detail elsewhere (Jensen, 1998). Some of the main points that were not demonstrated empirically in Spearman's own work seem

General Factor

Second-Order Factors

Primary Factors

Tests

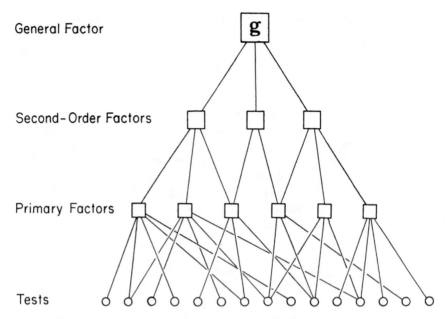

FIG. 6.2.   A three-strata factor hierarchy, showing first- and second-order factors (represented by squares) with *g* (the only third-order factor) at the apex. The factors increase in generality (i.e., the number of tests and lower order factors in which they are loaded) at each higher order in the hierarchy. Among virtually all of the tests of cognitive abilities that have been factor analyzed, there turn out to be about 20 to 30 well-identified primary factors and some 4 to 6 second-order factors. At the third order there appear to be no factors besides *g* (Jensen, 1998). Copyright © 1998 by Praeger Publishers. Reproduced with permission of Greenwood Publishing Group, Inc., Westport, CT.

worth indicating, if only briefly. Spearman would probably be happy to know that he had generally presaged many of these recent findings.

- The *g* loadings of a wide variety of psychometric tests that have been subjected to factor analysis represent a perfectly continuous variable ranging between about +.20 and +.80 and show a roughly normal distribution centered around +.50. Hence it is incorrect to think of *g* as reflected by just certain types of mental tests but not by others.
- The general factor in a diverse collection of learning tasks is the same factor as the *g* of psychometric tests.
- The *g* factor cannot be described in terms of the surface features of the tests that reflect it or even in any psychological terms. Highly dissimilar tests can be equally *g* loaded. Strictly speaking, *g* is not really an *ability* at all. It is a cause of individual differences in all cognitive abilities. It is a latent variable that presumably reflects certain properties of the brain elicited by all tests of mental ability, regardless of their form or information content as long as their

fundaments are appropriate for the persons tested. However, *g* should not be thought of as necessarily representing the essential design features of the brain, such as neural circuits, cell assemblies, functionally specialized modules, or the specific processes involved in perception, learning, and memory. Rather, *g* reflects individual differences in some property (or properties) of the brain that influences the speed and efficiency of all cognitive operations, thus causing them all to be positively correlated in the population. This property identified as *g* differs widely among individuals.

- Individuals' absolute levels of *g* rapidly increase with age from early childhood to maturity and then gradually decrease in later maturity and old age. Individuals differ in these rates of increase and decline.

- There is no pure test of *g*. Although all cognitive tests have some *g* loading, every test has some specificity (*s*). Most test batteries also measure one or more group factors in addition to *g* and *s*. A very large *g* loading (.70 to .80) is the *sine qua non* of the total score on all so-called IQ tests, which typically reflect certain group factors, such as verbal, spatial, and numerical.

- The *g* factor is not confined just to mental test scores. It is the chief active ingredient in the practical predictive validity of all test batteries used for selection—in college admissions, assignment of personnel to specialized training schools in the armed forces, and employment. This is because *g* is correlated with individual differences in actual performance in all these domains. The validity of *g* for predicting success in training and performance in various jobs depends on the complexity of the job's cognitive demands. Some types of work are much more *g* demanding than others, and the predictive validity of highly *g*-loaded tests is higher for the more *g*-demanding occupations. Statistically removing the *g* factor from selection tests would so drastically reduce their predictive validity as to render them practically useless. The group factors independent of *g* have relatively weak predictive validity, and then only for certain specialized types of jobs that require particular talents. Even general physical health is more highly related to *g* than to socioeconomic status. It is interesting to note that the g loadings of various tests are the best predictor of the degree to which spouses' test scores are correlated with each other. Group factors (independent of *g*) apparently contribute virtually nothing to the correlation.

- Spearman noted that across a wide variety of mental tests there was considerable variation in the magnitude of the average difference between groups of European ancestry and groups of sub-Saharan African ancestry. He conjectured that the size of these average differences for various tests is directly related to the difference in the size of the tests' *g* loadings. That is, the larger a test's *g* loading, the larger is the average White–Black difference. Spearman himself never tested this hypothesis. But his conjecture has since been borne out in more than 20 studies based on large samples and comprising nearly 100 different cognitive tests, including various measures of reaction times. (Details and references in Jensen, 1998, chapter 11; Jensen, in press; also comment by Neisser et al., 1996.) Every data set based on large and representative population samples of Black and White individuals that has been found displays the phenomenon predicted by Spearman, which therefore has the status of empirical fact.

- Spearman supposed that g was largely genetically determined and that the group factors were largely environmental. This has been shown by evidence on differences in the heritability of various psychometric tests based on studies of monozygotic (MZ, identical) and dizygotic (DZ, fraternal) twins. (The difference between the correlations for MZ and DZ twins affords an index of *heritability*, defined as the proportion of the total variance in test scores attributable to genetic factors.) It is found that tests' g loadings are a better predictor of their heritability coefficients than are any group factors independent of g, singly or in combination. Also predicted by a test's g loading is another genetic phenomenon known as *inbreeding depression*, or the decrement in the average test score of the offspring of genetically related parents (e.g., cousins) as compared with the average score of the offspring of unrelated parents. The higher a test's g loading, the greater is the effect of inbreeding depression in lowering the test scores.

- Spearman's hope that g would be found to have physical correlates in the brain has been realized in a number of studies, although most of these findings still need to be replicated to be regarded as firmly established (Jensen, 1993, 1998). Studies show correlations between g and a number of physical variables that have no conceptual connection with either psychometrics or factor analysis. Specifically, the magnitude of a test's g loading predicts that test's degree of correlation with the following variables: choice and discrimination reaction times; nerve conduction velocity in the brain's visual tract; head size and brain size; the brain's glucose metabolic rate (measured by PET scan); and the amplitude, rate of habituation, and complexity of the wave form of the average evoked potential (i.e., the brain's electrical reaction to an external stimulus, such as the sound of a sharp "click").

Knowing that these physical variables are correlated with g does not begin to explain g, of course. These findings only indicate that brain variables are in some way related to g, and they provide clues for further investigation of its physical basis. Exactly how or why these physical variables are related to g is still unknown. Discovering how many other anatomical, physiological, or biochemical brain variables may be involved and deciphering the whole causal chain resulting in g is a challenge for brain research. The explanation of g in terms of the brain should be a paramount scientific goal of future research. Its eventual accomplishment, given the accelerating pace of brain research, may be witnessed in the near future—in Spearman's hopeful words, "whereby physiology will achieve the greatest of all its triumphs" (1927, p. 407).

REFERENCES

Bartholomew, D. J. (1995). Spearman and the origin and development of factor analysis. *British Journal of Mathematical and Statistical Psychology, 48*, 211–220.

Boring, E. G. (1950). *A history of experimental psychology* (2nd ed.). New York: Appleton-Century-Crofts.

Burt, C. (1949). The two-factor theory. *British Journal of Psychology, Statistical, 2*, 151–178.

Carroll, J. B. (1991). Cognitive psychology's psychometric lawgiver. *Contemporary Psychology, 36*, 557–559.

Carroll, J. B. (1993). *Human cognitive abilities: A survey of factor analytic studies.* Cambridge: Cambridge University Press.

Cattell, R. B. (1978). Charles Edward Spearman. In W. H. Kruskal & J. M. Tanur (Eds.), *International encyclopedia of statistics* (Vol. 2). New York: Free Press.

Fancher, R. E. (1985). Spearman's original computation of *g*: A model for Burt? *British Journal of Psychology, 76*, 341–352.

Galton, F. (1869). *Heriditary genius.* London: Macmillan.

Galton, F. (1883). *Inquiries into human faculty and its development.* New York: AMS Press.

Hart, B., & Spearman, C. (1912). General ability, its existence and nature. *British Journal of Psychology, 5*, 51–84.

Jensen, A. R. (1993). Spearman's *g*: Links between psychometrics and biology. *Annals of the New York Academy of Sciences, 702*, 103–131.

Jensen, A. R. (1998). *The g factor.* Westport, CT: Praeger.

Jensen, A. R. (in press). "Spearman's hypothesis." In S. Messick & J. M. Collis (Eds.), *Intelligence and personality: Bridging the gap in theory and measurement.* Mahwah, NJ: Erlbaum.

Lovie, A. D., & Lovie, P. (1993). Charles Spearman, Cyril Burt, and the origins of factor analysis. *Journal of the History of the Behavioral Sciences, 29*, 308–321.

Neisser, U., Boodoo, G., Bouchard, T. J., Jr., Boykin, W. A., Brody, N., Ceci, S. J., Halpern, D. F., Loehlin, J. C., Perloff, R., & Sternberg, R. (1996). Intelligence: Knowns and unknowns. *American Psychologist, 51*, 77–101.

Spearman, C. E. (1904a). The proofs and measurement of association between two things. *American Journal of Psychology, 15*, 72–101.

Spearman, C. E. (1904b). "General intelligence" objectively determined and measured. *American Journal of Psychology, 15*, 201–293.

Spearman, C. E. (1914–1915). The heredity of abilities. *Eugenics Review, 6*, 219–237, 595–606.

Spearman, C. E. (1923). *The nature of "intelligence" and the principles of cognition.* London: Macmillan.

Spearman, C. E. (1927). *The abilities of man: Their nature and measurement.* London: Macmillan. (Reprinted by AMS Press, New York, 1970)

Spearman, C. E. (1930a). Autobiography. In C. Murchison (Ed.), *A history of psychology in autobiography*, Vol. 1 (pp. 299–333). Worcester, MA: Clark University Press. (Reprinted by Russell & Russell, New York, 1961)

Spearman, C. E. (1930b). *Creative mind.* London: Cambridge University Press.

Spearman, C. E. (1931). Our need of some science in place of the word "intelligence." *Journal of Educational Psychology, 22*, 401–410.

Spearman, C. E. (1937). *Psychology down the ages.* 2 vols. London: Macmillan.

Spearman, C. E., & Jones, L. W. (1950). *Human ability: A continuation of "The abilities of man."* London: Macmillan.

Thomson, G. (1947). Charles Spearman (1863–1945). *Obituary Notices of Fellows of the Royal Society, 5*, 373–385.

Zangwill, O. L. (1951). *Introduction to psychology.* London: Methuen.

Chapter 7

Hugo Münsterberg: Portrait of an Applied Psychologist

Ludy T. Benjamin, Jr.

On Saturday, December 16, 1916, Harvard University professor Hugo Münsterberg awoke to scenes of fresh snow outside the windows of his house on Ware Street. The sun was shining brightly, disguising the bitter cold of the day. Bundling himself in coat and hat, Münsterberg walked the several blocks to Radcliffe College, where he would meet the 60 young women students in his introductory psychology class. He began the lecture at the appointed hour of 9:00 a.m. Thirty minutes later he leaned suddenly against the lectern and then fell to the floor, knocking his watch and eyeglasses from the desk. His graduate assistant, Harold Burtt, reached him almost immediately, but within minutes Münsterberg was dead, apparently from a cerebral hemorrhage. He was 53 years old (Hale, 1980; M. Münsterberg, 1922).

When Münsterberg died, "He was arguably the best known psychologist in America" (Hale, 1980, p. 3). He was also one of the most hated individuals in America, because he was "the most prominent member of America's largest minority, the German-Americans" (Hale, 1980, p. 3) and the chief spokesperson for that group in justifying German aggression in Europe in World War I in the years before his death. No doubt there were many who cheered his death. His papers, housed today in the Rare Books and Manuscripts Collection of the Boston Public Library, include four folders of hate mail. The language is strong in many of the letters and extremely so in several. One wonders how he could have saved those letters. Some of them even made death threats.

Letters from the Münsterberg Collection quoted by courtesy of the Trustees of the Boston Public Library.

*Photo of Hugo Münsterberg courtesy of the Archives of the History of American Psychology, University of Akron.

In 1914, one former Harvard alumnus threatened to withdraw his promise of a $10 million gift to Harvard unless Münsterberg was fired. The man had no such money, however. In the middle of that controversy, Münsterberg even agreed to resign if the individual would pay $5 million to Harvard immediately. Certainly many Americans, including many of Münsterberg's colleagues at Harvard, would gladly have donated to that sum if it would have guaranteed his resignation from Harvard, and ideally, his transportation home to Germany.

There is no denying that the exceptional turbulence of the last years of Münsterberg's life contributed to his early death. But his life in America had not always been so difficult. Indeed for most of his years at Harvard he enjoyed great popularity, at least with the public if not always with his colleagues or with the administrators at Harvard. Münsterberg arrived in America in 1892, a psychologist and a German. Those two identities defined his life. This account will focus on Münsterberg the psychologist, particularly his diverse and pioneering efforts in applied psychology, yet it is not possible to tell that story without some understanding of his national identity.

BACKGROUND IN GERMANY

Münsterberg was born June 1, 1863, in Danzig, Germany (now Gdansk, Poland) into a moderately prominent Jewish family. He was the son of Moritz Münsterberg, a successful lumber merchant, and Minna Anna Bernhardi, an artist and homemaker. His mother died when Hugo was only 12 and his father died while he was completing his study at the Gymnasium (high school) in Danzig. Shortly thereafter Hugo converted to Christianity, a conversion of expediency that he deemed necessary to pursue his career goals in Germany. In 1882 he entered the University of Leipzig to study medicine, but he switched to psychology in the summer of 1883 after taking a course from Wilhelm Wundt (chap. 3, *Pioneers III*). Completing his PhD with Wundt in 1885, he resumed his medical studies at the University of Heidelberg, where he received an MD degree in 1887.

In that same year, Münsterberg applied for an unsalaried lecturer position at the University of Freiburg, where he was accepted in the fall of 1887, shortly after he married a distant cousin, Selma Oppler. At Freiberg, he built an outstanding laboratory in experimental psychology, funding much of it from his own pocket and housing some of it in his home. In 1892 Münsterberg became the equivalent of an associate professor, a faculty position that was unusual for someone only 28.

Also at Freiburg, Münsterberg established a reputation for research on will. In opposition to Wundt's ideas about voluntary action, he argued that the will was not experienced directly but was instead an awareness of the changes in muscles, joints, and tendons. Münsterberg had proposed research on this topic as his Leipzig dissertation, but Wundt had asked him to choose another subject. So

Münsterberg did no research on will until after he left Wundt's laboratory (Spill-mann & Spillmann, 1993). This research was well-known outside of Germany and was particularly admired by Harvard's William James (chap. 2, *Pioneers I*). James, who had met Münsterberg briefly in 1889 in Paris, no doubt felt a kin-ship with him because of the similarity of their views on the role of muscular sensations in the experience of emotion and will.

In the winter of 1892, James's admiration led to an invitation that would change Münsterberg's life forever. James wrote to him:

> Is it conceivable that if you should be invited, you might agree to come and take charge of the Psychological Laboratory and the higher instruction in that subject in Harvard University for three years . . . ? We are the best university in America, and we must lead in psychology. I, at the age of 50, disliking laboratory work [and] am certainly not the kind of stuff to make a first-rate director thereof. We could get younger men here who would be safe enough, but we need something more than a safe man, we need a man of genius if possible. (James, 1892)

James noted that although the position would be for three years, it was his hope that it would become a permanent arrangement.

Münsterberg expressed great interest in the invitation, although he worried about how easily he could master the English language for his lectures, and was especially concerned that in leaving Germany he would damage his chances for further advancement in the German university system (Hale, 1980). But he was able to arrange a three-year leave of absence and James was able to make the necessary arrangements with the Harvard administration. Thus Münsterberg came to America, intending not to stay beyond those three years. He envisioned the trip as an adventure, a chance to explore America and to sample American so-ciety (Hale, 1980). He held many of the prejudices about Americans—their lack of culture and the inferiority of their education—that were common among Ger-mans of his social and educational class. James, who no doubt sensed such reser-vations, offered faint praise for Harvard in his invitation letter, "Our university is one you need not be ashamed of" (James, 1892).

HARVARD UNIVERSITY: THE EARLY YEARS

Arriving in Boston for his American adventure in August 1892, Münsterberg was met at the train station by the philosopher Josiah Royce (who would become one of Münsterberg's strongest supporters at Harvard) and by Herbert Nichols, an in-structor at Harvard who would be his assistant in the laboratory (James was va-cationing in Italy and was not part of the welcoming party).

Although there were perhaps a dozen more productive psychology laborato-ries than Harvard's in American universities when Münsterberg arrived, he soon changed that. Working with Nichols and an excellent collection of psychological apparatus and research material already collected by James, and with Harvard's considerable financial resources, Münsterberg built a first-class laboratory that was described in detail by Nichols in an article for *McClure's Magazine*. The article discussed the ongoing research and included photographs and drawings of the laboratory rooms and equipment and a photograph and description of the new laboratory director. After only a year of Münsterberg's direction, Nichols (1893) wrote,

> Both for original research and for demonstration, this laboratory is the most unique, the richest, and the most complete in any country; and in witness of the fame and genius of its present director, and of the rapidly spreading interest in experimental psychology, particularly in America, there are already gathered here, under Professor Münsterberg's administration, a larger number of students specially devoted to mental science than ever previously studied together in any one place. (p. 406)

Surely that description would have rankled G. Stanley Hall, whose Clark University laboratory was arguably better equipped. And Wundt, if he had read the article, which is doubtful, would have been amused, if not offended, by such American braggadocio.

Nichols reminded *McClure's* readers that Münsterberg had been a student of Wundt and implied that he was more of an original thinker than Wundt, a criticism of Wundt often attributed to James. The article made it clear that, despite the slow start, Harvard expected to be the promised land of experimental psychology and Münsterberg would lead it there: ". . . in his genius the hopes and destiny of experimental psychology at Harvard are now centred" (Nichols, 1893, p. 409).

The three-year appointment went well for Münsterberg and for Harvard. He spent the first year and a half full-time in the laboratory, supervising graduate student research and training. His first lecture in English did not come until February 1894, to an undergraduate class at Radcliffe. Münsterberg actually did little research of his own during those three years, presumably because he felt uncomfortable writing for the English-language journals. But he was busy writing, working on his textbook, *Grundzüge der Psychologie*, that would be published in 1900.

When the appointment ended, Harvard made Münsterberg the offer of a permanent position. As Bruce Kuklick (1977) has noted, however, he "was not yet resigned to a career among the barbarians" (p. 196). Although Münsterberg's experience at Harvard had been very positive, he longed for his homeland and his place in German academia. Harvard understood the conflict he was in and offered him a two-year period to reach a decision. So Münsterberg returned to Freiburg in 1895 with the security of the Harvard position but seeking a professorship in one of the major German universities. Such a position never came.

Perhaps it was because of his birth as a Jew, or perhaps it was his conflict with the views of Wundt. Both have been offered as reasons. With some reluctance, and perhaps a sense of personal failure, Münsterberg returned to Harvard in the fall of 1897, beginning a tenure there that continued until his early death.

When he returned to Harvard, Münsterberg resumed the directorship of the psychology laboratory. That his work was well-respected in America was evidenced by his election to the presidency of the American Psychological Association (APA) in the following year, 1898. That year may have represented the peak of Münsterberg's popularity in the community of American psychologists, because he was about to step on the first of many professorial toes.

THE ATTACKS ON APPLIED PSYCHOLOGY

In the 1890s the most visible application of the new psychology in America was the Child Study Movement, a movement begun by G. Stanley Hall (Davidson & Benjamin, 1987). According to Hall, the most natural application of psychology was to education. Hall enlisted hundreds of child study researchers through a network of normal school professors and, especially, schoolteachers. Using questionnaires generated mostly by Hall, his colleagues, and graduate students at Clark, teachers sought to create a catalog of the contents of children's minds. The goal was to discover everything that could be known about the child: sensory capabilities, physical characteristics, sense of humor, play, religious ideas, memory, attention span, and so forth. With this new information, education would be a science. Teacher training would be improved, curricula could be individualized for students, and parents would have better information about child rearing. By 1898 child study was a principal topic of research and discussion at the annual meetings of the National Education Association, most states had their own child study societies, and Clark University was the data center distributing results from the many studies via special bulletins or in Hall's child study journal, *Pedagogical Seminary* (which began publication in 1891). There were certainly psychologists critical of the movement, but none of them was as public or as polemical as was Münsterberg. Writing in an 1898 issue of *Atlantic Monthly* he warned school teachers,

> This rush [of education] toward experimental psychology is an absurdity. Our laboratory work cannot teach you anything which is of direct use to you in your work as teachers. . . . You may collect thousands of experimental results with the chronoscope and kymograph, but you will not find anything in our laboratories which you could translate directly into a pedagogical prescription. (1898, p. 166)

The article was not really directed at schoolteachers; it was a frontal assault on the work of psychologists involved in child study, particularly Hall, Yale University's Edward Wheeler Scripture, and those who were identified with mental measurement, such as James McKeen Cattell, who worked with chronoscopes and kymographs. Münsterberg was careful not to name names but the targets knew who they were. The strong language of the article was perhaps unique among American psychologists to that point. There had been disagreements before, for example, over James's interest in psychic phenomena and seances in a time when his colleagues were working diligently to distance psychology from such spiritism. But Münsterberg was the first who could be said to hit below the belt in a public forum. The blows against child study would not be the only ones he delivered. In the next 18 months he published four more articles in *Atlantic Monthly*, all arguing for the limitations of experimental psychology in interpreting the meaning of phenomena experienced outside of the psychological laboratory—for example, spiritual events and aesthetic experiences. Three of them were published alongside other essays in his 1899 book, *Psychology and Life*.

Münsterberg's articles, especially the attack on child study, drew some heated responses from his colleagues, both in published replies in the popular literature and letters to Münsterberg. Cattell, Charles Bliss, John Dewey (chap. 4, *Pioneers II*), Joseph Jastrow (chap. 6, *Pioneers I*), Edward Thorndike (chap. 10, *Pioneers I*), and Lightner Witmer (chap. 5, *Pioneers II*) all published negative reactions. Münsterberg, never one to pass up what he perceived as an affront to his dignity or integrity, expressed his dismay over the attacks on him both in print and in personal correspondence. In an exchange of letters over Cattell's published reply in the *Psychological Review* (Cattell, 1898a), Cattell wrote one of the kinder responses:

> I quite think that the usefulness of experimental psychology to the teacher has been exaggerated in certain quarters. Still I think you go too far in saying that it is of no use at all. If psychology is of value to the teacher and experiment has enriched psychology, then it is scarcely fair to say that experiment and laboratory work—whether as training or as a professional help—are valueless. . . . In regard to the possibility and value of mental measurement we do really differ. . . . When you say that the time of mental processes cannot be measured you contradict not only me but Wundt, James, Ward, and, if I may be permitted to say so, also yourself. (Cattell, 1898b, May 26)

In the end, child study died a natural death. Psychologists abandoned their cooperative venture with schoolteachers and established their own child development research centers within their universities. Although the many ambitions of child study were never fulfilled, the movement was important in convincing psychologists and the public of the applicability of the new psychology.

MÜNSTERBERG, THE MEDIA DARLING

For Münsterberg, the controversy he raised in his article on the dangers of experimental psychology led to a new awareness for him that had great significance for the course of his career and life. As a writer, he stirred interest and emotions, a fact that led editors (including Willa Cather) to invite numerous contributions from his pen. For the rest of his life, Münsterberg was a frequent contributor to the popular press through numerous magazine articles, newspaper columns, and a series of popular books. These publications established him as America's psychological expert, and it seems that he never found a topic on which he felt unable to comment as expert. Invitations for public lectures, inquiries from the press, and consulting opportunities in business increasingly came his way. Münsterberg had a knack for sensationalism and he was often quoted in the press, partly because of his willingness to say outrageous things. In essence he was what reporters today call "good press."

In a span of fewer than 20 years Münsterberg wrote on a multitude of popular subjects such as the personality of Americans, school reform, hypnotism, women as unacceptable jurors, lie detection, criminality, democracy, native Americans, African Americans, political parties, the Monroe Doctrine, the Philippines, journalistic inaccuracy, motion pictures, psychotherapy, art and artists, communicating with the dead, murderers, gambling, prohibition, Christian Science, beauty, nervousness, vocational choice, bookstores, patriotism, coeducation, home economics, insanity, the subconscious, and being a scientific expert. Not surprisingly some of these articles and interviews caused consternation among his colleagues. At times Charles Eliot, president of Harvard, probably felt he needed a press secretary just to deal with the trouble caused by Münsterberg's utterances. He reminded Münsterberg that he should not feel compelled to comment on every question he was asked. In a 1909 letter to him Eliot wrote,

> You seem to me to work with too much intensity and too constantly, and to work on topics which are peculiarly stirring and exciting. I hope you will moderate your rate of work and of publication, and will take up some systematic course of interesting out-of-door exercise, with frequent absences from Cambridge between Friday night and Monday morning for change of scene and change of thoughts. (1909a)

Apparently to deal with the latest crisis, Eliot added, "I also advise you not to have anything to do here-after with the hypnotic treatment of women, even for the purposes of your laboratory research" (1909a).

As the same time that Münsterberg was discovering the delights of press clippings, he was growing disinterested in the laboratory. Hale (1980) reported that he began to lose interest in that work before his return to Harvard in 1897. If so, perhaps he kept it hidden for a while from Harvard's administration. Eventually, though, his change of heart was discovered. Eliot wrote to him in 1909 that some years earlier

> Professor James . . . wished to be wholly relieved of responsibility for an experimental laboratory that he might devote himself to the theoretical aspects of the sub-

ject; and I have been much interested to see in you a similar tendency. Perhaps this is an inevitable effect of advancing age in a philosopher. (1909b)

MÜNSTERBERG AS APPLIED PSYCHOLOGIST

After 1900 Münsterberg did very little original research in the laboratory and turned over much of his instruction there to assistants. He remained minimally involved, however, and he was instrumental in the design of the 24-room complex of the new psychological laboratory located in Emerson Hall, which opened in 1906 (see Münsterberg, 1906). But after 1906 his laboratory days were essentially over. He devoted himself virtually full-time to the field of applied psychology, the field he had so thoroughly trashed in 1898. Between 1906 and his death in 1916 he published 20 books (including one on psychology for teachers!), mostly on a variety of applied topics. Several of those books were collections of essays published in popular outlets.

Münsterberg's reputation in psychology today is chiefly based on his applied works. His book on psychology and the law, *On the Witness Stand* (1908), is considered one of the founding texts of forensic psychology. His 1909 book, *Psychotherapy*, was arguably the first book by a psychologist on that subject, as was his book on psychology and the motion pictures, *The Photoplay: A Psychological Study* (1916). His two books on industrial psychology, published in 1913 and 1915, were especially important in popularizing that field. Indeed, he has often been called the founder of industrial psychology in America, a label he does not merit given the earlier work by such figures as Harlow Gale, Walter Dill Scott, Daniel Starch, and Harry Hollingworth (chap. 9, *Pioneers II*). Still, there is no denying the importance of the 1913 book, *Psychology and Industrial Efficiency*, which was for a time on the list of nonfiction best-sellers. That book was particularly important in creating research and consulting opportunities for psychologists with American businesses and in spreading applied psychology's appeal to the general public. The scope of this work (and his other books) is much too broad to cover in this chapter. Instead, a brief description will be given of the two books that proved to be most influential in forensic and industrial psychology.

Psychology and Law

Then as now crime got lots of press coverage, and Münsterberg's interest in the subject comes as no surprise. He began his work in forensic psychology through his concerns about the accuracy of memory and thus the reliance on testimony of eye witnesses. The impetus for a series of a half dozen popular articles on psychology and law (compiled in his book, *On the Witness Stand*) was a murder case in Chicago in 1906. Both James and Münsterberg had taken up the cause of the convicted murderer, who had confessed under suspicious circumstances and later withdrew his confession. The man was mentally disabled and both James and Münsterberg, after studying the records supplied by his attorney, concluded that he was innocent. Their letters were released to the press, eliciting a reaction of outrage from the court that self-proclaimed experts who had not been part of the trial would deem to contradict the conclusion of a jury. The conviction stood and the man was hanged.

Münsterberg seemed especially upset by the outcome. "The failure of his and James's intercession involved more than a personal rebuff; it amounted to an attack on psychology itself" (Hale, 1980, p. 112). Münsterberg answered the attack of those in the legal profession in a series of articles that produced one of his most popular books, *On the Witness Stand*. In the introduction to that book, Münsterberg made his intent quite clear:

> The lawyer and the judge and the juryman are sure that they do not need the experimental psychologist. . . . They go on thinking that their legal instinct and their common sense supplies them with all that is needed and somewhat more; and if the time is ever to come when even the jurist is to show some concession to the spirit of modern psychology, public opinion will have to exert some pressure. Just in the line of the law it therefore seems necessary not to rely simply on the technical statements of scholarly treatises, but to carry the discussion in the most popular form possible before the wider tribunal of the general reader. (1908, pp. 10–11)

The book debunked the idea that crimes could be provoked by posthypnotic suggestion; it illustrated how suggestions could create memories and beliefs; it described the reasons why false confessions might be elicited (stimulated directly by the Chicago case); and discussed the ways in which emotions and gestures could be misread as signs of guilt. The chapter on the fallibility of recall in witnesses was particularly well developed; it drew many of the same conclusions that are part of contemporary psychology's admonitions about the inaccuracy of eyewitness testimony. In fact, these contemporary accounts often cite Münsterberg's writings as anticipations of this modern work.

The chapter that produced the most attention was "The Detection of Crime," a lengthy description of word association studies [pioneered independently by Carl Jung and Max Wertheimer (chaps. 11 and 13, respectively, *Pioneers I*)] and how they could be used to detect lying. Münsterberg described his lie-detection machine, a chronoscope used to record response latencies in thousandths of a second. He argued that individuals took longer to speak after words that were emotionally meaningful to the person. The time differences were small, Münsterberg acknowledged, but they were large enough to allow the trained investigator to tell truth from falsehood. Münsterberg gained considerable notoriety on the subject through his participation in a murder trial that drew national publicity. A labor organizer, Harry Orchard, confessed to killing a former Idaho governor who had been especially antilabor. His confession indicated that the killing was carried out under orders from William Haywood, the leader of the International Workers of the World. Münsterberg traveled to Idaho, at the request of the editor of *McClure's Magazine*, for part of the Haywood trial. He took his chronoscope with him to test Orchard. As he sat at the prosecutor's table in the Boise courtroom, Münsterberg watched Orchard's testimony. His physiognomic impressions are interesting coming from someone who argued so vehemently against such nonsense when it was often confused with the new experimental psychology:

> I had him [Orchard] only a few feet from me for careful observation. I cannot deny that the impression of that first morning was very bad. I saw him from the side and his profile, especially the jaw, appeared to me most brutal and most vulgar; I saw also at once the deformation of the ear, the irregularity in the movement of the eyes and the abnormal lower lip. That this was the profile of a murderer seemed to me not improbable. . . . I looked instinctively to the other side where Haywood sat, with the head of a thinker and leader. No sharper contrast was possible: all my sympathies went to this brilliant face of the defendant and all my disgust to the witness. (1907, p. 2)

Of course, the point is that physical impressions would have led Münsterberg to believe Haywood and brand Orchard as the liar. But after hours of testing Orchard, including several word-association tests, Münsterberg was convinced he was telling the truth about Haywood's involvement. His public expression of those views drew considerable attention. Some of it was negative, such as a scathing letter from Clarence Darrow, Haywood's attorney, who questioned Münsterberg's science: ". . . in my humble opinion you are in no more position to give any intelligent judgment upon the truthfulness of Orchard's story than the man in the moon. . . ." (Darrow, 1907).

The principal interest in Münsterberg's account of the trial and his investigations, however, centered on his lie-detection machine, or what one writer called his "Truth Compelling Machine" (Gilliams, 1907). Münsterberg (1908) gave mixed messages about the lie-detector. He was at times unequivocal in his faith in the method:

> The association experiments thus completely fulfilled their purpose; they . . . [answered] a definite question which could hardly be answered by other methods of evidence. The association experiments proved that the murderer [Orchard] did not try to hide anything. (p. 101)

Later in the same chapter he urged some caution: "The new method is still in many ways imperfect, and if clumsily applied it may be misleading; moreover there exists no hard and fast rule which fits every case mechanically" (p. 109).

Münsterberg continued his quest for a lie-detection procedure, eventually shifting his focus from the word-association procedure to measures of autonomic nervous system activity such as respiration, the resistance of the skin to transmitting electrical impulses [the Galvanic Skin Response (GSR)], and blood pressure. (One of his students who worked on blood pressure correlates of lying was William Moulton Marston, who later claimed credit for inventing the lie detector and who would gain fame as the creator of the super hero Wonder Woman. See Bunn, 1997.) Münsterberg acknowledged that his methods had no legal standing in court, but argued that "justice demands that truth and lies be disentangled. The time will come when the methods of experimental psychology cannot longer be excluded from the court of law" (Münsterberg, 1908, pp. 108–109). Although polygraph evidence is still inadmissible in American courts, the search for ways for psychology to serve the judicial system continues. The interface of psychology and law defines an important area of contemporary psychology, an area that began in America with Münsterberg's work.

Industrial Psychology

In the early 20th century, American business was preoccupied with efficiency. Efficiency meant more effective advertising, better training of workers, more scientific management, improved employee selection procedures, better accounting methods, and better ways to control the performance of workers and the quality of their output. Hale (1980) has written that, "No questions in applied psychology, in fact, attracted him [Münsterberg] more than those of industrial organization and efficiency. For more than half a decade . . . he extended his view to the entire range of economic psychology: vocational guidance, advertising, personnel management, mental testing, fatigue and monotony, motivation, and the 'mind' of labor" (p. 148).

Further, in recognizing business's growing concern with efficiency, Münsterberg touted the promise of psychology as the science of human efficiency. One of his chief interests regarding efficiency was in matching worker abilities to the requirements of the job. He argued that when job and worker were matched, an employer got a very satisfied employee and a good work output. Experimental psychology, he believed, had the tools to help create that perfect match by determining the mental traits required for any job.

Münsterberg's initial foray into the industrial world was a 1909 magazine article touting the applicability of psychology for the problems of business. He discussed what science, particularly chemistry, had contributed to the improvement of farming, and he lauded the federal government's Department of Agriculture for its role in establishing agricultural experimental stations around the country as a way to improve farming efficiency and production in different regions. He suggested that perhaps the "Department of Commerce and Labor at a future time may establish experimental stations which will bring corresponding help [from experimental psychology] to the mills and factories and even to the artisans everywhere" (Münsterberg, 1909b, p. 91). That article led to numerous consulting opportunities for Münsterberg, which he described in his popular 1913 book, *Psychology and Industrial Efficiency.*

Münsterberg indicated in that book that it was his intent to outline a new science that integrated the psychological laboratory and the world of business: "The psychological experiment is systematically to be placed at the service of commerce and industry" (Münsterberg, 1913b, p. 3). In introducing his book he gave little credit to colleagues in the field, such as Walter Dill Scott who, by 1911, had published four books on industrial psychology, including two on the psychology of advertising and another on increasing human efficiency in business. Worse, Münsterberg dismissed their work as "scattered beginnings" and "tentative efforts and disconnected attempts" (p. 3). It was not uncommon for him to take more credit than he deserved, a fact that annoyed many of his American colleagues.

Münsterberg's "new" applied science was focused on his tripartite model of industrial efficiency: (a) matching worker and job, (b) increasing productivity and quality of product, and (c) influencing workers to change in ways that would benefit the interests of the company. In his own work he focused almost exclusively on the first of those three.

One of his first opportunities came in October of 1911 (six months before the sinking of the *Titanic*) from the Hamburg–American shipping company asking him to devise a test that would allow the company to eliminate individuals who would be incompetent as ship captains. Münsterberg sought to design a test that involved the making of multiple rapid decisions simultaneously and that could be evaluated in terms of correct responses. After a series of unsatisfactory experiments he settled on a card-sorting task. The cards each contained 48 vowels on each card (A, E, O, and U). On each card one vowel occurred with greater frequency. Individuals being tested were to sort the deck of 24 cards into four piles according to which of the four vowels on the card was most frequent. Total sorting time was recorded, as were number of errors.

It is difficult to understand why Münsterberg thought that such a task would simulate the complexity of decisions a ship captain would have to make. We do not know if the shipping company actually used the test. Psychologist Guy Montrose Whipple did try the test on several samples in Cincinnati, including a sample of college students. He found that a "number of individuals who had displayed 'unusual quickness' in real emergencies scored low on the test . . . [and] the person most fitted for sea-captaincy of all those tested . . . turned out to be a co-ed" (Hale, 1980, p. 156).

It is clear that Münsterberg understood the concept of ecological validity because he created such a test for trolley car operators about the same time that he carried out his research on sea captains. The study on trolley operators ("motormen") was done at the request of the Boston Elevated Railway Company.

The company was in trouble because the trolley drivers had been involved in a number of fatal accidents involving pedestrians. Münsterberg was hired in March of 1912 to develop a test that would allow the company to weed out those drivers who were accident prone. A small moving belt was created to simulate a street with a window above the belt that exposed stimuli of differing kinds, for example, horses, automobiles, persons. Most stimuli moved parallel to the trolley track, but the danger came from stimuli approaching from either side. Performance was determined by errors (failure to avoid obstacles) and speed through the task.

Münsterberg was able to test Boston motormen whom he assigned to one of three groups, based on their accident records. The top group averaged 20 years of service with no accidents. The bottom group all had accident records and had been considered for dismissal by the company. He reported "the results show a far-reaching correspondence between efficiency in the experiment and efficiency in the actual service" (Münsterberg, 1913b, p. 75). The selection method was tried in other cities, for example, Milwaukee, Dallas, and Geneva, but with mixed results (Hale, 1980; Viteles, 1932).

Although Münsterberg conducted other studies of this nature, he was already focusing on a large-scale questionnaire study designed to identify the mental traits associated with many different jobs. Cattell, Hollingworth, and others had advocated the use of mental tests for selection, and a number of their students had been successful in such efforts. Thus in January 1912 Münsterberg sent hundreds of copies of a cover letter and questionnaire to business owners and executives asking them about the mental traits that they considered essential for the employees in their particular business. The Münsterberg papers contain several hundred replies. One from Tiffany and Company, for example, provided job descriptions of the physical and mental traits required for designers, "workmen at the bench," and "salesmen." Münsterberg was pleased enough with the responses that he planned a second wave of questionnaires to be sent in late 1913. He told his publisher, Doubleday Page, that he was planning to send out 15,000 questionnaires with stamped return envelopes "to men who are working in factories. Later I will send a similar set to men working in mines, etc. A third set of fifteen thousand will go to women workers, and so on" (Münsterberg, 1913a). There is no evidence that survey was ever started. Perhaps the growing conflict in Europe or the tensions surrounding Münsterberg's own life caused him to abandon those plans.

Although Münsterberg's career in industrial psychology was relatively brief, there is no denying that his 1913 book, *Psychology and Industrial Efficiency*, had an important impact on the growth of that field. Mental tests became a part of business practices in measuring advertising appeals, management styles, consumer behavior, sales strategies, and particularly personnel issues, including worker selection, job analysis, production, and efficiency. Personnel issues were part of the rise of big business in America in the early 20th century. As companies grew in size, as jobs grew more specialized, and as supervision grew both horizontally and vertically, businesses found that new practices were needed to ensure efficiency in workers. To meet these needs, companies established personnel departments that were centralized offices for hiring and job placement. These departments, which by the 1920s typically included psychologists as consultants or full-time employees, emphasized job analyses by which the individual components of all jobs were identified, and employee testing to make appropriate matches between employee skills and job requirements. It is what Münsterberg would have envisioned in his new applied science (Arthur & Benjamin, 1999).

ON BEING GERMAN IN AMERICA

As noted earlier, the last few years of Münsterberg's life were stressful. He was a German, never an American or even a German American. He maintained his German citizenship throughout his life in America and he never lost his love for German idealism, although he clearly came to appreciate some things American. Throughout his time in America he saw himself as an ambassador for both groups. He was at the time the principal interpreter of American culture to the Germans and German culture to the Americans (see Münsterberg, 1901, 1904).

As tensions grew in Europe in the early 20th century, Münsterberg became more outspoken on behalf of Germany. By 1907 his speeches, letters to newspapers, and magazine articles were causing serious tensions at Harvard. The situation got worse each year, especially after war broke out in Europe in 1914. Many in the public called for his resignation from Harvard; some wanted him deported. His continued defense of Germany after the sinking of the *Lusitania* in May 1915 was the final straw for many of his remaining friends and defenders. Ostracized by most of his Harvard colleagues, he withdrew from campus life other than his teaching obligations (see Keller, 1979).

When Münsterberg died on December 16, 1916, classes at Harvard were canceled for a day. Eulogies were kind and newspaper editorials focused mostly on his many achievements. There was an attempt by Robert Yerkes (chap. 7, *Pioneers II*) to continue his salary for the rest of the academic year for his widow, but Harvard refused. A similar request to secure a pension from Germany was also denied (Hale, 1980). Münsterberg was cremated and his ashes sent to his native Danzig, but his wife and two daughters remained in the United States (Keller, 1979).

CONCLUSION

Münsterberg is surely one of the most colorful figures in the history of psychology. Kuklick (1977) has described him as follows.

Vain and garrulous, Münsterberg was impressed with his organizational abilities in a variety of fields and with his talent for spreading good will both in and out of the scholarly community. In short, he was an early academic entrepreneur, but his entrepreneurial qualities were unfortunately wedded to bad judgment and political ineptitude. His pompous and authoritarian manner, heightened by his formal dress, waxed mustache, and pronounced German accent, did not contribute to his personal charm. In many respects he embodied what would become the American stereotype of the German. (pp. 435–436)

There is no denying that Münsterberg possessed personality traits that were problematic in his relations to many people. What could have been viewed as eccentricities earlier became harder and harder to tolerate as anti-German sentiment grew in the years before America entered the first world war.

Although he lived only 53 years, Münsterberg's achievements in that time are considerable. Moreover, some significant aspects of his professional contributions could not even be covered in this brief account—for example his works in philosophy (see Kuklick, 1977, for an excellent treatment). His mentoring of graduate students has not been discussed, and he produced some excellent ones— Edmund B. Delabarre, Ethel D. Puffer (chap. 8, *Pioneers I*), Robert M. Yerkes (chap. 7, *Pioneers II*), Mary Whiton Calkins (chap. 5, *Pioneers I*), Edwin B. Holt, Sidney Pressey, Edward C. Tolman (chap. 15, *Pioneers I*), Aaron Roback, Harold E. Burtt, Knight Dunlap, Gordon Allport, and Floyd Allport (chap. 8, *Pioneers III*)—individuals who made impressive contributions to the science and application of psychology.

It is clear that Münsterberg played an important role as an entrepreneur for the application of experimental psychology. His optimism, his grandiosity, and his reputation with the public as an expert psychologist helped sell the American public on the worth of psychology. He believed passionately in the value of psychological science applied in the public sphere, and he promoted that belief endlessly. He was a significant force in the growing professionalization of American psychology in the early 20th century and the exceptional popularity of psychology in the 1920s. Kuklick (1977) noted that James's first impression of Münsterberg was apt. James described him as

vain, loquacious, personally rather formal and fastidious . . . desiring to please and to shine . . . with probably a certain superficiality in his cleverness and lack of the deeper metaphysical humor [but] . . . a man of big ideas in all directions, a real genius. (p. 198)

His genius and his considerable talents as an entrepreneur are why he is remembered today.

REFERENCES

Arthur, W. E., Jr., & Benjamin, L. T., Jr. (1999). Psychology and business. In A. Stec & D. A. Bernstein (Eds.), *Psychology: Fields of application* (pp. 98–115). Boston: Houghton-Mifflin.

Bunn, G. C. (1997). The lie detector, Wonder Woman and liberty: The life and work of William Moulton Marston. *History of the Human Sciences, 10,* 91–119.

Cattell, J. McK. (1898a). Professor Münsterberg on "The danger from experimental psychology." *Psychological Review, 5,* 411–413.

Cattell, J. McK. (1898b). Letter to Hugo Münsterberg, May 26, 1898, Münsterberg Papers, Boston Public Library.

Darrow, C. (1907). Letter to Hugo Münsterberg, August 16, 1907, Münsterberg Papers, Boston Public Library.

Davidson, E. S., & Benjamin, L. T., Jr. (1987). A history of the child study movement. In J. Glover & R. Ronning (Eds.), *Historical foundations of educational psychology* (pp. 41–60). New York: Plenum Press.

Eliot, C. W. (1909a). Letter to Hugo Münsterberg, April 30, 1909, Münsterberg Papers, Boston Public Library.

Eliot, C. W. (1909b). Letter to Hugo Münsterberg, May 22, 1909, Münsterberg Papers, Boston Public Library.

Gilliams, E. L. (1907). Letter to Hugo Münsterberg, September 12, 1907, Münsterberg Papers, Boston Public Library.

Hale, M., Jr. (1980). *Human science and social order: Hugo Münsterberg and the origins of applied psychology.* Philadelphia: Temple University Press.

James, W. (1892). Letter to Hugo Münsterberg, February 21, 1892, Münsterberg Papers, Boston Public Library.

Keller, P. (1979). *States of belonging: German-American intellectuals and the first world war.* Cambridge, MA: Harvard University Press.

Kuklick, B. (1977). *The rise of American philosophy: Cambridge, Massachusetts, 1860–1930.* New Haven, CT: Yale University Press.

Münsterberg, H. (1898, February). The danger from experimental psychology. *Atlantic Monthly, 81,* 159–167.

Münsterberg, H. (1899). *Psychology and life.* Boston: Houghton, Mifflin.

Münsterberg, H. (1900). *Gründzuge der psychologie* [Principles of psychology]. Leipzig: J. A. Barth.

Münsterberg, H. (1901). *American traits: From the point of view of a German.* Boston: Houghton-Mifflin.

Münsterberg, H. (1904). *The Americans.* New York: McClure, Phillips.

Münsterberg, H. (1906). V. The psychological laboratory in Emerson Hall. *Harvard Psychological Bulletin, 2,* 34–39.

Münsterberg, H. (1907). Experiments with Harry Orchard. Münsterberg Papers. Boston Public Library.

Münsterberg, H. (1908). *On the witness stand: Essays on psychology and crime.* New York: Doubleday, Page.

Münsterberg, H. (1909a). *Psychotherapy.* New York: Moffat, Yard.

Münsterberg, H. (1909b, November). Psychology and the market. *McClure's Magazine, 34,* 87–93.

Münsterberg, H. (1909c). *Psychology and the teacher.* New York: D. Appleton.

Münsterberg, H. (1913a). Letter to Doubleday Page, September 27, 1913, Münsterberg Papers, Boston Public Library.

Münsterberg, H. (1913b). *Psychology and industrial efficiency*. Boston: Houghton-Mifflin.

Münsterberg, H. (1915). *Business psychology*. Chicago: Lasalle Extension Service.

Münsterberg, H. (1916). *The photoplay: A psychological study*. New York: D. Appleton.

Münsterberg, M. (1922). *Hugo Münsterberg: His life and work*. New York: D. Appleton.

Nichols, H. (1893, October). The psychological laboratory at Harvard. *McClure's Magazine, 1,* 399–409.

Spillmann, J., & Spillmann, L. (1993). The rise and fall of Hugo Münsterberg. *Journal of the History of the Behavioral Sciences, 29,* 322–338.

Viteles, M. S. (1932). *Industrial psychology*. New York: W. W. Norton.

Chapter 8

Lewis Terman: Scientist of Mental Measurement and Product of His Time

Jennifer Randall Crosby and Albert H. Hastorf

> It is not an easy task to give an accurate account of the influences which have worked together to give direction to one's interests and to determine the nature of one's professional output. As a more or less desultory student of biography, I have been much impressed by the daring that biographical writers have shown in their attempts to psychoanalyze the characters and careers of their subjects. (Terman, 1961, p. 297)

We will not attempt to psychoanalyze the life and work of Lewis Terman, but we will endeavor to trace his life, from his Indiana farm roots through his career, chronicling a variety topics, some of which might easily be excerpts from the tables of contents of psychology's journals at the beginning of the 21st century—the contributions of nature and nurture to intelligence, fairness in testing, sex differences in ability, and the constancy of the IQ. Charting such a course presents a challenge. As Terman himself observed, one's knowledge of the final outcome almost certainly biases the moments chosen as significant in one's past: "Memory of a given period of one's life is selective; what finally survives is determined partly by the nature of the events which follow" (1961, p. 297). We proceed, then, with an awareness of the biases inherent in examining a life with the benefit of hindsight.

Terman presents a biographer with a daunting array of apparent contradictions: He considered himself politically liberal, but he advocated eugenics. He recognized the unequal opportunities created by racism and sexism, but he often perpetuated biased views in his work and professional life. He recognized

---

*Photo of Lewis Terman courtesy of Stanford University Archives.

the role that environment played in his own life, but he adhered to a strongly hereditarian position in his views of intelligence. As a mentor, he served as a constructive critic, but he could not tolerate criticism of his own work. It is only by unraveling these contradictions, coupled with an understanding of Terman's deeply held belief in the power of quantitative methods to create a meritocratic society that we can begin to understand Terman as a person and as a scientist.

EARLY LIFE AND CAREER

Terman's roots were humble. He was born in Johnson County, Indiana, in 1877. As he pointed out, there was little in his background to suggest more in his future than a life as a farmer or schoolteacher. Even though we are reminded of Terman's caution to biographers—that history can be rewritten in hindsight—there are anecdotes in his early life that seem to us to suggest his future directions. Anticipating his interest in giftedness, Terman's autobiography describes a childhood fascination with children of unusual abilities or disabilities: a talented liar, a feeble-minded student, a "lightning calculator" (Terman, 1961, p. 300). Forecasting his contributions to the field of testing, he ran "introspective" psychological tests on himself (Minton, 1988, p. 7). Exercising what was to become his habitual style of work, he learned entire textbooks by heart, including footnotes (Terman, 1961, p. 301).

Education

Among the forces that drove Terman (1961, p. 302) toward an academic life was the perception that the one path out of a future of "forever ploughing the same fields" was teaching. In the hope of qualifying for such a career, he left home in 1892 for Central Normal College in Danville, Indiana. For five years Terman studied there for periods of 18 to 40 weeks and taught in the intervening periods, earning a BS, a BPd (Bachelor of Pedagogy), and finally an AB. Terman spoke fondly of his time at CNC and had great admiration for his teachers at that institution (1961, p. 306). He followed his normal college training with a stint as principal of a high school and, in 1901, borrowed money to attend Indiana University. It was there that Terman "became fired with the ambition to become professor of psychology and contribute something of [himself to that] science" (1961, p. 310). Hints as to the nature of that later contribution can be found in the seminar papers he wrote there on "Degeneracy" and "The Great Man Theory."

In 1903, Terman began graduate work at Clark University, which he called "the American Mecca for aspiring young psychologists" (1961, p. 312). He described the intellectual freedom of the university fondly, and saw it as crucial to his development as a scholar. In the German tradition, the University requirements were kept to a minimum, and students were encouraged to follow their own interests rather than a prescribed course of study—an arrangement that suited Terman's preferences. Terman asserted that he "never worked well under the restraint of rules and regulations," and that he found the environment at Clark ideally suited to his needs and temperament (1961, p. 314). G. Stanley Hall's Monday night seminar series was particularly crucial to his intellectual development. Terman's autobiography contains an almost breathless description of this series and its effect on him (1961, pp. 316–317). According to Terman "the Clark period was even richer in experience and stimulation than I expected" (1961, p. 320).

While at Clark, Terman's interest in gifted and "defective" children grew into an interest in mental testing. When he announced his decision to pursue this field to Hall, Hall "expressed very emphatically his disapproval of mental tests, but, finding that [Terman's] mind was made up, he finally gave [him] his blessing and some advice on the danger of being misled by the quasi-exactness of quantitative methods" (Terman, 1961, p. 318). Terman's thesis project dealt with the psychology of "bright and dull" children, and focused on the tests that might differentiate between them.

Academic Life

In his autobiography, Terman described the years following his time at Clark as "the fallow period" in his life. He was troubled by "mildly active tuberculosis" and chose positions in California in the interest of his health. He spent a year as a school principal in San Bernardino, California, followed by four years as a professor of child study and pedagogy at Los Angeles State Normal School (now California State University at Los Angeles). In 1910, Terman accepted a position in the School of Education at Stanford University, an appointment that he described as coming at an ideal time in his life and career (1961, p. 309). Later on at Stanford, Terman served as chair of the psychology department for two decades. He remained there until his death in 1956.

RESEARCH ON TESTING

On the advice of E. B. Huey, a Clark colleague and fellow advocate of testing, Terman (1961, p. 323) began revising Binet and Simon's 1908 intelligence scale. In his first volume of gifted studies, Terman stated "the importance of Binet's work for later studies of intelligence can hardly be overestimated" (1925, p. 1). In undertaking to bring Binet and Simon's work to the United States, Terman went beyond simple translation and performed extensive revisions on the test, both in the content and in the age norms. The first "Stanford Revision" was published in 1912 (Terman & Childs, 1912) and was finalized in 1915 (Terman et al., 1915). It came to be known as the Stanford–Binet (Minton, 1988, pp. 47–50). In response to problems with the 1915 scale, Terman undertook a series of revisions of the Stanford–Binet beginning in 1927.

Throughout the 10-year process of revision, Terman worked closely with Maude Merrill, who eventually became codirector of the project. The first revision addressed issues of standardization and validity, enlarged the range of the scale to include younger children and above-average adults, and provided two alternate test forms (labeled "L" for Lewis Terman and "M" for Maude Merrill) to reduce coaching and practice effects and to provide a powerful (alternate-forms) measure of the reliability of the scores obtained on the test. This well-received revision was published in 1937 (Terman & Merrill, 1937).

In 1917, Robert M. Yerkes (chap. 7, *Pioneers II*) invited Terman to join a small group of psychologists in designing a test for use by the U.S. Army in World War I. The significance of Terman's involvement in this project was two-fold: First, it provided him with a far larger and more representative sample to test than he would ever have access to among California schoolchildren—1.75 million men were tested (Minton, 1988, p. 71), although the testing conditions were far from ideal and discrepancies between Army data and Stanford–Binet data would help fuel testing critics (see Gould, 1996, and Lippman, 1922a, 1922b, 1922c, 1922d, 1923). Second, Terman's involvement with the creation of the Army test brought him into the fold of mainstream psychology. Before this time, Terman considered himself outside that fold. According to his biographer, Sea-goe (1975), "In his early years, he had felt like an outcast among psychologists because of his practical point of view and his orientation towards education" (p. 112). One result of this sense of alienation was that Terman did not belong to any of the professional psychological organizations. Immediately following his work with Yerkes, then president of the American Psychology Association (APA), however, he became a member of the APA and was elected president in 1923.

Throughout his work on a variety of tests (the Stanford–Binet, Stanford Achievement Test, Army Alpha, etc.) Terman maintained a faith in testing and test development. In his autobiography, he predicted

that mental testing is in its merest infancy and will develop to a lusty maturity within the next half-century; that its developments will include improved tests of general intelligence (in the reality of which I believe), tests of many kinds of special ability, and tests of personality traits which no one has yet even thought of measuring;

That within a few score years school children from the kindergarten to the university will be subjected to several times as many hours of testing as would now be thought reasonable;

That educational and vocational guidance will be based chiefly on test ratings. . . .
That it will some day be possible to identify, largely by means of tests, the pre-delinquent and the pre-psychotic, and that effective preventive methods will result from this advance;

That matrimonial clinics will become common and that couples in large numbers will subject themselves to extensive batteries of ability, personality, interest, and compatibility tests before deciding to embark together. (1961, p. 329)

Some of these predictions, such as the enormous number of hours dedicated to testing in kindergarten through college, have come to pass, whereas others, such as matrimonial testing clinics, remain largely unrealized. In this early segment of his career, Terman had no awareness of the criticism and controversy that, later on, would surround the testing movement and the tests in which he so ardently believed.

In his devotion to the quantification of human traits, intelligence in particular, Terman maintained an enduring faith in three principles: (a) that IQ tests measure a construct with physical reality, (b) that intelligence is largely of genetic origin, and (c) that intelligence is stable over time, despite environmental interventions. These principles drew criticism from Terman's contemporaries and conflict with our current understanding of the interplay between heredity and environment. But, for better or for worse, they were the bases on which Terman's belief in the validity of intelligence testing rested. They represent the foundation of his development of the Stanford–Binet Intelligence Scale. That test was Terman's most significant contribution to psychology and society. He gave the inherently fuzzy concept of intelligence a respectable measurability and made IQ a part of the general public's vocabulary.

THE GIFTED STUDY: "GENETIC STUDIES OF GENIUS"

Terman's other most significant contribution to psychology lies in his study of intellectually gifted adolescents, in which he created one of the richest longitudinal data sets in existence. The Terman "gifted study," as it is commonly known, began in 1911 in an effort to evaluate "the supposed evils of precocity" (Terman, 1925, p. 3). From 1913 to 1919, Terman systematically assembled a pool of participants in the study and refined his testing materials. In 1921, he received a grant from the Commonwealth Fund to follow 1000 precocious youngsters for ten years.

The youngsters who participated in the study came from schools in all of the major metropolitan areas of California. Teachers nominated from one to three students from their classrooms for inclusion in the study. The nominated students were then tested, and those with IQs of 140 or higher were selected for participation. By 1924, there were 1528 participants in Terman's group. For each selected child, Terman obtained the following information: scores on two intelligence tests; scores on the Stanford Achievement Test; a measure of general knowledge of science, history, literature, and the arts; a measure of knowledge of and interest in games; the information provided by an interest blank completed by the children; a two-month record of their reading completed by the children; a home information blank completed by the parents; a school information blank completed by the teachers; and, in some cases, home ratings on a standardized scale made by trained social workers (Terman, 1925, pp. 7–8).

Aims and Outcomes

When Terman began this study, his goals were modest: (a) to show that gifted children are not, as commonly thought, likely to "burn out" early or to show evidence of peculiarities or weaknesses of constitution, and (b) to demonstrate the constancy of their high IQs over time. From the earliest measures, it was clear that the gifted sample disproved the commonly held conception that youngsters who showed intellectual promise are somehow deficient in other ways. Terman's research participants had above-average physical health, an eager interest in games and play, and well-adjusted social behavior (Terman, 1925). In addition, follow-ups over time cast doubt on the notion that they would soon burn out and fail to maintain the promise of their youth. Many of the Terman participants went on to outstanding careers in academia, business, and the professions and, regardless of career path, seemed to retain their intellectual abilities (Terman & Oden, 1959, pp. 143–144).

As the gifted study progressed, Terman's research goals broadened, and his attention turned to a wide variety of other questions that might be answered by such a rich data set. He examined the personality characteristics that might differentiate the higher achievers in the group from the lowest achieving, and found positive correlations between achievement and persistence, integration toward goals, self-confidence, and freedom from inferiority feelings (Terman & Oden, 1959, pp. 148–149). Although these correlations cannot determine whether such traits produced or were produced by high achievement, Terman recognized that intellectual giftedness alone did not guarantee future success.

Descriptive—But Not Theoretical—Value of the Data

As Boring (1959) noted, "Terman's forte was description" (p. 432). In the gifted study, a great many variables were measured and followed over time, but Terman did not set out with a particular hypothesis, nor did he introduce any experimental conditions. He appears to use "experimental" and "control" group designations interchangeably with "selected" and "unselected" participants (see Terman, 1925). Thus the study provided (indeed, continues to provide) unique insight into the life course of intellectually gifted children, but very few definitive conclusions can be drawn from the data. Although Terman argued that these data provide evidence of the genetic nature of intelligence, his reasoning was sometimes faulty. For example, he argued that his participants seemed to exhibit "superior heredity" because their parents' socioeconomic status, income, and occupational achievement were higher than those of unselected students (Terman, 1925, p. 83), apparently failing to recognize that all these factors might contribute to a richer environment in which intelligence can blossom. Paradoxically, Terman acknowledged that the above-average physical health of his participants might be caused by the superior diet and medical care provided by higher economic status (Terman, 1925, p. 634), but he did not allow for the same possibility in the realm of intelligence.

ADDITIONAL RESEARCH DIRECTIONS

Although Terman is most closely associated with mental tests and the study of the gifted, he himself saw his work on sex roles as an equally important contribution: "If I am remembered very long after my death, it will probably be in connection with my studies of gifted children, the construction of mental tests, and the psychology of sex differences" (Terman, 1961, p. 328). With his gifted children and with other samples (such as gay men in the San Francisco Bay area), Terman concerned himself with the nature of sex differences, the determinants of homosexuality, factors in marital happiness, and sexual behavior. He and his collaborator, Catherine Cox Miles, described their research on masculinity and femininity in 1936, but were disappointed in the reception received by the volume by both professional and popular audiences. As Boring (1959) pointed out, "The results are characteristic of all of Terman's work, a mass of facts with no simple general theory emerging" (p. 434). Similarly, Terman's work on marital happiness, published in 1938, produced several useful insights (e.g., the greater importance of personal dispositions than sexual relations or differences in age and education in determining marital happiness), but it fell short of satisfying Terman's expectations (Boring, 1959, p. 435).

Terman retired from teaching in 1942, in good health and eager to continue his research. His plans were delayed, however, by a recurrence of the tuberculosis that had plagued him all his life, as well as burns from an accidental house fire. It was four years before he could return to work (see Minton, 1988, pp. 213–216). In 1946, Terman resumed his work, following up his gifted children (now middle-aged; Terman & Oden, 1947) and also publishing (Terman, 1948) a critique of Alfred Kinsey's 1948 study of sexual behavior. He continued to be active in writing and research until 1955, when he was again plagued by health problems. Terman died of a cerebral hemorrhage on December 21, 1956. At his request, there were no funeral services. Instead, a conference on gifted children was held in Terman's honor in 1957.

TERMAN AS SCIENTIST AND INDIVIDUAL: QUANTIFICATION AND CONTRADICTION

Terman has been hailed and vilified, throughout his life and in the decades since his death. One way to understand the variety and depth of feeling that Terman elicited—and continues to elicit—among lay persons, psychologists, and educators—is to examine a set of contradictions that existed in his life and work. In doing so, we may see how both Terman's supporters and detractors could have found fuel for their positions.

Environment Versus Heredity

As Terman examined his own life (Terman, 1961), he was quick to point out the ways in which circumstances were his benefactor at several crucial moments of his life. In his autobiography, he stated, "I know of nothing in my ancestry that would have led anyone to predict for me an intellectual career" (p. 298). Instead, he attributed the decision to follow such a career to several unplanned happenings: a chance interaction with a phrenologist, which led him to set more ambitious goals for himself (p. 303), his introduction to psychology at a "psychologically favorable time in [his] life" (p. 309), his hasty choice of a position in California instead of Florida (p. 322), and the series of coincidences that led him to Stanford, one of the turning points of his career (p. 323).

Yet for all of his acknowledgment of the role of environmental factors in his own life, Terman's views of intelligence and achievement emphasized heredity and stability and, like those of many psychologists in his time, left little room for the influence of the environment or circumstances. This passage from *Genetic Studies of Genius* expresses Terman's view:

> *Our data show that individuals of the various social classes present these same differences in early childhood, a fact which strongly suggests that the causal factor lies in the original endowment rather than the environmental influences.* (Terman, 1925, p. 66, emphasis in the original)

It occurs to us that the contradiction between Terman's explanations for the outcomes in his own life and career and his position on the determination of intelligence is an illustration of Jones and Nisbett's (1971) theory of actor–observer bias, a tendency of all people to attribute their own behavior to external situations, while at the same time attributing that of others to internal traits of character. We explain our own successes and shortcomings by environmental circumstances (we were late because of heavy traffic, short-tempered because of a hectic day, high achieving because of an outstanding teacher) but we attribute the accomplishments and failures of others to their personal characteristics (they were late because of unreliability, short-tempered because of grouchiness, high achieving because of genetic endowment). And in the process, there is a remarkable failure to see the incompatibility of the two types of attribution. Similarly, although Terman recognized the importance of (even accidental) environmental influences in determining the course of his own life and career, he placed responsibility for the accomplishments and failures of others entirely in their genes, without recognizing the conflict inherent in these two explanations.

Sociopolitical Views

A second contradiction, less easily explained by modern social psychology, is an apparent split between Terman's perception of himself as a political liberal and his endorsement of eugenic policies. As evidence of his liberalism, Terman argued against American isolationism in World War II and against McCarthy's anticommunist "witch hunts" in the 1950s. He was a vocal proponent of U.S. efforts to stop the spread of Nazism. He publicly opposed Stanford president Ray Wilbur and former U.S. president Herbert Hoover in their isolationist perspectives (Seagoe, 1975, pp. 150–162). He opposed the loyalty oath that University of California professors were required to sign in the early 1950s, supporting psychologist Edward C. Tolman's refusal to sign the loyalty oath, an act that led to Tolman's dismissal from the University of California at Berkeley (Minton, 1988, pp. 240–241). He was "disconcerted" when he was described as politically conservative in a thesis by Nicholas Pastore on the relationship between views on heredity and political affiliations (Minton, 1988, p. 235).

Yet at the same time Terman took a position on eugenics that could hardly be described as liberal. His belief in the biological nature of the IQ extended to the belief that the racial and ethnic differences measured by IQ tests reveal genuine differences in the innate capacities of individuals of different races. He asserted,

> It can not be disputed, however, that in the long run it is the races which excel in abstract thinking that eat while others starve. . . . The races which excel in conceptual thinking could, if they wished, quickly exterminate or enslave all the races notably their inferiors in this respect. (Terman, 1922, p. 118)

Terman maintained affiliations with eugenics groups such as the Advisory Council of the Eugenics Committee of the United States of America (later the American Eugenics Society) and the Human Betterment Foundation (later the Institute of Family Relations; Minton, 1988, pp. 148–149) and strongly supported "curtailing reproduction of feeble-mindedness" (Terman, 1916, pp. 6–7). In his reply to Walter Lippmann, Terman (1922) praised the intelligence-testing practices of Germany (p. 117) and, in his predictions regarding the future of testing, he asserted,

> That the major differences between children of high and low IQ, and the major differences in the intelligence test scores of certain races, as Negroes and whites, will never be fully accounted for in the environmental hypothesis. (1961, p. 329)

Terman's ties to eugenics organizations diminished as eugenics came to be associated with Nazi practices in the 1930s, although as late as 1938 he still supported the Institute of Family Relations in its sterilization research and propaganda (Minton, 1988, p. 149). It was not until much later in his life that his views on race and intelligence seem to have changed. In a note next to the preceding quote from his autobiography, Terman wrote that he was "less sure of this" in 1951 and "still less sure" in 1955 (Hilgard, 1957, p. 478).

In a related contradiction, Terman was keenly aware of the prejudices encountered by minority groups. For example, he attempted to bring Kurt Lewin (chap. 7, *Pioneers III*) to Stanford to secure Lewin's academic career outside of Nazi Germany. In addition, he was often angered by the sexism encountered by female academics, recognizing that they would receive wider acclaim if they were male. Seagoe mentioned that Terman "was especially helpful to female psychologists, for he felt they got the short end of things all along, from admission through graduate work and finding a position, to earning awards and offices" (Seagoe, 1975, p. 137).

Yet Terman often furthered these same stereotypes, both explicitly and implicitly. Although he was able to see some Jews as "exceptions" to the usual stereotypes, he held that most Jews were not free of "objectionable" traits, and used "Jewish" as a synonym for "shrewd" on the Stanford–Binet test. Further, Terman often perpetrated sexist ideas, normative at the time, of women's achievement in his own family (Minton, 1988, p. 250) and in his research. In explaining the increased proportion of males among his gifted sample as they reached high school, he asserted that "gifted girls do not maintain their intellectual superiority in adolescence as well as boys do" and that girls have "an earlier cessation of mental growth" (Burks, Jensen, & Terman, 1930, p. 161). Finally, Terman's interpretation of his own work on masculinity and femininity, as well as his critique of Kinsey's study on sexual behavior, demonstrated an adherence to the stereotypes about homosexuality common in Terman's day, despite the fact that Terman often served as a confidant for many of his gifted homosexual research participants (Minton, 1988, pp. 174–176, 228–232).

Dealing with Criticism

Another arena in which we see conflicting sides of Terman's character is in his relationship to criticism. Terman was a valuable and respected mentor to his students, to whom he always could be counted on to give honest, constructive criticism (Minton, 1988, p. 237), yet he seemed unable to tolerate criticism of his own contributions. For example, in reacting to the suggestion that there may be multiple intelligences that may all be equally valuable, Terman, as was his wont, took this as criticism of his own position and asserted, "It is difficult to argue with anyone whose sense of psychological values is disturbed to this extent" (1921, p. 128). When Lippmann (1922a, 1922b, 1922c, 1922d, 1923) published a series of critiques of Terman's work in the *New Republic*, Terman responded with articles that were sarcastic, personal attacks on Lippman. Instead of arguing with Lippman's interpretation of the data, he stated, "The validity of intelligence tests is hardly a question the psychologist would care to debate with Mr. Lippmann" (1922, p. 117).

It is not surprising that Terman's reply to Lippmann failed to satisfy the critics of mental testing. In the *Journal of Educational Research*, William C. Bagley (1922) criticized Terman's reply to Lippman, and, like Lippman, found evidence of environmental influences on intelligence in Terman's own data, pointing out that the most advanced nations are also those that supply universal education, that measured intelligence correlates with amount of time in school, and that performance on the Army intelligence tests correlates with the quality of educational facilities in the recruits' home states (pp. 375–377). Again, Terman avoided debating the merits of the data and dismissed Bagley as sentimental and unscientific (Minton, 1988, p. 105).

In 1940, George O. Stoddard and his colleagues at the University of Iowa, including Beth Wellman, undertook a study (Stoddard & Wellman, 1940; Wellman, 1940) to demonstrate that the IQ could be elevated through stimulating environmental influence. Terman seems to have taken this study as a direct attack on his own work, and he responded with force. He called on his junior colleague Quinn McNemar to issue a scathing critique of the work and tried to prevent the Iowa project from receiving publicity and funding. At Stanford, Terman engineered a conference in which he used his time as featured speaker to attack Stoddard's work, allowing Stoddard only 10 minutes to assert his own position (Minton, 1988, pp. 191–201).

Value of Unbiased Empiricism

In a final contradiction, although Terman valued unbiased quantitative methods above all else, he was occasionally guilty of biased interpretation of his own results. As Minton (1988) pointed out, the designs of Terman's studies and his interpretations often incorporated his own biases regarding race, sex, and class:

In reporting his results, Terman was generally able to confirm the expectations he had started with. He did have confirmatory evidence; but his interpretations contained biases, most notably with regard to class and sex. His hereditarian assumptions led him to neglect the intricate ways in which culture worked. Thus, he seemed insensitive to conditions that might exclude lower-class youngsters from a study of gifted children. Furthermore, he failed to consider the kinds of social pressures that might impede bright adolescent girls from excelling in the same way as their male peers. (p. 143)

In addition, several of Terman's actions in his study of gifted individuals, although motivated by no obvious biases, may have affected the results. Terman's communications with participants and their parents may have promoted the Pygmalion Effect described by Rosenthal and Jacobson (1968), whereby students for whom we have high expectations seem to rise to those expectations. Parents and teachers were aware that children were selected for the gifted study on the basis of perceived "genius." The impact of this information on the opportunities given to participants who were selected cannot be known, but it may have been significant. Further, in his early reports to parents, Terman advised parents to determine for themselves whether the students actually possessed any of the negative qualities attributed to them by teachers, and if they did to "undertake special training" to better them (1925, p. 13).

In contrast to these lapses into subjectivity, Terman devoted his career to the exhaustive quantitative analysis of every topic he pursued. In his research on testing, gifted individuals, gender, and marital happiness, he devoted himself to an unbiased assessment of the data at hand. Partly on this account, Terman has been criticized for amassing data without a guiding theory, and Terman himself admitted to this lack of theory, perhaps seeing it as allowing him to view his work objectively. He wrote, "I am in no sense a philosopher, and lord knows that as a psychologist I am not outstanding for either scholarship or originality," and "In all my books I have stuck pretty close to the data. . . . I guess I just don't have a theoretical mind" (letters to Boring, 1953 and 1955, cited in Minton, 1988, p. 243). This quantitative, data-oriented approach characterized Terman's work throughout his career.

EVALUATION AND LEGACY

With the contradictions evident in his life, the occasional shortcomings in his work, and the controversies that have persisted even after his death, what judgment are we to make about Terman's contributions to psychology? As Robert S. Woodworth (1942) wrote in his introduction to a volume of research papers dedicated to Terman on his retirement: "No one can say that Terman picked out easy tasks, and no one can deny that he has succeeded nobly in his early ambition to establish a direct relation between scientific psychology and the life of the people. He is truly to be numbered among the pioneers, whose example is an inspiration to the younger generation and whose work and influence will long endure" (1942. p. 11).

A Conspicuous Success

Perhaps Terman's most complete success was a major task he undertook outside research, building the department of psychology at Stanford. Terman went to great lengths to attract to Stanford the most promising faculty available, often seeking counsel from colleagues such as Boring and Yerkes on the strengths of various candidates. "He wanted the best in his appointments; his tolerant appreciation of scholarship and his zeal for excellence drew such men to him, and then his permissive democracy led them to flower" (Seagoe, 1975, p. 110).

Terman endeavored to create Stanford's department in the image of the Clark department of Terman's graduate school days. The German philosophy of intellectual independence prevailed, and Terman supported complete academic freedom. Terman was also described as a "revered mentor," and worked tirelessly to help secure the most prestigious positions possible for those whom he took under his wing (Minton, 1988, pp. 211–213, 259). In his autobiography, Terman commented, "Although I dislike doing work of an administrative nature, I think that nothing I have accomplished has given me a stronger or juster sense of pride than my part in helping to build up an outstanding department at Stanford" (1961, p. 326).

By all accounts, Terman's pride was well-founded. His efforts to secure financial support for large, long-term projects was unparalleled. His colleague Ernest Hilgard described him as a "remarkable head" (Minton, 1988, p. 211), and he built the Stanford department of psychology from an undistinguished one to one that many rankings call the best in this country (Seagoe, 1975, p. 111).

Impact on Gifted Education

Another of Terman's great successes was in the singular role he played in drawing attention to gifted individuals, and advocating enhanced educational opportunities for them. Gifted education programs, advanced placements classes, and magnet schools all owe a debt to Terman's efforts. According to Terman's biographer Minton,

> Terman deserves to be credited with pioneering an ambitious and thorough study of children with high ability. In terms of the amount of data generated, the sample size, the financial and staff support, and [its now over 60-year duration, it] represents the longest developmental investigation ever attempted, [and] ranks as a seminal longitudinal study. (1988, p. 225)

Robert Sears (1957), himself a participant in the gifted study and Terman's Stanford colleague, provided the following evaluation of the gifted study: "The social importance of this study . . . cannot be overestimated. In the field of education, it has given great impetus to the discovery and maximization of talent" (p. 979).

Indeed, Terman's work has allowed countless gifted individuals to be exposed to intellectual opportunities and challenges they would not have had if they had not been identified by Terman's tests. As Terman predicted, testing plays a greater role in the lives of all individuals than would have been imaginable before his time. A Ford Foundation study estimated that $100 million tax dollars and 20 million school days have been spent on standardized testing across the United States each year (cited in Steele, 1994). Terman's own tests (Stanford Binet and Stanford Achievement Test) continue to be used, and countless other tests have been created to sort individuals on a vast array of dimensions. Terman's dream of testing and identifying each individual's potential and "tracking" each individual into appropriate educational and vocational opportunities has largely come to pass. In fact, Terman's adherence to the power of tests continues to affect the structure of work and education, the expectations of educators, and the opportunities afforded all individuals.

Conflict and Controversy

As we have seen, throughout his life Terman's views were the center of controversy. What led Terman to these controversial positions appears to have been his faith in quantitative psychometric methods. Terman's mentor, G. Stanley Hall, once cautioned Terman "on the danger of being misled by the quasi-exactness of quantitative methods" (Terman, 1961, p. 318), and this warning does seem prescient. Enamored as he was of quantitative methods, Terman often failed to recognize the larger issues at work in his choice of research questions and in his interpretations of his results. For example, in his adherence to a primarily biological interpretation of test scores, Terman helped create an environment in which testing and the interpretation of individual differences cannot be disentangled from heredity, class, and race. Debates regarding the relative roles of heredity and environment in determining intelligence continue to rage (Fischer, Hout, Jankowski, & Swidler, 1996; Herrnstein & Murray, 1996), as do debates regarding the value of grouping individuals by tested ability (Oakes, 1985) and the relationship among test scores, achievement, and race (Bowen & Bok, 1998).

CONCLUSION

We often expect great scientists to be ahead of their times, but Terman was a scientist firmly planted in his own era. With his faith in the science of individual differences and the power of quantification to engineer social change, Terman represents a model of post-World War I enthusiasm for social engineering (Minton, 1988, p. 238). As Cravens (1992) described, Terman's work was "locked in time"—understandable only in the context in which it was created.

In Terman's day, the idea of using tests for the betterment of society, even creating a government managed by people with the necessary talents, as revealed by their scores on those tests —a "meritocracy"—seemed a noble and achievable goal (see Young, 1958). Looking back on those days, Boring (1959) put Terman's position in a light that is charitable and also realistic:

> Some persons, noting that he tended to believe in an hereditary intellectual elite, wonder how such an undemocratic view could be held by this tender-minded, sensitive, ambitious person, but the fact is that Terman thought of the intellectually elite as those who would save civilization for democracy. The gifted were given. You do not choose to have them, for they are there, whether you will or no. You can, however, choose to separate them from the crowd so that they may be trained to devote their special talents to benefit the crowd from which they have been taken. (p. 440)

These views belong squarely in a time in which political liberalism was not antithetical to hereditary views of individual differences, and in which an understanding of the consequences of racial biases did not preclude an endorsement of those same biases. As Cravens commented,

> One can extract from the corpus of Terman's work the answers he and his co-workers derived to many questions, but the questions themselves and the larger assumptions that undergirded them will not in almost any conceivable instance transfer from one age to another without becoming subtly but powerfully distorted beyond sensible recognition. (1992, p. 188)

Thus Terman, with his absolute faith in quantification and his many contradictions, was thoroughly a product of his time. Yet as Woodworth (1942) foresaw, "his influence will long endure" (p. 11).

REFERENCES

Bagley, W. C. (1922). Professor Terman's determinism: A rejoinder. *Journal of Educational Research, 6*, 371–385.

Binet, A., & Simon, T. (1908). Le développement de l'intelligence chez les enfants [The development of intelligence in children]. *L'Annee Psychologie, 14*, 1–94.

Boring, E. G. (1959). Lewis Madison Terman: 1877–1956. In *National Academy of Sciences Biographical Memoirs* (Vol. 33, pp. 414–461). New York: Columbia University Press.

Bowen, W. G., & Bok, D. (1998). *The shape of the river*. Princeton, NJ: Princeton University Press.

Burks, B. S., Jensen, D. W., & Terman, L. M. (1930). *The promise of youth: Follow-up studies of a thousand gifted children* (Vol. 3). Stanford, CA: Stanford University Press.

Cravens, H. (1992). A scientific project locked in time: The Terman genetic studies of genius, 1920s–1950s. *American Psychologist, 47,* 183–189.

Fischer, C. S., Hout, M., Jankowski, M. S., & Swidler, A. (1996). *Inequality by design: Cracking the bell curve myth.* Princeton, NJ: Princeton University Press.

Gould, S. J. (1996). *The mismeasure of man.* New York: Norton and Company.

Herrnstein, R. J., & Murray C. (1996). *The bell curve.* New York: Free Press.

Hilgard, E. R. (1957). Lewis Madison Terman. *American Journal of Psychology, 120,* 472–479.

Jones, E. E., & Nisbett, R. E. (1971). The actor and the observer: Divergent perceptions of the causes of behavior. In E. E. Jones, D. E. Kanhouse, H. H. Kelly, R. E. Nisbett, S. Valins, & B. Weiner (Eds.), *Attribution: Perceiving the causes of behavior* (pp. 79–94). Morristown, NJ: General Learning Press.

Lippmann, W. (1922a). The mental age of Americans. *New Republic, 32,* 213–215.

Lippmann, W. (1922b). The mystery of the "A" men. *New Republic, 32,* 246–248.

Lippmann, W. (1922c). The reliability of intelligence tests. *New Republic, 32,* 297–298.

Lippmann, W. (1922d). Tests of heridftary intelligence. *New Republic, 32,* 328–330.

Lippmann, W. (1923). A future for tests. *New Republic, 33,* 9–10.

Minton, H. L. (1988). *Lewis M. Terman: Pioneer in mental testing.* New York: New York University Press.

Oakes, J. (1985). *Keeping track: How schools structure inequality.* New Haven, CT: Yale University Press.

Rosenthal, R., & Jacobson, L. (1968). *Pygmalion in the classroom.* San Francisco: Holt, Rinehart & Winston.

Seagoe, M. V. (1975). *Terman and the gifted.* Los Altos, CA: William Kaufmann.

Sears, R. R. (1957). L. M. Terman, pioneer in mental measurement. *Science, 125,* 978–979.

Steele, D. M. (1994). *Teachers' attitudes regarding standardized tests and retention and promotion practices in kindergarten and first grade.* Unpublished doctoral dissertation, University of Michigan, Ann Arbor.

Stoddard, G. D., & Wellman, B. L. (1940). Environment and the IQ. *Yearbook of National Social Studies in Education, Part I, 39,* 504–542.

Terman, L. M. (1916). *The measurement of intelligence.* Boston: Houghton Mifflin.

Terman, L. M. (1921). Intelligence and its measurement: A symposium. *Journal of Educational Psychology, 8,* 127–133.

Terman, L. M. (1922). The great conspiracy on the impulse imperious of intelligence tests. *New Republic, 33,* 116–120.

Terman, L. M. (1925). *Genetic studies of genius, Volume I: Mental and physical traits of a thousand gifted children.* Stanford, CA: Stanford University Press.

Terman, L. M. (1948). Kinsey's 'Sexual behavior in the human male': Some comments and criticisms. *Psychological Bulletin, 45,* 443–459.

Terman, L. M. (1961). Trails to psychology. In C. Murchinson (Ed.), *A history of psychology in autobiography* (Vol. II, pp. 297–331). New York: Russell and Russell.

Terman, L. M., & Childs, H. G. (1912). A tentative revision and extension of the Binet-Simon measuring scale of intelligence. *Journal of Educational Psychology, 3,* 61–74, 133–143, 198–208, 277–289.

Terman, L. M., Lyman, G., Ordahl, G., Ordahl, L., Galbreath, N., & Talbert, W. (1915). The Stanford revision of the Binet-Simon scale and some results from its application to 1000 non-selected children. *Journal of Educational Psychology, 6,* 551–562.

Terman, L. M., & Merrill, M. A. (1937). *Revised Stanford-Binet scale.* Boston: Houghton Mifflin.

Terman, L. M., & Miles, C. C. (1936). *Sex and personality: Studies in masculinity and femininity.* New York: McGraw-Hill.

Terman, L. M., & Oden, M. H. (1947). *The gifted child grows up: Vol. 4.* Stanford, CA: Stanford University Press.

Terman, L. M., & Oden, M. H. (1959). *The gifted group at mid-life: Thirty five years' follow-up of the superior child.* Stanford, CA: Stanford University Press.

Wellman, B. L. (1940). Iowa studies on the effects of schooling. *Yearbook of National Social Science Studies in Education, Part II, 39,* 377–399.

Woodworth, R. S. (1942). Introduction. In Q. McNemar & M. A. Merrill (Eds.), *Studies in personality* (pp. 3–11). New York: Russell and Russell.

Young, M. O. (1958). *The rise of the meritocracy 1870–2033: An essay on education and equality.* London: Thames and Hudson.

Chapter 9

Sir Frederic Charles Bartlett:
Experimental and Applied Psychologist

Henry L. Roediger III

Sir Frederic C. Bartlett (1886–1969) is a legendary figure in British psychology. During his lifetime, his thinking affected psychologists around the world. Today he is chiefly remembered for his great book, *Remembering: A Study in Experimental and Social Psychology*, published in 1932. However, as with most great intellectual leaders, his interests and influence were much wider and deeper than reflected in this single work. He made contributions to the study of perceiving, thinking, skilled behavior, fatigue, and other topics. In addition, he helped train a generation or more of British psychologists who became famous in their own right and dominated the field of psychology in all of Great Britain.

At about the time of his death in 1969, Bartlett's ideas about mental life were gaining ascendancy in the cognitive revolution. Indeed, it can be fairly stated that many of the ideas put forward in Ulric Neisser's definitive 1967 text, *Cognitive Psychology*, derived from Bartlett's earlier work. Neisser's book became the rallying cry of the cognitive revolution in psychology, and his debt to Bartlett is clearly stated there.

EARLY LIFE

Bartlett was born October 20, 1886, at Stow-on-the-Wold, a very small country town in Gloucestershire, where his father ran a successful business making shoes and boots. The grammar school (more or less equivalent to a high school in North

---

*Photo of Walter Hunter (chap. 18, *Pioneers I*) and of Sir Frederic Bartlett at Brown University in 1947 courtesy of Gregory A. Kimble.

Quotations from Bartlett 1932 reprinted with the permission of Cambridge University Press.

America) in the town had closed, so his family contemplated sending him to boarding school. This option was closed off, however, by a severe childhood illness at age 14, so Bartlett remained in Stow and had to educate himself, with the help of his family. His father possessed a considerable library, as did a local minister, so Bartlett read voraciously. The decision was later made for him to take a course of study offered by the University College of the University of London, by which he could gain a degree. An offhand suggestion of an acquaintance led him to take logic as one of his subjects. This decision led eventually to his career in psychology. He later noted that "it seems odd that [an] apparently somewhat haphazard remark should have, indirectly, determined all my future, but so it turned out" (Oldfield, 1972, p. 133). Bartlett received an MA from the University of London in 1911, studying ethics and sociology, although he continued to study logic, too.

At this juncture Bartlett began his undergraduate studies anew at Cambridge University, with which he would be affiliated for the rest of his career. There he came under the influence of W. H. R. Rivers, who had just completed an intellectual migration from sensory physiology and psychophysics to anthropology. He led Bartlett to St. Johns College, which encouraged him to take psychology through its fellowship program. He received training in experimental psychology from Cyril Burt and C. S. Myers, although his heart seemed to lie in anthropology. He graduated in 1914 with First Class Honours. Burt was leaving Cambridge, so Myers offered Bartlett the opportunity to continue there and to teach Burt's experimental psychology courses. Bartlett's acceptance kept his primary influence in psychology rather than in anthropology.

WORLD WAR I

After Archduke Ferdinand was shot in 1914 in Sarajevo, World War I broke out and all of England was quickly affected. Normally placid university life was shattered. Most of Bartlett's colleagues at Cambridge enlisted to aid the war effort, but Bartlett's health barred him from doing the same. He remained at Cambridge in charge of the psychological laboratory. In addition to routine chores of teaching during the war, Bartlett began to write up his dissertation work, but much of it was not published until years later, as part of *Remembering (1932)*.

From an early age, Bartlett's career concentrated on practical problems, a focus that led him to study real-world issues. To help the war effort, Bartlett's research in the laboratory concentrated on the processes involved in detecting sounds of weak intensity. This research was relevant to attempts to construct better equipment to monitor German submarines. Later, in 1927, he published a book on *The Psychology of the Soldier*, which had its origins in the concerns that arose during World War I. His collaborator in the work on antisubmarine detection devices was Mary Smith, whom he later married.

THE CAMBRIDGE LABORATORY

After the war, Rivers and Myers returned to Cambridge and rejoined Bartlett. Rivers died suddenly in 1922, however, and Myers retired from academic life in that same year. As a result, Bartlett became director of the psychological laboratory and built it up over the next decades until his retirement from the post in 1952, at age 66.

In the 1920s Bartlett's interests returned to social anthropology and, in 1923, he published *Psychology and Primitive Culture*. Another significant event in this period, the Seventh International Congress of Psychology held at Oxford in 1923, afforded Bartlett the opportunity to make friends with contemporaries from around the world. These included Albert Michotte, Walter Miles, E. G. Boring, Wolfgang Köhler (chap. 17, *Pioneers I*), and Kurt Koffka, among others. By 1930 Bartlett had succeeded in establishing a first-rate program in experimental psychology at Cambridge, and for his efforts he was awarded the position professor of experimental psychology, the first at the university. In addition, during this time, Bartlett was influential in helping to establish psychology as a distinct discipline throughout Great Britain, with many Cambridge students taking posts at other universities when those universities developed their own departments.

A LANDMARK PUBLICATION

Bartlett's great book, *Remembering: A Study in Experimental and Social Psychology*, was published in 1932 when he was 46 years old—in mid-career and already famous. According to its preface, however, the origins of the book dated to 1913, when Bartlett became interested in the problem of the effects of attitudes and values on perceiving objects. Some of the work in the book had appeared in one form or another in previous reports (e.g., Bartlett, 1916, 1928), but the most famous work—on memory—was published in detail for the first time in the book. Although Bartlett was a strong empiricist and skeptical of introspection, the experimental methods in *Remembering* were quite unlike those following in the Ebbinghaus tradition. Ebbinghaus (chap. 4, *Pioneers III*) and his successors (see Münsterberg, chapter 7, this volume) conducted tightly controlled experiments using artificial stimuli (nonsense syllables) and with rigorous testing conditions. Bartlett's methods were casual in the extreme and it may be this feature of his work that caused the book to have relatively little impact on the study of memory for many years. Although the word "experimental" appears in the title of the book, his research was more anecdotal than experimental (Roediger, 1997).

The hallmark of experimental work is manipulating an independent variable and measuring the effects on some dependent variable, with other factors held constant. Bartlett did not conduct this kind of research, but rather tested people under fairly casual conditions, rarely manipulated any variable systematically, and his "data" were the protocols his research participants produced. He never converted the protocols to more systematic measures to which inferential statistics could be applied. He simply illustrated points he wished to make by reference to the protocols, drawing examples from especially apt spots.

Bartlett noted at the outset that he wanted to test people under more natural conditions than was typical of experimental studies of learning and memory and he did. Kintsch (1995), in his foreword to the reprint of *Remembering*, noted that the informal conduct and reporting of the experiments "is the weakest aspect of the book and something that has limited its historical influence" (p. xiv). Putting a more positive spin on this aspect of the work, however, Donald Broadbent (one of Bartlett's students) noted that Bartlett's penchant for expressing his results by "selecting significant incidents which happened during the experiments . . . to illustrate the general truths about the processes of perceiving and remembering . . . places an enormous strain upon the ability of the experimenter to grasp what is truly significant, and in some ways a measure of Bartlett's stature is that nobody seriously questions the factual results of his experiments" (Broadbent, 1970, p. 3). In the years since those in which Bartlett made his major contributions, such questions about his findings have sometimes been raised (e.g., Wynn & Logie, 1998), but Bartlett's basic results can be replicated under more tightly controlled conditions than the ones he used (e.g., Roediger, Bergman, & Meade, 2000; also see Bergman & Roediger, 1999). Despite its experimental limitations, the achievements in *Remembering* were great. The book was wide ranging and reflected Bartlett's interest in perceiving and attention, on the one hand, and in social anthropology and the transmission of culture on the other.

Bartlett devised two primary methods for studying memory. In his most famous work, he asked people to remember a native American folktale, "The War of Ghosts," which is rather disjointed and has supernatural elements unfamiliar to the British participants who served in his studies. He read the story twice and then tested his participants' memory of it. One method of testing was that of serial reproduction. In the serial reproduction technique, a first person recalls the story as well as possible after hearing it twice. Then the second person reads the first person's story twice and, after a period, tries to recall it. A third person reads the story as recalled by the second person and later tries to recall it, and so on, for as many participants as desired. The method of serial reproduction is like the game called telephone or rumor, in which the same method is used. The result is the same, too: Bartlett showed that remarkable transformations of the story (and of other material) occurred as the story was passed through one person's memory to the next person. The participants' errors and omissions cumulated, so that the final story produced by the last person often bore only a faint resemblance to the original. An interesting sidelight to this history (Oldfield, 1972) is that the idea for this method arose in a graduate school conversation between Bartlett and his friend, Norbert Wiener, who was studying philosophy at Cambridge with Bertrand Russell and who later went on to help found the field of cybernetics.

Bartlett (1932) viewed the method of serial reproduction as a way of studying how social memories can change from one person to another over time. Later in the book he endorsed the method as one for studying change in cultures, when some practice becomes changed over time as it is passed from one group to another. More pertinent to the study of individual memory and how it might change over time and repeated retellings is the method of repeated reproduction. In this method, Bartlett again had participants listen to the story twice and recall it 15 minutes later. He did not present the story again. After a period of time, the original participants would recall it again, and then again, with repeated recall sometimes occurring over several sessions. The periods of time between repeated tests varied rather unsystematically from participant to participant. Bartlett reported a number of systematic changes across repeated reproductions of the story: The stories got shorter, they became simpler, many supernatural elements dropped out, and other elements would be reinterpreted. Bartlett coined the term *rationalization* to account for the process responsible for some of these errors. Rationalization meant that "whenever anything appeared incomprehensible, it was either omitted or explained" by adding material (1932, p. 68), and he said that it occurred "in practically every reproduction or series of reproductions" (p. 71). Rationalization occurred over repeated retellings and gradually caused the story "to be robbed of all its surprising, jerky and inconsequential form, and reduced to an orderly narration" (p. 86).

Bartlett emphasized the individual's "effort after meaning" throughout his book. Perceiving involves trying to comprehend the world, and Bartlett published studies in chapter 3 of *Remembering* on this topic, showing that when people glimpsed a painting or other scene very briefly and were instructed to guess what it was, their hypotheses would persist through many successive presentations of the scene, even when the presentations were so long that most people seeing it for the first time would have been able to interpret the scene correctly. Similarly, in repeated retellings with short intervals between tests, the general form of the story would often remain the same, although some details changed. People seemed to be trying to fit the strange story of the ghosts at war into more familiar and comfortable forms. This effort to impose structure caused rememberers to tie together unrelated elements in some cases, and Bartlett emphasized that "the process of fitting is an active process, depending directly upon the preformed tendencies and bias which the subject brings to the task" (1932, p. 85). Indeed, Bartlett wrote, "the most general characteristic of the whole of this group of experiments was the persistence, for any single subject, of the form of his first reproduction," and the use of "a general form, order and arrangement of material seems to be dominant, both in initial reception and in subsequent remembering"

(p. 83). Bartlett called the idea of a "general form" a *schema* (after somewhat different use of the term by his friend, Henry Head, in a 1920 book *Studies in Neurology*).

A schema is the general organization of a story or event. One of Bartlett's key ideas is that, although schemata can aid remembering by providing a coherent form, they can also lead to errors. People "remember," as fact, details consistent with the schema, whether or not those details are accurate. In retelling a story, people rely on the schema and therefore may insert into their accounts details, or even whole episodes, that were not actually in a story but that are consistent with its schema, or general theme.

Both Bartlett's serial reproduction and repeated reproduction studies became famous. Although the former technique produced greater distortion than the latter over repeated reproductions, Bartlett believed the processes involved in producing distortions were similar in the two paradigms. Serial reproduction produced more dramatic change, because the features that different people learning and recounting the story selected formed a chain that was only as strong as its weakest link or links. One person could be wildly off in remembering the previous person's account and thereby undermine any possibility of success in the reports of persons responding later in the chain.

Because Bartlett stressed that inaccuracy in memory is the rule and not the exception, his work is generally mentioned in any discussion of memory errors, false memories, or memory illusions, as these are variously called (e.g., Roediger, 1996; Schacter, 1995). One of Bartlett's key theoretical pronouncements was an argument against the notion that perceiving (or encoding) creates memory traces that are accurate representations of events in the world. Rather, events of the world are recoded [to use a term made popular years later, by Miller (1956)] and this recoding process could introduce errors. Retrieval from memory, then, is not the calling back of perfectly recorded information stored in packets or memory traces, as if examining a videotape of the original event. Rather, remembering is the process of retrieving certain features of the event and, with organization provided by the schema, weaving these into a coherent story that would probably contain truth mixed with falsehood. The individual is unlikely to be able to tell the difference between true and false occurrences, as long as they are consistent with the overall schema. In Bartlett's (1932) words, "Remembering is not the re-excitation of innumerable fixed, lifeless and fragmentary traces" (p. 213). Rather, "remembering appears to be far more decisively an affair of construction rather than mere reproduction" (p. 205). "It is an imaginative reconstruction, or construction, built out of the relation of our attitude towards a mass of organized past reactions or experiences" (p. 213).

The schema theory propounded by Bartlett came in for criticism as being too loose and difficult to test. Bartlett himself worried that it could be said that his "theory after all does very little. It merely jumbles together innumerable traces and calls them 'schemata'" (1932, p. 214). In fact, the criticism of schema theory by others was so frequent and effective that, when Broadbent wrote his obituary of Bartlett in 1970, he would comment that although the concept of schema had "provoked enormous discussion. . . . it is fair to say . . . that this discussion is now dead, and that the term 'schema' appears to have become completely disused" (p. 4). Broadbent goes on to say that the concept of schema was too complex and too vague and that "theoretical concepts of this kind, without public definitions, are almost bound to be self-defeating. Like others of its breed, schema expired unregretted among mutual misunderstanding" (Broadbent, 1970, p. 4).

If ever there was a case of the premature announcement of the death of an idea, this is it. The concept of schema came roaring back, propelled both by cognitive psychologists interested in remembering and by researchers in social cognition and artificial intelligence, who conducted research on packets of knowledge that we all carry about the world with us. These were variously referred to as schemata, scripts, or other names (see Schank & Abelson 1977), but the underlying concept was close to that developed by Bartlett (1932) in *Remembering*. In addition, the original criticisms miss the main point, which is that Bartlett was proposing a radically different theory from the standard trace theory of memory. Instead of viewing memories as static little packets of information in the brain, put there during acquisition and called back in retrieval, Bartlett saw remembering as an active process that is heavily influenced by the individual's current attitudes and thoughts. Perceiving, attending, remembering, and thinking are all intertwined, all constructive, and all involve active processes. The spirit of these ideas was very different from the stimulus–response zeitgeist that dominated psychology in the 1930s through 1960s, so it was probably no accident that Bartlett's great book was "rediscovered" in the late 1960s and early 1970s and has guided research to this day.

The latter part of Bartlett's *Remembering* was on social influences on cognition, on acculturation, and on similar processes. The evidence came from anthropological reports of acculturation in African societies, when they came into contact with the people of the West. The ideas are often interesting but they have not been systematically pursued.

During the late 1930s, Bartlett continued to serve as director of the psychological laboratory, but much of his attention turned again to providing a synthesis of psychology and anthropology, as in evidence in the last chapters of *Remembering*. He worked with sociologists, anthropologists, and other psychologists in meetings held twice a year to try to thrash out common problems and research methods. A book, *The Study of Society: Methods and Problems*, resulted from their efforts in 1939 but it had little impact, because World War II soon consumed people's attention.

WORLD WAR II AND ITS IMPACT

As it became clear that England would be drawn into World War II, psychologists, like others, began to organize to do what they could for the war effort. A brilliant young psychologist named Kenneth Craik had joined the junior research staff at the lab in 1936, and he and Bartlett were to have great mutual influence on one another. As the senior member of the lab, Bartlett was appointed to the Royal Air Force's Flying Personnel Research Committee. Craik was interested in the study of bodily skills and Bartlett had long been interested in such issues, chiefly through his love of skilled sports such as tennis and cricket. Bartlett and Craik teamed together to study the acquisition of skills and how the knowledge gained could be applied in training the bomber and fighter pilots who were holding the Germans at bay. They also studied topics such as the effects of fatigue on performance and other issues, with the lab becoming increasingly large. In 1944 the British Medical Research Council established the famous Applied Psychology Research Unit, usually called the APU, and named Craik its director. The Cambridge psychological lab and the APU greatly aided the British war effort—and the APU was so successful that it continued well after the war. Sadly, Craik died in an automobile accident two days before the end of the war in Europe in 1945. His death was a huge blow to Bartlett, because the two had become best friends as well as close collaborators. Bartlett (1946) wrote a moving obituary notice for Craik.

AFTER WORLD WAR II

Bartlett had been intensely interested in skill during and after the war years. Although he published individual papers and lectures on this topic, he never wrote a treatise on skill. After the war he turned his attention to the important, but difficult, topic of thinking. He had hoped that the methods developed to study remembering would be applicable in this realm, too. But the perspective he took, relying on his more recent interests, was in thinking as skilled behavior. Just as one could run off expert motor skills after much practice, so thinking could be analyzed in similar terms, as processes in solving problems that could become practiced with numerous examples. The approach is again one that seems modern today, as contemporary research on topics such as problem solving and concept learning consider the development of skill from numerous examples of analyzing similar situations as a key process in thinking. Bartlett's book, *Thinking: An Experimental and Social Study (1958)*, has as yet not gained a wide scientific following. If the fate of his book on *Remembering* is any guide, however, *Thinking* may yet have an impact on work in that field.

THE LATER YEARS

Bartlett retired from the chair in experimental psychology at Cambridge and as director of the psychological laboratory in 1952. He maintained his affiliation with the Applied Psychology Unit, which was independent of Cambridge. He also continued to serve on many important committees in which his long experience and keen insight were useful. Many of his students had gone on to great success and fortune and frequently called on him for advice. He could spend his remaining years as the grand elder statesperson of British psychology. Although troubled by hearing loss in his later years, he remained generally robust and healthy. He died at age 82, on September 30, 1969, after a brief illness.

Bartlett was a captivating person and he attracted many outstanding students to work at Cambridge. The list includes Donald Broadbent, Richard Conrad, Richard Gregory, R. Carolus Oldfield, Christopher Poulton, Alan T. Welford, and Oliver Zangwill, among numerous others. These individuals went on to become the next generation of leading psychologists in the United Kingdom and, in the case of Welford, in Australia. These individuals, in turn, have trained many of the current generation of psychologists, so Bartlett's influence continues to the present both in his own scholarly works and in his more indirect influence as a teacher and mentor.

DISCOVERING WHAT BARLETT WAS LIKE

The foregoing provides a sketch of Bartlett's career and contributions, but does not answer the question of what he was actually like as a person and a scientist. Of course, more than 30 years after his death, it is difficult to answer. Many psychologists and students do not leave their impressions of their colleagues and mentors. However, in Bartlett's case some information can be provided. In R. C. Oldfield's obituary (1972), he wrote, "Bartlett's presence was so immediately compelling and impressive that he wielded influence over territory far outside his own academic and scientific pastures" (1972, p. 139). People who knew Bartlett well still found him enigmatic. Sometimes he could be blunt and direct, nearly off-putting. At other times people found his comments so oblique that they would have to reflect before understanding what he meant.

In "A personal homage" to Bartlett, Richard Conrad wrote of his first meeting with Bartlett:

> After the Second World War I wanted to read psychology at Cambridge, and Bartlett invited me to visit the Laboratory. That was the first time I met him. Still in uniform, I sat in his large office where he was reading a book by the gas fire. For an hour he terrorized me with a rich monologue concerned with the futility of my entering on a career in psychology. I listened, fearful and dumb. Suddenly Sir Fred-

eric rose up on his very lengthy legs, shook me warmly by the hand and said he
would be delighted to have me; Bartlett, as I knew him, was warm, generous, simple and talkative. He loved to talk. There was a legend that Norbert Wiener fell
asleep on one occasion, but that was after a long transatlantic flight. He loved to
talk—on any topic—and he talked brilliantly. (1979, p. 159)

Bartlett held a famous seminar that met twice weekly and included faculty,
students, and occasional visiting researchers. The topics were varied and discussion lively. Bartlett was the great presence at these meetings, overseeing them,
commenting on the ideas. The meetings seem to have been both a prime means
of educating the students and of pushing forward the research agenda of the Cambridge laboratory.

People writing about Bartlett's personal qualities often portray him as composed of conflicting dual qualities. Oldfield (1972) wrote that "as a person,
Bartlett could at times appear austere, impassive—even withdrawn. At other
times, and more frequently as he got older, a robust and striking boyish gaiety
would seize him" (p. 139). Conrad wrote of his generosity toward others and
their fondness for him, while commenting, "But he was also authoritarian. He
ran his Laboratory the way he wanted it. He could, and sometimes did, quell
protest with a look; and because he was anything but colorless, he had his detractors" (p. 160).

Bartlett apparently had a forceful, magnetic personality, and was someone of
whom others found themselves in awe. Again, Conrad commented,

What a man he was: what a teacher: what a humble giant. . . . He was honored
everywhere, Greek, Turkish, Egyptian, Italian, American psychology students visiting Cambridge gazed in awe at "Sir Bartlett." Yet for us, his own students, he
was always available, always willing to discuss. . . . He had the gift of appearing
to take you deeply and secretly into his confidence. . . . And he had the *charisma*
of the great. (p. 160)

Broadbent (1970) offered the opinion that Bartlett's great influence on psychology lay more in his personality than in his research and publications:

Bartlett's writings would frankly not explain his extraordinary dominance inside
his profession. . . . His technical writing is obscure, even though shot through with
brilliant observation. It was rather his handling of everyday relations in his department which gave him influence. . . . His weekly lecture-discussions were a fes-
tive performance which nobody would have dreamed of missing. (Broadbent, 1970,
p. 7)

Broadbent maintained that the compelling features of Bartlett's personality,
along with the important lessons he always taught about the importance of empiricism, his willingness to consider ideas on their merit based on evidence, and

his ability to admit past errors were imbued into his students through example and served them in good stead.

ACHIEVEMENTS, HONORS, AND AWARDS

Bartlett's achievements were greatly celebrated during his lifetime. His fame rested both on his great scholarly achievements and perhaps equally on his charisma and his training of many students who went on to greatness themselves. Bartlett was editor of the influential *British Journal of Psychology* from 1924 to 1948 (Bruce, 2000). In the 1930s, Carl Murchison (chap. 11, *Pioneers II*) began editing a series of volumes on *The History of Psychology in Autobiography*, inviting the world's most eminent psychologists to write brief autobiographies for publication. It is worth noting that Bartlett was selected for inclusion in Volume III and that his selection process probably occurred before the publication of *Remembering*, his most influential work. His fame was so great that he received honorary doctoral degrees from seven universities (Athens, Edinburgh, London, Louvain, Oxford, Padua and Princeton). In the United States he was elected to the American Philosophical Society, the National Academy of Sciences, and the American Association of Arts and Sciences. In his homeland, he was a Fellow of the Royal Society of London in 1932 and received its Baly and Huxley Medals in 1943. He was knighted in 1948 and awarded the Royal Medal, the highest distinction a scientist in Britain can receive, in 1952.

CONCLUSION

Bartlett was clearly one of the great psychologists of the 20th century. Conrad (1970, p. 160) said the account of Bartlett's greatness was "simplicity, realism, empiricism." Bartlett could take a broad perspective on human behavior from his training in social anthropology, but he could also use the logic of psychological experimentation. When confronted with the practical difficulties faced by pilots, submariners, and soldiers in two world wars, he could develop concepts of skill, study them, and apply the knowledge gained to practical ends. As with most great historical figures, today he is remembered for only a fraction of his great scholarly work. His study of remembering will certainly be deemed his primary achievement. Therefore, it is fitting to end this chapter with a quote from *Remembering* that captures its main message, the ease with which memory may be led astray:

> The one overwhelming impression produced by this more "realistic" type of memory experiment is that human remembering is normally exceedingly subject to error. It looks as if what is said to be reproduced is, far more generally than is com-

monly admitted, really a construction, serving to justify whatever impression may have been left by the original. It is this "impression," rarely defined as with much exactitude, which most readily persists. So long as the details which can be built up around it are such that they would give it a "reasonable" setting, most of us are fairly content, and we are apt to think that what we have built we have literally retained. (Bartlett, 1932, pp. 175–176)

REFERENCES

Bartlett, F. C. (1916). An experimental study of some problems of perceiving and imaging. *British Journal of Psychology, 8,* 222–266.

Bartlett, F. C. (1923). *Psychology and primitive culture.* Cambridge: Cambridge University Press.

Bartlett, F. C. (1927). *Psychology and the soldier.* Cambridge: Cambridge University Press.

Bartlett, F. C. (1928). An experiment upon repeated reproduction. *Journal of General Psychology, 1,* 54–63.

Bartlett, F. C. (1932). *Remembering: A study in experimental and social psychology.* Cambridge: Cambridge University Press.

Bartlett, F. C. (1936). Autobiography. In C. Murchison (Ed.), *A history of psychology in autobiography* (Vol. III, pp. 39–52). Worcester, MA: Clark University Press.

Bartlett, F. C. (1946). Obituary notice: K. J. W. Craik, 1914–1945. *British Journal of Psychology, 36,* 109–116.

Bartlett, F. C. (1958). *Thinking: An experimental and social study.* London: Allen and Unwin.

Bartlett, F. C., Ginsberg, M., Lindgren, E. J., & Thouless, R. H. (Eds.). (1939). *The study of society: Methods and problems.* London: Kegan, Paul.

Bergman, E., & Roediger, H. L. (1999). Can Bartlett's repeated reproduction experiments be replicated? *Memory & Cognition, 27,* 937–947.

Broadbent, D. E. (1970). Frederic Charles Bartlett 1886–1969. *Biographical Memoirs of Fellows of the Royal Society, 16,* 1–13.

Bruce, D. (in press). Bartlett, Sir Frederic Charles. In A. E. Kazdin (Ed.), *Encyclopedia of psychology.* (in press). New York: Oxford University Press.

Conrad, R. (1979). Sir Frederic Bartlett: 1886–1969. A personal homage. *Ergonomics, 13,* 159–161.

Head, H. (1920). *Studies in neurology.* Oxford, England: Oxford University Press.

Kintsch, W. (1995). Foreword. In reprint of F. C. Bartlett's *Remembering: A study in experimental and social psychology.* Cambridge, England: Cambridge University Press

Miller, G. A. (1956). The magical number seven plus or minus two: Some limits on our capacity for processing information. *Psychological Review, 63,* 81–97.

Neisser, U. (1967). *Cognitive psychology.* New York: Appleton-Century Crofts.

Oldfield, R.C. (1972). Frederic Charles Bartlett: 1886–1969. *American Journal of Psychology, 85,* 132–140.

Roediger, H. L. (1996). Memory illusions. *Journal of Memory and Language, 35,* 76–100.

Roediger, H. L. (1997). Remembering [Retrospective review of the book *Remembering: A study in experimental and social psychology*]. *Contemporary Psychology, 42,* 488–492.

Roediger, H. L., Bergman, E. T., & Meade, M. L. (2000). Repeated reproduction from memory. In A. Saito (Ed.), *Bartlett, cognition and culture* (pp. 115–134). London: Routledge.

Schacter, D. L. (1995). Memory distortion: History and current status. In D. L. Schacter, J. T. Coyle, G. D. Fischbach, M. M. Mesulam, & L. E. Sullivan (Eds.), *Memory distortion* (pp. 1–43). Cambridge, MA: Harvard University Press.

Schank, R. C., & Abelson, R. P. (1977). *Scripts, plans, goals and understanding: An inquiry into human knowledge structures.* Hillsdale, NJ: Erlbaum.

Wynn, V. E., & Logie, R. H. (1998). The veracity of long-term memories: Did Bartlett get it right? *Applied Cognitive Psychology, 12*, 1–20.

Zangwill, O. L. (1970). Obituary notice. Sir Frederic Bartlett (1886–1969) *Quarterly Journal of Experimental Psychology, 22*, 77–81.

Chapter 10

Karen Horney: The Three Phases of Her Thought

Bernard J. Paris

Karen Horney occupies a prominent place among the pioneers in psychology. Her thought went through three distinct phases, in each of which she made major contributions to psychoanalytic theory. During the first phase, in the 1920s and early 1930s, she wrote a series of essays in which she tried to modify orthodox ideas about feminine psychology while staying within the framework of Freudian theory. In the second phase, she tried to redefine psychoanalysis, replacing Freud's biological orientation with an emphasis on culture and interpersonal relationships. Her major works in this phase were *The Neurotic Personality of Our Time* (1937) and *New Ways in Psychoanalysis* (1939). In the third phase, represented by *Our Inner Conflicts* (1945) and *Neurosis and Human Growth* (1950), she developed her mature theory, which posited that individuals cope with the anxiety produced by feeling unsafe, unloved, and unvalued by disowning their spontaneous feelings and developing elaborate strategies of defense.

Horney's thought was important in its own time and continues to be significant today. Forty years ahead of their time, her early essays were largely ignored until they were collected in *Feminine Psychology* (1967). Since then, they have been widely read and cited, and Horney is now recognized as the first great psychoanalytic feminist (Chodorow, 1989). Her emphasis on culture and disturbed human relationships had a great influence on subsequent theory, and her focus on current character structure rather than the infantile origins of personality is

---

*Photo of Karen Horney used by permission of Marianne Horney Eckardt.

reflected in many present-oriented therapies. Her most distinctive contribution is her mature theory, which has never been superseded. Students of human behavior must still go to Horney for an account of the defenses and conflicts she so brilliantly described in her last two books. Her contributions continue to have an impact not only on analytic theory and clinical practice, but also on the study of literature, culture, gender, religion, philosophy, and biography (see Paris, 1994).

PERSONAL HISTORY

Born Karen Danielsen in a suburb of Hamburg on September 15, 1885, Horney was the daughter of a Norwegian sea captain and a Dutch-German mother. Horney sided with her mother in the fierce conflicts between her parents, who were ill-matched in age and background; and her mother supported Horney in her desire for an education, despite her father's opposition. Horney had a brother, Berndt, who was four years older than she.

Overview of Horney's Career

Having decided that she wanted to be a physician when she was 13, Horney became one of the first women in Germany to be admitted to medical school. She received her medical education at the universities of Freiburg, Göttingen, and Berlin. In 1910, she entered analysis with Karl Abraham, a member of Freud's inner circle and the first psychoanalyst to practice in Germany. She decided to become an analyst herself, and in 1920 was one of the six founding members of the Berlin Psychoanalytic Institute. She taught there until 1932, when Franz Alexander invited her to become associate director of the newly formed Chicago Psychoanalytic Institute. She joined the faculty of the New York Psychoanalytic Institute in 1934 but was driven out in 1941 as a result of her criticism of Freud in *New Ways in Psychoanalysis (1939)*. She founded the American Institute for Psychoanalysis the same year and was dean until her death in 1952.

Personal Development

Horney was introspective and self-analytical in her youth, partly because of her temperament and partly because of her unhappy childhood. She felt that she had been unwanted and that her brother was much more highly valued than she, principally because he was a male. Because she disliked her father, whom she regarded as a religious hypocrite, and because her mother confided in her brother more than in her, she felt alone and unsupported in the family. To compensate, she attached herself to her brother, with whom she seems to have engaged in some kind of sex play between the ages of 5 and 9. When her brother distanced himself from her on reaching puberty, Horney felt rejected and tried to gain a sense of worth by becoming fiercely competitive in school.

As a child, Horney was bitter, angry, and rebellious, but when she reached puberty she could no longer tolerate her isolation and won a position in the family by denying her anger and joining the circle of her mother's admirers. At the age of 13, she began keeping a diary (Horney, 1980) in which she expressed adoration of her mother and brother. Her buried hostility toward them erupted, however, when she was 21, and her relations with them were strained thereafter. Because Horney had been repressing her resentments, the diaries give a misleading picture of her relations with her family members and must be read in light of the case of Clare in her 1942 book, *Self-Analysis*, which is highly autobiographical. Clare, who also appears in three of Horney's other publications, provides information about Horney's earlier history and explains her behavior during adolescence (Paris, 1994).

Although Horney's diaries are misleading about her relations with her family, they clearly reveal her emotional problems. She suffered from depression, timidity, and paralyzing fatigue. She could not bear being without a boyfriend, was insecure about her intellectual abilities, and felt like an ugly duckling who could not compete with her beautiful mother. She had great difficulty focusing on her school work and succeeded academically only because of her exceptional intelligence.

Horney's diaries were mostly devoted to her relationships with men, from whom she desperately needed attention. The typical pattern of her relationships was first idealization of the man, followed by disappointment, depression, and efforts to comprehend why the relationship failed. Because of her disappointments, she moved from man to man, often trying to hold onto several at once because each satisfied different demands. She hoped to find a great man who could fulfill her conflicting needs for dominance and submission, crude force and refined sensibility, but she was perpetually disappointed. Deeply unhappy, she tried to understand the sources of her misery, first in her diaries and then in her psychoanalytic writings, many of which are covert autobiography.

Marriage and Divorce

In 1909, Horney married Oskar Horney, a social scientist whom she had met while they were both students in Freiburg. When they were courting, she thought that he was the great man for whom she had been looking, but she soon realized that he was not forceful enough for her. Although Oskar and Horney remained together for nearly 20 years, the marriage was in trouble almost from the beginning. Horney sought help in her analysis with Karl Abraham, but her symptoms were the same after two years of treatment as they had been when she began. The failure of her analysis is one reason why she began to question orthodox theory, especially with respect to the psychology of women.

After having three children, Horney and Oskar separated in 1926 and divorced in 1938. Horney never remarried, but she had many troubled relationships of the kind she described in her essays on feminine psychology and the Clare case in *Self-Analysis* (1942).

ESSAYS ON FEMININE PSYCHOLOGY

In her earliest essays on feminine psychology, Horney strove to show that girls and women have intrinsic biological constitutions and patterns of development that must be understood in their own terms—not just as products of their difference from and presumed inferiority to men. She argued that psychoanalysis regards women as defective when compared to men, because that theory is the product of a male genius (Freud) and a male-dominated culture. The male view of the female has been incorporated into psychoanalysis as an alleged scientific picture of woman's essential nature.

An important question for Horney was why men see women as they do. She contended that male envy of pregnancy, childbirth, motherhood, breasts and suckling gives rise to an unconscious tendency to devalue women, and that men's impulse toward creative work is an overcompensation for their small role in procreation. The "womb-envy" of the male must be stronger than the "penis-envy" of the female, because men need to depreciate women more than women need to depreciate men.

In later essays, Horney continued to analyze the male view of woman in an effort to expose its lack of scientific foundation. In "The Distrust Between the Sexes" (1931), she argued that woman is seen as

> a second-rate being [because] at any given time, the more powerful side will create an ideology suitable to help maintain its position. . . . In this ideology the differentness of the weaker one will be interpreted as inferiority, and it will be proven that these differences are unchangeable, basic, or God's will. (Horney, 1931, 1967, p. 116)

In "The Dread of Woman" (1932), Horney traced the male dread of woman to the boy's fear that his genital is inadequate in relation to the mother. The threat of woman is not castration but humiliation; the threat is to his masculine self-regard. As he grows up, the male continues to have a deeply hidden anxiety about the size of his penis or his potency, an anxiety that has no counterpart for the female, who "performs her part by merely *being*" (Horney, 1932, 1967, p. 145) and is not obliged to go on proving her womanhood. There is, therefore, no corresponding female dread of men. The male deals with his anxiety by identifying himself with his work, by seeking sexual conquests, and by debasing the love object.

In her essays on feminine psychology, Horney moved steadily away from Freud's belief that anatomy is destiny and toward a greater emphasis on cultural factors as a source of women's problems and of gender identity. She acknowledged that little girls envy the male "plumbing" but regarded this as psychologically insignificant. What women chiefly envy is male privilege, and what women need is greater opportunity to develop their human capacities. The patriarchal ideal of woman does not necessarily correspond to the inherent female character, but the cultural power of that ideal often makes women behave in accordance with it.

In "The Problem of Feminine Masochism," Horney challenged the idea that "masochistic trends are inherent in, or akin to, the very essence of female nature" (Horney, 1935b, 1967, p. 214). This is the position of classic Freudian psychoanalysis, which reflects the stereotypes of male culture, but Horney identified a number of social conditions that have made women more masochistic than men. Moreover, comparative studies show that these conditions are not universal and that some societies are more unfavorable to women's development than others.

Horney did not deny that women often envy men and are uncomfortable with their feminine role. Indeed, many of her essays deal with the "masculinity complex," which she defined as "the entire complex of feelings and fantasies that have for their content the woman's feeling of being discriminated against, her envy of the male, her wish to be a man and to discard the female role" (Horney, 1926b, 1967, p. 74). Although she initially argued that women are bound to have a masculinity complex because of their need to escape the guilt and anxiety that result from their oedipal situation, she soon came to believe that the masculinity complex is not inevitable but is the product of a male-dominated culture and of particular kinds of family dynamics. A girl's exposure "from birth onward to the suggestion—inevitable, whether conveyed brutally or delicately—of her inferiority [is an experience] that constantly stimulates her masculinity complex" (Horney, 1926a, 1967, p. 69).

In discussing family dynamics, Horney focused at first on the girl's relationship with male members of the family, but later she derived the masculinity complex and all the phenomena traditionally associated with penis envy—such as feelings of inferiority, vindictiveness, and competitiveness toward men—from the girl's relationship with females in the family, particularly the mother. In "Maternal Conflicts" she brought together the separate features of childhood to which she had attributed the masculinity complex in previous essays:

A girl may have reasons to acquire a dislike for her own female world very early, perhaps because her mother has intimidated her, or she has experienced a thoroughly disillusioning disappointment from the side of the father or brother; she may have had early sexual experiences that frightened her; or she may have found that her brother was greatly preferred to herself. (Horney, 1933, 1967, p. 179)

All of these features were present in Horney's childhood.

"The Overvaluation of Love" is the culmination of Horney's attempt to analyze herself in terms of feminine psychology. The essay draws on the cases of seven women whose family histories, symptoms, and social backgrounds are similar to Horney's, and she may well have included herself in her clinical sample. Most of the essay is devoted to trying to explain why these women have an obsessive need for a male but are unable to form satisfactory relationships. Their obsession is traced to a childhood situation in which each "had come off second best in the competition for a man" (Horney, 1934, 1967, p. 193). It is the typical fate of the girl to be frustrated in her love for her father, but for these women the consequences are unusually severe because of the presence of a mother or sister who dominates the situation erotically.

These women respond to their sense of defeat either by withdrawing from the competition for a male or by developing a compulsive rivalry with other women in which they try to demonstrate their erotic appeal. For members of the latter group, their relationships with men may be paramount but are never satisfactory. They tend to lose interest in a man as soon as he is conquered because they have "a profound fear of the disappointments and humiliations that they expect to result from falling in love" (Horney, 1934, 1967, p. 205). Having been rejected by father or brother in childhood, they simultaneously need to prove their worth through erotic conquests and to make themselves invulnerable by avoiding deep emotional bonds. They tend to change partners frequently because after securing a man they need to get out of the relationship before they get hurt. However attractive they may be, they do not believe that a man can actually love them. Moreover, they have a "deep-seated desire for revenge because of their original defeat: the desire is to get the better of a man, to cast him aside, to reject him just as [they themselves] once felt cast aside and rejected" (Horney, 1934, 1967, p. 206). All of this describes Horney herself.

Although Horney had devoted most of her previous professional life to writing about feminine psychology, she abandoned the topic in 1935 because she believed that the role of culture in shaping the female psyche makes it impossible to determine what is distinctively feminine. In a lecture titled "Woman's Fear of Action" (delivered in 1935), she argued that only when women have been freed from the conceptions of femininity fostered by male dominated cultures can they discover how they really differ from men psychologically. Our primary objective must not be to identify what is essentially feminine but to foster "the full development of the human personalities of all" (Horney, 1937, 2000, p. 123). At this point in her career, Horney began to develop a theory that she considered gender-neutral, one that applied equally to males and females.

CRITIQUE OF FREUD AND DEVELOPMENT
OF A NEW PARADIGM

Although Horney had begun to emphasize culture in her writings in the 1920s, it was her move to the United States in 1932 that convinced her that Freud had given too much importance to biology and too little to social factors. First in Chicago and then in New York she found patients with very different kinds of problems from those that she had encountered in Germany. This experience, combined with her reading in the burgeoning sciences of sociology and anthropology, made her doubt the universality of the Oedipus complex and led her to explore the impact of culture on individual psychology. In 1935, she lectured on this topic at the New School for Social Research and was invited by the publisher, W. W. Norton, to write the book that became *The Neurotic Personality of Our Time* (1937). As Horney's disagreements with Freud deepened, she felt it important to contrast her thinking with his in a systematic way, which she did in *New Ways in Psychoanalysis* (1939).

In that book, Horney argued that because of his overemphasis on the biological sources of human behavior, Freud had incorrectly assumed the universality of the feelings, attitudes, and kinds of relationships that were common in his culture. Moreover, she rejected Freud's attribution of neurosis to the clash between culture and instinct. In Freud's view, as Horney saw it, we must have culture to survive, and we must repress or sublimate our instincts to have culture. Horney did not believe that collision between the individual and society is inevitable but rather that it occurs when a bad environment frustrates emotional needs and inspires fear and hostility. Freud depicted human beings as inherently insatiable, destructive, and antisocial, but according to Horney these traits are not expressions of instinct, but neurotic responses to adverse conditions.

Horney did not reject the significance of childhood in emotional development, as is sometimes thought, but emphasized pathogenic conditions in the family that make children feel unsafe, unloved, and unvalued rather than the frustration of libidinal desires. As a result of these conditions, children develop "basic anxiety," a feeling of being helpless in a potentially hostile world, which they try to reduce by adopting such strategies of defense as the pursuit of love, power, or detachment.

Horney believed that these defensive strategies are doomed to failure because they generate vicious circles in which the means used to allay anxiety tend to increase it. For example, the frustration of the need for love makes that need insatiable, and the demandingness and jealousy that follow make it less likely than ever that the person will receive affection. People who have not been loved develop a feeling of being unlovable that leads them to discount any evidence to the contrary. Being deprived of affection has made them dependent on others, but they are afraid of that dependency because it makes them too vulnerable.

Horney compared the situation created in this way to that "of a person who is starving for food yet does not dare to take any for fear that it might be poisoned" (Horney, 1937, p. 114).

Although Horney devoted much of *The Neurotic Personality of Our Time* (1937) to the neurotic need for love, she gave a good deal of space to the quest for power, prestige, and possessions that develops when a person feels hopeless about gaining affection. She also discussed detachment and some of the intrapsychic strategies of defense, such as guilt, neurotic suffering, and self-inflation, which she examined in more detail in later books (Horney, 1945, 1950).

In her first two books, Horney developed a paradigm for the structure of neurosis in which disturbances in human relationships generate a basic anxiety that leads to the development of strategies of defense that are not only self-defeating but are in conflict with each other, because people adopt not just one but several of them. Although her thinking continued to develop in many ways, this paradigm formed the basis of her mature theory.

Perhaps the most significant aspect of Horney's new version of psychoanalysis was her shift in emphasis, both in theory and in clinical practice, from the past to the present. She replaced Freud's focus on genesis with a structural approach, arguing that psychoanalysis should be less concerned with infantile origins than with the current constellation of defenses and inner conflicts. This feature of her theory sharply differentiated it from classical psychoanalysis, which seeks to explain the present by trying to recover the past.

In *New Ways in Psychoanalysis* (1939), Horney distinguished between her own "evolutionistic" thinking and what she called Freud's "mechanistic–evolutionistic" thought. Evolutionistic thinking presupposes "that things which exist today have not existed in the same form from the very beginning, but have developed out of previous stages. These preceding stages may have little resemblance to the present forms, but the present forms would be unthinkable without the preceding ones" (1939, p. 42). Mechanistic–evolutionistic thinking holds that "nothing really new is created in the process of development [that] what we see today is only the old in a changed form" (1939, p. 42). For Horney, the profound influence of early experiences does not preclude continued development, whereas for Freud nothing much new happens after the age of five, and later reactions or experiences are to be considered as a repetition of earlier ones.

At the heart of Freud's conception of the relation between childhood experience and adult behavior is the doctrine of the timelessness of the unconscious. Fears and desires, or entire experiences, that are repressed in childhood remain uninfluenced by further experiences or growth. These repressed emotions persist in the form of fixations, attachments of libido—perhaps to a person in the early environment, such as father or mother, perhaps to a stage of libidinal development. The concept of fixation makes it possible to see later attachments and other behavior as repetitions of the past, which has remained encapsulated and unchanged in the unconscious.

Horney did not attempt to refute the doctrine of the timelessness of the unconscious or the cluster of concepts related to it, but rather built her own theory on a different set of premises. The "non-mechanistic viewpoint is that in organic development there can never be a simple repetition or regression to former stages" (Horney, 1939, p. 44). The past is always contained in the present, but through a developmental process rather than through repetition. In "Conceptions and Misconceptions of the Analytical Method," Horney observed that the way in which lives really develop is that "each step condition the next one." Thus "interpretations which connect the present difficulties immediately with influences in childhood are scientifically only half truths and practically useless" (Horney, 1935a, 1999, p. 39).

Horney's model was one in which early experiences profoundly affect the individual, not by producing fixations that cause people to repeat earlier patterns but by conditioning the ways in which they respond to the world. These in turn are modulated by subsequent experience and eventually evolve into adult defensive strategies and character structures. Early experiences may have a greater impact than later ones because they determine the direction of development, but the character of the adult is the evolved product of all previous interactions between psychic structure and environment.

Another important difference between Horney and Freud is that whereas for Freud the experiences in childhood that determine neurotic adjustments are relatively few in number and mostly of a sexual nature, for Horney the sum total of childhood experience is responsible for neurotic development. Things go wrong because of all the factors in the culture, including relationships with peers and especially the family, that make a child feel unsafe, unloved, and unvalued, and give rise to basic anxiety. This anxiety leads to the development of defensive strategies that form a neurotic character structure. It is this character structure from which later difficulties emanate. Horney sees sexual difficulties as the result rather than the cause of personality problems.

HORNEY'S MATURE THEORY

At the heart of Horney's mature theory is the idea that people have a real self that requires favorable conditions to be actualized. When they are motivated by defensive strategies instead of genuine feelings, however, they become alienated from their real selves. Horney divided defensive strategies into two kinds: interpersonal, which we use in our dealings with other people, and intrapsychic, which we use in our own minds. She focused mainly on interpersonal strategies in *Our Inner Conflicts* (1945) and on the intrapsychic in *Neurosis and Human Growth* (1950).

Horney came to see the central feature of neurosis as alienation from the real self because of oppressive forces in the environment. The object of psychotherapy is to "restore the individual to himself, to help him regain his spontaneity and find his center of gravity in himself" (Horney, 1939, p. 11). The real self is not a fixed entity but a set of intrinsic potentialities—including temperament, talents, capacities, and predispositions—that are part of a person's genetic makeup and need a favorable environment in which to develop. The self is not a product of learning because one cannot be taught to be one's self. But neither is it impervious to external influence, because it is actualized through interactions with an external world that can provide many paths of development.

People actualize themselves in different ways under different conditions, but there are certain conditions in childhood that everyone requires for self-realization. These include an atmosphere of warmth that enables children to express their own thoughts and feelings, the good will of others to satisfy their various needs, and "healthy friction with the wishes and will" of those around them (Horney, 1950, p. 18). When their own neuroses prevent parents from loving the child or even thinking "of him as the particular individual he is," the child develops a feeling of basic anxiety that prevents him "from relating himself to others with the spontaneity of his real feelings" and forces him to develop defensive strategies (Horney, 1950, p. 18).

Interpersonal Strategies of Defense

According to Horney, people try to cope with their basic anxiety by adopting a compliant or self-effacing solution and moving toward people, an aggressive or expansive solution and moving against people, or a detached, resigned solution and moving away from people. Each solution involves a constellation of behavioral patterns and personality traits, a conception of justice, and a set of beliefs about human nature, human values, and the human condition. Each also involves a "deal" or bargain with fate in which obedience to the dictates of that solution is supposed to be rewarded.

Healthy people move appropriately and flexibly in all three directions—toward, against, and away from people—but in neurotic development these moves become compulsive and indiscriminate. In each of the interpersonal defenses, one of the elements involved in basic anxiety is overemphasized: helplessness in the compliant solution, hostility in the aggressive solution, and isolation in the detached solution. Because under pathogenic conditions all of these feelings are likely to occur, individuals will come to make all three of the defensive moves, giving rise to inner conflicts.

To gain some sense of wholeness, people will emphasize one move more than the others and will become predominantly self-effacing, expansive, or detached. Which move they emphasize will depend on the particular combination of temperamental and environmental factors at work in their situation. The other trends will continue to exist but will operate unconsciously and manifest themselves in disguised and devious ways. The inner conflicts will not have been resolved but will simply have gone underground. When the submerged trends are for some reason brought closer to the surface, individuals will experience severe inner turmoil and may be unable to move in any direction at all. Under the impetus of some powerful influence or the dramatic failure of their predominant solution, they may embrace one of their repressed defensive strategies. They will experience this as conversion or education, but it will merely be the substitution of one neurotic solution for another.

Self-Effacing Solution.   People in whom compliant trends are dominant try to overcome their basic anxiety by gaining affection and approval and controlling others through their dependency. Their values "lie in the direction of goodness, sympathy, love, generosity, unselfishness, humility; while egotism, ambition, callousness, unscrupulousness, wielding of power are abhorred" (Horney, 1945, p. 54). They embrace Christian values, but in a compulsive way, because they are necessary to their defense system. They must believe in turning the other cheek, and they must see the world as displaying a providential order in which virtue is rewarded. Their bargain is that if they are good, loving people who shun pride and do not seek their own gain or glory, they will be well-treated by fate and other people. If their bargain is not honored, they may despair of divine justice, they may conclude that they are at fault, or they may have recourse to belief in a justice that transcends human understanding. They need to believe not only in the fairness of the world order but also in the goodness of human nature, and here, too, they are vulnerable to disappointment. Self-effacing people must repress their aggressive tendencies to make their bargain work, but they are frequently attracted to expansive people through whom they can participate vicariously in the mastery of life. They often develop a "morbid dependency" on their partner.

Expansive Solutions.   People in whom expansive tendencies are dominant have goals, traits, and values that are opposite to those of the self-effacing solution. What appeals to them most is not love but mastery. They abhor helplessness, are ashamed of suffering, and need to achieve success, prestige, or recognition. In *Neurosis and Human Growth* (1950), Horney divided the expansive solutions into three distinct kinds: narcissistic, perfectionistic, and arrogant–vindictive.

Narcissistic people seek to master life "by self-admiration and the exercise of charm" (Horney, 1950, p. 212). They were often favored and admired children, gifted beyond average, who grew up feeling that the world was a fostering parent and that they were the favorites of fortune. They have an unquestioned belief in their abilities and feel that there is no one they cannot win. Their insecurity is manifested in their tendency to speak incessantly of their exploits and their wonderful qualities, and their need for endless confirmation of their estimate of themselves in the form of admiration and devotion. Their bargain is that if they hold on to their dreams and their exaggerated claims for themselves, life is bound to give them what they want. If it does not, they may experience a psychological collapse, because they are ill-equipped to cope with reality.

Perfectionistic people have extremely high standards, moral and intellectual, on the basis of which they look down on others. They take great pride in their rectitude and aim for a "flawless excellence" in the whole conduct of life. Because of the difficulty of living up to their standards, they tend to equate knowing moral values with being a good person. While they deceive themselves in this way, they may insist that others live up to their standards of perfection and despise them for failing to do so, thus externalizing their self-condemnation. Perfectionists have a legalistic bargain in which being fair, just, and dutiful entitles them "to fair treatment by others and by life in general. This conviction of an infallible justice operating in life gives [them] a feeling of mastery" (Horney, 1950, p. 197). Through the height of their standards, they compel fate. Ill-fortune or errors of their own making threaten their bargain and may overwhelm them with feelings of helplessness or self-hate.

Arrogant–vindictive people are motivated chiefly by a need for triumphs and "getting even." Whereas the narcissists received early admiration and the perfectionists grew up under the pressure of rigid standards, the arrogant–vindictive people were harshly treated in childhood and have a need to retaliate for the injuries they suffered. They feel "that the world is an arena where, in the Darwinian sense, only the fittest survive and the strong annihilate the weak" (Horney, 1945, p. 64). The only moral law inherent in the order of things is that might makes right. In their relations with others they are competitive, ruthless, and cynical. They want to be hard and tough, and they regard every manifestation of feeling as a sign of weakness. Their bargain is essentially with themselves. They do not count on the world to give them anything, but are convinced that they can reach their ambitious goals if they remain true to their vision of life as a battle and do not allow themselves to be influenced by traditional morality or their softer feelings. If their expansive solution collapses, self-effacing trends may emerge.

Detached Solution.   Predominantly detached people pursue neither love nor mastery but rather worship freedom, peace, and self-sufficiency. They disdain the pursuit of worldly success and have a profound aversion to effort. They have a strong need for superiority and usually look on their fellows with condescension, but they realize their ambition in imagination rather than through actual accomplishments. They handle a threatening world by removing themselves from its power and shutting others out of their inner lives. To avoid being dependent on the environment, they try to subdue their inner cravings and to be content with little. They do not usually rail against life but resign themselves to things as they are and accept their fate with ironic humor or stoical dignity. Their bargain is that if they ask nothing of others, others will not bother them; that if they try for nothing, they will not fail; and that if they expect little of life, they will not be disappointed.

Intrapsychic Strategies of Defense

While interpersonal difficulties are creating the moves toward, against, and away from people, and the conflicts between them, concomitant intrapsychic problems are producing their own defensive strategies. Self-idealization generates what Horney calls the pride system, which includes neurotic pride, neurotic claims, "tyrannical shoulds," and increased self-hate.

Creation of the Idealized Image.   To compensate for feelings of weakness, worthlessness, and inadequacy, people create—with the aid of imagination—an idealized image of themselves, an image they endow with "unlimited powers and exalted faculties" (Horney, 1950, p. 222). The process of self-idealization must be understood in relation to the interpersonal strategies, because people's idealized images are based on their predominant defense and the attributes it exalts.

The idealized self-image of self-effacing people "is a composite of 'lovable' qualities, such as unselfishness, goodness, generosity, humility, saintliness, nobility, sympathy" (Horney, 1950, p. 222). It also glorifies "helplessness, suffering, and martyrdom" and deep feelings for art, nature, and other human beings (Horney, 1950, p. 222). Arrogant–vindictive people see themselves as invincible masters of all situations. They are smarter, tougher, more realistic than other people and therefore can get the better of them. They take pride in their vigilance, foresight, and planning and feel that nothing can hurt them. The narcissistic person is "the anointed, the man of destiny, the prophet, the great giver, the benefactor of mankind" (Horney, 1950, p. 194). Narcissists see themselves as having unlimited energies and as being capable of great achievements, effortlessly attained. Perfectionists see themselves as models of rectitude whose performance is invariably excellent. They have perfect judgment and are just and dutiful in their human relationships. The idealized image of detached or resigned people "is a composite of self-sufficiency, independence, self-contained serenity, freedom from desires and passions," and stoic indifference to the slings and arrows of outrageous fortune (Horney, 1950, p. 277). They aspire to be free from restraint and impervious to pressure. In each solution, the idealized image may be modeled in whole or in part on a religious or cultural ideal or an example from history or personal experience.

The idealized image does not ultimately make people feel better about themselves but rather leads to increased self-hate and additional inner conflict. Although the qualities with which they endow themselves are dictated by their predominant interpersonal strategy, the subordinate solutions are also represented; and because each solution glorifies a different set of traits, the idealized image has contradictory aspects, all of which the individual must try to actualize. Moreover, because people can feel worthwhile only if they *are* their idealized image, everything that falls short is deemed worthless, and there develops a despised image that becomes the focus of self-contempt. Horney observed that a great many people shuttle between feelings of arrogant omnipotence and feelings of extreme worthlessness (1950, p. 188).

Search for Glory.   With the formation of the idealized image, people embark on a search for glory, the object of which is to actualize their idealized self. What is considered to be glorious will vary with each solution. The search for glory constitutes a private religion, the rules of which are determined by the individual's particular neurosis, but people may also participate in the glory systems that are a prominent feature of every culture. These include organized religions, various forms of group identification, wars and military service, and competitions, honors, and hierarchical arrangements of all kinds.

Pride, Claims, and Shoulds.   The creation of the idealized self-image produces not only a search for glory but also neurotic pride, neurotic claims, "tyrannical shoulds," and self-hate, all of which will vary with the individual's predominant solution. Neurotic pride substitutes a pride in the attributes of the idealized self for realistic self-confidence and self-esteem. Threats to pride produce anxiety and hostility; its collapse results in self-contempt and despair.

On the basis of their pride, people make neurotic claims on the world, in which they demand to be treated by others in accordance with their grandiose conceptions of themselves. Their claims are "pervaded by expectations of magic" (Horney, 1950, p. 62). People's claims intensify their vulnerability, because frustration of claims deflates their pride and confronts them with the sense of powerlessness and inadequacy from which they are fleeing.

The idealized self-image generates not only pride and claims but also what Horney calls "the tyranny of the should." The function of their "shoulds" is to compel people to live up to their grandiose conception of themselves. The "shoulds" are determined largely by the character traits and values associated with people's predominant solutions, but because their subordinate trends are also represented in the idealized image, they are often caught in a "crossfire of conflicting shoulds." For example, self-effacing people want to be good, noble, loving, forgiving, and generous; but they also have an aggressive side that tells them to go all out for their own advantage and to hit back at anybody who offends them. Accordingly, they despise themselves when they show any trace of cowardice, ineffectuality, or compliance. Thus they are under a constant cross fire: damned if they are either aggressive or compliant (Horney, 1950, p. 221). "It is the threat of a punitive self-hate that lurks behind [the shoulds]," observed Horney, that "truly makes them a regime of terror" (Horney, 1950, p. 85).

The shoulds are the basis of people's bargains with fate. No matter what the solution, their bargain is that their claims will be honored if they live up to their shoulds. They seek magically to control external reality by obeying inner dictates. They do not see their claims as unreasonable, of course, but only as what they have a right to expect, given their grandiose conceptions of themselves, and they feel that life is unfair if their expectations are frustrated. Their sense of justice is determined by their predominant solution and the bargain associated with it.

Self-Hate.   Self-hate is the end product of the intrapsychic strategies of defense, each of which tends to magnify a person's feelings of inadequacy and failure. Self-hate is essentially the rage the idealized self feels toward the self one actually is for not being what it "should" be. Horney sees self-hate as "perhaps the greatest tragedy of the human mind. Man in reaching out for the Infinite and Absolute also starts destroying himself. When he makes a pact with the devil, who promises him glory, he has to go to hell—to the hell within himself" (Horney, 1950, p. 154).

Horney's theory has a dynamic quality that a description of its structure does not convey. Solutions combine, conflict, become stronger or weaker, need to be defended, generate vicious circles, and are replaced by others when they collapse. Conflicts between the defenses cause oscillations, inconsistencies, and self-hate. Within the pride system, there is a seesawing between the idealized and despised selves and a cross fire of conflicting shoulds.

HORNEY'S LATER LIFE

Horney's third book, *Self-Analysis* (1942), was an outgrowth of the breakdown of her relationship with Erich Fromm. She had known Fromm when he was a student at the Berlin Psychoanalytic Institute (he was 15 years younger than she), and she met him again when he lectured at the University of Chicago in 1933. They became lovers when both moved to New York in 1934. Their relationship was intellectual as well as emotional, with Fromm teaching Horney sociology and Horney teaching Fromm psychoanalysis. The relationship deteriorated in the late 1930s, after Horney sent her daughter Marianne, who was specializing in psychiatry, to Fromm for a training analysis. When Marianne's hostilities toward her mother emerged in the course of analysis—as was to be expected—Horney blamed Fromm. The breakdown of the relationship was extremely painful to Horney and led to a period of intense self-analysis. This issued in the writing of *Self-Analysis*, in which the story of Clare and Peter is a fictionalized account of what happened between Horney and Fromm. Despite their estrangement, Fromm became a member of the American Institute for Psychoanalysis when it was founded in 1941, but Horney drove him out in 1942, using his status as a lay analyst (he had a PhD rather than an MD) as a pretext.

The 1930s were a turbulent period for Horney, culminating with the hostile reaction of her colleagues at the New York Psychoanalytic Institute to her criticisms of Freud and with her separation from Fromm. The 1940s were equally turbulent, because many of Horney's most distinguished colleagues (including Fromm, Harry Stack Sullivan [chap. 21, *Pioneers I*], and Clara Thompson) left the American Institute to form the William Alanson White Institute or to join the New York Medical College. These splits were partly the result of Horney's need for dominance and her inability to grant others the kind of academic freedom she had demanded for herself at the New York Psychoanalytic Institute. Horney continued to have difficulties in her love life, and these often contributed to dissension at the institute, because she tended to place men with whom she was having relationships in positions of power. Despite the political turmoil it involved, however, heading her own institute enabled Horney to flourish. It gave her the intellectual freedom she had always sought and facilitated the development of her mature theory. Toward the end of the decade, Horney became interested in Zen, and not long before her death in 1952, she traveled to Japan with D. T. Suzuki, who had written and lectured about Zen in America, to visit Zen monasteries (see Quinn, 1987; Rubins, 1978).

CONCLUSION

Although Horney was a brilliant clinician, she suffered all her life from not having had an analyst who could really help her. After her disappointing experiences, first with Karl Abraham and then with Hanns Sachs in the early 1920s, she turned to self-analysis in an effort to gain relief from her emotional difficulties. Combined with her clinical experience, her self-analysis generated many of her psychoanalytic theories. Her constant struggle to obtain relief from her problems was largely responsible for the continual evolution of her theory and the deepening of her insights. Horney had a remarkable ability to see herself clearly and to be brutally honest about her problems. With the exception of her earliest essays, she did not construct a theory that universalized or normalized her difficulties.

Although Horney made little progress with some of her problems, she was remarkably successful with others. As a young woman, she had suffered severely from depression, fatigue, and inability to work, but she eventually became extraordinarily creative, energetic, and productive. Like Clare in *Self-Analysis*, she was a late bloomer. She did not write very much until she was in her 40s, but the last 15 years of her life were remarkable. She published five ground-breaking books; she was in great demand as an analyst, supervisor, and speaker; she founded and directed the American Institute for Psychoanalysis; she founded and edited *The American Journal of Psychoanalysis*; she taught at the New School on a regular basis; she read widely; she learned how to paint; she had many eminent friends and a busy social life; she spent much time in the summers with her daughters; and she traveled a great deal. Her failure to overcome some of her problems made her realistic, and her successes were the source of her optimism. Her belief both in the human potential for growth and in the difficulty of achieving it was based on her own experience.

REFERENCES

Chodorow, N. (1989). *Feminism and psychoanalytic thought*. New Haven, CT: Yale University Press.

Horney, K. (1926a). The flight from womanhood: The masculinity complex in women as viewed by men and by women. *International Journal of Psycho-Analysis, 7,* 324–329.

Horney, K. (1926b). Gehemmte Weiblichkeit: Psychoanalytischer Beitrag zum Problem der Fridigität [Inhibited femininity: Psychoanalytical contribution to the problem of frigidity]. *Zeitschrift für Sexualwissenschaft, 13,* 67–77.

Horney, K. (1931). Das Misstrauen zwischen den Geschlechtern [The distrust between the sexes]. *Die Ärztin, 7,* 5–12.

Horney, K. (1932). The dread of woman: Observations on a specific difference in the dread felt by men and women for the opposite sex. *International Journal of Psycho-Analysis, 13,* 348–360.

Horney, K. (1933). Maternal conflicts. *American Journal of Orthopsychiatry, 3,* 455–463.

Horney, K. (1934). The overvaluation of love: A study of a common present-day feminine type. *Psychoanalytic Quarterly, 3,* 605–638.

Horney, K. (1935a). Conceptions and misconceptions of the analytical method. *Journal of Nervous and Mental Disease, 91,* 399–410.

Horney, K. (1935b). The problem of feminine masochism. *Psychoanalytic Review, 22,* 241–257.

Horney, K. (1937). *The neurotic personality of our time*. New York: Norton.

Horney, K. (1939). *New ways in psychoanalysis*. New York: Norton.

Horney, K. (1942). *Self-analysis*. New York: Norton.

Horney, K. (1945). *Our inner conflicts*. New York: Norton.

Horney, K. (1950). *Neurosis and human growth*. New York: Norton.

Horney, K. (1967). *Feminine psychology* (H. Kelvin, ed.). New York: Norton.

Horney, K. (1980). *The adolescent diaries of Karen Horney*. New York: Basic Books.

Horney, K. (1999). *The therapeutic process: Essays and lectures*, ed. B. Paris. New Haven, CT: Yale University Press.

Horney, K. (2000). *The unknown Karen Horney: Essays on gender, culture, and psychoanalysis* (B. Paris, ed.). New Haven, CT: Yale University Press.

Paris, B. (1994). *Karen Horney: A psychoanalyst's search for self-understanding*. New Haven, CT: Yale University Press.

Quinn, S. (1987). *A mind of her own: The life of Karen Horney*. New York: Summit Books.

Rubins, J. (1978). *Karen Horney: Gentle rebel of psychoanalysis*. New York: Dial Press.

Chapter 11

Francis Cecil Sumner: The First African American Pioneer in Psychology

Robert V. Guthrie

Francis Cecil Sumner was an American psychologist whose perseverance in his struggle against racial prejudice led to academic and professional successes despite the era in which he lived. Sumner lived his entire life in a racially segregated America. He did not live to witness the Supreme Court's landmark *Brown v. Board of Education* decision that sounded the death knell for racially separate schools and also served as a precursor for legislation barring separate public accommodations based on race. He lived during an age in which inequitable and disproportionate academic programs were permitted and governmental financial support for Black students was rare. He also lived at a time when there were significant differences between the professional activities of White scholars and those of the few Black scholars who persevered despite the obstacles. For instance, although high rewards came to White psychologists who built and tested theories, established laboratories, conducted experiments, published books, and wrote journal articles, Black psychologists struggled to establish undergraduate degree programs, without which Black students would not have been able to pursue degrees in psychology.

CAREER

In 1920, Sumner, a 25-year-old Black World War I veteran, successfully defended his doctoral dissertation before a group of prominent scholars and psy-

---

*Photo of Francis Cecil Sumner courtesy of Robert V. Guthrie.

chologists at Clark University in Worcester, Massachusetts. Sumner thus became the first Black person to receive the PhD in psychology.

Sumner was born in Pine Bluff, Arkansas, on December 7, 1895, just 30 years after the abolishment of slavery in the United States. Because most Black Americans who had been slaves had no last names, Sumner's parents had adopted their last name out of respect for a one-time Massachusetts senator, Charles Sumner. Young Francis received his early education in the elementary schools of Norfolk, Virginia, and Plainfield, New Jersey. But because secondary education for Blacks was rare in the early 1900s, he did not have a formal high school education. Instead, as his father had done before him, Sumner advanced his own education through intense reading and discussion on a wide variety of subjects. His parents provided guidance in his quest for knowledge by securing for him old textbooks and other reading materials.

LINCOLN UNIVERSITY: 1911–1915

In the fall of 1911, at the age of 15, Sumner was permitted to enroll as a freshman at Lincoln University on the basis of his passing a written examination. As mentioned previously, he had no high school diploma because no academic high school was available to him. He had received private instruction from his father in secondary-school subjects. Sumner's parents worked to pay their son's fees and tuition at Lincoln, and Sumner himself worked, part-time and during the summer breaks, at many odd jobs to contribute to his college expenses. In 1915, at the age of 20, he graduated from Lincoln magna cum laude, with special honors in English, modern language, Greek, Latin, and philosophy.

During this time, Sumner began a correspondence with James P. Porter, a professor of psychology and dean of the College at Clark University, concerning his possible enrollment there.

Relevant to Sumner's fate was the fact that G. Stanley Hall, then president of Clark, was a study in contradictions. He sometimes expressed views that were obviously anti-Black, but his actual behavior toward Black individuals would be considered liberal even by today's standards. Hall openly solicited Black students to enroll at Clark, and to facilitate this he encouraged a connection with a Black institution, Howard University in Washington, DC, and allowed Clark's entrance examination to be taken at several Black colleges.

In the spring of 1915, Porter (1915) notified Sumner of his acceptance to Clark's undergraduate college for the fall semester and later arranged for Sumner to live with a "fine colored family in Worcester" (Porter, 1915, p. 2).

Sumner's fondness for reading led him to want to become a great writer, and there was little doubt he succeeded. His talent as a writer had been recognized by most of his teachers at Lincoln University. Later on, G. Stanley Hall (1918) noted Sumner's literary skills and interest and observed that he was an "extraordinarily voracious reader." Sumner (1915) himself wrote, "My sole ambition is to write. Yet I shall have to fall back on something—teaching—or government employ as an immediate means of livelihood" (Sumner, 1915, p. 2). He continued, "Many have endeavored to discourage me in my projected career and yet a few old heads have advised me to follow my own bent rather than in the least to be dissuaded by anyone" (Sumner, 1915, p. 2).

CLARK COLLEGE: 1915–1916

When Sumner enrolled at Clark College in 1915, he pursued his literary interests by enrolling in English courses. He took foreign languages and psychology as electives. This combination of studies led him to be described a year later in the *Clark College Yearbook* (1916) as "more or less of a psychologist, and you can usually find him at the last table at the further end of the library reading something in the line of 'psychological' novels" (p. 14). In June 1916, Sumner was awarded his second bachelor's degree in English.

SUMNER AND HALL

The relationship between Sumner and Hall steadily grew into one of mutual respect. There is little doubt that Sumner's admiration for Hall led him to consider seriously psychology as a graduate major. Hall always found time to maintain correspondence during Sumner's World War I military service. Sumner's admiration for Hall is evident in the dedication in his manuscript, "The Structure of Religion" (Sumner, 1934) "To the Memory of G. Stanley Hall 1844–1924." In this manuscript, Sumner recalled the support and guidance that Hall had provided during his days at Clark, and he remembered with great pride Hall's enthusiasm for his writings during a seminar in the autumn of 1917:

> Dr. Hall proposed at the time that I enlarge upon ["The Structure of Religion"] under the title, "Modern Surrogates for Old Religious Ideas," as my doctoral thesis. However, it appeared that my interest in the subject had terminated for try as I might, I could not kindle a passion for the proposed study. (p. 1)

In further discussing Hall's strong suggestion that he pursue the religious treatise as a possible dissertation, Sumner wrote, "It was then as it was always . . . against my nature to write to order. [Moreover] I was at Clark University among people who believe for the most part as I did, hence there was no inspiration from opposition" (Sumner, 1934, p. 1).

LINCOLN UNIVERSITY: 1916–1917

In the fall of 1916, Sumner returned to Lincoln University as a graduate student and instructor of psychology and German. During the year at Lincoln he studied religious psychology, philosophy, and German. Teaching, which was part of his graduate course assignment, constituted the bulk of his program; he taught psychology of religion, mysticism, and rationalism; experimental psychology; social psychology; and intermediate and advanced German.

Near the end of his first semester of work at Lincoln, Sumner recognized a desire to continue in the field of psychology and a need for further advanced training. He began to investigate graduate schools, including the American University and the University of Illinois, for possible admission and financial assistance. Early in 1917, he again sought the advice and assistance of Dean Porter at Clark:

> The old problem of getting situated or of finding one's level is again before me. I am convinced that I can't do the work I want to do without further study. The chief hindrance to carrying out the latter is financial backing. (Sumner, 1917, p. 1)

Although Sumner was strongly interested in psychology, he vacillated between psychology and German as his possible major, because he felt that graduate courses in German offered the best chances for financial assistance. Nevertheless, his leaning toward psychology was evident:

> Psychology appears the most vital subject in which I would specialize. Many have tried to discourage me from that subject, saying it was not much in demand among colored people. However I seem to see a great latent demand for it. (Sumner, 1917, p. 2)

Porter's (1917) reply reinforced Sumner's bias toward psychology, and this seemed to provide the turning point for Sumner's decision:

> I would not say one word to dissuade you from the study of German if you feel that is your strongest interest. I thoroly [sic] believe that if you make of your study of psychology a practical matter you can be of the greatest service to your own people. (p. 3)

Porter (1917) continued to spell out occupational possibilities in psychology:

> This need not be confined to teaching, for the reason that many opportunities are more in evidence in which the knowledge of psychology may be turned to practical account for those in whom you may be interested. (p. 3)

Finally on March 28, 1917, after discouraging responses from American University and the University of Illinois, Sumner wrote all to ask his consideration for a junior fellowship in psychology award "to study race psychology." Because Sumner's teaching and graduate study arrangement at Lincoln University was without pay, he further impressed on Hall his need for financial assistance and his inability to find a teaching position: "I would drop out of school and teach for a while if I could get an appointment but so far none has appeared" (Sumner, 1917, p. 3). Shortly after Sumner received his MA degree from Lincoln in 1917, he received word that he had been accepted at Clark and awarded a fellowship as a senior scholar in psychology.

CLARK UNIVERSITY: 1917–1918

As Sumner prepared to return to Massachusetts and to enter the PhD program at Clark, the American Expeditionary Forces began landings in France. The United States had entered World War I, Sumner was immediately classified 1-A for military service, and he was well aware that he might be drafted in spite of the government's intention "to limit the number of colored troops in the Army" (Hall, 1918, p. 1). Nevertheless, Sumner began his graduate studies, and on October 15, 1917, Hall, Sumner's advising professor, approved his application for candidacy for the PhD degree in psychology. The following week, Sumner passed his French and German language qualifying examinations and was well into his course of studies.

Sumner's acute awareness of social injustice against Black people in the United States led him to recognize the inconsistencies of popular accusations against World War I German *Kultur* as being "symbolic of barbarity, immorality, and irreligiousness" (*Worcester Gazette,* 1918). The ensuing conflict in his mind resulted in his writing several letters to the local newspaper expressing what was to become an unpopular view to several of Worcester's leading White citizens. Sumner's first letter (Sumner, 1918a) to the editor said,

> Within the soul of each member of my race the conscious self is saying, serve your country, while the unconscious from the depths is thundering, you have a poor cause to serve. On the one side the martial music and the tramp of soldiers exhort to arms and patriotism, on the other side in movements of sweet, silent thought the words "God punish America" ring of salvation. (p. 8)

Several months later, as the fighting in Europe increased, Sumner wrote another lengthy letter (Sumner, 1918b) criticizing the claim that the United States was "a self-appointed paragon of virtue" (p. 4). In the letter, Sumner made an interesting psychoanalytic analysis of racism in the United States—which inflamed the local citizenry.

Sumner's statements, with their detailed arguments, resulted in several verbal attacks against the "Fellow in Psychology who has raised a traitor's voice in defamation of American ideals and of the spirit of American people" (Chamberlin, 1918, p. 2). The reaction to Sumner's letters reached such proportions that he was summoned to the U.S. Post Office in Worcester to give reason why he should not be listed as an enemy alien and his mail held up. The case was referred to the Boston regional post office; Sumner convinced the postal authorities of his good intentions and his loyalty to the United States, and no further action was initiated by the post office.

On May 29, Sumner (1918c) formally apologized in a letter to the newspaper for the circumstances of his "disloyalty to my native country" (p. 9). A later unsigned memorandum, undoubtedly written by Hall (1918), cleared the air by suggesting further explanations for Sumner's actions:

> Having lived in the South, [Sumner] has taken a great interest, under the influence of the colored leader Du Bois, who was Booker Washington's chief rival, in lynching, of which he has a ghastly collection of newspaper accounts, and some of which have come pretty near to him. . . . He was also smarting under the fact that by a rearrangement of the tables at the dining-hall, there happened to be at least some one at each table who preferred not to eat with a Negro, so that a special table had been arranged for him and others who had befriended him. (Hall, 1918, p. 1)

As the spring semester drew to a close, so did much of the discussion of Sumner's letters to the newspaper.

During this time, Sumner had finished a study, "Psychoanalysis of Freud and Adler," and was attempting to have it published by Badger Publishing. In the summer of 1918, he wrote Hall (Sumner, 1918d, p. 2) to ask him to consider the merits of this work as a potential doctoral dissertation. Before he was able to elicit a response from Hall, Sumner was drafted into the army.

MILITARY SERVICE: 1918–1919

As soon as he had completed his basic training with the 48th Company, 154 Depot Brigade at Camp Meade, Maryland, Sumner (1918d, p. 1) wrote to Hall. Sumner expressed disappointment over the interruption of his graduate studies and commented that he was "trying hard to take my medicine with the courage befitting a regular soldier" (p. 3). Sumner found time to humor his mentor in the same letter by drawing a parallel between army food and one of Hall's theoretical postulates,

> I noticed here at camp that they feed one so much of raw onion to give one long wind. I find that it does have something of that effect upon me and that the fact has caused me to associate it with the "second breath" phenomena. (p. 3)

Sumner felt he had a good chance of attending the army officer training camp and in another letter asked Hall to write his commanding officer to recommend him for such training. Hall promptly responded with a recommendation for officer training, but it was too late; Sumner had been transferred to Company M, 808th Pioneer Infantry, and he was on his way to the battlefields of France as a 22-year-old company sergeant.

Recalling his overseas experiences, Sumner (1925) described the horrifying effects of the war:

> The greatest fear I have ever experienced was that which I experienced when first introduced to the cannonade of German artillery. I did not fear submarines in crossing the Atlantic against which so many precautions were being taken; I did not fear exposure to the elements, to sleeping on the frozen ground, or in rain-drenched fields; I did not fear the ravages of influenza, but my resistances broke when quartered in a little shell-raked town upon which enemy artillery was trained. The man-sized projectiles would burst with the fury of gigantic explosion, causing to shudder within me every fiber. (p. 27)

Although the Armistice was signed on November 11, 1918, Sumner's unit remained in France until 1919. During this time, he took leave and went to southern France (Chambery, Lyons, Dijon) and to Paris. He also began to prepare for his return to the United States and to Clark University. In a letter to Hall early in 1919 he asked for reappointment as a senior Fellow in psychology and readmission for the 1919–1920 school year. On May 2, 1919, Hall approved Sumner's appointment as a senior fellow for the academic year 1919–1920. Writing from the Pontanezen Barracks at Brest, Sumner expressed his appreciation to Hall and spoke of his travels in France, telling how much he enjoyed that country and expressing a desire to live there (Sumner, 1919).

After his discharge in the fall of 1919, Sumner returned to Clark. With the assistance of a YMCA scholarship for veterans and the money he had saved during the war, he enrolled in psychology courses taught by Hall, E. G. Boring, S. W. Fernberger, and K. J. Karlson. On June 11, 1920, Sumner, Hall's last graduate student, defended his doctoral dissertation, "Psychoanalysis of Freud and Adler." Sumner's defense was approved and his thesis was accepted by his committee on the same day. The following day, an "Action of the Faculty" labeled his doctoral candidacy "passed." On June 14, 1920, Francis Sumner became the first Black American to receive the PhD degree in psychology.

Sumner's dissertation (Sumner, 1922), published in the *Pedagogic Seminary* (later renamed the *Journal of Genetic Psychology*), was called an outstanding interpretation of psychoanalytic theories. Hall (1920) commented on Sumner's work:

> [He] has made what I think a remarkable compilation of opinions, with a genuinely new contribution, for his Doctor's thesis on the Freudian psychanalysis [sic]. . . .

Sumner had a strong penchant for [psychoanalysis] and really has shown unusual facility in mastering and even pointing out the limitations and defects of the great authorities in that field. (Hall, 1920, p. 1)

The one journalistic account (Allison, 1920) of Sumner's graduation was in the *Crisis Magazine* in an article published annually, "The Year in Negro Education." The article noted that only two PhD degrees and twelve MA degrees had been awarded to Black graduate students in 1920:

Since the cessation of the war many Negroes who ordinarily would have continued their education, instead have entered into industry. [Although this is inevitable] we are especially proud of those of our race who keep the ranks in education [for example,] Francis C. Sumner in psychology. (p. 47)

WEST VIRGINIA COLLEGIATE INSTITUTE: 1921–1928

Sumner's first teaching position was as a professor of psychology and philosophy at Wilberforce University (Ohio) during the 1920–1921 school year. In the summer of 1921, he taught at Southern University (Louisiana). In February, 1921, Carter G. Woodson (1921), dean at West Virginia, wrote Dr. Porter of Clark:

I am looking for an instructor in Experimental Psychology to head this department in this college. Dr. Francis C. Sumner has applied for this position. What can you say of his qualifications in this field? I understand that he has worked under you. Have you another Negro graduate better qualified? (p. 1)

Professor Porter's (1921) reply spoke of Sumner's "good work as a member of my class in Social Psychology" and his graduate work under his instruction in comparative psychology. Porter continued, "He not only did good work in my courses but I know of his work in other courses. . . . He is an able and serious student. He has personal qualities which should make him a very useful man on your faculty . . . . I strongly suggest that you give him favorable consideration." (p. 1). In the fall of 1921, Sumner accepted an appointment as instructor of psychology and philosophy in the college department at West Virginia Collegiate Institute.

Shortly following his arrival at West Virginia, his lifelong emotional reaction to lightning and fire inspired him to make a contribution to the *American Journal of Psychology* on being awakened one morning by a spring thunderstorm. Sumner's description of the "Core and Context in the Drowsy State" (Sumner, 1924a) was the first of a number of significant journal articles during his seven-year tenure at West Virginia.

In one of Sumner's most timely articles (1928), he attacked the conclusion favoring genetics that had been reached by some of the contestants in the heredity and environment dispute of the 1920s:

In the current struggle between the respective protagonists of heredity and environment, the bone of contention [should not have] been whether heredity or environment contributes all but rather whether heredity or environment contributes more in the determination of an individual's achievement. The proponents of [heredity] in their eagerness to defend the myth of Nordic superiority have intentionally or unintentionally assumed that which is to be proved, namely, that heredity counts all. (p. 11)

All of Sumner's research studies at West Virginia were done without outside financial assistance. He bitterly complained of the refusals he received when applying to White agencies for funding his research projects. His own field of psychology had to be neglected because of what he referred to as the factor of race prejudice that barred him from positions in northern universities, isolated him from his White colleagues, and, worst of all, exerted a peculiar effect on his scholarship. He referred to this effect as the obsession of race persecution and observed its attendant pathological symptoms, which forced him to engage most of his mental energies in contending with race prejudice. Moreover, he called attention to the many Black institutions of higher learning that were located in out-of-the-way sections of the country and were generally difficult to get to. In Sumner's (1928) words:

The intellectual Negro is often deprived by reason of the fact that Negro universities and colleges are frequently located in almost inaccessible rural districts. In order to increase one's income that was at best half of that of a White professor, he is forced to seek ways and means of increasing the family income. These side occupations run from preaching to common labor. (p. 43)

In a series of controversial articles in 1926 and 1927, Sumner strongly endorsed some of the fundamentalist reforms of Booker T. Washington. Sumner (1926) declared, "Negro education is cryingly in need of a new dispensation. It needs awakening to the serious responsibility of morally redeeming the soul of Black folk" (p. 43). To accomplish this "new dispensation," he suggested that certain virtues be instilled in Black students:

Physical Well-Being; Simplicity in Living; Belief in God; Fondness for Literature, Art, and Music; Industry; A Contempt for Loud and Indiscreet Laughing and Talking; Thrift; Honesty; Courteousness; Respect; Race Pride; and Punctuality. (p. 43)

Sumner believed that their acceptance as a part of western culture would clear the path for Black people to enter the mainstream of U.S. society. He also believed that there were far too many substandard Black colleges and universities; he proposed (1927a) "a drastic reduction in the number of Negro colleges from 40 to about five." He wrote,

With only four or five large colleges advantageously located, . . . the resources of [the existing] forty institutions [would be] merged into the support of the smaller number. . . . Salaries [would be] placed on a standardized basis [and] the teaching personnel [would be] rigorously selected on the basis of academic and professional qualifications. (p. 43)

This was Sumner's plan for the creation of first-class institutions of higher learning. He also suggested a division of labor among the five new colleges. Two, at least, should be technical—that is, devoted to applied sciences such as home economics, business administration, electrical, chemical, civil, and mechanical engineering, social service education, library science, and agriculture. One college should specialize in the fine arts and literature, giving thorough training in music, painting, architecture, commercial art, sculpture, drama, and the writing of poetry and fiction. Two colleges should specialize in the liberal arts and sciences and should also have added to them professional schools of medicine, dentistry, law, and religion.

Finally, Sumner criticized the semester system of instruction. He believed that the division of the school year into semesters did not allow adequate time for content mastery: "It is far more important for a student to learn thoroughly and in all their ramifications three subjects a year (rather) than in isolated fragments ten or twelve subjects" (Sumner, 1926, p. 45).

Writing for the *Institute Monthly*, Sumner (1927b) tackled the issues concerning the earmarks of high intelligence when he assigned self-education and creativeness as "two infallible signs of high intelligence" (p. 6). And in one of Sumner's final articles at West Virginia, his treatise on "The Nature of Emotion," he systematically evaluated several concepts of emotion from a behavioristic stance. In this evaluation, Sumner called for the importance of understanding and training the emotions of children. He criticized the "great evil of undisciplined emotions in the home" and illustrated how this resulted in an "unfortunate augmentation of the conflict of the individual with the social milieu" (p. 52).

Sumner became restless at West Virginia because of its rural setting, the absence of other psychologists, and a felt need to fulfill his mission in a larger institution. The administration at West Virginia, sensing that Sumner might leave for a better offer and aware of the frequent faculty "raids" by Howard University—many of Howard's early faculty had taught at West Virginia State College—urged the State Board of Education to change Sumner's annual salary from $2400 to $2700, in the belief that "We shall be able to hold Dr. Sumner for this amount" (Davis, 1927, p. 1). President John Davis (1927) further commented to the Board, "I do not need to call your attention to the result which would come to this institution if Dr. Sumner accepted one of the positions to which he is now being called. You will note that we have just lost, to Howard University, Professor Julian, Head of our Department of Chemistry" (p. 1). But Davis's effort was futile. Sumner resigned from West Virginia effective August 31, 1928, and headed eastward to Howard.

HOWARD UNIVERSITY: 1928–1954

When Sumner left West Virginia, he became the acting chair of the department of psychology at Howard University. He was convinced that to develop a strong program to train psychologists adequately, psychology departments needed to be autonomous units divorced from departments of philosophy and schools of education. The inclusion of psychology in these other units of the university, then current in most Black schools, left psychology to be taught as a subject that was ancillary to education or linked to philosophy, as had been the case at West Virginia. With the aid of Howard's relatively new president, Mordecai W. Johnson, a separate department of psychology was permanently established at Howard, and Sumner was appointed full professor and head of the department in 1930.

A young graduate assistant, Frederick P. Watts, was at Howard when Sumner arrived in 1928, and he assisted Sumner during the early days; but it was clear that more help was needed to carry out Sumner's plans for an expanded department. With the recommendations of E. G. Boring, one of his former professors at Clark University, Sumner sought 30-year-old Max Meenes at Lehigh University in Pennsylvania as a new colleague. Meenes, a White man holding a PhD degree from Clark, had been trained as a "brass-instrument"[1] psychologist and had the desired specialization and credentials. Meenes elected to join Sumner at Howard in 1930. In a taped interview conducted at Howard University by the author, Max Meenes remembered his decision this way:

I was teaching at Lehigh from 1926 to 1930 and I had received a promotion from instructor to assistant professor and it seemed clear that the next step to associate professor might take quite many years, and in the meantime I had received a letter in early 1929 from Dr. Sumner at Howard University. He wanted another psychologist. . . . He made me an offer that was attractive, so I said goodbye to Lehigh and came down here. I knew that Dr. Sumner was Black and that Howard was a Black school, but I was a teacher of psychology and I wanted to teach students in psychology wherever they were. Dr. Sumner had an excellent reputation and was a brilliant scholar, so I joined him. (personal communication, Nov. 28, 1972)

A lifelong association was formed among Sumner, Meenes, and Watts. One of their most important accomplishments was creating a three-person psychology department for training Black students. As Meenes recalled, during World War II, Sumner stressed the need for Howard to train more psychologists:

The demand for Negroes trained in psychology has been larger during the present emergency than heretofore, in fact larger than the supply. It is believed that the greatest immediate need . . . is the . . . training of specialized personnel, particularly in the case of the better student. (personal communication, Nov. 28, 1972)

In 1946, as the program produced more psychologists, the enrollment at the graduate and undergraduate level was the highest in the history of the department, and

---

[1]During this era psychological laboratories became so overidentified with gadgets and other paraphernalia that they were caricaturized as "brass-instrument" laboratories. Psychologists studying in these laboratories were called "brass-instrument psychologists," as opposed to the "questionnaire"-type psychologists.

the scholastic ability was also higher. It was clear, as the 1940s came to an end, that Sumner's plan for a first-class department of psychology had reached fruition.

CONCLUSION

Sumner made significant scholarly contributions to his chosen field. Sumner, who professed religion publicly at the age of sixteen, read exhaustively in the American literature on religious psychology, and subsequently he drafted a paper titled "The Idea of Holiness" (later retitled; see Sumner, 1934). In May 1931, Sumner had the opportunity to attend the First International Congress for Religious Psychology held at the University of Vienna. At this conference he presented a paper titled "Mental Hygiene and Religion" and met many leaders among European psychologists of religion. After being inspired at this conference by the vast religion–psychology movement in Europe, Sumner began to build an extensive library of works from Europe in that area. He also began offering courses in the subject during the 1940s. Sumner's massive 1934 manuscript, *The Structure of Religion: A History of European Psychology of Religion,* is proof of his growing interest.

Sumner was also responsible for instigating studies and research into the relationship between psychology and the law. Along these lines, his research expanded into several additional areas. Among them, in the late 1930s and 1940s, was a series of important studies assessing the attitudes of Black and White individuals toward the administration of justice. Sumner, with his graduate students, surveyed more than 2000 college students. Their data led to the recommendation of several procedures that promised to administer justice on a more democratic basis.

Sumner's enjoyment of reading and his constant quest for knowledge led him to write many reviews of a wide variety of books. He became an official abstractor for the *Psychological Bulletin* and for the *Journal of Social Psychology.* In this capacity, he wrote English abstracts of more than 3000 articles in German, French, and Spanish.

Sumner was described by former students as a low-keyed and very dedicated psychologist; as a very quiet and unassuming individual who was brilliant with a tremendous capacity to make an analysis of an individual's personality; and as Howard's most stimulating scholar. His colleagues spoke of his deep interest in his students and recalled that he prepared a mimeographed newsletter, *The Record,* which he issued periodically, publishing items of interest about graduates from his department, their accomplishments, and various statistical summaries.

Sumner was a Fellow of the American Psychological Association and held memberships in the American Association for the Advancement of Science, American Educational Research Association, Eastern Psychological Association, Southern Society for Philosophy and Psychology, and the District of Columbia Psychological Association. His fraternal memberships included Psi Chi, Pi Gamma Mu, and Kappa Alpha Psi. His lifelong membership in Kappa Alpha Psi was active and dedicated; he wrote frequent articles in their national journal. His first marriage was to Francees H. Hughston in 1922, and his second marriage was to Nettie M. Brooker in 1946. He had no children.

On January 12, 1954, Sumner suffered a fatal heart attack while shoveling snow at his home in Washington, DC. President Mordecai Johnson of Howard University delivered the eulogy at the University Chapel, and J. St. Clair Price, dean of the College of Liberal Arts at Howard, paid a tribute. There was a military honor guard in memory of his service in World War I and he was buried at Arlington Cemetery in Virginia. Sumner's role in the development of Black psychologists is a monument to perseverance, scholarship, and dedication.

REFERENCES

Allison, M. G. (1920). The year in Negro education. *Crisis Magazine*, 126.

Chamberlin, H. (1918, May 27). Letter to the editor. In "The Forum of the People," *Worcester Gazette*, p. 4, col. 2.

Clark College Yearbook. (1916). "Who's Who, 1916." Worcester, MA: Clark University Press.

Davis, J. (1927). Letter to the West Virginia State Board of Education and Advisory Council, July 19.

Hall, G. S. (1918). Letter. *University Archives*, Clark University, Worcester, MA.

Hall, G. S. (1920). Letter. *University Archives*, Clark University, Worcester, MA.

Porter, J. P. (1915). Letter to F. C. Sumner, *University Archives*, Clark University, Worcester, MA.

Porter, J. P. (1917). Letter to F. C. Sumner, *University Archives*, Clark University, Worcester, MA.

Porter, J. P. (1921). Letter to F. C. Sumner, *University Archives*, Clark University, Worcester, MA.

Sumner, F. C. (1915). Letter to J. P. Porter, *University Archives*, Clark University, Worcester, MA.

Sumner, F. C. (1917). Letter to J. P. Porter, *University Archives*, Clark University, Worcester, MA.

Sumner, F. C. (1918a, February 15). Letter to the editor. In "Forum of the People," *Worcester Gazette*, p. 7, col. 2.

Sumner, F. C. (1918b, May 25). Letter to the editor. In "Forum of the People," *Worcester Gazette*, p. 6, col. 2.

Sumner, F. C. (1918c, May 29). Letter to the editor. In " Forum of the People," *Worcester Gazette*, p. 5, col. 4.

Sumner, F. C. (1918d), June 18). Letter to G. S. Hall, University Archives, Clark University, Worcester, MA.

Sumner, F. C. (1919). Letter to G. S. Hall, *University Archives*, Clark University Worcester, MA.

Sumner, F. C. (1921). Letter to J. P. Porter, *University Archives*, Clark University Worcester, MA.

Sumner, F. C. (1922). Psychoanalysis of Freud and Adler on sex-determinism and character formation. *Pedagogical Seminary, 29,* 139–168.

Sumner, F. C. (1924a). Core and context in the drowsy states. *American Journal of Psychology, 35,* 307–308.

Sumner, F. C. (1924b). The nature of emotion. *Howard Review, 1,* 1–38.

Sumner, F. C. (1925). The fear of death and the belief in a future life. *Kappa Alpha Psi Journal, 12.*

Sumner, F. C. (1926). The philosophy of Negro educating. *Educational Review, 71,* 42–45.

Sumner, F. C. (1927a). Morale and the Negro college. *Educational Review, 73,* 168–172.

Sumner, F. C. (1927b). Earmarks of high grade intelligence. *The Institute Monthly,* 6–8.

Sumner, F. C. (1928). Environic factors which prohibit creative scholarship among Negroes. *School and Society, 22,* 294–296.

Sumner, F. C. (1934). *The structure of religion: A history of European psychology of religion.* Unpublished manuscript. Howard University, Washington, DC.

Woodson, C. G. (1921). Letter to J. P. Porter, *University Archives*, Clark University, Worcester, MA.

Worcester Gazette. (1918). May 25, p. 8.

Chapter 12

Fritz Heider: Philosopher and Social Psychologist

Bertram F. Malle and William Ickes

> Whenever I begin to think about specific experiments that I might do, I am confronted with theoretical problems whose solution does not require experiments but which can be thought through on the basis of the ordinary experience of everyday life. Only when I have cleared up the basic concepts would I feel it proper to proceed to experiments. (Heider, 1983, p. 87)

Fritz Heider was a wanderer, someone who liked to survey and take the measure of whatever he encountered. In his formative years, he was a wanderer in the geographical sense—hiking in his beloved Austrian mountains and traveling through much of Europe. In his professional years, he was a wanderer in the intellectual sense—taking daily walks for the purpose of analyzing a difficult concept or conducting a thought experiment. Because he was rarely in a hurry and took the time to look more closely and to deliberate more thoroughly than most of his peers, Heider was able to achieve profound insights about essential aspects of human behavior and experience.

There are few social psychologists who have had more influence on their field than Heider. There are also few psychologists whose ideas have been so often underestimated and misrepresented. In this chapter we follow the development of Heider's contributions to psychology along the tread marks of his own life path—from philosophy to psychology, from Europe to America. By tracing the development and interrelation of Heider's ideas we hope to emphasize their originality and scope and speak out against the sometimes narrow reading of Heider's work.

---

*Photo of Fritz Heider courtesy of Heider Archives.

GRAZ

Heider was born in Vienna in 1896 but he grew up in and around Graz, the second largest Austrian city, which lies at the southeast end of the Alps. Heider's childhood was happy, carefree, and protected. During adolescence, the previously extroverted Heider became serious and quite shy, perhaps as the result of a serious eye injury he sustained at the age of 9 and some bewildering experiences that taught him about the harsher realities outside of family life.

Two of Heider's lifelong preoccupations were already evident: his interest in human perception (initially in the context of drawing) and his fascination with human relations, about which he wrote in small notebooks. After completing his Gymnasium years, Heider wanted to become a painter, but his father—a prosperous architect—suggested that he make a living through more traditional means and keep art as his hobby. Thus began a tortuous path for Heider toward finding such traditional means.

Because of his bad eye, Heider was not drafted into military service during World War I and, in 1914, he enrolled as an architecture student at the Technical University in Graz. Soon, however, he grew tired of the tedious reproductive exercises (for example, making copies of Greek temple blueprints) that were required of architecture students. So in 1915 he once more expressed to his family the desire to become a painter. His father again discouraged the idea, this time persuading him to study law. Heider gave that a try but soon lost interest. He decided to admit frankly to his father that he was interested in learning for its own sake, not as a means to a particular profession. His father, always more of a friend than an authority figure for Heider, offered him four years of intellectual luxury—auditing courses in all his areas of interest—if he agreed to study agriculture afterward and raise pigs on a piece of land they owned.

Heider was happy to accept this offer, and his studies over the next years spanned the fields of premedical science, zoology, philosophy, and art history. He spent semesters in Innsbruck and in Munich, where he took his first course in psychology with Karl and Charlotte Bühler. Returning to Graz, Heider focused his studies increasingly on philosophy and, to the extent that it was possible, on the fledgling field of psychology.

The major figure at the Graz Institute of Philosophy was Alexius Meinong, and Heider took many courses with him. Meinong's ontology and epistemology were extensively discussed by G. E. Moore and Bertrand Russell in the early years of analytical philosophy, and Meinong is still well-known in today's philosophical circles for his analysis of how we can know and refer to nonexisting objects (see Zalta, 1988). A philosopher at heart, Meinong was also a strong proponent of empirical psychology, even though he did not conduct experiments himself. On his initiative, the University of Graz offered a proseminar on psychological experiments as early as 1886 and funded an experimental laboratory in 1894. Christian von Ehrenfels, often identified as a predecessor of Gestalt psychology, was one of Meinong's students and also a teacher of Max Wertheimer (chap. 13, *Pioneers I*) in Prague. During Heider's time at Graz, the most active empirical researcher was Vittorio Benussi, also a student of Meinong's. Often overlooked in histories of psychology, Benussi published some of the earliest experimental papers on Gestalt principles in perception (Benussi, 1906, 1914). His work made a strong impression on the emerging group around Wertheimer in Berlin (e.g., Koffka, 1915).

Much of the thinking and research at the Graz Institute focused on sensation and perception, topics that enabled the philosophers to integrate the classic puzzles of epistemology with their nascent commitment to an empirical study of psychological processes. Heider became Meinong's last doctoral student, and he fit well into the Graz school's focus on perception, even though his interest in perception was initially fueled more by drawing and painting than by philosophical puzzles. At first Heider merely audited seminars and lectures, but it eventually occurred to him that, like his fellow students, he too had the potential to write a doctoral thesis. He broached this idea to Meinong, who referred him to one of his books on epistemology, and Heider began to read, analyze, and expand on the core problem of Meinong's current thinking: the relation between sense qualities and real objects. Meinong and Heider asked how it is possible that we take sense qualities to be qualities of objects, given that sense qualities are "in here," in the mind, whereas object qualities are "out there," in the physical world. Heider's solution to this puzzle was one of the first causal theories of perception—a theory that describes the causal chain between properties of objects and properties of the perceptions to which they correspond (Heider, 1920).

At the heart of Heider's theory lies the distinction between *things* (physical objects) and the *media* through which things "reach" the perceiver (see also Heider, 1925). Things, according to Heider, are coherent units that have mutually dependent parts and are thus causally potent in shaping their surrounding forms and processes. Heider liked to use the example of a ticking watch that causes systematic air vibrations (sound), which stimulate the eardrum and lead to perception. Heider argued that things shape media and not vice versa, so the perceptual apparatus must reconstruct things from their effects on media, and ultimately on the senses. Heider termed this reconstructive process in perception *attribution*, and he argued that it focuses not on the specifics of the media but on the dispositional qualities of things, for these qualities shape the media surrounding them. Thus when we look at a house we say, "I see a house," not "I see sunlight," even though the sunlight is the necessary medium by which we are able to see the house.

Readers who are familiar with Heider's later thinking will recognize that several of its defining features were already present in his dissertation work: (a) the method of developing conceptual distinctions and relations from an analysis of linguistic use and familiar domains of knowledge, (b) the notion of *units*, (c) the notion of *attribution* as a reconstructive process, and (d) the notion of *dispositions*. When Heider later applied these concepts to the domain of social perception, he expanded their meaning to fit the more complex social domain, but he also retained much of their core meaning. As a result, misunderstandings ensued because readers who were not familiar with the original core meaning mistook the expanded meaning (e.g., personality traits as one type of dispositions that social perceivers reconstruct) for the exclusive meaning (i.e., dispositions are always personality traits). We will return to these misunderstandings in a later section.

Despite the focus on object perception in his dissertation work, Heider's deepest concern was already with the topic of social perception—the perception of social "objects" such as people, conversations, or relationships. However, neither among his fellow students and mentors nor in the field of psychology as a whole did Heider find scholars who shared his interest in social perception, and he feared that the academic path might not allow him to study this topic most dear to him. So in spite of delivering a creative dissertation in an impressively short span of nine months, Heider did not, on receiving his doctorate in 1920, enter the academic world.

Heider's four years of luxurious studies came to an end, and the arrangement with his father committed him to start reading about pigs and cows, in preparation for going to agricultural school and taking up farming. Luckily, however, Heider was offered a reprieve in the form of an applied psychology position with the provincial government—a position that required him to devise aptitude tests and provide vocational guidance for adolescents. After a year and a half in this occupation, Heider became restless and contemplated leaving Graz. World War I had degraded the culturally and intellectually rich Imperial Austria to a frail, destitute nation, and postwar inflation made educational positions such as Heider's acutely vulnerable to funding cuts. Moreover, with Meinong's death in 1920 and Benussi's move to Italy, the Graz school not only had lost its most active scholars but also surrendered to the Berlin school all control over the research agenda in Gestalt psychology.

Intellectual life was indeed blossoming in Berlin, and because Heider's uncle (and friend) Karl Heider was a professor in Berlin, it seemed natural for him to move there.

BERLIN

Soon after arriving in Berlin in the fall of 1921, Heider attended psychology courses offered by Max Wertheimer, Wolfgang Köhler (chap. 17, *Pioneers I*), and Kurt Lewin (chap. 7, *Pioneers III*) with whom he developed a lasting friendship. While earning a modest living through dozens of small jobs and enjoying the excitement and intoxication of big-city life, Heider continued to work on his theory of perception. In the spring of 1923, Lewin invited him to give a talk about his work at a gathering of the Philosophical Society in Erlangen, and the reception was positive. Among the speakers were Rudolf Carnap and Hans Reichenbach (major proponents of the emerging "Logical Empiricism" movement in philosophy), but Heider found himself unimpressed by Carnap's tangled attempt to explicate logically the simple statement "1 + 1 = 2." Heider strongly endorsed the use of conceptual explication as a scientific tool, but deemed it more appropriate for elucidating real-world social phenomena such as emotions, action, and conflict.

As Heider's thinking about social perception developed, he recognized its commonalities with Lewin's work on thought and action. Both theorists, for example, were interested in the subjective representation of reality. Lewin was concerned with explaining action as locomotion through a subjectively represented life space; Heider was concerned with explaining one person's subjective perception of another person's action. Moreover, Heider learned from Lewin (himself influenced by the philosopher Ernst Cassirer) the value of having a well-organized system of concepts when describing any phenomenon—in particular, any psychological phenomenon. Lewin grounded his system of concepts in topology, perhaps influenced by the high status of mathematics in the rapidly growing philosophy of science community in Europe. Interpersonal phenomena, however, were not readily explicable within Lewin's topological system, and Heider realized that he had to develop his own system of concepts (an endeavor that took more than 30 years to complete).

Heider's exciting years in Berlin came to an end in 1924 when, strapped for money, he took a position at an orphanage in Northern Germany. He stayed for a summer but then returned to Austria, unsure what he should do with his life. A gift offered by a generous relative came in the form of a monthly allowance, which enabled Heider to live for the next two years without worrying about regular work. He spent much of this time painting, reading, and thinking about psychology, while traveling among Graz, Czechoslovakia, Florence, and Naples.

As his 30th birthday approached, however, Heider felt that his years of wandering were coming to an end. After considering his options and interests, he recommitted himself to an academic career in psychology. Through the years he had continued to keep notes on his psychological thinking about the problems of perception and interpersonal relations. He also enjoyed the support and encouragement of Kurt Lewin, who was instrumental in helping Heider publish *Ding und Medium* around that time (Heider, 1925). It therefore seemed natural for him to move back to Germany, where his chances of finding an assistantship appeared to be the greatest.

HAMBURG

By 1927, Heider had three academic positions to choose from—in Graz, Vienna, and Hamburg. The Austrian positions promised familiarity and comfort, but they also signified a step back. Heider chose to go forward and became a lecturer in educational psychology at the Psychology Institute in Hamburg, which was chaired by William Stern (chap. 6, *Pioneers II*).

Heider comfortably slid into the academic role. He enjoyed lecturing on educational psychology and exploring themes of interpersonal relations between students and teachers. With some disappointment, he noticed that there was no literature on this topic, so he began to collect free-response data on students' experiences that were formative for teacher–student relations. However, Heider was unable to find order in the richness of these data because, as he later confessed, "I lacked a network of clear concepts and a knowledge of their interrelations" (Heider, 1983, p. 86). He also thought a good deal about trait words and suspected that they might reveal something fundamental about interpersonal relations. He eventually concluded that the opposite was true: that the meaning of trait terms will become clearer if one first develops a theory of interpersonal behavior.

Even more than his teaching, Heider enjoyed the collegial interactions and intellectual exchanges at this high-powered university, which was then in its golden age. He had contact, among others, with Ernst Cassirer, the eminent philosopher; Heinz Werner, an influential psychologist; and Jakob von Uexküll, the well-known biologist. In collaboration with Werner he organized a meeting in Rostock between the Hamburg and the Berlin psychologists, including Lewin, Wertheimer, and Köhler, who were joined by Albert Michotte from Belgium.

During his years at Hamburg, Heider did not publish experimental work. Instead, he refined the concepts he had first developed in his dissertation, resulting in a lens model of perception (Heider, 1930) that inspired Egon Brunswik's well-known work (e.g., Brunswik, 1934). In 1929 Heider met Brunswik at a conference in Vienna (where he was an assistant with Karl Bühler) and exchanged ideas with him, Bühler, and Else Frenkel. Bühler invited Heider to an informal evening discussion among psychoanalysts and empirical psychologists. At the time, there was little common ground between the two emerging traditions; it was Frenkel who later identified such common ground (e.g., Frenkel-Brunswik, 1940, 1954). Frenkel, perhaps one of the most broad-minded psychologists of her time, also had contacts with the emerging Vienna Circle (the groundbreaking group of philosophers of science led by Moritz Schlick and Otto Neurath), and she took Heider to one of their meetings.

This wide variety of intellectual connections was perhaps typical for that time, and it was certainly typical for Heider: "All my life, wherever I have been, I have tried to get people together for discussions" (Heider, 1983, p. 88). Heider interacted with philosophers, psychologists of all denominations, biologists, writers, and artists. At one point he even became interested in astrology and graphology, more for their refined systems of describing personality, life tasks, and interpersonal relations than for their alleged connections to planets or handwriting. This breadth and open-mindedness is seldom found in today's academic psychology.

Heider's career might have stalled had he stayed in Hamburg without publishing. Or perhaps he might have returned to Vienna, where he was highly regarded, and eventually become a full professor there. In either case, he would not have helped revolutionize American social psychology. Fortune had it that Kurt Koffka, who had just begun a five-year visiting position at Smith College to develop a research department in psychology, was searching for an assistant to supervise some of the burgeoning research at Smith and at the neighboring Clarke School for the Deaf. Because Koffka could not find a suitable person in America, he asked Stern to recommend someone, and Stern recommended Heider. Without hesitation Heider accepted the position, expecting to return after a year. Apart from a few memorable visits, however, Heider was never to return to Europe.

NORTHAMPTON

In the fall of 1930, Heider began his research appointment at the Clarke School in Northampton and his teaching position at Smith College, where he would stay for 17 years. Heider's time in America began well—he liked the little town of Northampton and its surrounding hills, and he was welcomed warmly by the people there.

On arriving he met Grace Moore, who had graduated from Mount Holyoke College and was working on her master's degree at Smith. Moore had also an interest in strengthening the ties between the Clarke School (where her only sister, who was deaf, had been educated) and Smith College, so she volunteered to help Heider settle into his role as the head of research at the newly formed Clarke Research Department. Both were also members of Koffka's lab, and within a few weeks Grace and Fritz had fallen deeply in love. Because of both their differences (diverse cultural backgrounds and experiences) and their similarities (shared interests and knowledge, agreement on many issues, and common acquaintances), the two had much to talk about. It was quite natural for them to spend increasing amounts of time together, and they quickly became inseparable. They were married after three months.

In the summer of 1932, the Heiders embarked on extended travels in Europe, visiting many friends and colleagues and attending conferences. It was less than a year before the Nazi party, under Hitler's lead, would gain power in Germany. The international conference of psychology in Copenhagen, which the Heiders attended, was the last occasion to unite the elite of psychology in Europe. Then the massive exodus began. Wertheimer and Lewin left in 1933. Stern was dismissed from his professorship in Hamburg, his books were burned, and he fled to America in 1935. Köhler, not Jewish himself, fought courageously for academic freedom for a while but eventually had to escape. Karl Duncker, Paul Lazarsfeld, Egon Brunswik, and Else Frenkel were among the others who left Europe after 1935, and many of them passed through Northampton. Around that time, perhaps to strengthen the ties between the many exiles, Lewin initiated an annual meeting of "Topological Psychologists." The meeting grew in membership and eminence over the decades, hosting many outstanding psychologist [e.g., Gregory Bateson, Erik Erikson, Leon Festinger (chap. 20, *Pioneers III*), James Gibson (chap. 17, *Pioneers II*), George Herbert Mead, Henry Murray], until the meetings ended in the 1960s.

During the first years in Northampton, Heider struggled with the challenges of expressing his thoughts in English (his second language) and finding sources of intellectual inspiration. To bridge this time of "ebb tides" (Heider, 1983, p. 112), he immersed himself in the study of statistics and taught a seminar on experimental psychology at Smith College. Working collaboratively with Grace, he also translated Lewin's *Principles of Topological Psychology* during the summer of 1935 and his own article *Thing and Medium* in 1936. His work on the latter translation led Heider to return briefly to issues of perception, but despite praise from such eminent thinkers as Kurt Lewin, Rudolf Carnap, Hans Reichenbach, Karl Bühler, and Egon Brunswik, his work in this area found little reception or acknowledgment in the academic community.

Perhaps spurred by this lack of acknowledgment, and certainly because of their involvement with the Clarke School for the Deaf, the Heiders began a program of original research on aspects of language learning in deaf children—a program that led to two well-known publications in this field (Heider & Moore Heider, 1940, 1941). They found, for example, that lip-reading ability is correlated not with general intellectual aptitude but with the ability to follow a rhythm (e.g., in dancing) and the ability to empathize with other people. Through observing the social detriments that can accompany deafness, Heider also gained a greater appreciation for the social function of language—the many ways in which it enables and advances interaction with others.

In the early 1940s, Heider returned to what he had come to recognize as his primary concern: describing the manifold of social relations in more general, theoretically coherent terms. In all his previous analyses of interpersonal behavior—from his early observations of quarreling relatives to his more recent studies of deaf children—Heider felt the need for a general framework of concepts with which to describe that behavior. He was convinced that a systematic psychological theory of social relations must start with a well-formed network of concepts applicable to that domain. The breakthrough came when Heider realized that there already existed such a powerful conceptual network: It was commonsense psychology, the system of concepts ordinary people use to describe and understand human behavior. Just as Lewin and Solomon Asch had before him, Heider recognized that a psychology of social interaction must chart out the subjective concepts and perceptions of the social perceiver, "studying interpersonal relations at the level of their meaning for the participants" (Ickes & Harvey, 1978).

The significance of Heider's insight cannot be overstated. Today, the importance of commonsense psychology (typically labeled *theory of mind*) is widely accepted and enthusiastically discussed across disciplinary boundaries (e.g., Carruthers & Smith, 1996; Davies & Stone, 1995). Fifty years ago, however, its study was extremely unusual and suspect because of its own nonscientific status. Heider was one of the first theorists to recognize that the conceptual network of commonsense psychology has a fundamental influence on people's social perception and action—an influence comparable to that which the Kantian categories of space, time, and causality have on people's perception and action in the physical world.

There was, already at this early stage of Heider's ambitious project, a fundamental ambiguity that has plagued the interpretation of his opus ever since. On the one hand, Heider wanted to develop a *theory of social behavior* grounded in an organized network of scientific concepts and their relations. On the other, he wanted to reconstruct commonsense concepts and their relations as they are already used by ordinary people, summarized in a *theory of social perception*— a theory of how people *think* about social behavior. Heider reconciled these different goals in two ways (see Heider, 1958, p. 5). First, he asserted that a theory of social perception can predict a good deal of human behavior because people's social behavior is based to a large extent on their commonsense concepts of social perception. Second, he made the even bolder assertion that commonsense concepts provide a good starting point for a scientific theory of social behavior.

Researchers who followed Heider were less careful in reconciling, or even distinguishing, the two aspects of Heider's project (see Fletcher, 1995). For example, the two aspects are strikingly confounded in Smedslund's (1997) heroic attempt to build an axiomatic system of commonsense concepts (see Malle, 1998). In addition, most attribution researchers ignored Heider's advice that "scientific psychology has a good deal to learn from common-sense psychology" (Heider, 1958, p. 5). Instead, they compared people's thinking about social behavior to normative models that psychologists proposed (e.g., Kelley, 1967; Nisbett & Ross, 1980).

From 1943 on, Heider worked on this immense, initially amorphous project of laying out a conceptual network of interpersonal behavior. He read children's stories, fables, dramas, and novels, trying to extract from them basic principles of how people perceive and relate to each other. In 1944 he published two papers (Heider, 1944; Heider & Simmel, 1944) based on the famous studies with

Marianne Simmel, one of his students at Smith College. In these studies, participants were presented with films of geometric figures that were animated as if moving around in relation to each other. Heider and Simmel found that the observers almost invariably treated these figures as agents and interpreted their movements in terms of interpersonal relations such as love, hate, power, fights, and reunions.

These results are usually interpreted as evidence that people inevitably use social perception concepts such as intention and emotion and project them even onto geometric shapes (e.g., Dittrich & Lea, 1994). A sentence in Heider's autobiography, however, suggests a slightly different interpretation: "As I planned the action of the film, I thought of the small triangle and the circle as a pair of lovers or friends and I thought of the big triangle as a bully who intruded on them" (Heider, 1983, p. 148). In this light, one realizes that the participants did not freely project intentionality and emotion onto the geometric figures but instead were able to understand what Heider tried to communicate to them. The geometric shapes and their movements served as a kind of language in which Heider communicated a human interest story. How he translated this story into the language of moving geometric shapes is at least as intriguing as the fact that observers were able to infer the story from the movements. Indeed, recent research in developmental psychology has begun to examine the features of objects and movements that compel people (and infants in particular) to perceive things as agents and ascribe intentions and other mental states to them (e.g., Baldwin & Baird, 1999; Gergely, Nadasdy, Csibra, & Biro, 1995; Premack & Premack, 1995).

Despite the publication of these two papers, Heider did not feel that he had made much progress toward his larger project of developing a systematic conceptual framework for describing interpersonal relations. His teaching load was heavy at Smith College (he had taken over for the late Koffka); no federal funding was available during wartime for work on conceptual projects; and few people appreciated, let alone understood, Heider's vision. Even after the publication of another groundbreaking paper in which Heider first formulated his balance hypotheses (Heider, 1946), he became discouraged by the apparent lack of interest in his ideas and fell victim to a series of anxiety attacks.

Symptomatic of his frustration during these years was an incident in 1946, which occurred during a conference at Harvard on social perception that Lewin organized. Heider gave a one-hour talk on his ideas about interpersonal relations, which appeared to rouse no one except Roger Barker and Lewin himself. The feeble response from the scientific community lasted for quite some time. Heider reported, for example, that Jerome Bruner, who was also at the Harvard conference, did not once refer to Heider's talk, despite many subsequent conversations between the two. To some extent, Bruner may have been attempting to atone for this slight when, decades later, he emphasized the fundamental importance of folk psychology and acknowledged Heider's role in illuminating it (Bruner, 1990).

Heider's health, both physical and psychological, was of concern to his friends and supporters, and one of them practically forced him to take a summer vacation on Martha's Vineyard. There Heider found time to work on his ideas and build up some strength. His friends also encouraged him to apply for a Guggenheim fellowship, which would allow him to work uninterrupted for a whole year on his "book project." Shortly before Lewin's death in 1946, Heider had a last, long conversation with him about psychological theory, the topic of so many mutually inspiring discussions in the past. From Lewin and his supportive friends, Heider had regained hope and verve.

In fact, Heider received a Guggenheim fellowship in the academic year of 1947–1948 and was also offered a new academic position. Barker (a former postdoctoral student of Lewin's at the University of Iowa) was about to take the chair in psychology at the University of Kansas and he invited a few of his colleagues—people from the Lewin group, including Heider—to join him there. Heider cherished the prospect of working with graduate students and developing his ideas in the safety of a permanent academic position. The Heiders accepted the offer swiftly and enthusiastically, relocating to Kansas in the summer of 1947.

KANSAS

The new environment was intellectually stimulating. The psychology department at Kansas benefited from the influx of a number of young and active researchers, and the Menninger clinic was just an hour away, giving Grace a base from which to conduct her own research. The Heiders quickly established friendships and were never at a loss for discussion partners. They also welcomed several visitors from Europe, New England, and other parts of the United States, many of them originating from the Gestalt psychology school or from Lewin's group of graduate and postdoctoral students at Iowa, Stanford, and MIT.

During his first years in Kansas, Heider found the time and freedom to work on his book, a theoretical account of interpersonal relations. From 1948 on, rough drafts of his developing chapters were mimeographed and circulated among various colleagues in the field. As Robert Krauss (1983) recalled, "A graduate student thought to be deserving and (more importantly) neat would be permitted to borrow it overnight, one chapter at a time."

Although Heider believed that his thinking had become clearer and more orderly, he was working, characteristically, at a slow pace toward completing the book. It took another Guggenheim fellowship (1951–1952), a Ford Foundation fellowship (1956–1957), and nine additional years of work—toward the end with the enormous help of Beatrice Wright, a former graduate student with Lewin at

Iowa—until the book was sent off to publishers. After 15 years of work on this project and more than 40 years of thinking about interpersonal relations, after numerous rejections, misunderstandings, and much indifference, Heider finally published what eventually would be recognized as a seminal contribution to psychology. His patience and persistence through decades of indifference are deeply admirable and inspiring.

THE PSYCHOLOGY OF INTERPERSONAL RELATIONS (1958)

By the time the book was published, Heider was known for his work on perception and primarily for his influential balance theory (Heider, 1946), which set in motion an enduring research program on cognitive consistency (see Abelson, 1968). Heider's balance theory applied the Gestalt principle of unit formation to the realm of sentiments (emotions and values) and predicted the conditions under which relations among people, and between people and entities, would be perceived as harmonious.

In *The Psychology of Interpersonal Relations*, Heider elaborated on his balance theory, but the truly novel aim of his book was to explore thoroughly the network of commonsense concepts that people use to describe human behavior (including terms such as *can*, *want*, *intend*, *ought*). Heider's blend of empirical observation with conceptual and linguistic analysis was visionary and unlike anything psychology had seen before—resembling much more the tradition of ordinary language philosophy (Austin, 1962; Ryle, 1949; Searle, 1969) and anticipating contemporary cognitive linguistics by about 40 years (e.g., Jackendoff, 1985; Lakoff, 1987).

How was the book received? According to Krauss (1998), its initial reception was ambivalent and cautious, in good part because Heider's treatise lacked explicitly stated hypotheses and empirical support at a time when experimentation had great currency. Moreover, Heider's appreciation of the insights to be gleaned from commonsense psychology stood in direct opposition to the contemporary emphasis on the counterintuitive predictions of dissonance theory (Festinger, 1957) and other emerging cognitive theories (e.g., Miller, Galanter, & Pribram, 1960). These theories—depicting humans as complex biological machines guided by (often unconscious) cognitive processes—seemed to cater to many psychologists' desire to do actual science, not "just philosophy." But for Heider, who had been trained as a philosopher, it seemed only natural to use conceptual analysis (a philosopher's tool) to reconstruct commonsense concepts in social perception and to depict people as what they perceive each other to be: intentional agents with motives and purposes, navigating planfully in a complex environment.

Even though Heider's book was at odds with the zeitgeist, it received a favorable review by Kelley (1960) and was followed by seminal papers on attribution processes that drew heavily on Heider's analysis (Jones & Davis, 1965; Kelley, 1967). *The Psychology of Interpersonal Relations* eventually became a classic, and it is still widely read and cited today.

We propose that this continued popularity has been possible for reasons that perhaps are not flattering either to Heider or to his interpreters. We suggest that *The Psychology of Interpersonal Relations* became a classic in part through the selective attention and resulting misunderstandings of its interpreters, facilitated by ambiguities in the work itself. In the spirit of examining closely Heider's work as well as his life, we invite the reader to engage briefly in a revisionary exegesis.

In his earlier work on the perception of physical objects, Heider used the concept of attribution to refer to the reconstruction of distal objects from features of perceptual experience. In *The Psychology of Interpersonal Relations*, he extended the concept of attribution to the perception of other persons and was then obliged to deal with the more complex structures in which person–perception is embedded. For it was clear to Heider that persons are very different "objects of perception" than inanimate objects. Persons are "perceived as action centers and as such can do something to us. They can benefit or harm us intentionally, and we can benefit or harm them. Persons have abilities, wishes and sentiments; they can act purposefully, and can perceive or watch us" (Heider, 1958, p. 21). Note that twice in this short quote Heider refers to the *intentionality/purposefulness* of persons, which he considered to be a fundamental concept in commonsense psychology. Even so, most of the subsequent research on attribution downplayed this concept and thereby missed what is perhaps Heider's most significant contribution.

The tendency to downplay Heider's thinking about intentionality can best be illustrated with respect to the famous chapter 4 of *The Psychology of Interpersonal Relations*, in which Heider laid out in detail what he termed people's "naive analysis of action." The first two sections of this chapter, "Dispositional Properties" and "Forces of the Person and the Environment," provided the basis for subsequent attribution theory revolving around the person–situation dichotomy. In contrast, the next two sections, "Personal and Impersonal Causality" and "The Concept of Trying," which both focused on the social perception of intentionality, did not enter mainstream attribution research.

We suggest that this process of selective attention is associated with four related misunderstandings. First, researchers interpreted Heider's notion of *disposition* rather narrowly as stable personality traits or abilities. Although Heider (1958) did occasionally refer to traits and abilities when talking about dispositions (e.g., p. 30, p. 80), it is clear that he considered "motives, intentions, sentiments . . . the core processes which manifest themselves in overt behavior" (p. 34). They are "the psychological entities that bring consistency and meaning to the behavior" (p. 34). Similarly, when Heider characterized the inference of "invariances" as an essential component of perception, and therefore of social perception, his readers interpreted these invariances as stable, enduring factors (such as personality traits). Heider's notion of invariances, however, included "perceptions, intentions, desires, pleasures, abilities, and sentiments" (p. 26), which are all invariant relative to the stream of ongoing behavior. Among these factors, motives—not personality traits—occupied a special role: "The underlying causes of events, especially the motives of other persons, are the invariances of the environment that are relevant to [the perceiver]; they give meaning to what [the perceiver] experiences" (p. 81).

Second, many of Heider's readers have considered the distinction between personal factors and environmental factors to be the centerpiece of his theorizing. However, for Heider this distinction was only one of many within the conceptual network, and to him perhaps less important than the distinction between personal (i.e., intentional) and impersonal (i.e., unintentional) causality. Worse yet, his readers were much too eager to equate person factors with traits. As a result, the study of people's commonsense analysis of behavior turned into requests for simplistic ratings about the extent to which "traits" versus "the situation" influenced a given behavior.

Third, Heider's distinction between personal and impersonal causality—the terms he used to characterize intentional versus unintentional behavior (Heider, 1958, pp. 100–101)—was falsely equated with the distinction between personal causes (traits) and situational causes. As a result, attribution research applied the person–situation dichotomy to all behaviors alike, whether intentional or unintentional, and thereby eliminated (since Kelley, 1967) the central concepts of intention, purpose, and motive from later models of social perception.

Heider may have contributed to this misinterpretation by claiming that "in the case of impersonal causality, a wide range of environmental conditions will lead to a wide range of effects" (1958, p. 102), as if suggesting that impersonal causality always involves environmental (situational) causes. However, he also identified "effects involving persons but not intentions . . . as cases of impersonal causality" (p. 101), thus acknowledging unintentional behaviors caused by person factors (e.g., sadness because of a thought about one's dead brother). Most important, he clearly stated that "personal causality refers to instances in which p causes x intentionally. That is to say, the action is purposive" (p. 100). Thus at the heart of his analysis lies the distinction between intentional and unintentional behavior, not the distinction between person causes and situation causes.

Fourth, Heider's analysis of *trying* and the attribution of actions to motives have been forgotten, because many readers subsumed them under the broad category of "person attributions." A careful reading of Heider's book reveals (and an interview by Harvey, Ickes, & Kidd, 1978, confirms) that Heider clearly distinguished between (a) attributing outcomes to causal factors (i.e., providing answers to questions of the type, "Why did A succeed/fail?"), and (b) attributing actions to the actor's motivation (i.e., providing answers to questions of the type "Why did A do it?"). Heider believed that outcome attribution was well-developed in Bernard Weiner's attributional model, but that motive attribution was inadequately treated by Kelley's causal schemata or by other contemporary attribution work (Harvey, Ickes, & Kidd, 1978, p. 14).

Part of the blame for this state of affairs may reside with Heider himself, because he never developed the attribution of motives in much detail. He primarily noted that intention refers to "*what* a person is trying to do . . . and not *why* he is trying to do it. The latter applies more particularly to the reasons behind the intention" (1958, p. 110). Heider briefly analyzed reasons as desires and beliefs (pp. 125–128) but then seldom referred back to this crucial analysis. Forty years later, after several unsuccessful attempts to reintroduce the vocabulary of intentionality into theory about social perception (Buss, 1978), psychological researchers are only now beginning to take an active interest in the phenomenon of reason explanations (Kalish, 1998; Malle, 1999) and the ascription of motives (Fein, 1996; Vonk, 1998).

Finally, two general aspects of Heider's thinking remain to be fully appreciated. First, Heider adopted a truly interpersonal perspective. For him, social perception was a tool to be used instrumentally to accomplish one's goals in social interaction. In contemporary social cognition research, by contrast, the continuing focus on cognitive processes has not been adequately balanced by attention to the interpersonal processes and tasks that provide the functional context in which these cognitive processes operate (e.g., Ickes & Dugosh, in press; Ickes & Gonzalez, 1996). Second, Heider analyzed the concepts of commonsense psychology in their everyday conversational usage, much in line with philosophy of language and cognitive semantics. Despite the important precedent he established, however, contemporary American social psychology has, with rare exceptions, neither used this method nor extensively explored social regularities in naturally occurring conversation.

Given the Heiders' intensive study of the challenges of deaf children, it is fitting that the research domain that has made the greatest progress in the exploration of commonsense psychology is the developmental study of children's theory of mind. It is also encouraging that philosophers, anthropologists, and psychologists have recently engaged each other in interdisciplinary debates about these and related issues (see Carruthers & Boucher, 1998; Carruthers & Smith, 1996; Davies & Stone, 1995). Sadly, however, Heider's psychology of interpersonal relations is rarely cited in these areas of research, even though they address many of the same questions that Heider had considered. Even more disconcerting, perhaps, is the fact that current psychological research on social cognition largely ignores both contemporary work on theory of mind and Heider's classic study of commonsense psychology. An integration of these different strands of work is clearly needed.

CONCLUSION

Over the first 40 years of his professional career, Heider made many friends and colleagues throughout the United States and Europe. In the wake of publishing his 1958 book, Heider often traveled to visit these colleagues and give guest lectures, and he spent sabbatical years at the University of Oslo, Cornell, and Duke. By habit as well as by preference, he continued to write his thoughts in small notebooks that he always carried with him, and a large portion of the ideas that he compiled through this process is now available in print (Benesh-Weiner, 1987–1990). Heider also published a few more articles, mostly historical in nature (e.g., Heider, 1970). But his life's work had culminated in 1958, and he had 30 more years to see its repercussions unfold. Even in Heider's unusually modest autobiography, one senses his pride in having contributed something to the field of psychology that was finally well-received. The influence his work had on social psychology has been enormous, and if we are right that some of the best parts of it have been neglected, it is possible that a more enlightened rediscovery of Heider could result in another 40 years of influence on the field.

After the publication of his 1958 book, Heider finally enjoyed due recognition in the academic community. He received the Lewin Memorial Award in 1959, was designated as a University of Kansas Distinguished Professor in 1963, and received the APA Distinguished Scientific Contribution Award in 1965, some years before the first major wave of attribution research swept over the field of social psychology (e.g., Harvey, Ickes, & Kidd, 1976; Jones et al., 1972). Heider retired from teaching in 1966 and lived the remaining 22 years of his life doing what he liked most: being with Grace, taking daily walks and naps, drawing, reading, and thinking.

Heider was first and foremost a wanderer, a person who chose his own path and took his own time to see the sights. But he was also—in his own quiet way—a revolutionary figure in the history of psychology. It is a fitting irony, therefore, that the reverberations of the Heiderian revolution in psychological theory have been anything but quiet. They have, on the contrary, acquired an increasing force and resonance over time.

REFERENCES

Abelson, R. P. (Ed.). (1968). *Theories of cognitive consistency: A sourcebook*. Chicago: Rand McNally.

Austin, J. L. (1962). *How to do things with words*. Cambridge, MA: Harvard University Press.

Baldwin, D. A., & Baird, J. A. (1999). Action analysis: A gateway to intentional inference. In P. Rochat (Ed.), *Early social cognition* (pp. 215–240). Mahwah, NJ: Erlbaum.

Benesh-Weiner, M. (Ed.). (1987–1990). *Fritz Heider: The notebooks* (Vols. 1–6). Munich: Psychologie Verlags Union.

Benussi, V. (1906). Experimentelles über Vorstellungsinadäquatheit [Experiments on representational inadequacy]. *Zeitschrift für Psychologie, 42,* 22–55.

Benussi, V. (1914). Gesetze der inadäquaten Gestaltauffassung [Laws of inadequate gestalt representation]. *Archiv für die gesamte Psychologie, 32,* 396–419.

Bruner, J. (1990). *Acts of meaning*. Cambridge, MA: Harvard University Press.

Brunswik, E. (1934). *Wahrnehmung und Gegenstandswelt* [Perception and the object world]. Leipzig and Vienna: Deuticke.

Buss, A. R. (1978). Causes and reasons in attribution theory: A conceptual critique. *Journal of Personality and Social Psychology, 36,* 1311–1321.

Carruthers, P., & Boucher, J. (Eds.). (1998). *Language and thought: Interdisciplinary themes*. New York: Cambridge University Press.

Carruthers, P., & Smith, P. K. (Eds.). (1996). *Theories of mind*. New York: Cambridge University Press.

Davies, M., & Stone, T. (Eds.). (1995). *Mental simulation: Evaluations and applications*. Cambridge, MA: Blackwell.

Dittrich, W. H., & Lea, S. E. G. (1994). Visual perception of intentional motion. *Perception, 23,* 253–268.

Fein, S. (1996). Effects of suspicion on attributional thinking and the correspondence bias. *Journal of Personality and Social Psychology, 70,* 1164–1184.

Festinger, L. (1957). *A theory of cognitive dissonance*. Stanford, CA: Stanford University Press.

Fletcher, G. J. O. (1995). Two uses of folk psychology: Implications for psychological science. *Philosophical Psychology, 8,* 221–238.

Frenkel-Brunswik, E. (1940). Psychoanalysis and personality research. *Journal of Abnormal and Social Psychology, 35,* 176–197.

Frenkel-Brunswik, E. (1954). Psychoanalysis and the unity of science. *Proceedings of the American Academy of Arts and Sciences, 80,* 273–347.

Gergely, G., Nadasdy, Z., Csibra, G., & Biro, S. (1995). Taking the intentional stance at 12 months of age. *Cognition, 56,* 165–193.

Harvey, J. H., Ickes, W., & Kidd, R. F. (Eds.). (1976). *New directions in attribution research* (Vol. 1). Hillsdale, NJ: Erlbaum.

Harvey, J. H., Ickes, W., & Kidd, R. F. (1978). A conversation with Fritz Heider. In J. H. Harvey, W. Ickes, & R. F. Kidd (Eds.), *New directions in attribution research* (Vol. 2, pp. 3–18). Hillsdale, NJ: Erlbaum.

Heider, F. (1920). *Zur Subjektivität der Sinnesqualitäten* [On the subjectivity of sense qualities]. Unpublished doctoral dissertation. University of Graz, Austria.

Heider, F. (1925). Ding und Medium [Thing and media]. *Symposium, 1,* 109–157. In F. Heider (1959), On perception, event-structure and psychological environment (selected papers). *Psychological Issues, 1,* 1–123.

Heider, F. (1930). Die Leistung des Wahrnehmungssystems [The function of the perceptual system]. *Zeitschrift für Psychologie, 114,* 371–394.

Heider, F. (1944). Social perception and phenomenal causality. *Psychological Review, 51,* 358–374.

Heider, F. (1946). Attitudes and cognitive organization. *Journal of Psychology, 21,* 107–112.

Heider, F. (1958). *The psychology of interpersonal relations*. Hillsdale, NJ: Erlbaum.

Heider, F. (1959). *Thing and medium*. In F. Heider, On perception, event-structure, and psychological environment (selected papers, pp. 1–34). *Psychological Issues, 1,* 1–123.

Heider, F. (1970). Gestalt theory: Early history and reminiscences. *Journal of the History of the Behavioral Sciences, 6,* 131–139.

Heider, F. (1983). *The life of a psychologist: An autobiography*. Lawrence: University Press of Kansas.

Heider, F., & Moore Heider, G. (1940). *Studies in the psychology of the deaf* (Vol. 1). Psychological monographs, 52 (1), whole no. 232. Evanston, IL: American Psychological Association.

Heider, F., & Moore Heider, G. (1941). *Studies in the psychology of the deaf* (Vol. 2). Psychological monographs, 53 (5), whole no. 242. Evanston, IL: American Psychological Association.

Heider, F., & Simmel, M. (1944). An experimental study of apparent behavior. *American Journal of Psychology, 57,* 243–259.

Ickes. W., & Dugosh, J. (in press). An intersubjective perspective on social cognition and aging. *Basic and Applied Social Psychology*.

Ickes, W., & Gonzalez, R. (1996). "Social" cognition and social cognition: From the subjective to the intersubjective. In J. L. Nye, & A. M. Bower (Eds.), *What's social about social cognition? Research on socially shared cognition in small groups* (pp. 285–308). Thousand Oaks, CA: Sage.

Ickes, W., & Harvey, J. H. (1978). Fritz Heider: A biographical sketch. *Journal of Psychology, 98,* 159–170.

Jones, E. E., & Davis, K. E. (1965). From acts to dispositions: The attribution process in person perception. In L. Berkowitz (Ed.), *Advances in experimental social psychology* (Vol. 2, pp. 219–266). New York: Academic Press.

Jones, E. E., Kanouse, D., Kelley, H. H., Nisbett, R. E., Valins, S., & Weiner, B. (Eds.). (1972). *Attribution: Perceiving the causes of behavior*. Morristown, NJ: General Learning Press.

Kalish, C. (1998). Reasons and causes: Children's understanding of conformity to social rules and physical laws. *Child Development, 69,* 706–720.

Kelley, H. H. (1960). The analysis of common sense. A review of "The psychology of interpersonal relations" by Fritz Heider. *Contemporary Psychology, 5,* 1–3.

Kelley, H. H. (1967). Attribution theory in social psychology. In D. Levine (Ed.), *Nebraska Symposium on Motivation* (Vol. 15, pp. 192–240). Lincoln: University of Nebraska Press.

Koffka, K. (1915). Zur Grundlegung der Wahrnehmungspsychologie: Eine Auseinandersetzung mit V. Benussi [On the foundation of perceptual psychology: A debate with V. Benussi]. *Zeitschrift für Psychologie, 73,* 11–90.

Krauss, R. M. (1983). Introduction to the reprint of "The Psychology of Interpersonal Relations." In F. Heider (1958). *The psychology of interpersonal relations*. Hillsdale, NJ: Erlbaum.

Krauss, R. M. (1988, May). *"The Psychology of Interpersonal Relations" in the context of its time*. Paper presented at the Annual Preconference of the Society for Personality and Social Psychology, Washington, DC.

Lakoff, G. (1987). *Women, fire, and dangerous things: What categories reveal about the mind*. Chicago: University of Chicago Press.

Lewin, K. (1936). *Principles of topological psychology* (F. Heider & G. M. Heider, trans.). New York: McGraw-Hill.

Malle, B. F. (1999). How people explain behavior: A new theoretical framework. *Personality and Social Psychology Review, 3,* 23–48.

Malle, B. F. (1998). Whose psychological concepts? A review of J. Smedlsund's "The structure of psychological common sense." *Contemporary Psychology, 43,* 671–672.

Miller, G. A., Galanter, E., & Pribram, K. H. (1960). *Plans and the structure of behavior*. New York: Holt.

Nisbett, R. E., Ross, L. D. (1980). *Human inference: Strategies and shortcomings of social judgment*. Englewood Cliffs, NJ: Prentice-Hall.

Premack, D., & Premack, A. J. (1995). Intention as psychological cause. In D. Sperber, D. Premack, & A. J. Premack (Eds.), *Causal cognition: A multidisciplinary debate* (pp. 185–199). New York: Clarendon.

Ryle, G. (1949). *The concept of mind*. London, New York: Hutchinson.

Searle, J. R. (1969). *Speech acts: An essay in the philosophy of language*. London: Cambridge University Press.

Smedslund, J. (1997). *The structure of psychological common sense*. Mahwah, NJ: Erlbaum.
Vonk, R. (1998). The slime effect: Suspicion and dislike of likeable behavior toward superiors. *Journal of Personality and Social Psychology, 74*, 849–864.
Zalta, E. N. (1988). *Intentional logic and the metaphysics of intentionality*. Cambridge: MIT Press.

Chapter 13

T. C. Schneirla: Pioneer in Field and Laboratory Research

Ethel Tobach

By tradition, comparative psychologists and animal behaviorists have defined the "field" as the environment, the life space, or the ecological niche in which animals evolved and may be found today. Field research presents the investigator an opportunity to study animals in their natural habitats, but it also presents obstacles and problems: uncomfortable weather, or the presence of life-threatening micro- or macroorganisms. Special instruments may be needed depending on the animal's habitat. Those required for observations in a rainforest canopy are different from those needed for work in the ocean, meadows, or the desert. It is possible that such difficulties played a role in turning comparative psychologists away from the field and toward the laboratory at the beginning of the 20th century.

Another influence contributing to the preference for laboratory work was that most psychologists who worked with animals at that time were driven by the aim to make psychology "scientific." To reach this goal, they believed that they must record behavior under carefully controlled conditions in human-manufactured environments (laboratories) in which studies could be repeated under precisely prescribed conditions (experiments). From this point of view, field research appeared to involve uncontrollable and unsuitable experimental procedures.

Although T. C. Schneirla did important laboratory work throughout his whole career, he did not give in to the arguments against field research. He was introduced to the wonders and excitement of doing observations in the field by his

I thank Sue Berlin, without whose bibliographic assistance this chapter could not have been written.

*Photo of T. C. Schneirla courtesy of Charles Tobach.

215

teacher J. F. Shepard, who taught comparative psychology at the University of Michigan and interested Schneirla in an integrated approach to behavior. Shepard's course included field trips to study the behavior of the common carpenter ant in the wooded areas around Ann Arbor. This was a minimally threatening introduction to field work for undergraduate students. This experience stimulated Schneirla to combine his intellectual interest in comparative psychology with the adventures of studying the so-called army ant in exotic locales in the Panama Canal Zone, Mexico, and the Philippines. His work in those areas earned him membership in the Explorers Club, a private club of individuals who explore areas of the world previously unexplored by Europeans. It also resulted in his taking a great deal of quinine to protect him from malaria, which left him with a troublesome tinnitus for the rest of his life.

BIOGRAPHY

Theodore Christian Schneirla was born July 23, 1902, in Bay City, Michigan. His family ran a celery farm, and he worked after school and summers delivering celery in town. In high school, he learned the Gregg shorthand system, typing, and how to play the trumpet, although later he preferred the flute. Throughout his career, he kept his stenographic skills at sharp efficiency. He used shorthand to record his field notes, and annotated the books and reprints in his library in shorthand. As a typist, he prided himself on "never making a typo requiring erasure."

College Education and Early Career

After high school, Schneirla went to the University of Michigan, where he joined the university band and became its president. He continued at Michigan through his graduate studies and was awarded the DSc (doctor of science) degree in 1929. Schneirla and Leone Warner, a student of library science at the university, were married in Michigan, and on her graduation, the newlyweds moved to New York City in 1927. Schneirla had not yet finished his dissertation, but he was given a position as an instructor in the psychology department at New York University (NYU).

In 1930, the Schneirlas went to Chicago, where Schneirla was a Fellow of the National Research Council in the laboratory of K. S. Lashley (chap. 20, *Pioneers I*). There he did research on maze learning in ants (Schneirla, 1934), and met Norman and Ayesha Maier. From Chicago, the Maiers went to Michigan and the Schneirlas returned to New York City, but the two couples remained close friends for life.

Schneirla became a full professor at NYU, a position he held for some time even after Frank Beach (chap. 16, this volume) invited him in 1943 to become an associate curator at the American Museum of Natural History and a member of the staff of the department of animal behavior that Beach chaired. Schneirla became a curator in 1947, and remained in the department until his death on August 20, 1968.

Schneirla made his first field trip to the Panama Canal Zone to study army ants in 1932, and during his tenure at NYU and the museum, he studied various species of ants in their natural habitats. While at NYU, however, he also studied the maze behavior of ants as well as that of rats in the laboratory. He supervised graduate students, including Daniel S. Lehrman, whose doctoral dissertation was on the parental behavior of ring doves. In the late 1940s, Schneirla began a series of studies of cat behavior culminating in a major research collaboration with Jay S. Rosenblatt on maternal behavior in cats.

Early Battles

The word "pioneer" derives from the word "peon," originally meaning "foot soldier." And indeed, one might say that Schneirla was a foot soldier. When he came to NYU, he found himself in one battle or another from the beginning. One of these was with the laboratory psychologists who were seeking unifying principles for all behavior. Species were not of intrinsic interest to these psychologists because they studied every animal as representative of animals in general. From this perspective, human beings have the same status as any other animal, and any law or principle discovered in the behavior of the rat also applies to people. The commonly held view, based on reading Darwin's writings on emotion in man and animals (Darwin, 1872; chap. 2, *Pioneers III*), was that emotion and motivation are the same in people as in other animals. Psychologists of this persuasion ignored species differences in behavior and emphasized the similarities. The white laboratory rat became their model for the behavior of human beings and all other animals.

Schneirla did not ignore research with the laboratory rat, but he looked at the behavior of the rat in comparison with that of ants and people. For example, he and Witkin showed that although ants were capable of learning a complex maze, their behavior in running from the end of a learned maze back to the start box was not as efficient as that of rats (Witkin & Schneirla, 1937).

Schneirla also was engaged in a battle against vitalism, the acceptance of nonmaterial causes of behavior instincts, for example. Vitalistic theories were generally accepted in comparative psychology when Schneirla started as an instructor at NYU. They were still popular later in his career, when ethology elaborated the instinct concept and came to dominate the field.

In choosing the army ant, Schneirla focused on an organism that was commonly thought to be driven by instinct, expressed in alternating periods of (statary) inactivity and (nomadic) activity, or "raiding," as foraging was called. But in a monograph based on his doctoral dissertation Schneirla showed that the complex behavior exhibited by ants during foraging did not reflect an "inner direction sense" (p. 9) or "an internal factor that could not have been either visual, olfactory, or tactual in nature" (stated by Cornetz and cited by Schneirla, 1929, p. 9) but was rather a result of visual, tactual, sometimes chemical, and to a large extent kinesthetic, stimulation.

In his studies of the maze behavior of ants, and in his field observations of the ants' complex migrations to and from their nests (1944), Schneirla showed that ants are capable of complex learning and storing of information. Explanations based on instinct are not necessary. Schneirla's view of learning as development was also already evident in this early period of his work: "The orienting factors [in leaving and returning to the nest] are operative . . . to the extent permitted by . . . environmental stimuli, and their respective influences vary *according to the stage attained in the learning"* (italics added) (Schneirla, 1929, p. 28).

Schneirla saw that vitalism leads to overlooking the relationship between the physiological characteristics and behavior of the animal. In a paper on modifiability of behavior in starfish, he and Maier pointed out the limitations of the nervous system of that echinoderm for complex behavior patterns (Schneirla & Maier, 1940). He also demonstrated the fallacies inherent in attributing human characteristics to other animals in an article on "cruelty" in ants (Schneirla, 1942b).

It should be mentioned at this point, to correct a possible wrong impression, that Schneirla's demeanor was not combative. When I came to know him in 1950, he was quietly firm in his thinking, talk, and action. He preferred quiet discourse to excited exchanges or confrontational interactions. He handled living ants with particular delicacy—an application of the concept of biphasic processes in behavior (to be considered later) that living organisms approach sources of low stimulation of regular periodicity, and withdraw from irregular, high-intensity stimulation. He was persistent, even stubborn, in his beliefs, but he always took the ideas and possibilities posed by others seriously. The sharpness of his thinking about issues he deemed worthy of battle reflected the steel in the man.

A Pioneer in Integrating Societal Responsibility and Science

While Schneirla was on the faculty at NYU, he was not only an energetic teacher and researcher but was also active in organizing a teachers' union—an effort that left him disillusioned with his colleagues (personal conversations, 1953–1968). In 1935, he signed a resolution presented to the American Psychological Association to "approach the Federal government immediately with a request that money be made available from the works-relief fund to unemployed psychologists" (Tobach & Aronson, 1970, p. xiv). In the mid-1930s he was a leader in organizing scholars to support the democratically elected Spanish government in its fight against Spanish, German, and Italian fascism (Finison, 1977).

History of a Pioneering Book

It is not clear from available material when Schneirla and N. R. F. Maier decided to collaborate on the book *Principles of Animal Psychology* (Maier & Schneirla, 1935, 1964), but it is evident in Schneirla's early writings that he was interested in an integrated approach to behavior. Among Schneirla's papers there is the typed manuscript of a full-length book titled, *A Systematic View of Psychology,* possibly written to fulfill some course or degree requirement, possibly intended for a publisher. This unpublished book must have been written at about the same time as another typewritten volume, *Outline of Comparative Psychology,* while he was Shepard's student. The latter book—beautifully illustrated and leather bound—is clearly the prototype of *Principles of Animal Psychology.* That Maier and Schneirla may have used the first of these books in the preparation of *Principles of Animal Psychology* is evident from notations in the margins of the pages of the "Outline of Comparative Psychology." There are short-hand modifications of the text by Schneirla, as well as sections marked for the attention of "Norman." *Principles of Animal Psychology* was published in 1935 and, in 1964, the book was republished by the Dover Press, with additional material by Schneirla on the theory of biphasic processes and instinctive behavior and two papers by Maier on frustration theory and selector–integrator mechanisms in behavior. One additional paper on conditioning was jointly authored by the two friends.

SCHNEIRLA'S RESPONSE TO ANOTHER PUBLICATION ON COMPARATIVE PSYCHOLOGY

Schneirla's views of contemporary psychology in general and comparative psychology in particular are also evident in his review in 1941 of three volumes on comparative psychology by Warden, Jenkins, and Warner (1934, 1936, 1940) that were published at about the same time as *Principles of Animal Psychology.*

Schneirla's notes in short-hand and script in *Introduction to Comparative Psychology* (Warden et al., 1934) indicate that he probably used that book in his own teaching. In the margin next to the table of contents for Chapter I (The Development of Modern Comparative Psychology), he wrote "for September 28," possibly for his course in animal psychology. Next to the title of Chapter III (The Biological Foundations of Comparative Psychology), he noted in short-hand: "Assign in connection with ants." On page 354, next to a discussion about pulmonates, he wrote "get this for lab."

There are also critical notations in the book. On page 36, Warden et al. stated "a reaction against elementalism in comparative psychology has already set in and the dominant trend is now toward an organismic viewpoint. . . . These together with the more thoroughgoing Action–Tendency theory of Warden will be discussed in the next chapter." On pages 50–51, that theory was described as follows: "We have termed these . . . [common animal drives—hunger, thirst, sex, and the maternal impulse] . . . the primary action-tendencies. Since they represent the functional aspect of the species pattern, they are essentially hereditary in character. They are *directly related to the basic biological needs* of the organism and derive from evolutionary sources." The words in italics were underlined by Schneirla and were next to his short-hand question: "why?"—that question indicating Schneirla's critical view of formulations based on the assumption of hereditary or instinctive "needs," even when they are called "impulses."

On page 191, the authors wrote, "According to Kepner, the Ameba closes its pseudopodia tightly around prey when there is no danger that the latter will escape. However, the pseudopods are extended in a wide embrace so as to cut off retreat if the prey is still struggling to escape." Next to this set of statements, Schneirla drew a line in red with a question mark next to it. In a chapter on fish, Warden et al. wrote (p. 430), "The bubbles are supposed to aid in floating the materials utilized in making the nest." Next to "supposed" Schneirla questioned "by the fish?"

Although Schneirla was polite in his review of *Plants and Invertebrates* (1940), he noted that the authors did not critically examine the sources from which they gathered the "facts" that they report, particularly in regard to learning in invertebrates, resulting in "much confusion" (Schneirla, 1941, p. 107). He praised their meticulous scholarship (sic!) but went on to say,

> there is no development of a theory for each animal type and no progressive construction of a theory which embraces all invertebrate types. . . . The seriatim reporting of evidence under the dominance of a pre-established set of rubrics does not facilitate appropriately dealing with the problem of organization and interrelationship of capacities in particular animal groups. (p. 107)

He concluded the review by saying that the volumes "are a fine scientific tool and a monumental contribution to the field . . . particularly because such a consistent and devoted application of their high capacities reveals an unbounded confidence in the future of the science" (p. 107). Schneirla's concern with the survival of comparative psychology as a science was apparently an important consideration in his evaluation of the volumes.

SCHNEIRLA'S FUNDAMENTAL CONTRIBUTIONS

After 1945, Schneirla's pioneering research and theoretical formulations became more clearly integrated. He elaborated concepts proposed by others in significant new ways, extending them beyond the comparative psychology of his time. Four of Schneirla's key contributions to psychology in general and to comparative psychology in particular illustrate this point. (a) He sharpened psychology's understanding of the significance of individual and species differences in the development and evolution of behavior by applying the concept of levels of integration to a variety of life processes, including human behavior. (b) He focused on the stimulative aspect of trophallaxis, formulated by Wheeler (1928), primarily in terms of the exchange of nutrients between insects. Schneirla broadened the significance of trophallaxis by proposing the concept of "reciprocal stimulation" as a basis for the development of social behavior in all animals. (c) He enriched the generally accepted approach–avoidance (appetitive–aversive) formulation by treating approach and withdrawal behavior as the primary patterns of response to the intensity of stimulation. He saw that approach and withdrawal to different stimulus intensities vary according to ontogenetic stages and phyletic levels and are central in the developmental processes involved in motivation, emotion, and socialization. (d) He not only criticized instinctive, "unlearned," or hereditary explanations of behavior, but offered the study of development as a heuristic and theoretically sound alternative to the dichotomization of heredity and environment, maturation and learning, and other such appositions.

The Concept of Integrative Levels

In the introduction to the "Systematic View of Psychology" (n.d.) Schneirla stated that the behavior of organisms may be studied from either of two points of view: the psychological, in which the organism is studied as a whole, an individual, an entity; or the physiological, in which "the organism is studied from the standpoint of the interactions of units, the study extending even to the examination of cells in their various interactions," but this division of behavior "cannot be carried on as separate [because] the psychological and the physiological are inseparably related studies of the behavior of the organism" (p. 2). This integrative approach in which organisms subsume many levels of organization was eventually elaborated in Schneirla's concept of levels of integration (see Aronson, Tobach, Rosenblatt, & Lehrman, 1972).

The concept of integrative levels informed Schneirla's research. For example, in 1957 (Aronson et al., 1972, pp. 806–852), he offered a scientific explanation of the army ants' apparently "instinctive" behavior that integrated his knowledge and experience. By analyzing the material processes at different levels of individual organization (chemical, tactile, behavioral) that produce the ants' "instinctive" behavior, he showed how their relative quiescence, with little foraging (statary phase) and their active raiding or foraging (nomadic phase), are the result of changes within the integrative levels of brood cycle (development from eggs, larvae, pupae into callows, and so forth). The presence of individuals at different developmental stages results in changes in activity level within the colony, making for increased foraging. When there is less interindividual activity, the colony is quiescent.

The next nodal stage in Schneirla's development of the concept of integrative levels occurred in response to a symposium at the University of Chicago organized in 1941 by the anthropologist Robert Redfield on "Levels of Integration in Biological and Social Systems" (Redfield, 1942). At that symposium, Alfred E. Emerson (1942), a noted entomologist, gave a paper on "Basic Comparisons of Human and Insect Societies," which emphasized the similarities of the two groups. Emerson, in agreement with other biologists and philosophers, also proposed that socially organized species, such as insects and human beings, produce superorganisms that are more than the sum of the activity of the individuals. Novikoff (1945a, 1945b) took issue with Emerson and offered the concept of integrative levels to account for species differences. Even earlier, in 1940, Schneirla had rejected the superorganismic concept and, in later papers (1952, 1972b, 1972e, 1972f, 1972g) he elaborated the concept of integrative levels to counter it (Aronson et al., 1972). In the 1972g (originally published in 1946) paper he applied the concept of integrative levels to deal with the differences between human beings and ants and developed the concepts of biosocial and psychosocial levels (Aronson et al., 1972, p. 420). He also showed that the exchange of nutriment (Wheeler's concept of trophallaxis) is integrated differently in the two groups because of differences in their levels of learning and problem solving (Aronson et al., 1972, p. 420). Later, Schneirla listed three main differences between the biosocial and the psychosocial levels. "Outstanding contrasts are found especially [1] in the nature of communication, [2] in the occurrence of castes and [3] in 'tradition'" (Aronson et al., 1972, p. 420). The outstanding characteristics that contrast communication among people and ants are symbolism, the intentional use of symbols to influence others in social situations, and "capacity for arrangement . . . according to requirements of meaning. . . . These characteristics are mastered in the socialization of the child and are apparent both in linguistic and written communications" (Aronson et al., 1972, p. 420).

In "caste determination" in insects, "the determination is based upon biological processes that developed through long series of generations in a given species . . . stereotyped . . . and essentially changeless unless new developments occur through genetic evolution" (Aronson et al., 1972, p. 421). "On the human level . . . castes in the sense of social or functional classes of different social ranks exist essentially on a psychological basis. The one clear biological foundation for a human functional 'caste' differentiation is a sexual dichotomy, in which the organic differentiation of sexes imposes a qualitative differentiation of general reproductive function." In a footnote, Schneirla added, "that is to say, genetico-physiological differences such as muscular strength existing between the sexes would facilitate certain differences in social function, but such differences are quantitative or relative rather than absolute, and are subject to alteration under appropriate social conditions" (Aronson et al., 1972, p. 421n).

Finally, Schneirla demonstrated that, within species, forms of social organization vary among populations. Biological evolution produced different forms of social organization in different species of insects. The diversity of human cultural behavior contrasts significantly. Citing Veblen (1931), he argued that, from ancient times to the present, castes have been a social practice designed to limit or block upward shifting across the traditional class lines of a given society. "In each cultural setting man exhibits somewhat differently his capacity for transmitting the conceptualized traditions of previous generations to his descendants; yet all are alike in possessing some form of 'social heritage'" (Aronson et al., 1972, p. 423).

The prescient use of the concept of integrative levels to discuss differences of gender, class, and intelligence is an example of Schneirla's ability to see the significance of integrative levels in human behavior. He extended this application to issues of war and peace as well. During World War II, he wrote an article on Nazism for the Psychologists League (Schneirla, 1942a), an avowedly antifascist group. He defended the military activities of the antifascist nations in World War II (Schneirla, 1946), but he also postulated that human beings could solve the problem of the persistence of war by using their human characteristics in 1949 (Aronson et al., 1972, pp. 199–237).

Trophallaxis and Reciprocal Stimulation: Levels in Socialization

E. O. Wilson, the eminent sociobiologist, chided Schneirla for making a "forgivable mistake" in extending Wheeler's concept of trophallaxis beyond what Wilson interpreted Wheeler to mean: chemical communication (Wilson, 1975, p. 30). At an international colloquium of the National Center for Scientific Research on "The Structure and Physiology of Animal Societies" in Paris in March 1950 (Grasse, 1952), Schneirla had analyzed Wheeler's work, and cited Wheeler's own listing of the interactions among the members of the ant colony to illustrate trophallaxis. Wheeler had included antennal stroking of the queen by the workers, the handling of the eggs, and "the frequent contact with one another in the nest situation, touching antennae . . . as well as regurgitating food to one another" (Schneirla, 1952, p. 251). Further, Schneirla said,

> Wheeler reached the conclusion that such relationships must be basic to colony unity and organization, and conceptualized them under the term "trophallaxis." This term may be interpreted to signify relationships of reciprocal stimulation and response involved in the various forms of food-delivery, or in processes related to feeding or equivalent to food in their sensory and organic effects. (p. 252)

Even though the conference participants did not seem to accept "reciprocal stimulation" as an elaboration of trophallaxis (Grasse, 1952, pp. 267–269), Schneirla continued in 1956 to support that conceptualization, proposing that "reciprocal stimulation" includes Wheeler's trophallaxis (Aronson et al., 1972, pp. 131–188). Schneirla made the concept useful in all socialization, even as it varies according to species level and to developmental stage. In 1951 he wrote,

> On the human level the initial organic processes have substantially the same role in principle, and their effect as a basis for some kind of trophallactic reciprocal relationship between mother and young is also the same in principle. Yet it is manifest that the socialization process may be very different in its outcome, depending upon the social context in which the early family relationships develop. . . . The chimpanzee mother is much quicker to become attached emotionally and perceptually to the infant as a social object than are the mothers in lower mammals, yet the relative complexity of her perceptual schema and understanding of this object has its limitations far below the psychological level attainable by the human mother. (Aronson et al., 1972, p. 460)

Approach–Withdrawal in Ontogeny and Phylogeny

In *Principles of Animal Psychology (1935)*, Maier and Schneirla tied the approach and withdrawal behavior of amoeba to stimulus intensity:

> Other things equal, the energy value of the stimulus determines whether the Amoeba moves toward or away from the source. Stimuli of weak intensity characteristically elicit movement toward the stimulated locality. . . . The more intense the stimulus applied to Amoeba the more does the next movement diverge in direction from the stimulated locality. (Maier & Schneirla, 1935, p. 16)

They then cited an experiment by Mast (1931) and observations by Hyman (1917) in which photic and tactile stimuli of graded intensity resulted in approach or withdrawal (positive or negative responses) based on intensity (pp. 17–18). Maier and Schneirla's comments about the appropriate interpretations of the amoebas behavior are significant:

> The response [to weaker stimulation] might therefore be called a "positive" one, in contrast with the "negative" response to the strongest intensity. . . . But one doubts the value of such arbitrary expressions as "positive," since they poorly express the important fact that the effect of a stimulus depends upon its intensity. . . . The "positive" and the "negative" in amoeboid behavior do not represent a mysterious ability on the part of the organism to diagnose the "beneficiality" of the stimulus but are only the crude and arbitrary designations of some observers for the different effects exerted upon protoplasmic activity by stimuli of different intensities. (1935, pp. 17–18)

Maier and Schneirla understood the relevance of "Occam's razor" to such interpretations: Do not resort to divine or otherwise mysterious causation when explanations without the agency of God are available (cf. Hamilton, 1859, pp.

550–558; Ockham, 1957, pp. 84–88; Schneirla, 1942b; Scotus, 1987, pp. 166–167).

Maier and Schneirla recognized that intensity in and of itself is not enough to bring about approach or withdrawal. They cited the internal conditions of the organism, repetition of stimuli (adaptation and summation effects), the inherited constitution of the protoplasm, and other characteristics of the environment as important modifiers of these responses.

Extending the Application of Approach–Withdrawal.   Much has been learned about the neurophysiology of behavior since the *Principles of Animal Psychology* was written and, today, the approach–withdrawal formulations of 1935 are mainly of historical interest. But Schneirla's interest in the problem stayed with him, and in 1939 he gave a talk on approach–withdrawal at the American Psychological Association annual convention. Only an abstract of the talk exists, but it anticipates Schneirla's later application of the concept to human motivation and development:

> Stimuli at high intensities typically elicit a general reaction in which the predominance of a differentiated excitation-reaction system virtually insures withdrawal from the source. Conversely, weak stimuli predominantly arouse the antagonistic system and typically produce an approach to the source of stimulation. . . . Through natural selection, we may hypothecate the evolution of such mechanisms along adaptive lines. This view has utility as a hypothetical basis for understanding approach/withdrawal behavior in man. . . . The bearing of this "reaction-system-threshold" theory upon concepts such as "appetite-aversion," "vectors," "sign-gestalt," and the like will be considered. (Schneirla, 1939, p. 643)

Twenty years later, in 1959, in the Nebraska Symposium on Motivation, Schneirla pointed out that

> the aspect of towardness or awayness is common in animal behavior. Our problem is to consider, from the phyletic and the ontogenetic approaches, the question of how animals generally manage to reach beneficial conditions and stay away from the harmful, that is, how survivors do this. . . . My purpose is to discuss some promising theoretical ideas and evidence bearing on [the evolutionary and developmental aspects of the motivation problem]. (Schneirla, 1972d, p. 137)

Significance of Ontogenetic Processes.   As indicated in *Principles of Animal Psychology*, the biphasic processes, approach and withdrawal, depend on the state of the organism, implicating developmental and phyletic differences. Although "stimulative energy fundamentally dominates the approach and withdrawal responses of all animals" (Schneirla, 1972d, p. 113), and "In early ontogeny in all animals, the quantitative aspects of stimulation evidently dominate both the direction and vigor of action" (Schneirla, 1972d), "mammalian ontogeny leads into further stages in which 'attitudes' become effective, involving readiness to organize adjustments relevantly to discriminated situation meanings. In mammalian ontogeny, it is likely that motivated learning of the anticipative type enters [and dominates the] processes of orientation and adaptation carried over from earlier stages" (Schneirla, 1972d).

For Schneirla these biphasic processes in motivation and emotion were basic to his criticisms of the psychological term "drive" and the etholgical term "releaser," both of which stress endogenous processes without recognizing their changing role in ontogeny (Aronson et al., 1972, p. 319). In 1959, he called for research on the role of developmental experience. "From the phyletic and ontogenetic perspectives, the changing relationships of stimulation, organic processes and reaction in animal motivation, although grounded in biphasic conditions in all phyla, are seen as different kinds of processes at each level" (Schneirla, 1972c, p. 319).

Some six years later, in 1965, Schneirla was asked by his former students who were editing the new and important series, "Advances in the Study of Behavior," to write the first article in the first volume (Aronson et al., 1972, pp. 344–412). He took this invitation as an opportunity to respond to some of the criticisms that had been leveled at his earlier papers. His primary response was to remind the reader that the biphasic processes, although effective for all phyla, are "based on the utilization, through development, of the animal's inclusive resources for adaptive behavior" (Aronson et al., 1972, p. 348). This is a holistic theory designed for studying all adaptive patterns of behavior attainable in species under the conditions of individual development. He emphasized this again:

> Through evolution, then, biphasic mechanisms underlying directionally opposed orientative responses, governed first of all by quantitative properties of stimulation, are present in all animals from protozoans to primates. But, through natural selection, specializations have appeared in all the mechanisms underlying adaptive behavior. They have emerged in a variety of types which have brought sensory-neural input effects increasingly under the influence of species properties bearing on behavioral plasticity through experience. (Aronson et al., 1972, pp. 348–349)

Schneirla's emphasis on developmental processes that are related to the experiential differences in phyletic history of the organism is one of the most significant aspects of Schneirla's work and was his solution to the Gordian knot of heredity versus environment.

Instinct Theory: Ethology and Sociobiology

Schneirla's major theoretical battle against vitalism was expressed in his critical analysis of ethological instinct theory (Lorenz, 1937). In a 1949 article on "Levels in the Psychological Capacities of Animals" he criticized psychologists like McDougall, who are "proponent[s] of purposivistic theory in biology and psychology" (Aronson et al., 1972, p. 210). Schneirla believed that basic to purposivism is the faulty argument that "since materialistic procedures in science cannot account for . . . (a) growth and (b) adaptivity in behavior, only Animism remains adequate as a basis for metaphysical theory" (Aronson et al., 1972, p. 210). Schneirla also noted that the second argument bears most "directly upon animal psychology, where its considerable contemporary influence is evident in the writings of . . . Lorenz" (p. 210).

Schneirla used Lorenz's "abrupt comment" in 1949 (Aronson et al., 1972, p. 888) on the failures of American comparative psychology as the starting point for his own analysis of the problems of comparative psychology and of ethology as developed by Lorenz and his associates. He criticized the behavioral studies of the ethologists for their derivation from a traditional, morphological method that uses organ systems for taxonomic analyses and then uses behavior patterns in the same way for behavioral analyses (Aronson et al., 1972, pp. 896–898). Some critics saw this approach as "too simple" but Schneirla called it a "rigid, nativistic ideology" and, "with all due credit to its emphasis on behavior," wondered "about the validity of its basic postulates" (Aronson et al., 1972, p. 897). Schneirla also discussed problems with ethological experimental work (Aronson et al., 1972, p. 905), citing the 1953 paper by Lehrman that was then in press. His concluding paragraph stated the centrality of developmental processes in his argument: "It is doubtful whether any methodology can be successfully comparative without a thoroughgoing concern for ascertaining the characteristics of ontogeny in each behavior system studied, as a step preliminary to the intellectual process of comparing behavior patterns and personality in different animals" (Aronson et al., 1972, p. 898). Schneirla elaborated on the purposivist character of Lorenz' theory (Aronson et al., 1972, p. 913) and also used the concept of integrative levels to criticize the reductionism in ethology (Aronson et al., 1972, p. 914).

Sociobiology: A Battle That Might Have Been

Although Schneirla was an early and persistent critic of vitalistic theorizing in biology and psychology, he was not present for the more recent iteration of such theorizing, E. O. Wilson's (1975) germinal book, *Sociobiology*. Schneirla and Wilson were aware of each other's work in entomology, but there was minimal collegial interaction between them. In *Sociobiology*, Wilson accepted Emerson's superorganismic concept without mentioning Schneirla's criticisms. Emerson and Schneirla had both presented their views in the 1952 symposium (Grasse, 1952), which Wilson must have read because he cited some of the papers in *Sociobiology*. Wilson (1963, 1987) had cited Schneirla's work and his book edited posthumously by Topoff (Schneirla, 1971), but he did not discuss that work in relation to sociobiology. In *Sociobiology*, Wilson described Schneirla's research on ants in great detail and praised his studies (1975, pp. 424–427). Schneirla never wrote about Wilson's theoretical approach.

CONCLUSION

Someone described scientific progress as the clearing of a space in the darkness of a forest. The result is an ever-widening circle of light bordered by a darker forest that still needs clearing. Schneirla left a legacy in the work of many people whose research and writing, inspired by some aspect of his theoretical approach, enlarged that circle of light. There is too little space to present all of them, or to analyze their contributions, but brief references to some of them will give an indication of Schneirla's status as a pioneer in comparative and developmental psychology. Among these followers were Herbert Birch, Daniel Lehrman, Jay S. Rosenblatt, Gerald Turkewitz, Richard M. Lerner, Gilbert Gottlieb, and Howard R. Topoff.

Birch was an instructor at New York University when Schneirla was an assistant professor there. He received his PhD from NYU after World War II, went on to teach at City College, and studied self-grooming in rats at the American Museum of Natural History. Birch left City College and became a medical researcher studying child development. He introduced the physicians Stella Chess, Alexander Thomas, and Margaret Hertzig to Schneirla's theories of development. Birch's collaboration with Chess, Thomas, and Hertzig produced a monumental study reflecting Schneirla's theories (Thomas, Chess, Birch, Hertzig, & Korn, 1963). Their study of neonates, their parents, and their subsequent development has yielded fundamental information about human behavior.

It is fitting that this study, which began in the late 1950s, is continuing in the hands of Richard and Jacqueline Lerner. Richard Lerner was introduced to Schneirla's ideas at Hunter College by his mentor Sam Korn, who had been Birch's student at City College. He went on to become a prominent developmental psychologist, whose scholarship was stimulated by Schneirla's theories (Lerner, 1978, 1984). His book on Nazi ideology and ethology (Lerner, 1992) is a further development of the Lorenzian critique begun by Schneirla and Lehrman.

When Rosenblatt approached Schneirla seeking to study with him, Schneirla introduced him to Lehrman, who at that time was at the American Museum of Natural History—and had been active there since he was 10 years old—and was a graduate student at City College. As a graduate student himself, Rosenblatt studied sexual behavior and experience in cats. After earning his doctorate, he continued as a postdoctoral fellow with Schneirla working on maternal behavior in cats. Rosenblatt carries on the tradition of Schneirla's concept of integrative levels in an impressive body of research. He has ingeniously teased out the biochemical, physiological, and experiential processes that are implicated in parental behavior in mammals (Rosenblatt, Factor, & Mayer, 1994; Rosenblatt, Matthews-Felton, Corodimas, & Morrell, 1995; Rosenblatt and Mayer, 1998).

Lehrman's classic paper on ethology (Lehrman, 1953) is an example of Schneirla's way with the people who worked around him. Schneirla was available for discussion and gave advice, when asked, but was most supportive in giving younger people opportunities to develop in their own ways. Lehrman's work, which emphasized, as Schneirla did, developmental processes and the role of experience is a fitting testimony to his often-expressed debt to Schneirla, as described by Silver and Rosenblatt (1987).

Both Lehrman and Rosenblatt discussed ethology and comparative psychology with Robert Hinde from time to time, and Hinde acknowledged these interactions in an article commemorating the publication of his 1966 book, *Animal Behaviour*:

> The book was intended as a synthesis, to focus on the conceptual problems that divided . . . extreme ethologists (characterized by Lorenz) . . . and extreme comparative psychologists (characterized by T. C. Schneirla). . . . Occasional discussion with Danny and Jay Rosenblatt helped me a great deal to understand the viewpoint of the Schneirla group. (Hinde, 1993, p. 8)

When Turkewitz, an undergraduate at City College, spoke with Birch about his interest in animal behavior, Birch recommended him to Schneirla, who then suggested that he work with Rosenblatt on the cat–kitten project. Turkewitz has studied aspects of stimulus intensity and approach–withdrawal behavior, among other processes in development (Turkewitz, Gardner, & Lewkowicz, 1984). In his article on Schneirla's influence on human developmental psychology, he concluded, "Schneirla has already had at least an influence on the study of human development, and judging by how long it took for his views to have a major impact on developmental psychobiology, it is likely that his influence will continue to grow. I believe the field will be a more exciting one because of it" (Turkewitz, 1987, p. 374).

Gottlieb was not connected with City College, New York University, or the American Museum of Natural History but had corresponded with Schneirla about his 1959 motivation paper and, when he had the opportunity, invited Schneirla to give a seminar in North Carolina where Gottlieb lived and worked. This was the beginning of a deep personal friendship. In his pursuit of understanding of the development of behavior, Gottlieb went into the embryological territory pioneered by Zing-Yang Kuo (chap. 12, *Pioneers III*; Gottlieb & Kuo, 1965), making careful observations of the behavior of ducklings and female parents (Gottlieb, 1961). As he stated in the introductory chapter to the *Behavioral Embryology* series that he established, his search into preceding levels of integration and earlier developmental stages is a direct response to Schneirla's approach–withdrawal theory of neonatal behavior (Gottlieb, 1973, p. 37).

Topoff, Schneirla's graduate student, is the only person who worked with Schneirla in the field. When Topoff was a biology student at City College (after Birch, Lehrman, and Rosenblatt had left), he applied to an undergraduate research training program in the department of animal behavior at the American Museum of Natural History and met Schneirla. Topoff now teaches comparative psychology and animal behavior in the department of psychology at Hunter College. He attracts many doctoral students and is a productive researcher, working mostly in Arizona with a variety of ants. Topoff brings to his meticulous work a theoretical understanding of comparative psychology that seems likely to have an impact on new generations of followers of Schneirla's pioneering work with ants.

In his paper "Adaptations for Social Parasitism" (1997), Topoff drew on Schneirla's approach to compare social parasitism in birds and insects:

> The differences in the mechanisms and processes underlying these matching adaptations are also the productions of evolution, as they reflect qualitatively different neuroanatomical specializations, ecological requirements and divergent historical origins. Indeed, it is by concentrating equally on these two aspects of animal behavior that comparative psychology stands apart from, and in some respects is more comprehensive than, classical ethology. (p. 191)

These, of course, are some of the themes to which Schneirla devoted a lifetime of research and theorizing.

REFERENCES

Aronson, L. R., Tobach, E., Rosenblatt, J. S., & Lehrman, D. S. (Eds.). (1972). *Selected writings of T. C. Schneirla*. San Francisco: W. H. Freeman.

Darwin, C. (1872). *The expression of the emotions in man and animals*. London: Murray.

Emerson, A. E. (1942). Basic comparisons of human and insect societies. In R. Redfield (Ed.), *Levels of integration in biological and social systems* (pp. 163–176). Lancaster, PA: Jacques Cattell Press.

Finison, L. J. (1977). Psychologists and Spain: A historical note. *American Psychologist, 32,* 1080–1084.

Gottlieb, G. (1961). The following-response and imprinting in wild and domestic ducklings of the same species (Anas platyrhynchos). *Behaviour, 18,* 205–228.

Gottlieb, G. (1973). Introduction to behavioral embryology. In G. Gottlieb (Ed.), *Behavioral embryology* (Vol. I, pp. 3–45). New York: Academic Press.

Gottlieb, G., & Kuo, Z. Y. (1965). Development of behavior in the duck embryo. *Journal of Comparative and Physiological Psychology, 59,* 183–188.

Grasse, P.-P. (1952). Structure et physiologie des sociétés animales [Structure and physiology of animal societies]. *Colloques Internationaux du Centre National de la Recherche Scientifique* (Vol. 35). Paris: Centre National de la Recherche Scientifique.

Hamilton, W. B. (1859). *Lectures on metaphysics* (H. L. Mansel & J. Veitch, Eds.). Boston: Gould and Lincoln.

Hinde, R. A. (1993). *Animal behaviour: A synthesis of ethology and comparative psychology*. This week's citation classic. *Current Contents, 40,* 8.

Hyman, L. (1917). Metabolic gradients in Amoeba and their relation to the mechanism of amoeboid movement. *Journal of Experimental Biology, 24,* 381–407.

Lehrman, D. S. (1953). A critique of Konrad Lorenz's theory of instinctive behavior. *Quarterly Review of Biology, 28,* 337–363.

Lerner, R. M. (1978). Nature, nurture and dynamic interactionism. *Human Development, 21,* 1–20.

Lerner, R. M. (1984). *On the nature of human plasticity.* New York: Cambridge University Press.

Lerner, R. M. (1992). *Final solutions: Biology, prejudice and genocide.* University Park: Pennsylvania State University Press.

Lorenz, K. (1937). The companion in the bird's world. *Auk, 54,* 245–273.

Maier, N. R. F., & Schneirla, T. C. (1935). *Principles of animal psychology.* New York: McGraw-Hill.

Maier, N. R. F., & Schneirla, T. C. (1964). *Principles of animal psychology* (Reprinted with supplemental articles). New York: Dover.

Mast, S. O. (1931). The nature of response to light in Amoeba proteus (Leidy) *Zeitschrift für vergleichende Physiologie, 15,* 139–147.

Novikoff, A. B. (1945a). The concept of integrative levels and biology. *Science, 101,* 209–215.

Novikoff, A. B. (1945b). Continuity and discontinuity in evolution. *Science, 102,* 404–405.

Ockham, William of (1957). *Philosophical writings* (P. Boehner, Ed.). New York: Thomas Nelson and Sons.

Redfield, R. (Ed.). (1942). *Levels of integration in biological and social systems. Biological Symposia* (Vol. VIII). Lancaster, PA: Jacques Cattell Press.

Rosenblatt, J. S., Factor, E. M., & Mayer, A. D. (1994). The relationship between maternal aggression and maternal care in the rat. *Aggressive Behavior, 20,* 243–255.

Rosenblatt, J. S., Matthews-Felton, T., Corodimas, K. P., & Morrell, J. I. (1995). Lateral habenula neurons are necessary for the hormonal onset of maternal behavior and for the delay of postpartum estrus in naturally parturient female rats. *Behavioral Neuroscience, 109,* 1172–1188.

Rosenblatt, J. S., & Mayer, A. D. (1998). A method for regulating duration of pregnancy and the time of parturition in Sprague-Dawley rats (Charles River CD strain). *Developmental Psychobiology, 32,* 131–136.

Schneirla, T. C. (n.d.). *Outline of comparative psychology.* Unpublished manuscript, American Museum of Natural History, New York.

Schneirla, T. C. (n.d.). *A systematic view of psychology.* Unpublished manuscript, American Museum of Natural History, New York.

Schneirla, T. C. (1929). Learning and orientation in ants. *Comparative Psychology Monographs, 6,* 1–143.

Schneirla, T. C. (1934). The process and mechanism of ant learning. *Journal of Comparative Psychology, 17,* 303–328.

Schneirla, T. C. (1939). A theoretical consideration of the basis for approach-withdrawal adjustments in behavior. *Psychological Abstracts, 13,* 643.

Schneirla, T. C. (1940). Further studies on the army-ant behavior pattern. *Journal of Comparative Psychology, 29,* 401–460.

Schneirla, T. C. (1941). Review of C. S. Warden, T. N., Jenkins, and L. H. Warner, *Comparative psychology: A comprehensive treatise. Vol. II: Plants and invertebrates* (New York: Ronald Press, 1940). *Psychological Bulletin, 38,* 105–108.

Schneirla, T. C. (1942a). German psychological warfare. *Psychologists League Journal, 5,* 9–18.

Schneirla, T. C. (1942b). "Cruel" ants—and Occam's razor. *Journal of Comparative Psychology, 34,* 79–83.

Schneirla, T. C. (1944). A unique case of circular milling in ants, considered in relation to trail following and the general problem of orientation. *American Museum Novitiates, 1253,* 1–26.

Schneirla, T. C. (1946). Contemporary American animal psychology in perspective. In P. L. Harriman (Ed.), *Twentieth century psychology* (pp. 306-316). New York: Philosophical Library.

Schneirla, T. C. (1952). Basic correlations and coordinations in insect societies with special reference to ants. In Pierre-P. Grasse (Ed.), Structure et physiologie des sociétés animales. *Colloques Internationaux du Centre National de la Recherche Scientifique* (Vol. 35, pp. 247–269). Paris: Centre National de la Recherche Scientifique.

Schneirla, T. C. (1971). *Army ants: A study in social organization.* San Francisco: W. H. Freeman.

Schneirla, T. C. (1972a). Aspects of stimulation and organization in approach/withdrawal processes underlying vertebrate behavioral development. In L. R. Aronson, E. Tobach, J. S. Rosenblatt, & D. S. Lehrman (Eds.), *Selected writings of T. C. Schneirla* (pp. 344–412). San Francisco: W. H. Freeman.

Schneirla, T. C. (1972b). A consideration of some conceptual trends in comparative psychology. In L. R. Aronson, E. Tobach, J. S. Rosenblatt, & D.S. Lehrman (Eds.), *Selected writings of T. C. Schneirla* (pp. 887–925). San Francisco. W. H. Freeman.

Schneirla, T. C. (1972c). An evolutionary and developmental theory of biphasic processes underlying approach and withdrawal. In L. R. Aronson, E. Tobach, J. S. Rosenblatt, & D.S. Lehrman (Eds.), *Selected writings of T. C. Schneirla* (pp. 297–339). San Francisco: W. H. Freeman.

Schneirla, T. C. (1972d). Interrelationships of the "innate" and the "acquired" in instinctive behavior. In L. R. Aronson, E. Tobach, J. S. Rosenblatt, & D. S. Lehrman (Eds.), *Selected writings of T. C. Schneirla* (pp. 131–188). San Francisco: W. H. Freeman.

Schneirla, T. C. (1972e). The "levels" concept in the study of social organization in animals. In L. R. Aronson, E. Tobach, J. S. Rosenblatt, & D. S. Lehrman (Eds.), *Selected writings of T. C. Schneirla* (pp. 440–472). San Francisco: W. H. Freeman.

Schneirla, T. C. (1972f). Levels in the psychological capacities of animals. In L. R. Aronson, E. Tobach, J. S. Rosenblatt, & D. S. Lehrman. (Eds.), *Selected writings of T. C. Schneirla* (pp. 199–237). San Francisco. W. H. Freeman.

Schneirla, T. C. (1972g). Problems in the biopsychology of social organization. In L. R. Aronson, E. Tobach, J. S. Rosenblatt, & D. S. Lehrman (Eds.), *Selected writings of T. C. Schneirla* (pp. 417–439). San Francisco: W. H. Freeman.

Schneirla, T. C. (1972h). Theoretical considerations of cyclic processes in doryline ants. In L. R. Aronson, E. Tobach, J. S. Rosenblatt, & D. S. Lehrman (Eds.), *Selected writings of T. C. Schneirla* (pp. 806–852). San Francisco: W. H. Freeman.

Schneirla, T. C., & Maier, N. R. F. (1940). Concerning the status of the starfish. *Journal of Comparative Psychology, 30,* 103–110.

Scotus, J. D. (1987). *Philosophical writings.* Indianapolis, IN: Hackett.

Silver, R., & Rosenblatt, J. S. (1987). The development of a developmentalist: Daniel S. Lehrman. *Developmental Psychobiology, 20,* 563–570.

Thomas, A., Chess S., Birch H., Hertzig M., & Korn, S. (1963). *Behavioral individuality in early childhood.* New York: New York University Press.

Tobach, E., & Aronson, L. R. (1970). T. C. Schneirla: A biographical note. In L. R. Aronson, E. Tobach, D. S. Lehrman, & J. S. Rosenblatt (Eds.), *Development and evolution of behavior: Essays in memory of T. C. Schneirla* (pp. x–xviii). San Francisco: W. H. Freeman.

Topoff, H. R. (1997). Adaptations for social parasitism. In G. Greenberg & E. Tobach (Eds.), *Comparative psychology of invertebrates. The field and laboratory study of insect behavior* (pp. 177–192). New York: Garland.

Turkewitz, G. (1987). Psychobiology and developmental psychology: The influence of T. C. Schneirla on human developmental psychology. *Developmental Psychobiology, 20,* 369–375.

Turkewitz, G., Gardner, J. M., & Lewkowicz, D. J. (1984). Sensory/perceptual functioning during early infancy: The implications of a quantitative basis for responding. In G. Greenberg & E. Tobach (Eds.), *Behavioral evolution and integrative levels* (pp. 167–195). Hillsdale, NJ: Erlbaum.

Veblen, T. (1931). *The theory of the leisure class.* New York: Viking.

Warden, C. J., Jenkins, T. N., & Warner, L. H. (1934). *Introduction to comparative psychology.* New York: Ronald Press.

Warden, C. J., Jenkins, T. N., & Warner, L. H. (1936). *Comparative psychology: A comprehensive treatise. Vol. III: Vertebrates*. New York: Ronald Press.

Warden, C. J., Jenkins, T. N., & Warner, L. H. (1940). *Plants and invertebrates, Vol. II*. New York: Ronald Press.

Wheeler, W. M. (1928). *The social insects*. New York: Harcourt Brace.

Wilson, E. O. (1963). The social biology of ants. *Annual Review of Entomology, 8,* 345–368.

Wilson, E. O. (1975). *Sociobiology: The new synthesis*. Cambridge, MA: Harvard University Press.

Wilson, E. O. (1987). Causes of ecological success: The case of the ants. Sixth Tansley Lecture. *Journal of Animal Ecology, 56,* 1–9.

Witkin, H. A., & Schneirla, T. C. (1937). Initial maze behavior as a function of maze design. *Journal of Comparative Psychology, 23,* 275–304.

Chapter 14

Starke Rosecrans Hathaway: Biography of an Empiricist

James N. Butcher

The four-wheel-drive vehicle plied its way through the ancient Sinai desert as the somewhat scruffy, quiet Egyptian tour driver occasionally turned the vehicle sharply to avoid rock formations embedded in the sand. The passengers in the vehicle, an American woman psychologist[1] and her son, gazed intently at the picturesque landscape, only occasionally glancing at the nomadic-appearing driver. After a long day's ride through the desert the driver broke his characteristic silence and asked the passengers, "Where do you come from in America?" The woman replied, "We're from Minnesota in the Midwest." The driver looked at her, smiled, and said in broken English "Ah, the home of the MMPI!" As their subsequent conversation soon revealed, the driver had obtained a masters degree from the University of Cairo, where he had conducted research on the Egyptian version of this widely used personality inventory.

AN INTRODUCTION TO THE
MMPI AND ITS CREATORS

What is the MMPI (Minnesota Multiphasic Personality Inventory) and how did a paper-and-pencil personality scale that was developed for clinical assessment in the United States in the 1930s and 1940s come to be so widely used—even more than half a century later—to evaluate personality? Did Starke Hathaway, the originator of the MMPI, realize the potential impact this test would have on

---

[1] I would like to thank Gloria Leon for providing this anecdote.
*Photo of Starke Hathaway courtesy of the Archives of the University of Minnesota.

subsequent generations of psychologists? What was the personality makeup of the man who conceived and developed this instrument that has been so influential in contemporary psychology? This chapter will provide a glimpse into the life and work of this pioneer in personality scale development.

The MMPI is an empirically based objective personality assessment inventory that was originally made up of 550 true–false items covering a broad range of physical and psychological symptoms, behaviors, beliefs, and attitudes, to which clients responded true or false (true, I have that attribute; or false, I do not). The MMPI was developed as an aid to clinical diagnosis. The responses of patients who take the inventory are scored on scales derived from groups of items that represent such clinical problems as depression and schizophrenia. Over the years these scales have been empirically validated against external criteria and provide reliable and valid personality descriptions of clinical patients, job applicants, and convicted felons, with whom the instrument is widely used.

The MMPI scales have also been found to have substantial cross-cultural validity. When the items are carefully translated, they assess similar traits and behavior across cultures (Butcher, 1996; Butcher & Pancheri, 1976). The original MMPI has been translated more than 150 times and is widely used in 46 countries. The revised version of the instrument (MMPI-2) published in 1989 (Butcher, Dahlstrom, Graham, Tellegen, & Kaemmer, 1989a, 1989b) has been translated into 22 languages and several more translations are currently underway.

The MMPI's great success is a testimony to the personal qualities of two men: Hathaway, an empirical psychologist devoted to practical solutions to problems, and J. C. McKinley, chief of psychiatry at the University of Minnesota Hospital. They developed the MMPI as a clinical assessment tool that was simple to use and more accurate in its evaluations of personality than other then-available techniques.

THE EARLY YEARS

Hathaway was born in Central Lake, Michigan, on August 22, 1903, but he lived there only until he was 7, when his family moved to Kansas. Shortly afterward, the family moved again—this time to Ohio, where young Hathaway spent the remainder of his childhood. Those years provided the experiences that formed his geographic identity. As an adult he always thought of himself as an Ohioan.

One of the most predictive features of Hathaway's developmental history was that, from childhood on, he was interested in things mechanical, electrical, and quantitative. When he was 8 years old his family allowed him to set up a workshop in an old crate outside the family home. Throughout his life such workshops provided him the opportunity to test out mechanical principles, build devices to solve practical problems, and to create pieces of jewelry, a hobby he later cultivated. Wherever he went, even in the psychiatric hospital setting where he devoted most of his professional career, he was never far from a workshop. Once when he was in his late 70s (after having had a stroke that weakened his memory and cognitive functioning) he still showed his mechanical interests and drive. With this interest in building and taking apart mechanical devices, it is no wonder, when he made his initial career choice and selected a college program, that he chose electrical engineering. In the early 1920s he entered the school of engineering at Ohio University in Athens.

As it turned out, however, engineering disappointed Hathaway. The curriculum provided neither the outlets that his talents needed nor the challenge he had hoped to find. The textbook used in his second-year course on electricity was the same book he had studied in high school, and the extracurricular activities offered in his engineering courses were not sufficiently advanced or interesting. It is likely that he had attained more than an adequate engineering background in his high school studies.

Faced with that disappointment, Hathaway began to look for more challenging material. Influenced by friends at Ohio University, he found himself attracted to psychology and switched his major. From that point forward, psychological matters occupied his attention, although his approach to psychological issues— flowing naturally from his early preparation—was mechanistic and quantitative. He obtained a bachelor's degree in psychology with a minor in mathematics from the Ohio University in 1927, and stayed on for advanced study. As a graduate student, he studied under James P. Porter, whom he considered to be a powerful force in his development as a psychologist. Hathaway obtained a master's degree in psychology that was actually awarded by the Ohio State University because, at that time, Ohio University did not offer advanced degrees.

After graduation, and before going on for doctoral study, Hathaway served for a brief period in 1929 as a research assistant to Harry Johnson at Carnegie Mellon University in Pittsburgh, Pennsylvania—a job that was 95% engineering and 5% psychology. In this work, he developed an automatic camera that enabled Johnson to record the movements of people while they slept. Some of Johnson's films, using this equipment, made it into movie comedies and were later used for advertising. This invention was a part of what the American Psychological Association acknowledged in awarding him the Distinguished Scientific Award for Applications of Psychology in 1977.

Hathaway studied for the PhD degree at the University of Minnesota in the 1930s and was influenced by such outstanding psychologists as Karl Lashley (chap. 20, *Pioneers I*), Edna Heidbreder (chap. 19, *Pioneers I*), Donald G. Patterson, and B. F. Skinner (chap. 16, *Pioneers III*), with whom he apparently had a number of stimulating debates about psychological matters. He received his PhD degree in physiological psychology and stayed on at Minnesota, where he taught in the department of psychology for three years and did postgraduate studies in anatomy. During these early years at Minnesota, Hathaway also taught a course in physics.

In 1932 Hathaway was offered a permanent job at the University of Minnesota Hospital, with a joint appointment in the department of anatomy. His chief responsibility was to establish a division of clinical psychology in the department of psychiatry at the University of Minnesota Medical School. It is interesting to note that it was his engineering and mechanical background as much as his training in psychology that suited him for the job. Much of what he initially did was to put his engineering background to use, designing an ideal psychiatric facility and building amplification equipment to measure neuromuscular potentials for research conducted at the hospital (Butcher, 1977). During his tenure as a member of the faculty of the medical school, Hathaway worked closely with the medical staff, particularly the neurosurgeons, and often observed them conducting brain surgery.

PERSONAL QUALITIES

If one were to find the single word that best characterized him as an individual, that word would be "pragmatic," a trait that was central to the approach he took to every area he pursued. He was not theoretically inclined and did not think much of the deductive method or of looking at problems from a grand perspective. When he faced theoretical issues, he began by breaking them down into component parts. By his own admission, he was a "nuts and bolts" empiricist in everything he undertook.

He had an interest in applying rigorous quantification to human problems, particularly those involving mental health. He assumed that human qualities could be "engineered" in much the same way as physical matter could be influenced by electrical and mechanical forces. That idea was one he shared with B. F. Skinner.

He believed that biological processes underlie psychological phenomena and that a knowledge of human anatomy and physiology is essential to understanding psychological processes.

He was avidly interested in other languages. He had a working knowledge of French and German, and was facile in Spanish. He often lectured or led discussions in Spanish at the National Autonomous University during his annual trips to Mexico.

He was quantitatively and mechanically gifted and had an uncanny knack of seeing practical solutions to complex problems. But he was not particularly articulate in communicating with others. In fact, some have noted that at times he was almost incoherent (Buchanan, 1994).

He was a master clinician, with great sensitivity to the problems of others and skill at helping others see their problems clearly. His practical orientation well-suited him to helping patients with psychiatric disabilities, particularly those with chronic, long-term problems.

Along with his mechanical tinkering, Hathaway was an avid fisherman. He tied his own flies and made his own lures—to which fish were reportedly mysteriously attracted. He owned a cabin in northern Minnesota, where he spent a great deal of time fishing for Walleyes. (This author was once invited there, to try his hand at walleye fishing—without conspicuous success.) Hathaway's most unusual catch came in the 1970s, during his retirement years at his home in Melbourne, Florida. Early one morning, he cast a line from his dock and hooked a large bale of marijuana that must have been set adrift by smugglers. After considerable inspection of the unusual packaging—and to the dismay of some of his younger colleagues—he turned the contents over to the local police.

No better characterization of the personal side of Hathaway has been provided than the letter that Roland Peek (former chief of Psychological Services for the Department of Public Welfare of Minnesota) wrote in 1969 for the collection of letters presented to Hathaway at a ceremony honoring his contributions to psychology:

> Starke Hathaway? One of those unforgettable characters, as everyone knows, of course. But why? Well for me there is a kaleidoscopic glitter of images and memories, all unforgettable: his eyes, kindly and penetrating; the unsettling frequency of his mind-reading in clinical settings; his absent-minded combing of a brain model as he paced and lectured in physiological psychology, with a scrap of comb rescued from the floor; unmatched shoes cocked comfortably on a VA desk-top; his quiet encouragement of an uncertain student, and his skillful reshaping of a brash one; white duck trousers made greasy from crawling under a car just before the lecture; incisive cuts through words to the essence of things. If psychology has some kind of soul, Starke Hathaway is surely part of it.

PROFESSIONAL CONTRIBUTIONS

To give a picture of the breadth of Hathaway's professional contributions, our discussion will be divided into eight areas of activity and professional endeavor in which he was engaged during his long academic career. Although these areas do not have equal weight, they illustrate the diversity of his interests and underscore the empirically oriented manner in which he approached all tasks that he undertook.

Instrumentation in Psychology

In a pattern consistent with his life-long interests and his engineering background, Hathaway's early work centered around developing mechanical and electrical devices to measure psychological processes. His first publication, in 1929 when he was still a student at Ohio University, "A Comparative Study of Psychogalvanic and Association Time Measures: A New Psychogalvanic Apparatus," demonstrated Hathaway's ability to conceptualize psychological processes and to use electronic methods to measure them.

This article also illustrated his experimental, inventive approach to psychological problems. In an effort to study emotions in a quantifiable manner, Hathaway had developed a device to measure galvanic skin responses in a reliable manner. He patented this apparatus as a "lie detector" and built 30 machines, which he sold to other psychology departments. Incidentally, this commercial venture also provided the money that he needed to marry his wife Jinny—an important relationship that lasted the remainder of his life.[2] His work on the psychogalvanometer also thrust him into the national limelight for the first time as the inventor of a lie-detection machine.

Physiological Psychology

Early in his career, in 1942, at about the same time that the MMPI was in the final stages of development, Hathaway published a textbook, titled *Physiological Psychology*. This text was a state-of-the-art description of the physiological and neurological mechanisms of behavior and provided students in the expanding field of clinical psychology a necessary grounding. In his introduction to the book, Hathaway wrote,

> Physiological psychology is not a separate science but is, as the name implies, a link between two basically similar sciences, physiology and psychology. Its content and definitions are determined by its raison d'etre; namely, by the need felt by psychologists working in the fields of general, clinical, and animal psychology for an enriched vocabulary and for a simplified but fundamentally workable grounding in the allied biological sciences. (Hathaway, 1942, p. vii)

This book, which revealed Hathaway's great depth of knowledge of neuroanatomy and physiology, was published in Appleton-Century-Croft's prestigious Century Psychology Series. It was both a practical introduction to physiological psychology and a highly influential resource in the training of clinical psychologists in the years following World War II. It is interesting to note that Hathaway not only wrote the book but crafted its anatomical drawings.

Hathaway taught physiological psychology at Minnesota for many years and influenced many psychologists who later came to be important in the field. One of them, Kenneth MacCorquodale (1969), on the occasion of a ceremony honoring Hathaway and his contributions to psychology, wrote,

---

[2]Starke and Jinny had no children. Hathaway's estate went to the University Minnesota, where an endowed Hathaway Chair in Psychology is funded by his MMPI royalties.

It seems incredible that I have known you for twenty-eight years. I took physio-logical psychology from you in 1941, beginning then an association which I have continued to enjoy and profit from always. I remember many intellectual illumi-nations and personal kindnesses throughout these years. Your professional contri-butions and recognition have been a source of pride to us all, and have reflected their excellence upon our department. I am grateful that you will be here to help us through what comes next.

Development of the MMPI

In the years following World War I, psychologists published numerous paper-and-pencil tests of personality. These instruments followed in the wake of the first published personality inventory, Woodworth's (1920) "Personal Data Sheet," developed as a screening instrument for draftees during World War I. Most of these postwar scales were rationally or theoretically derived. They were aimed at assessing vague concepts or processes such as "will" or "temperament." Few of them presumed to detect clinical problems or to serve as aids in psychiatric diagnosis. Typically, they had not been validated against external criteria.

For such reasons, Hathaway was disenchanted with existing instruments, as well as with the standard practice of arriving at classifications of mental health problems on the basis of clinical interviews and observation. Those methods led to clinical diagnoses that were often wrong or seriously off target. The MMPI remedied those deficits and provided the practitioner with a means of clinical di-agnosis that could be used by the general medical practitioner or the nonmedical mental health professional.

The MMPI was a product of Hathaway's tinkering mode of problem solving. He and McKinley built a machine (made up of true–false statements rather than electrical wires) to measure clinical problems. In developing the MMPI, they ap-proached the task in a strictly empirical manner. Without resorting to theory or any preconceived idea about what they might assess, they put together a large array of items: beliefs, attitudes, behaviors based on case material, textbooks, and existing tests. They wanted a broad range of content for the inventory and de-veloped items that provided a universe of "interesting" symptoms. It was their intention to let empirical experience determine which of the items were effective at discriminating particular patient groups (e.g., depressed patients) from the nor-mal sample. Items that were found, in fact, to discriminate between a designated clinical group and a normal sample was made up of a provisional psychometric scale that measured that clinical condition. These scales, which addressed such clinical problems as depression, schizophrenia, and hypochondria, were made up of items that empirically separated patients in a clinical group from a large sam-ple of normal individuals. When new patients obtained an extreme score on a particular scale they were considered to belong to that clinical group and to have the personality characteristics and symptoms that other members of that group possessed. The primary reason for the success of the MMPI in psychiatric screening was that it provided diagnoses of clinical patients' problems in a quantifiable form. Psychologists at last had an instrument that enabled them to diagnose patients' behavior and their problems in an objective manner.

Shortly after the publication of the MMPI in 1943 an article appeared in *Time* magazine describing the test's publication and heralding its utility in assessing clinical problems in an objective manner. By that early date, the MMPI was already gaining a broad following and was becoming the most favored personality instrument to use in clinical assessment.

Harrison Gough (1988), himself a substantial contributor to objective personality assessment, described his exposure to the utility of the MMPI in clinical assessment during World War II. Gough had been a student at Minnesota before the war and had some knowledge of the MMPI but had not learned how to use the test. When he went into the service during the war and was assigned to an 1800-bed station hospital as a clinical psychologist, he acknowledged that he "knew next to nothing of the clinical arts." He described his situation as follows:

> One of the things that hastened my participation was an Army circular announcing the availability of the MMPI for use in military installations. At that time I had never seen the test, but remembered hearing . . . about it, and decided we should get it for our psychiatric service. In due time, a box of cards, a manual, recording sheets, scoring templates, and a pamphlet telling how to use the test arrived. I read everything, took the test myself, and began to administer it to all of our new patients. We were admitting from 5 to 10 patients a day, so my sample grew rapidly. It soon became apparent that there was a strong correspondence between the MMPI findings and those from the interview and psychiatric examinations. Very often the MMPI suggested something important that had either been overlooked elsewhere or that was not really detectable in other appraisals. (1988, p. 10)

By the 1970s the MMPI was the most widely used personality test for research and clinical assessment purposes but, throughout his career, Hathaway himself avoided involvement in the promotion of his test:

> I have always avoided the business and promotion activities connected with the MMPI, as well as involvements with the publications policies and procedural decisions or questions concerning the instrument. Indeed, I have avoided teaching the subject and any intimations of promoting the test. Certainly, I am less expert in the knowledge of the literature and interpretation of the MMPI than are many routine users of it, and considerably less than the many contributors to the knowledge of the MMPI. At times I have become impatient, wishing that my connection with the MMPI could be forgotten in favor of my other work and interests. (1978, p. 117)

Lie Detection and "Profiling" Criminals

Although it may seem unlikely for a psychologist, Hathaway had a strong interest in crime detection. The local police department frequently called on him to assist in developing "criminal profiles" of likely suspects in unsolved crimes, particularly when the crime involved unusual aspects that stumped the police. Hathaway's crime-detection hobby probably evolved from his interest in physiological psychology and his work, described earlier, on measuring emotions through galvanic skin response recording.

We do not know how much success Hathaway or the police detectives experienced with Hathaway's consultation on these matters or much about how he assisted them in their profiling tasks. Hathaway's work in the area of criminal consultation, in all likelihood, provided less in the way of formal techniques or instruments for use in law enforcement than it did in serving as a role model for other psychologists to apply psychology for solving practical problems.

Pioneer in Medical Psychology

Hathaway's work in the medical school at Minnesota helped define the field of medical psychology. His vision of what clinical psychology as a profession should be like included bringing laboratory psychology into the clinic. In his view, experimental psychology, with its rigorous examination of psychological phenomena, could be applied in the clinical context to aid in the development of methods that would help people with severe mental problems.

Hathaway spent much of his later career heading the division of clinical psychology at the University of Minnesota and serving as assistant head of the department of psychiatry. He built the division of clinical psychology into a large and active medical psychology program. His professional contribution was likely to have been the fruition of his relationship with medical professionals and his conversance with medicine. In this connection, Buchanan pointed out the significance of Hathaway's relationship with J. C. McKinley:

> In his partnership with McKinley, Hathaway enjoyed certain privileges that guaranteed the pertinence of his work. Hathaway's role as a research-oriented psychologist holding a responsible and influential position in a psychiatric setting was, at the time, almost unique. His occupational profile differed markedly from that of the average clinical psychologist of the inter-war period. The professional pecking order within the mental institutions usually precluded psychologists from a share of the resources necessary for large-scale research. For those working in the clinics, particularly child guidance establishments, access to an adult psychiatric population was limited. Hathaway's access to a varied psychiatric population and the power of his medical co-worker McKinley to mobilize hospital staff and garner resources constituted an enormous practical advantage. It provided the opportunity

to develop a test adapted to the diagnostic problems of the period and suitable for use with all patient groups. (1994, p. 155)

Experimental Model in Psychotherapy

During the latter part of his career, Hathaway moved beyond his earlier interest in psychophysiology and diagnosis and became interested in psychotherapy (Hathaway, 1951). In this endeavor, as in all others, he was a pragmatist. He was opposed to theories of psychotherapy and to theoretical orientations that dictated treatment strategies. He favored therapeutic methods that were designed to fit particular cases. Hathaway's own methods, which he called pragmatical or "redirective psychotherapy" (Hathaway, 1978), most closely resembled Albert Ellis's rational–emotive therapy. Ellis wrote the following, in a letter to honor Hathaway:

> I . . . want to remind your well wishers that you have been, for the last quarter of a century, one of the foremost proponents of a sane and objective approach to psychotherapy, and that you have helped turn out some unusually good clinicians in this area. My warmest greetings and best wishes for continued effective functioning to you this happy day. (1969)

Hathaway was a sensitive clinician and had a proclivity toward working with long-term and difficult to treat patients—in some cases following them for decades. His major contributions during this period were in teaching others how to do psychotherapy, in founding an experimental inpatient treatment unit (Station 61) at the University of Minnesota Hospital during the 1960s, and in supervising psychiatric residents and clinical psychology interns in mental health treatment. These treatment efforts were, however, not to bring as much recognition to Hathaway as the MMPI had done. Even though he minimized the contribution of the MMPI to the field, it rather than psychotherapeutic intervention was Hathaway's most visible and lasting contribution to the field of psychology.

International Collaboration

Although, as noted earlier, Hathaway did not view himself as a "promoter" of the MMPI and did not accept invitations to lecture or conduct workshops on the topic, he was much interested in extending the use of the instrument to other cultures, particularly Mexico, and making it available in other languages. He collaborated in and provided consultation on the translation of the MMPI into Spanish in Cuba, Puerto Rico, and Mexico. He assisted Rafael Nuñez, of the University of the Americas in Mexico City, in developing and publishing the MMPI in Mexico in 1967.

Moreover, when Nuñez and the author of this chapter organized and conducted the first International Conference on Personality Assessment in 1970 in Mexico, Hathaway provided us with a great deal of advice, emotional support, and introductions to his Spanish-speaking colleagues in Latin America. He also aided the program by being a keynote speaker in a talk titled, "Research Pertinent to Spanish-American Cross-Validation of the MMPI."

Analyzing and Predicting Delinquency

In the late 1940s, Hathaway became interested in the possibility of using personality-based information on adolescents to predict later outcomes such as school dropout and delinquency. In collaboration with Elio Monachesi, a sociologist at Minnesota, he conducted an extensive longitudinal study of adolescent personality and behavior. Hathaway and Monachesi (1953) believed that factors leading up to delinquency were poorly understood because the act of delinquency changes a person, and that assessments after the beginning of adolescence might mask the effect of important personality factors. They thought that the only way to determine the extent to which such factors encourage or suppress delinquency was to obtain preadolescence personality appraisals and follow individuals over time, noting the presence or absence of later behavior problems. In 1947, these investigators tested more than 4000 students from the Minneapolis public schools with the goal of following them up later when they were in high school to determine if measured personality factors were associated with later negative outcomes. Again, in 1954 Hathaway and Monachesi administered the MMPI to a far broader sample of ninth graders, nearly 12,000 boys and girls from school districts throughout Minnesota, to incorporate rural as well as urban youth in their sample.

Hathaway and Monachesi followed these adolescents into the last year of high school to determine those who had obtained police records for delinquent acts (approximately 34% of both samples had police records). Next, using interviews and official school records, they documented the extent of their delinquent behavior and school performance to assess the "level" of delinquent behavior.

Hathaway and Monachesi determined through analysis of the students' MMPI scores that delinquent boys and girls had common personality patterns on the earlier MMPI. Extreme scores on scales PD (psychopathic deviate), SC (schizophrenia), and MA (mania), referred to as the "activator scales," were frequent among adolescents who became delinquent. But extreme scores on scales D (depression), MF (masculinity–femininity), and SI (social introversion), referred to as "suppressor" scales, were associated with low rates of delinquency. Hathaway and Monachesi described these results in several influential publications (Hathaway & Monachesi, 1953, 1963; Hathaway, Monachesi, & Young, 1960). These results show that elevated scores on certain of the MMPI scales, obtained when young people are in the ninth grade, are associated with high rates of delinquency and school dropout later on in high school.

LASTING CONTRIBUTIONS TO THE
FIELD OF PERSONALITY ASSESSMENT

On the occasion honoring Hathaway's contributions to psychology in 1969, Harry Harlow wrote,

> I have always been pleased by the fact that it took an experimental-physiological psychologist to create the most meritorious personality test ever achieved. Frankly, I have often meditated on the intervening variables that must have operated during this intellectual transition, but whatever they may have been, the fact is that you remain psychologists' greatest contribution to the psychiatric process.

As a summary of Hathaway's lasting contributions will attest, Harlow was not being overly extravagant.

Objective Personality Assessment

Hathaway and McKinley brought into the field of personality assessment a desperately needed objective portrayal of clinical symptoms and problems. Their method of developing personality scales through "blind empiricism" provided clinical measures that have stood the test of time. This work brought refreshing clarity to the field of personality assessment by applying empirical scale-construction methods, which took the subjectivity out of personality research and promoted a more rigorous understanding of personality.

The MMPI (in but slightly altered form) is the most widely used and effective clinical instrument today. Now, some 60 years after it emerged from "dust bowl empiricism," the MMPI has spun off more than 13,000 books and articles and the research is currently being published at the rate of about 200 or more publications a year. And even 20 years after his death people still write to and try to telephone Hathaway to discuss his test.

Development of Measures to Detect Protocol Validity

Although Hathaway was not the first psychologist to address the impact of response bias on the quality of the data obtained through self-report, his work on the development of validity scales for the MMPI—the lie and faking scales, along with the K or defensiveness scale developed by Meehl and Hathaway (1946)—represented a major contribution to the science of personality assessment. These measures allow the researcher or practitioner to determine whether the person taking the test responded in a frank and open manner. This work substantially influenced later personality test development, and the most effective personality scales developed later use such measures of validity.

Norms as Invariant Standards

One of the distinguishing features of Hathaway and McKinley's questionnaire was the use of a large "normal" population to serve as a reference group against which clinical samples could be compared to develop scales that would empirically differentiate different groups. Hathaway was a staunch believer in test norms and had a "one size fits all" view of how they should function. There should be one standard unit of measure for assessing clinical dimensions, just as there is for physical measures—the 12-inch foot for length and the 16-ounce pound for weight, and so forth. He insisted that one should not develop special norms for subsets of the population, and that the MMPI norms should be the same for such varying groups as old people, adolescents, and those from foreign countries who take translated versions of the test. The science of personality assessment needs a standard reference against which the performance of any individual can be compared. This view has influenced subsequent researchers, for example, in developing MMPI-2 (Butcher et al., 1989b).

Rigorous Empirical Conceptualization of Clinical Cases

Hathaway's way of conceptualizing clinical cases might be described as a "naive empiricism." Rather than imposing his own biases or preconceptions on data, Hathaway chose to let the data speak for themselves. He let patterns (profile types) on the MMPI that differed from others in the population serve as the identifiers of traits and clinical categories and as predictors of behavior. He interpreted MMPI profiles with high scores on certain scales by referring to the characteristics of cases with similar patterns. So that practitioners could determine the meaning of particular scale elevations or profile patterns, Hathaway and his colleagues cataloged cases in reference guides known as "atlases" (e.g., Hathaway & Meehl, 1951). One could determine what behavior could be expected from a particular profile by referring to similar cases in the atlas. Similar profile types were found to have similar background and personality characteristics.

Pioneer in Computer-Based Personality Assessment

Hathaway's objective clinical perspective was influential in the creation of automated personality assessment and its culmination in computer-based interpretation. Although Hathaway was an advocate of mechanical or actuarial test-interpretation strategies, he did not develop a computer-based personality assessment system. His career was coming toward its end as the computer age dawned. However, he contributed conceptually to the early development of the first computer-based interpretation system at Mayo Clinic in the early 1960s.

Hathaway was a coauthor of a widely cited article that provided intellectual support for later computer-based interpretive programs (Rome et al., 1962). In a collection of letters written to the memory of Hathaway, John Pearson (1992), one of his early students (who along with Wendell Swenson developed the first computer-based MMPI interpretation system at Mayo Clinic in Rochester, Minnesota, with Hathaway's consultation) wrote the following about Hathaway's contribution to computer-based assessment:

> In 1962, when Wendell Swenson and I launched the automated MMPI project at Mayo Clinic, Hathaway was totally supportive and very vocal in his efforts to convince doubters that this was a good idea. He stated repeatedly that this was a logical technologic extension of the original purposes of the test, that it could serve as a screening device for internists and other physicians, leaving the more detailed analysis of the MMPI along with interview and other techniques to clinical psychologists or psychiatrists. (p. 29)

Hathaway (1972a) summarized his views on computer-based interpretation as being an important development that would allow for the "voluminous" actuarial database on the MMPI to improve interpretation of the test. He noted that "the immense storage of a computer provides an opportunity to receive in a short time all the interpretative statements that may be directly and indirectly used as a basis for further clinical evaluation" (p. 277).

Challenge to Improve Personality Assessment

When asked to offer an appraisal of the field of personality assessment, Hathaway expressed disappointment with what he saw as the lack of progress in the field. In 1972, following a 1969 conference devoted to the issue of "whether the MMPI should be revised and if so how?" Hathaway (1972b) asked, "With so many competent efforts over so many years, why have we not yet developed better personality tests? I could extend the question to a more arbitrary one: Why are we today unable to confidently undertake the development of significantly more valid and useful tests?" (p. 23).

This query is still appropriate today. Several new instruments, developed with different and supposedly more sophisticated methods, have failed to improve on the MMPI or to gain favor among test users. During the early stages of the MMPI revision in 1981, the MMPI-2 Restandardization Committee asked Hathaway for comments on the plan for revising the instrument. In his response, he approved of the idea of maintaining continuity with the original MMPI by keeping clinical and validity scales relatively intact. He also thought that it was time to eliminate some of the original MMPI items in favor of new ones that focus on more contemporary problems. As a result, in the revision a number of these items were deleted and replaced with others with a broader range of content—for example, the items "I like tall women" and "I believe there is a god" were deleted.

CONCLUSION

Hathaway's empirical orientation, his desire to apply rigorous, objective methods in the study of psychology—from physiological psychology to personality—advanced the field substantially. A number of his contributions were highlighted and his lasting mark on objective personality assessment noted.

Hathaway discouraged developing a "cult" or following for himself or for the MMPI. At a conference dedicated to the question of whether the MMPI could and should be revised, he opened the meeting with a lamentation about what he saw as a "mystery of missing progress" and advised against accepting any standard (even the MMPI) (Hathaway, 1972b) and encouraged psychologists to strive for innovation and for building better assessment devices. He ended his professional career with the same down-to-earth, questioning, pragmatic approach he used when he began it.

REFERENCES

Buchanan, R. D. (1994). The development of the Minnesota Multiphasic Personality Inventory. *Journal of the History of the Behavioral Sciences, 25,* 148–161.

Butcher, J. N. (1977) Videotaped interview of Starke R. Hathaway. *MMPI-2 Workshops.* Minneapolis: University of Minnesota.

Butcher, J. N. (1996). *International adaptations of the MMPI-2: Research and clinical applications.* Minneapolis: University of Minnesota Press.

Butcher, J. N., Dahlstrom, W. G., Graham, J. R., Tellegen, A., & Kaemmer, B. (1989a). *Manual for the restandardized Minnesota Multiphasic Personality Inventory: MMPI-2. An administrative and interpretive guide.* Minneapolis: University of Minnesota Press.

Butcher, J. N., Dahlstrom, W. G., Graham, J. R., Tellegen, A., & Kaemmer, B. (1989b). *Minnesota Multiphasic Personality Inventory-2 (MMPI-2): Manual for administration and scoring.* Minneapolis: University of Minnesota Press.

Butcher, J. N., & Pancheri, P. (1976). *Handbook of cross-national MMPI research.* Minneapolis: University of Minnesota Press.

Ellis, A. (1969). Letter honoring the contribution of Starke Hathaway. In J. N. Butcher (Ed.), *Letters to Hathaway.* Archives of the University of Minnesota, Minneapolis.

Gough, H. G. (1988). Along the way: Recollections of some major contributors to personality assessment. *Journal of Personality Assessment, 52,* 5–29.

Harlow, H. (1969). Letter honoring the contribution of Starke Hathaway. In J. N. Butcher (Ed.), *Letters to Hathaway.* Archives of the University of Minnesota, Minneapolis.

Hathaway, S. R. (1929). A comparative study of psychogalvanic and association time measures: A new psychogalvanic apparatus. *Journal of Applied Psychology, 13,* 632–646.

Hathaway, S. R. (1942). *Physiological psychology.* New York: Appleton-Century-Crofts.

Hathaway, S. R. (1951). Clinical methods in psychotherapy. *Annual Review of Psychology, 2,* 259–280.

Hathaway, S. R. (1972a). MMPI and the computer. *Psychologie, 31,* 277–280.

Hathaway, S. R. (1972b). Where have we gone wrong? The mystery of missing progress. In J. N. Butcher (Ed.), *Objective personality assessment: Changing perspectives* (pp. 21–43). New York: Academic Press.

Hathaway, S. R. (1978). Through psychology my way. In T. S. Krawiec (Ed), *The psychologists: Autobiographies of distinguished living psychologists* (Vol. 3, pp. 105–123). Brandon, VT: Clinical Psychology Publishing.

Hathaway, S. R., & Meehl, P. E. (1951). *An atlas for the clinical use of the MMPI.* Minneapolis: University of Minnesota Press.

Hathaway, S. R., & Monachesi, E. D. (1953). *Analyzing and predicting juvenile delinquency with the MMPI.* Minneapolis: University of Minnesota Press.

Hathaway, S. R., & Monachesi, E. D. (1963). *Adolescent personality and behavior.* Minneapolis: University of Minnesota Press.

Hathaway, S. R., Monachesi, E. D., & Young, L. A. (1960). Delinquency rates and personality. *Journal of Criminal Law, Criminology and Police Science, 50,* 433–440.

MacCorquodale, K. (1969). Letter honoring the contribution of Starke Hathaway. In J. N. Butcher (Ed.), *Letters to Hathaway.* Archives of the University of Minnesota, Minneapolis.

Meehl, P. E., & Hathaway, S. R. (1946). The K factor as a suppressor variable in the Minnesota Multiphasic Personality Inventory. *Journal of Applied Psychology, 30,* 525–564.

Pearson, J. (1992). Memory of Starke Hathaway. In D. S. Nichols & P. A. Marks (Eds.), *Reflections and remembrances.* Minneapolis: University of Minnesota Press.

Peek, R. (1969). Letter honoring the contribution of Starke Hathaway. In J. N. Butcher (Ed.), *Letters to Hathaway.* Archives of the University of Minnesota, Minneapolis.

Rome, H. P., Swenson, W. M., Mataya, P., McCarthy, C. E., Pearson, J. S., Keating, F. R., & Hathaway, S. R. (1962). *Symposium on automation technics in personality assessment. Proceedings of the Staff Meetings of the Mayo Clinic, 37,* 61–82.

Time. (1943). Truth & consequences. May 3.

Woodworth, R. S. (1920). *The Personal Data Sheet.* Chicago: Stoelting.

Chapter 15

What a Light It Shed: The Life of Evelyn Hooker

Douglas C. Kimmel and Linda D. Garnets

Evelyn Gentry was born into a farm family and grew up in the hard life on the plains of Nebraska and Colorado. In 1924 she entered the University of Colorado and majored in psychology, earning a bachelor's degree in 1928 and a master's degree in 1930. In 1932 she received her PhD from Johns Hopkins University. Some years later she moved to California to recover from tuberculosis and stayed two years in a sanitarium. In 1939 she became an adjunct faculty member at the University of California at Los Angeles (UCLA), where she taught through the extension program. While she and her second husband, Edward Hooker, a Distinguished Professor of History at UCLA, fought the anticommunist loyalty-oath issue of the 1950s, Evelyn began collecting the data that would change the psychological understanding of human sexuality. After her ground-breaking paper was presented at the American Psychological Association (APA) annual meeting in Chicago in 1955, one member of the audience commented, "What a light it shed" (Harrison & Schmiechen, 1991).

When Hooker died at her home in Los Angeles on November 18, 1996, she was surrounded by awards and tributes to her work and by persons whose lives had been directly touched by her research four decades earlier. That research changed the meaning of same-gender love from an illness to a gift. She was, in many ways, the recipient of that gift, and became an "honorary homosexual."

The authors of this brief review of the life of Hooker are among the direct beneficiaries of her work. We came to discover our same-gender attractions and love when the impact of the research and writings of Hooker and other pioneers began to offer a perspective different from the pathology, illness, deviance mod-

---

*Photo of Evelyn Hooker from the documentary film *Changing Our Minds: The Story of Dr. Evelyn Hooker,* directed by Richard Schmiechen. Used by permission.

els that were prevalent in the 1950s and 1960s. By the time we entered our careers, Alfred Kinsey, Hooker, and William Masters and Virginia Johnson were
as well-known to us as B. F. Skinner, Carl Rogers, Virginia Satir, and Abraham
Maslow. Hooker was then in the final period of her life: one of fame, awards,
and a surprising bequest; and also a period of health problems and limitations.
We begin with this period of her life, for we knew her well then. Then we focus on the specific details of her life in two parts: first, as a remarkable woman
of her time; second, as a psychologist who was the foremother of the gay liberation movement. We conclude with a discussion of the lasting legacy of her contributions to psychology.

TWO PERSONAL REFLECTIONS
ON THE LATER YEARS

Hooker touched people in many different ways. She cared about people and attracted a circle of friends of all ages. She was a teacher, mentor, colleague, psychotherapist, and bon vivant. She enjoyed knowing everyone as an individual
who had stories to share with a good listener.

Hooker's Kitchen Cabinet

The second author (LG) first met Hooker in 1986 at the home of Nora Weckler.
Hooker had been given the first Outstanding Achievement Award from the APA
Committee on Lesbian and Gay Concerns. She was unable to attend the convention, so we presented the award to her in Los Angeles. I was immediately
impressed with her wit, incisive comments, and astute mind. I was thrilled to be
in the presence of this woman whose research had given me such hope as I was
coming out in the early 1970s. We became friends over the next several years,
and I often visited her at her home in Santa Monica.

I had the good fortune to meet with Hooker regularly as part of what she called
her "kitchen cabinet"—a group made up of Anne Peplau, Jackie Goodchilds, and
me. We used to arrive at Hooker's apartment laden with food and wine and settle in for an afternoon of lively conversation and much good humor. We would
sit in her living room, surrounded by books and awards that she had received.
Hooker was eager to discuss art, literature, politics, and the issues of the day;
she was always open to new ideas. The conversations moved between intense
intellectual and political debate to sharing intimate secrets about our lives. And
when Hooker had sufficiently tired the three of us out, we would leave filled
with this woman who conveyed such a great strength of character. She was smart,
well-read, iconoclastic, opinionated, and able to have a good time.

One experience with Hooker exemplifies the kind of impact that she had on
my life. In the summer of 1995, my parents were visiting me and I wanted them

to meet Hooker. We went to see her with my life partner and my uncle, who is gay. Earlier in the day, I had showed my parents "Changing Our Minds," the film about Hooker's life and work. Eventually our conversation turned to a discussion about homosexuality. Hooker remarked that she believed that homosexuality was genetic, at which point my father jumped up and exclaimed, "It's not my fault!" When he realized the effect of what he had said, he confided in Hooker, "You know I've always wished that Linda was heterosexual and I still do." Now it was Hooker's turn to jump out of her seat. She said, "Ira, how sad! Here you have a daughter who has done every thing to make a parent happy. She has a loving, stable, long-term relationship; she's successful in her work; and she has a happy and fulfilling life. What more could any parent want?" What Hooker did for me that day is what her research has done for all of us.

Hooker's work and friendship encouraged me to pursue a career in gay, lesbian, and bisexual psychology. During the 1990s, when Hooker and I served on the review committee for the American Psychological Foundation's Wayne Placek Fund, we developed an important group ritual. The committee would first meet at my home to narrow down the applications. The next day, we would go over to Hooker's to make the final decisions. I was continually impressed with how carefully Hooker (in her late 80s at this point) had reviewed each proposal and would engage us for hours in discussions of the nuances of the research and its implications for gay, lesbian, and bisexual psychology. She punctuated all of her scholarly comments by regaling us with stories about when she was conducting her own research in the 1950s. For example, to learn about the gay community, Hooker not only interviewed people but she also went with friends to gay bars and parties. She made it clear that she enjoyed being the only woman at these events. And then she would lament one of her favorite refrains: "But alas, I am hopelessly heterosexual!"

She Knew My Work Before We Met

It was at the annual APA convention in San Francisco, on August 26, 1977, where the first author (DK) was chairing the meeting of the four-year-old Association of Gay Psychologists, that Hooker walked into the room. The business meeting was nearly over, so after asking a colleague if that in fact was Dr. Hooker, I introduced her. She was a tall woman with a distinctive voice, raspy from years of cigarette smoking. According to a report of the meeting, she said that "when she began her research 25 years ago she never dreamed that gay men and women would come together openly at a meeting of the American Psychological Association during her lifetime" (Kimmel, 1978, p. 1). This was greeted with a standing ovation in her honor. After the meeting adjourned, I met her in person and was overwhelmed: She began to give citations of papers I had written on gay male aging. I listened in amazement as others in the room met her for the first time and she cited their publications and, clearly, had read them. At this time she was nearly 70, retired from UCLA, and in private practice.

We corresponded occasionally over the years. One letter I received troubled me deeply because she was apparently depressed when she wrote it. Later I learned she had struggled for many years with bipolar affective disorder and was often on medication for it.

My correspondence with her intensified when she received a bequest from one of the participants in her classic study. I offered my assistance in resolving the disposition of the moneys, which eventually became the Wayne Placek Fund of the American Psychological Foundation. I also was a member of the APA Board of Social and Ethical Responsibility for Psychology and, in that role, nominated her year after year for the award she eventually received from the APA. Although she was unable physically to be present at the award ceremony, a telephone hook-up was arranged so she could listen as her paper was read the following year and then she engaged in a long-distance audio discussion with the audience. The whole event was videotaped for her to view later.

By now we had become friends and I visited her at her home on a few occasions. She was a delightful conversationalist, sharp and incisive in her wit and comments, and blessed with a good memory and sense of humor. As a bequest, she left me a watercolor portrait of a young man that had hung in her home, a gift to her from the artist, Don Bachardy; it is a treasured reminder of those visits. Eventually her health began to fail. During one particularly bad episode, I was able to reassure her that her memory would return, that she was suffering from the aftereffects from the acute illness and not from dementia. After one bad fall that made it no longer feasible for her to be alone, I contacted some geropsychology colleagues and they found a home-care service. One of the key people at that service knew of Hooker's research and made a personal commitment that she be cared for with all the loving skill that was possible.

A REMARKABLE WOMAN OF HER TIME

It is important to understand Hooker's life and professional experiences in the social context of the status of women in society and psychology. As we look at some of the key aspects of her upbringing, education, and highlights of her career, it becomes clear how she created many opportunities for herself, but she also encountered repeated instances of sexism. Hooker had the ability to focus on the opportunities and to surmount those obstacles she faced simply because she was female.

The sixth of nine children, Hooker began school in a succession of one-room schoolhouses. As a young girl she experienced the burden of social stigma—both for being poor and for being a girl: "Growing up for me was a very painful process. . . . I was very tall, very tall when I was an adolescent. I grew to be almost six feet . . . and girls at that time, especially in a small high school, were not favored, let us say we didn't learn to stand up straight for example" (Schmiechen & Haugland interview with Evelyn Hooker, as cited in Boxer & Carrier, 1998, pp. 5–6).

Hooker's mother was a pioneer of another sort who had crossed the plains in a covered wagon. Although her mother had only a third-grade education, she advised Hooker, "Get an education and they can never take it away from you" (Anonymous, 1992b, p. 502). She moved the family to the county seat so that Hooker could attend a large high school, where she entered an honors program that included a course in psychology. At the urging of a female teacher to pursue a college education, Hooker entered the University of Colorado at Boulder in 1924 at the age of 17. To supplement her tuition scholarship, Hooker supported herself by doing housework—one of the few jobs then available for women. Later she became a teaching assistant and, working with Karl Muenzinger in her senior year, she was offered an instructorship.

Hooker completed a master's degree at Colorado, and the topic of her research—vicarious learning in rats—scarcely hinted at the career that lay ahead. When it came time for a PhD program, Hooker chose Yale, but the male department chair at Colorado (whose doctoral degree was from Yale) refused to recommend a woman. So Hooker went to Johns Hopkins University. After receiving her PhD, she held a succession of short-term positions, first at the Maryland College for Women and later at Whittier College in California. Her teaching was interrupted by a two-year bout with tuberculosis that began in 1934. After recovering, she had a fellowship to study in Germany (1937–1938).

When Hooker applied for an appointment in the psychology department at UCLA, she experienced more sex discrimination. As she told the story, the department chair turned her down, explaining that the department already had three women, which were more than enough for his male colleagues. Instead, he only offered her an opportunity to teach through the UCLA Extension Program. She never joined the full-time faculty at UCLA, maintaining her affiliation as an adjunct with an NIMH Research Career Award until 1970 (Anonymous, 1992b).

Hooker's determination and tenacity in dealing with the sexism that she experienced as a student in the 1920s and 1930s and throughout her professional life make her a role model for all women psychologists. Hooker drew from her own life experiences an appreciation and awareness of social stigma: "The fact that I should end up studying an oppressed, a deprived people comes from my own experiences, in part, of being stigmatized" (quoted in Humphreys, 1978, p. 199).

"ANOTHER ELEANOR ROOSEVELT": FOREMOTHER OF THE LESBIAN AND GAY LIBERATION MOVEMENT

When Hooker died in 1996, several major newspapers carried a full obituary. The *Los Angeles Times* article began, "Evelyn Hooker, the psychologist whose 1950s research showing that homosexuality is not a mental illness helped fuel gay liberation, has died" (Oliver, 1996, p. A32). The *New York Times* lead was, "Dr. Evelyn Hooker, a psychologist who defied conventional wisdom and greatly emboldened the fledgling gay rights movement in the 1950s by finding there was no measurable psychological difference between homosexual and heterosexual men, died on Monday at her home in Santa Monica, Calif. She was 89" (Dunlap, 1996, p. D-19). D'Emilio (1996) in his obituary in the newsletter of the National Gay and Lesbian Task Force, reprinted in the *APA Monitor*, wrote, "I'm willing to lay odds that not many of us know who she is or what she did. Yet she deserves the status of hero in our community as a pioneering psychologist whose research has changed our world. Her career is also a fascinating case study of the potentially productive relationship between 'the expert' and a social movement."

A documentary film, *Changing Our Minds: The Story of Dr. Evelyn Hooker,* was selected as the best documentary in the 1992 San Francisco Lesbian & Gay Film Festival and was nominated for "best documentary feature" at the 65th Academy Awards (Harrison & Schmiechen, 1991). It was shown widely at film festivals, added to library collections, and distributed commercially.

Hooker received many awards from lesbian, gay, bisexual, and allied groups. In the documentary film, she is shown speaking at the award presentation for the Lesbian and Gay Community Services Center in Los Angeles. Her apartment proudly displayed awards from the Association of Lesbian and Gay Psychologists, the Gay Caucus of the American Psychiatric Association, and the Parents and Friends of Lesbians and Gays. In the film, she quotes one homophile leader who introduced her as "another Eleanor Roosevelt."

In 1991 Hooker received the APA Award for Distinguished Contribution to Psychology in the Public Interest. The citation was written by the first author (DK):

> When homosexuals were considered to be mentally ill, were forced out of government jobs, and were arrested in police raids, Evelyn Hooker courageously sought and obtained research support from the National Institute of Mental Health (NIMH) to compare a matched sample of homosexual and heterosexual men. Her pioneering study, published in 1957, challenged the widespread belief that homosexuality is a pathology by demonstrating that experienced clinicians using psychological tests widely believed at the time to be appropriate could not identify the nonclinical homosexual group. This revolutionary study provided empirical evidence that normal homosexuals existed, and supported the radical idea then emerging that homosexuality is within the normal range of human behavior. Despite the stigma associated with homosexuality, she received an NIMH Research Career Award in 1961 to continue her work. In 1967, she became chair of the NIMH Task Force on Homosexuality, which provided a stamp of validation and research support for other major empirical studies. Her research, leadership, mentorship, and tireless advocacy for an accurate scientific view of homosexuality for more than three decades has been an outstanding contribution to psychology in the public interest. (Anonymous, 1992b, pp. 501–502)

Until a few months before her death in 1996, Hooker continued to participate in professional activities related to the psychological study of lesbian and gay issues as a member of a review panel for the Placek Fund research awards.

The Research Project

As Hooker described in *Changing Our Minds* (also described in Boxer & Carrier, 1998), she was teaching an undergraduate course at UCLA when one very good student, Sam From, sensing that she could be trusted, befriended her and eventually confided to her that he and other friends to whom he had introduced her were homosexual. They took her to parties, clubs, and bars, where she was accepted as a heterosexual woman who was "in the know." Finally, they confronted her with the urgent request that she conduct scientific research to show that they were not abnormal or mentally ill. She refused, because she could not study this group objectively. Unconvinced, they introduced her at meetings of homophile organizations in Los Angeles where she could recruit participants she did not know. At one meeting she asked, "How many of you are married?" When many raised their hands, she was aghast, because she thought that meant that they must be bisexual and not suitable for her study. It turned out, however, that they were in long-term same-sex relationships. Thus she gathered a sample of exclusively homosexual men (although three had a few heterosexual experiences, all identified as homosexual) who were not in psychotherapy and did not show overt signs of disturbance.

It was difficult to find a matched comparison sample. Her study became known as "the fairy project," and no heterosexual man would want to be seen going to her office at UCLA. She used a building on the estate of her private home for conducting the interviews and projective tests. Her husband once commented that "no man is safe on Saltaire Avenue" (Harrison & Schmiechen, 1991) because she needed to find a group of heterosexual men matched (in terms of age, IQ, and educational level) with the homosexual men recruited from the homophile organizations. In her published report (Hooker, 1957) she described the process by which she was referred heterosexual participants by community leaders and eliminated any from the study who had had more than a single postadolescent homosexual experience. Likewise, she attempted to exclude any who showed evidence of latent or covert homosexuality. As with the homosexual sample, none were in psychotherapy at the time of the study. They were matched with the homosexual sample pair-wise on age, Otis self-administered intelligence scale scores (Otis, 1922), and education level.

Funding was difficult to obtain. She once told the story of the site visit by the chief of extramural grants of the NIMH, John Eberhart, who, she said, wanted to meet this "kook" who claimed that she had access to a large number of normal homosexual males. At that time, of course, the concept of "normal homosexual" was an oxymoron. She was a charming and strikingly attractive woman, and obviously convinced the NIMH to provide funding for the study.

Clinical psychology was in its infancy at the end of World War II and the measures that were thought to be valid were projective tests. She shared an office with Bruno Klopfer, one of the foremost experts on the Rorschach test, and he too urged her to conduct the study. Klopfer scored the Rorschach protocols (Rorschach, 1921) for the matched pairs of heterosexual and homosexual respondents. Edwin Shneidman, who had developed a projective test using cut-out figures called the Make-A-Picture-Story (MAPS) test (Shneidman, 1947), scored those results. Mortimer Meyer scored the Thematic Apperception Test (TAT; Murray, 1943). Each test was scored by two judges. The protocols were then reviewed by three expert clinicians in Los Angeles who rated the individuals' overall adjustment. Finally, the three experts were presented with the 30 matched pairs and were asked to determine which of the pair was homosexual.

The then-startling result was that the homosexual and heterosexual samples could not be distinguished from one another. "Can you imagine what it was like when I examined the results of the three judges of the adjustment ratings from the projective techniques? I knew the men for whom the ratings were made, and I was certain as a clinician that they were relatively free or psychopathology. But what would these superb clinicians find? You know now that the two groups, homosexuals and heterosexuals, did not differ in adjustment or psychopathology. When I saw that, I wept with joy. I knew that the psychiatrists would not accept it then. But sometime!" (Hooker, 1993, p. 452).

After the paper was presented at the 1955 APA meeting in Chicago, it was published in the *Journal of Projective Techniques* (Hooker, 1957) with the unusual footnote by the editor: "A study such as Dr. Hooker's challenges several widespread and emotional convictions. In view of the importance of her findings it seemed desirable to the editors that they be made public, even in their preliminary form" (p. 18n). Several follow-up articles appeared in subsequent issues (Hooker, 1958, 1959, 1960, 1961). Although the study was open to criticism on several empirical grounds, it did call into question the belief that homosexuality is a form of mental illness. As Hooker once commented, "After all, if Bruno Klopfer couldn't tell one was homosexual on the Rorschach, who could?" (Harrison & Schmiechen, 1991).

In 1972 Siegelman replicated the Hooker study with a larger sample, using objective measures. "I wrote to him when I had read his article, saying that I wished I had done it. What Dr. Siegelman had demonstrated was that the results of my research were not dependent on projective tests. The results were not artifacts. They were true" (Hooker, 1993, p. 452).

NIMH Task Force on Homosexuality

Dr. Eberhard's successor at NIMH, Philip Sapir, encouraged Hooker and her work in countless ways, including extending her research grants until she received the Career Research Award (1961). In 1967, she was invited to form the NIMH Task Force on Homosexuality, which lasted until 1969. Bayer (1981) observed, "The Task Force placed enormous emphasis on the extent to which the misery of homosexuals could be alleviated through an end to the discriminatory social practices of the heterosexual world" (p. 53). Judd Marmor was a member; a few years later he would play an important role as a member of the Executive Committee, when the American Psychiatric Association made the decision to remove homosexuality from the revised third edition of the *Diagnostic and Statistical Manual of Mental Disorders* (American Psychiatric Association, 1987). Although publication of the task force report was delayed on the election of Richard Nixon as U.S. president, it was circulated by homophile organizations. The task force also encouraged NIMH funding of important research projects on homosexuality.

Social Context of Hooker's Contribution

During the 1950s, a repressive attitude was widespread regarding homosexuality. The U.S. armed services sought out and dishonorably discharged lesbians and gay men, and often engaged in witch hunts, forcing one suspect to reveal others, using deceit and undercover surveillance, and generally created an openly hostile atmosphere. U.S. Rep. Joseph McCarthy (R-WI), as chair of the House Un-American Activities Committee, specialized in uncovering secret homosexuals, especially in the government bureaucracy. The policy that homosexuals could not have high-level security clearance led to the firing of many government employees and to subsequent protests by those discharged.

Homosexual parties, private clubs, and public bars were sometimes raided by the police and, if people were arrested, their names were published in the newspaper, often causing loss of employment, divorce, and public humiliation. These raids were especially likely to occur at the time of elections as a sign that the incumbent was intolerant of "sexual perversion."

Until the mid-1970s, homosexuality was "treated" by mental health professionals with electroshock, hospitalization, hormone therapy, psychotherapy, and aversive conditioning. There was also a stigma applied to the mothers and fathers of homosexuals, who were portrayed as engaging in pathological parenting. Distinctions were blurred among homosexuality, cross-dressing, and pedophilia in both the public mind and the professional literature. Nearly all empirical research was based on clinical, hospitalized, or prisoner samples. Morin (1977) documented the heterosexist bias that dominated psychology during this period.

Impact of Hooker's Contributions

In the obituary for the *American Psychologist*, Shneidman (1998) wrote, "Many homosexual men have stated that they owe improvements in the attitudes of society and in their acceptance of themselves directly and indirectly to the work of Evelyn Hooker" (p. 481). An example of this impact is her entry in the 1968 *International Encyclopedia of the Social Sciences* (Hooker, 1968):

> The only obvious difference between homosexuals and heterosexuals is in psychosexual object choice. All experienced clinicians and research workers report that the personality differences among individual homosexuals are far more apparent than the similarities. Investigators who include the data on individual differences in their studies have found a great diversity of personality patterns. (p. 227)

Homosexual communities in large cities are made up of constantly changing aggregates of persons who are loosely linked by friendship and sexual interests in an extended and overlapping series of networks. Some network clusters form tightly knit cliques of friends and homosexually "married" pairs, while in others, informal groups or social organizations develop. The structure of the communication, friendship, and sexual network among members of the community is complex. [p. 231]

Female homosexual, or lesbian, communities apparently develop on a smaller scale, with informal groups, cliques, and special gathering places. But a formal organization of lesbians and an official publication with national circulation indicate that the collective aspects of female homosexuality have some importance. No empirical studies of these aspects are currently available. Although homophile organizations, whether male or female, constitute and represent a very small minority of the total homosexual population, they achieve social significance by the role they assume in openly protesting the status assigned to homosexuals by the larger society. [p. 231]

These ideas were published one year before the sociopolitical event triggered by the 1969 police raid on the Stonewall bar in New York City. Word of the raid, the riot, and several days of civil disobedience that followed spread through an underground network and began the modern era of a gay, lesbian, and bisexual community identity.

Bayer (1981) noted,

The appearance of Hooker's work in the mid-1950s was of critical importance for the evolution of the homophile movement. Her findings provided "facts" that could buttress the position of homosexuals who rejected the pathological view of their conditions. She had met the psychiatrists on their own terms and provided their critics with clinical data with which to do battle. As important as her findings was her willingness to share them with the ordinary men and women of the homophile movement. . . . She became not only a source of ideological support, but an active participant in the homosexual struggle. (p. 53)

On February 8, 1973, Charles Silverstein made a presentation to the Nomenclature Committee of the American Psychiatric Association urging that homosexuality be removed from the list of disorders. His presentation began with the work of Hooker, Kinsey, Clellan Ford, and Frank Beach (chap. 16, this volume; Bayer, 1981). Silverstein concluded, "It is no sin to have made an error in the past, but surely you will mock the principles of scientific research upon which the diagnostic system is based if you turn your backs on the only objective evidence we have" (quoted in Bayer, 1981, p. 120).

The Silverstein presentation apparently made a significant impression on the committee, which undertook a serious review of the matter and announced it to the *New York Times,* which reported the event the next day, February 9. Opponents of the change also mobilized their supporters. On December 15, 1973, the Board of

Trustees of the American Psychiatric Association met and, in a vote of 13 to 0 with two abstentions, homosexuality was deleted and replaced with "sexual orientation disturbance." The trustees also approved a significant civil rights statement:

> Whereas homosexuality in and of itself implies no impairment in judgment, stability, reliability, or vocational capabilities, therefore be it resolved, that the American Psychiatric Association deplores all public and private discrimination against homosexuals in such areas as employment, housing, public accommodation, and licensing, and declares that no burden of proof of such judgment, capacity, or reliability shall be placed upon homosexuals greater than that imposed on any other persons. Further, the APA supports and urges the enactment of civil rights legislation at local, state, and federal levels that would insure homosexual citizens the same protections now guaranteed to others. Further, the APA supports and urges the repeal of all legislation making criminal offenses of sexual acts performed by consenting adults in private. (American Psychiatric Association, 1973, quoted in Bayer, 1981, p. 137)

The decision was supported in a subsequent referendum of the membership; 58% of the voters supported the board's decision.

In August 1973 a group of openly gay and lesbian psychologists met at the APA convention in Montreal to form the Association of Gay Psychologists. Two of the "demands" the group made to the APA Board of Directors were to establish a task force on homosexuality and to depathologize homosexuality. The task force was established in 1974 and the APA Council of Representatives adopted the following two resolutions in 1975 to remove the stigma of mental illness that had long been associated with homosexuality.

> 1. The American Psychological Association supports the action taken on December 15, 1973, by the American Psychiatric Association, removing homosexuality from that Association's official list of mental disorders. The American Psychological Association therefore adopts the following resolution:

> Homosexuality per se implies no impairment in judgment, stability, reliability, or general social and vocational capabilities; Further, the American Psychological Association urges all mental health professionals to take the lead in removing the stigma of mental illness that has long been associated with homosexual orientations.

> 2. Regarding discrimination against homosexuals, the American Psychological Association adopts the following resolution concerning their civil and legal rights:

> The American Psychological Association deplores all public and private discrimination in such areas as employment, housing, public accommodation, and licensing against those who engage in or have engaged in homosexual activities and declares that no burden of proof of such judgment, capacity, or reliability shall be placed upon these individuals greater than that imposed on any other persons. Further, the American Psychological Association supports and urges the enactment of civil rights legislation at the local, state, and federal level that would offer citizens

who engage in acts of homosexuality the same protections now guaranteed to others on the basis of race, creed, color, etc. Further, the American Psychological Association supports and urges the repeal of all discriminatory legislation singling out homosexual acts by consenting adults in private. (Conger, 1975, p. 633)

Many additional resolutions by professional organizations have followed.

Within the APA, a standing Committee on Lesbian, Gay, and Bisexual Concerns was established in 1980 and an official division, called the Society for the Psychological Study of Lesbian and Gay Issues (Division 44 of the APA) was approved in 1985. Hooker was a discussant at the symposium titled, "From Mental Illness to an APA Division: Homosexuality and Psychology," presented by the new division at the 1986 APA convention (Kimmel & Browning, 1999).

HER LEGACY

Hooker's research has had far-ranging impact. It has affected psychological science by encouraging a new generation of researchers to study the lives of gay men and lesbians, and her demonstration that homosexuality is not a form of mental illness cleared the way for researchers to ask new questions. In 1978, with the support of Jackie Goodchilds, then editor of the *Journal of Social Issues*, a special issue on "psychology and the gay community" was a landmark. This issue was an outgrowth of the APA Task Force on the Status of Lesbian and Gay Male Psychologists. Steve Morin and Dorothy Riddle were the editors of this special issue. As Hooker wrote in her epilogue to the volume, "This is a first in publishing in the social and behavioral sciences," noting that "the entire issue is devoted to social issues which are problematic for gay/lesbian individuals, and not to clinical problems" (Hooker, 1978, p. 132).

Her research has directly affected psychological practice. She laid the groundwork for a new affirmative approach that has as its premise that being gay or lesbian is a capacity, an ability—not a disability—and that focuses on finding ways to enhance the functioning of gay and bisexual men and lesbian and bisexual women. Both authors are personally aware of the trail blazed by Hooker as we worked over the past 20 years on boards and committees within the APA that have been addressing issues of concern for gay men and lesbians. We have seen the ways that organized psychology has taken steps to remove the stigma and to advance an affirmative psychology for lesbians and gay men.

The APA has influenced public policy by participating in *amicus* briefs concerning the civil rights of lesbians and gay men, by disseminating social science research that demonstrates that same-gender sexual orientation is not pathological, and by educating other professionals and the public about the reality of gay and lesbian lives. Moreover, the APA Council of Representatives has passed numerous policy statements on gay and lesbian issues, including discrimination against homosexuals, child custody, hate crimes, sodomy laws, gay and lesbian youth, treatments to alter sexual orientation, and same-sex marriage benefits. Hooker helped legitimate gay, lesbian, and bisexual research as well as gay, lesbian, bisexual, and heterosexual researchers conducting investigations in this field. Hooker was greatly pleased in her later years by the growing numbers of gay and lesbian psychologists and the development within the APA of a division devoted to the study of gay, lesbian, and bisexual issues. Hooker took great satisfaction in knowing that she helped to launch these new directions within psychology.

Her legacy lives on in several concrete ways. The University of Chicago established the Evelyn Hooker Center for the Mental Health of Gays and Lesbians in 1992. Through its interdisciplinary research programs and multidisciplinary training programs, the center contributes new knowledge about lesbians and gay men and applies that knowledge through clinical services. An Evelyn Hooker archive has been established in the Division of Special Collections of the UCLA Library (Boxer & Carrier, 1998).

In 1992, Hooker received a telephone call from a bank in Nebraska informing her that she had been named to head a committee entrusted to distribute the Wayne F. Placek bequest. Wayne Placek was one of the participants in Hooker's classic 1957 study. She had worked with Placek for only two days and remembered him as someone who expressed unhappiness at being gay. Placek's explicit goals for this fund were to support research and to increase information and to change attitudes and beliefs about lesbians and gay men. Hooker said, "It is highly unlikely that a half million dollars will ever again be available for research on homosexual orientation. This bequest makes possible a sustained research attack on homophobia, the most serious problem facing gays and lesbians today" (Anonymous, 1992a, p. 1).

Since 1994, the American Psychological Foundation's (APF) Wayne Placek Trust has been awarding annual research grants to meet these important goals. In 2000, APF created the Evelyn Hooker Programs to include the Placek Trust and all other APF funds dealing with gay, lesbian, and bisexual issues. Through the Evelyn Hooker Center and through the Evelyn Hooker Programs and the APF, the values and goals that Hooker practiced and encouraged remain as vital reminders of her work and contributions.

Most important, Hooker's legacy lives on in the improved quality of lives for so many sexual-minority individuals. Hooker cherished the letters, cards, and calls that she received over the years from gay men and lesbians who let her know how directly and deeply she had affected their lives. One such letter is quoted.

Dear Dr. Evelyn Hooker, Feb. 20, 1992, Berlin

My boyfriend and I just saw the documentary about you at the Berlin Film Festival. We want to say thank you for all the work you did. We're pretty sure that life would have been a lot different and a lot worse for us if you hadn't done your research.

I asked a close, straight friend of mine, who is a medical student at Berlin, why you wanted to do this work. I mean, it just didn't make sense. Why did this straight lady care about gays? My friend replied that it was probably because you felt that it had to be done by somebody, sooner or later. He said that you must have thought that the studies you undertook would help people in some way. He called it scientific altruism.

Well, whatever the reason is, I think that your work was more than just doing a good turn for man. I think you did it because you knew what love was when you saw it and you knew that gay love was like all other love. No better, no worse.

So I guess if we are thanking you, we should thank you not for the work itself, but for your desire to show to the world what you had already understood, or at least suspected, on your own.

With much respect and admiration. . . . (quoted in Hooker, 1993, p. 453)

CONCLUSION

For more than 40 years, Hooker used the methods of her discipline of empirical psychology to advance knowledge of same-gender sexual and erotic attraction, which she often termed "love"; and to change scientific and public misconceptions about lesbians, gay men, and bisexual persons. Her work has had major impact in four interrelated areas.

1. Her research and its replication is often cited in *amicus curiae* briefs presented to courts making determinations about child custody and adoption, laws prohibiting same-sex sexual behavior between consenting adults in private, the integration of lesbians and gay men into the U.S. armed services, in cases of discrimination on the basis of sexual orientation, and in same-gender marriage cases in Hawaii and Vermont.
2. Her research and personal mentorship have stimulated a generation of researchers and research topics that are based on sexual orientation as one dimension of human diversity, not as a pathology to be explained.
3. Her research and professional influence helped to create the practice of gay-affirmative psychotherapy, which she also practiced after retiring from her research career at UCLA.
4. Her research, combined with the cultural impact of the 1969 Stonewall Uprising and the emergence of the contemporary lesbian and gay movement, produced a paradigm shift in the psychological view of homosexuality from a mental illness to a lesbian, gay, or bisexual identity that links one with others—locally, nationally, internationally, and also historically. It is not an individual's illness or condition but a natural variant of sexual expression that provides some individuals a community with which to identify.

REFERENCES

American Psychiatric Association. (1987). *Diagnostic and statistical manual of mental disorders* (3rd ed., rev.). Washington, DC: Author.

Anonymous. (1992a, Fall). APF receives $510,000 trust: Largest gift in foundation's history. *American Psychological Foundation, 4*, 1.

Anonymous. (1992b). Awards for distinguished contribution to psychology in the public interest. *American Psychologist, 47*, 498–503.

Bayer, R. (1981). *Homosexuality and American psychiatry: The politics of diagnosis*. New York: Basic Books.

Boxer, A. M., & Carrier, J. M. (1998). Evelyn Hooker: A life remembered. *Journal of Homosexuality, 36*(1), 1–17.

Conger, J. J. (1975). Proceedings of the American Psychological Association, Incorporated, for the year 1974: Minutes of the annual meeting of the Council of Representatives. *American Psychologist, 30*, 620–651.

D'Emilio, J. (1996). Evelyn Hooker: Unsung hero. *National Gay and Lesbian Task Force Newsletter*. [Reprinted in *APA Monitor*].

Dunlap, D. W. (1996, November 22). Evelyn Hooker, 89, is dead: Recast the view of gay men. *New York Times*, D-19.

Harrison, J. (Producer), & Schmiechen, R. (Director). (1991). *Changing our minds: The Story of Dr. Evelyn Hooker* [Film/Video]. (Distributed by Frameline, 346 Ninth St., San Francisco, CA 94103; http://www.framline.org.)

Hooker, E. (1957). The adjustment of the male overt homosexual. *Journal of Projective Techniques, 21*, 18–31.

Hooker, E. (1958). Male homosexuality in the Rorschach. *Journal of Projective Techniques, 22*, 33–54.

Hooker, E. (1959). What is a criterion? *Journal of Projective Techniques, 23*, 278–281.

Hooker, E. (1960). The fable. *Journal of Projective Techniques, 24*, 240–245.

Hooker, E. (1961). The case of El: A biography. *Journal of Projective Techniques, 25*, 252–267.

Hooker, E. (1968). Sexual behavior: Homosexuality. *International Encyclopedia of the Social Sciences* (pp. 222–233). New York: Crowell Collier and Macmillan.

Hooker, E. (1978). Epilogue. *Journal of Social Issues, 34*(3), 131–135.

Hooker, E. (1993). Reflections of a 40-year exploration: A scientific view on homosexuality. *American Psychologist, 48*, 450–453.

Humphreys, L. (1978). An interview with Evelyn Hooker. *Alternative Lifestyles, 1*(2), 191–206.

Kimmel, D. C. (1978, January). Kimmel reports on convention activities. *Association of Gay Psychologists Newsletter, 1*(3), 1.

Kimmel, D. C., & Browning, C. (1999). A history of Division 44 (Society for the psychological study of lesbian, gay, and bisexual issues). In D. A. Dewsbury (Ed.), *Unification through division: Histories of the divisions of the American Psychological Association* (Vol. IV, pp. 129–150). Washington, DC: American Psychological Association.

Morin, S. (1977). Heterosexual bias in psychological research on lesbianism and male homosexuality. *American Psychologist, 32*, 629–637.

Murray, H. A. (1943). *Thematic apperception test pictures and manual*. Cambridge, MA: Harvard University Press.

Oliver, M. (1996, November 22). Evelyn Hooker: Her study fueled gay liberation. *Los Angeles Times*, A32.

Otis, A. S. (1922). *Otis self-administering tests of mental ability*. Yonkers, NY: World.

Rorschach, H. (1921). *Psychodiagnostik*. Berne, Switzerland: Birchen.

Shneidman, E. S. (1947). The make-a-picture story (MAPS) projective personality test. *Journal of Consulting Psychology, 11*, 315–325.

Shneidman, E. S. (1998). Obituaries: Evelyn Hooker (1907–1996). *American Psychologist, 53*, 480–481.

Chapter 16

Frank A. Beach, Master Teacher

Donald A. Dewsbury

Great teachers come in many varieties, but Frank Beach was one of a kind. His first job after leaving graduate school at the University of Chicago in 1936 was as a research assistant in neuropsychology with Karl S. Lashley at Harvard University. A year later he moved to the American Museum of Natural History in New York City. Both jobs were free of teaching responsibilities. Thus in 1946 when he arrived at his third job as a professor of psychology at Yale University, he was completely unprepared for teaching. As he described it:

> My first attempt at graduate teaching was a complete disaster. After twenty minutes of the first session I was perspiring excessively, my heart rate was accelerated, and waves of nausea threatened to overcome me. It was a classic case of stage fright. I dismissed the class, went home, and spent the rest of the day in bed. The situation improved with practice but the symptoms recurred in full force the first time I tried to lecture to an undergraduate class in comparative psychology. (Beach, 1974, p. 51)

Beach solved the problem of stage fright by limiting his subsequent teaching at Yale to seminars for graduate students and hand-picked undergraduates and research supervision—an approach made easier by his appointment as a Sterling Professor in 1950. He described his teaching load at Yale as "quite light and completely self-determined" (Beach, 1974, p. 52).

I thank Terry Christenson, Randy Nelson, and Laura Smale for their reminiscences of Frank Beach as a teacher and mentor.

*Photo of Frank A. Beach courtesy of Donald A. Dewsbury.

Eventually, in 1958 Beach was successfully recruited for a position at the University of California, Berkeley. Striking a bargain with Clark Kerr, then the Berkeley chancellor, and Leo Postman, department chair, Beach received "the prerogatives I had enjoyed at Yale, namely determination of my own teaching assignments, *if any*; assignment of a full-time secretary, ample research space; and a promise I would never be asked to serve as departmental chairman" (Beach, 1974, p. 56, italics added). Typically, in the early Berkeley years he taught one seminar, meeting once a week for two or three hours per semester.

Beach "retired" in 1978, and in 1986 received the American Psychological Foundation's Award for Distinguished Teaching in Biopsychology. What had happened? Had the selection committee made some kind of mistake in honoring as a great teacher one who shirked classroom teaching responsibilities during much of his career and described himself as ineffective when he could not? I leave the reader hanging with these questions while I treat the life and works of Beach in the hope of providing context and understanding of Beach's recognition as a teacher. I will present an informal and personal view of Beach; more formal treatments of his life are available in various autobiographical chapters and obituaries (Beach, 1974, 1978, 1985; Dewsbury, 1989, 1997a; Glickman & Zucker, 1989; Sachs, 1988a).

LIFE HISTORY

Frank Ambrose Beach Jr. (he never used the "Jr.") was born April 13, 1911, the first-born among the three children of Frank A. and Bertha Robinson Beach. Although lacking a PhD, his father succeeded in building the Department of Music of the then-Kansas State Teachers College at Emporia from an operation of two or three persons into a full-blown music department of 30 to 40 people; the music building there is named for him. Young Frank's relations with his father were complex and not always peaceful. Although he respected his father, he had little affection for him and spent much of his youth rebelling against him. By contrast, he remembered his mother as firm but gentler and more understanding (Beach, 1952, in Roe, n.d.).

After his start in college in Emporia as an English major (where he was noted for his poor grades) Beach's parents sent him to Antioch College for his sophomore year. He returned to Emporia the next year motivated for successful work. A psychology course from a new instructor at Emporia, James B. Stroud, piqued Beach's interest and Stroud served as something of a father substitute for Beach (Roe, n.d.). When Beach graduated in 1932 the Depression was in full swing and, unable to find a job, he accepted a fellowship in clinical psychology at Emporia on the condition that he work toward an MS degree in experimental psychology. He accomplished this in one year, completing a thesis on color vision in rats (they are color blind).

Beach then moved on to the University of Chicago, where he met physiological psychologist Karl S. Lashley (chap. 20, *Pioneers I*). Much of Beach's subsequent research career can be viewed as a highly creative and original extension of the work of Lashley, who was probably the strongest influence on his professional life. Lashley may have shaped Beach's primary approach to teaching as well. Beach (1961, p. 182) quoted Lashley as saying that teaching is useless, because "those who need to be taught can't learn, and those who can learn don't need to be taught." Beach noted that Lashley "did a great deal of teaching, but this took place in small groups, the traditional coffee hour in his laboratory, or in individual conversations in his own office or the student's lab" (p. 183). He described Lashley's relations with students as characterized by an aloofness and lack of intimacy but without coldness.

Unable to continue at Chicago after one year because of financial problems, Beach landed a job teaching high school English in Yates Center, Kansas. There he met and married his first wife, a marriage that soon ended in divorce when Beach returned to Chicago and both partners sought new mates.

On returning to Chicago, Beach found that Lashley had departed for Harvard. He completed his PhD thesis on the neural basis of innate behavior under the nominal supervision of Harvey Carr (chap. 9, *Pioneers I*). During this period he married his second wife, Anna Beth Odenweller; they had two children. In 1936 Beach followed Lashley to Harvard and then made successive moves to Yale and Berkeley, as described earlier. He did not complete his PhD until 1940, well into his term at the American Museum—foreign languages (required for the doctorate in those days) were not Beach's strength.

The move to Berkeley was Beach's last. He would remark that it is good that young faculty members remain in cold climates because once they sampled warm ones they would never want to leave. After Beach's second wife died in 1971, he married Noel Gaustad. Although Beach technically retired in 1978, he remained active in research and writing. He discussed data to the end with colleague Stephen Glickman, projecting slides for a planned talk on his hospital room wall when he was near death.

Beach received many honors. Among them were honorary degrees from McGill University, Williams College, and Emporia State University; the Warren Medal from the Society of Experimental Psychologists; the Distinguished Scientific Contribution Award from the American Psychological Association (APA); the Carl G. Hartman Award for Research in Reproductive Physiology; and the Kenneth Craik Research Award of St. John's College, Cambridge, England. He was president of such organizations as the Eastern Psychological Association, the Western Psychological Association, Division 3 (Experimental Psychology) of the APA, and the International Academy of Sex Research. Beach was elected to membership in the American Philosophical Society, the National Academy of Sciences, and the Society of Experimental Psychologists; he was a Fellow of the

New York Academy of Sciences and the American Academy of Arts and Sciences.

RESEARCH

Beach was first and foremost a researcher. He was deeply motivated by an abiding yearning to understand how nature works. Few things gave him more pleasure than massaging a data set to ask interesting questions and extract from it some understanding about what made his animals tick. Although he loved to design experiments that would test speculative hypotheses, his grasp of statistical concepts was not great. His was a down-to-earth, midwestern, seat-of-the-pants approach, in contrast to the more sophisticated, more abstract, methods used by many of his colleagues. Gordon Bermant called his approach "rigor illuminated by common sense, rather than constrained by the expectation of doctrinaire allegiance" (quoted in Sachs, 1988a, p. 312). Beach would write that "I am illogically distrustful of statistical procedures that go far beyond means, sigmas, simple correlations and the like" (Beach, 1974, p. 39). Beach had a set of stock phrases, packed with wisdom, with which he would stop contentious colleagues dead in their tracks; one was "simply because certain statistical operations are possible it does not follow automatically that they are worth carrying out" (p. 39). Yet he had an ability to see the significant question that needed answering and to design straightforward experiments that would provide clear-cut answers. In the same spirit, he would quip that "the last thing a discipline finds out is what the important questions are" and "if an experiment is not worth doing, it is not worth doing well" (personal communication).

Beach set the tone for his research career with his first article, "The neural basis of innate behavior. I. Effects of cortical lesions on the maternal behavior pattern in the rat" (Beach, 1937). The bulk of the research that would follow over the course of the next half century would deal with the physiological correlates of species-specific behavioral patterns in nonhuman animals.

In an era when the bulk of experimentally oriented psychologists were focused on the study of learning, Beach concentrated on behavioral patterns that are in some sense innate, or, as he preferred, species-specific. His primary focus was on sexual behavior. One must remember that much of this work was conducted before the "sexual revolution," at a time when such research was viewed with considerably more suspicion than it is today. It took a good bit of courage to address problems of sexuality as intensively as he did and at the time that he did it.

Beach advocated the study of a wide range of species. His research record is spotted with studies of alligators, hamsters, and marsupials, but laboratory rats were his most frequent subjects, and his favorite subjects were dogs. He started a research program on dogs during the Yale years and continued it in Berkeley.

He established the Field Station for Behavioral Research on a beautiful site in the Berkeley Hills overlooking San Francisco Bay. There he and his students and associates established a long-term program of research primarily on the consequences of early hormone manipulations on the social and sexual behavior of dogs. After Beach's retirement, Glickman transformed the station into a site for the study of hyena behavior, an endeavor in which Beach was a much interested, if clearly secondary, collaborator.

As noted earlier, from the beginning of his career Beach was interested in the physiological correlates of behavior. For Beach "physiological correlates" defined a two-way street because he recognized that behavior affects physiological processes just as physiological processes affect behavior. His research career spanned some 50 years, during which he published more than 100 articles, the bulk of which dealt with the physiological correlates of species-specific social and sexual patterns in mammals.

Much of Beach's early research used brain lesions, in the tradition of Lashley and others. As his career developed, however, he became more interested in the role of hormones in behavior. This interest started during the American Museum years, when he took a course in endocrinology. He found little on behavior in that course and library research revealed no integrative summary of work in the field. Beach soon provided one, however, with his first book, *Hormones and Behavior* (Beach, 1948). This book and his correlated research made him the cofounder, along with William C. Young, of the burgeoning field of behavioral endocrinology.

INTEGRATIONS

Beach prided himself on being an experimenter and loved the process of conducting and analyzing the results of experiments. I believe, however, that his greatest impact was as a synthesizer of research results. Beach not only contributed original research data but was an avid consumer of the results generated by others. He read professional journals religiously and attended many conferences at which he was not only a registrant but one likely to attend every session sitting near the front. He was not afraid to ask questions that seemed naive to others, but when he left the room one got the feeling that his grasp of what had been presented was exceptional. Laura Smale (personal communication, September 10, 1998) recalled "several times when I was in graduate school, he stopped me in the halls to tell me about some new hormone/behavior research that he'd been reading about. It seemed that he just would get excited about it and want to share what he had just learned with someone."

Beach, however, did not just absorb information; he integrated it. It was his capacity to fit together the puzzle pieces and to provide a whole that set him apart from many of his contemporaries. He had a genius for integrating disparate information at a time when an approach was just beginning to mature and creating a document that would provide its definition. The example of behavioral endocrinology is paradigmatic. Scattered results on the effects of hormones on behavior were accumulating in the literature. Beach saw this, integrated the information, packaged it, and, in the process, provided a new synthesis.

The formula worked again and again. He synthesized information on the central nervous mechanisms involved in vertebrate reproductive behavior (Beach, 1942a), on the factors producing sexual arousal (Beach, 1942b), and on the evolution of physiological control of mammalian mating behavior (Beach, 1947). He provided a synthesis of research on play in animals (Beach, 1945). Just as research was beginning to reveal the complexity of female sexual behavior, Beach (1976a) differentiated attractivity, receptivity, and proceptivity, and made the field his own. He was clever in his choice of titles. His treatment of the use of the instinct concept was in "The De-scent of Instinct" (Beach, 1955). Who else would combine experimental data from rats, hamsters, and guinea pigs into a mythical "ramstergig?" (Beach, 1971). When dogs copulate, a mechanical tie or "lock" holds the male's penis in the female's vagina; his summary of research on sexual behavior in dogs was titled "Locks and Beagles" (Beach, 1969). Arguably his most influential article was "The Snark Was a Boojum" (Beach, 1950; the title, of course, taken from Lewis Carroll), in which he advocated a broadening of the range of species and behavioral patterns studied by comparative psychologists. It is not clear who first called him "the conscience of comparative psychology," but that reputation stems from this article.

An example of the impact of the naming of experimental phenomena, and of the fun Beach could have while doing serious research, is evident in his naming the so-called "Coolidge effect" (Dewsbury, 1981). The term refers to the fact that male rats, like the males of many species, that seem satiated for sexual activity often appear revived if a novel female replaces the female with which they have been copulating. Beach related the origin of the neologism

> to an old joke about Calvin Coolidge when he was President. . . . The President and Mrs. Coolidge were being shown [separately] around an experimental government farm. When [Mrs. Coolidge] came to the chicken yard she noticed that a rooster was mating very frequently. She asked the attendant how often that happened and was told, "Dozens of times each day." Mrs. Coolidge said, "Tell that to the President when he comes by." Upon being told, Coolidge asked, "Same hen every time?" The reply was, "Oh, no, Mr. President, a different hen every time." Coolidge: "Tell that to Mrs. Coolidge." (Kimble, Garmezy, & Zigler, 1984, p. 249)

The term, introduced by one of Beach's students at a psychological convention in 1955, has stuck ever since.

Beach was among the first in North America to recognize the value of the work of the European ethologists, and he served on the editorial board of the ethological journal *Behaviour* for many years.

He rarely wrote for popular audiences, preferring to interact with other scientists. An interesting exception is a series of articles published in the American Museum of Natural History's *Natural History* magazine in the 1940s (Dewsbury, 1997b).

Although Beach's experimental work was confined to nonhuman animals, he was interested in human sexuality and tried to examine human and nonhuman sexual activity in similar ways to reveal their similarities and differences. This interest produced an early collaborative synthesis, *Patterns of Sexual Behavior* (Ford & Beach, 1952) and a later edited volume, *Human Sexuality in Four Perspectives* (Beach, 1977).

WHAT KIND OF MAN

In some respects, Beach was a study in contradictions. He was a gifted writer who was first and foremost a scientist, an award-winning teacher who did little teaching until late in life, an influential psychologist who worked at the borders of psychology, and a serious scholar and academician who had a lot of fun (Dewsbury, 1988, p. 433).

In addition, Beach was a deeply serious person. He believed in research for its own sake as a highly valued human endeavor and wrote, "increasing knowledge, in and of itself, is a justifiable way to spend your life. I don't think that research workers should be compelled any more than artists, or magazine editors, or musicians to justify the way they spend their energies and live their lives" (Beach, 1975, p. 71). Beach believed that knowledge is good and ignorance is evil and devoted his professional life to the pursuit of knowledge. "He didn't take himself seriously, but, oh, how he took his work seriously. The intellectual values first" (Tiefer, 1988, p. 441). At the same time, however, he believed that those who create knowledge are proficient only in their own fields and was skeptical of those who used academic positions to pontificate about issues outside their realm of primary competence (Beach, 1975).

Beach insisted that the creation of knowledge should not be confused with the accumulation of facts. Facts must be structured and placed into a context that gives them meaning: "'Ant-like' industry, unaccompanied by any major philosophical or theoretical reorientation, would only lead to an overwhelming accumulation of empirical evidence incapable of organization or interpretation" (Beach, 1984, p. 1).

Among all the areas about which knowledge is needed, Beach prized the study of behavior above all: "Man's greatest problem today is not to understand and exploit his physical environment, but to understand and govern his own conduct" (Beach, 1966, p. 949). Beach helped develop the study of neural mechanisms of behavior and was a founder of the study of endocrine influences on behavior. In some respects, however, as it matured, he came to dislike some aspects of the approach that he helped to create. He saw too many young scientists confusing figure and ground—focusing on the physiology and not the behavior. Like B. F. Skinner (chap. 16, *Pioneers III*), he believed that "laws pertaining to behavior stand in no need of 'validation' by correlating behavioral and neurophysiological phenomena" (Beach, 1971, p. 282). As psychologists, our focus should be on behavior, not tissue.

It is likely that his commitment to accumulating knowledge explains Beach's disdain for administration. Actually, Beach was an able administrator, as indicated by his saving of the American Museum's Department of Experimental Biology in a time of crisis and transforming it into a prominent Department of Animal Behavior. He chaired the Committee for Research on Problems of Sex of the National Research Council for many years—and oversaw its disbanding when its function seemed outmoded.

Beach was known for his intellectual honesty and his willingness to be a builder of steps in the pursuit of scientific knowledge that would give rise to higher steps created by those coming after him. In judgments of his theories and research, it was extremely important to Beach that critics recognize that he had done a first-rate job, given the knowledge and methods available at the time. Once that was understood, he was quite willing for new research and theory to supercede his own. I recall his returning from a trip and informing me that he had just read a journal article improving on his earlier work and invalidating his conclusions. He appeared joyful that science was advancing rather than morose that his hard work would be discarded. He noted that "my scientific mentor, Karl Lashley, once expressed the opinion that all scientific papers should be printed on paper that automatically disintegrates in five years" (Beach, 1984, p. 1).

Beach was conservative in many respects. He took the public trust very seriously and went so far as to return unused grant money to the government—a practice almost unheard of. He would not let me spend all of the research allowance associated with my postdoctoral stipend—the balance went back to Uncle Sam. He let me stay only one year as a postdoctoral fellow in his laboratory and was distressed that all three of his graduating students elected to take postdoctoral fellowships that year. He viewed postdocs as freeloading on the public dole; one should get out and earn a living. He noted "grant money comes from taxes; taxes come from a lot of folks who don't have much money. Spend that money wisely" (quoted in Clemens, 1988, p. 429). A product of his generation, through much of his early career Beach did not want women in his laboratory, or as he put it, he "would never have ovaries in his lab" (quoted in Sachs, 1988a, p. 312). As was often the case, however, he changed with the times and actively supported numerous women students during the later parts of his career.

The picture presented thus far is incomplete because it fails to capture the bawdy side of Beach. He was as much at home in a barroom as in a laboratory. Like many of his generation, he drank and smoked more than was good for him. In his interview with Anne Roe (1952 in Roe, n.d.) he was candid about his drinking, noting that he might consume between a pint and a fifth of whiskey per 24 hours. He drank especially before he had to give a lecture and when things were going well. The earthy Beach was ever present and complemented the serious side of his personality. There are many anecdotes. For example, Lester Aronson and Arthur Zitrin (1988) recalled an incident in which they, along with Beach, were about to attend their first psychological convention, and Beach had several drinks on the train to loosen up his tongue for his talk. The three marched into the hotel lobby singing a chorus of "Hail, hail, the gang's all here" (Aronson & Zitrin, 1988). Sachs (1988b, pp. 439–440) recalled another:

> At one memorable gathering, in a peanut-shell littered nightspot in Berkeley, Frank accepted a shuffleboard challenge from a very street-smart student. Frank proceeded to beat him badly, and the student then opined that pool was really his game, and offered to spot Frank 25 points, best two out of three games. Frank took three straight, having given up his handicap after the first game.

Beach socialized readily. It was hard not to like this outgoing, direct, and honest man. People naturally liked him, and he liked people, though he did not tolerate fools easily. His language in conversation could be earthy and his comments direct. One rarely had to guess where one stood in his view at any particular moment.

FRANK BEACH, THE TEACHER

We can now return to the opening theme of Beach as a teacher. During most of his career, Beach's teaching was in small classes or in interactions with graduate students doing research. It was primarily for his work as a mentor of graduate students and postdoctoral fellows that Beach was honored as a teacher. In his years at Yale and Berkeley he had a steady stream of graduate students, many of whom went on to be productive psychologists of many stripes. Their affection for their mentor is exceptional. It is apparent, for example, in the Festschrift prepared for the occasion of his 65th birthday (McGill, Dewsbury, & Sachs, 1978) and in a series of reminiscences published in *Hormones and Behavior*, the journal he helped to found, in 1988, soon after his death.

His students honor Beach in the same critical spirit that he lived his life. Some mentors produce sets of students who seem to carve the master's words in stone and regard deviations from them as indications of disloyalty. Beach's students are a more feisty bunch who do not hesitate to criticize the pronouncements of their mentor. Recognizing the validity of his efforts at the time they were made, they rarely hesitate to criticize them in the context of the present. This is not an indication of disrespect but rather of high respect in carrying on the critical tradition that he represented. Data, not false loyalties, take precedence.

Beach could be a hard task master. Reminiscences are especially notable for their tales of his legendary concern for writing style and the sea of red ink that would cover the manuscripts one gave to him to read. Remember that he started out to be an English teacher. Adler (1988) recalled that he wrote seven drafts of his thesis before Beach was satisfied. Clemens (1988) topped that, counting 19 revisions—after he had already thrown away many earlier drafts. But he added that the thesis was later accepted for publication without a single change.

For Beach, a cardinal sin in writing was the use of the word "data" as a singular, rather than a plural, noun.

> Therefore it was fitting that, when Steve Glickman asked Frank whether he had any messages for his students attending the Conference on Reproductive Behavior in the days just before he died, Frank said, "Just tell them, 'Data are.'" Frank may only have had the grammatical joke in mind, but the message also captured Frank's feeling that in science solid data endure, and all else is transient. (Sachs, 1988b, p. 440)

Beach's directness could be intimidating. Davidson (1988, p. 430) noted that "though he sometimes affected the role of some kind of country bumpkin from Kansas, nobody dared to talk down to him. He could be fierce and didn't tolerate foolishness lightly." Adler recalled one incident:

> Trying to impress him following a point he had made (which I now repress), I said something like, "I think I understand, but in my humble opinion. . . ." I never finished the sentence. Beach cut me off (as he did often during the next 25 years), saying, "Adler, you've never had a humble opinion in your whole goddamned life. Now what do you want?" (Adler, 1988, p. 427)

Once, when Adler complained to Beach about the excessive rewriting that Beach required of him, Beach noted "if the dancing master tells you to dance in chains, you will do so—if only because when you remove the chains you will feel so free" (Adler, 1988, p. 427). I recall an incident when I thought I had caught him being inconsistent in his thinking. He stopped me dead in my tracks with "consistency is the sole virtue of a jackass." Randy Nelson (personal communication, October 13, 1998) recalled a seminar in which students were to present their term paper research to the class. He recalled that Beach "was very kind to the undergraduates and his questions were intellectually curious, but he would follow-up with a series of probing questions to find out where the limits of your knowledge were." And "Lively debate was spiced by Frank's ample wit and rapier-like turns of phrase, which could, with a stroke, deflate pomposity or uncover poor preparation" (Sachs, 1988a, p. 312).

Like Lashley, Beach was not really close to his students. Students called him "Dr. Beach" and it was only through a gradual process over years after schooling that one got to be on a first-name basis with him. Beach noted, "I don't see how you can be a pal and a father figure at the same time" (Adler, 1988, p. 427).

On the other hand, Beach was a master at providing exactly what his students needed at the time they needed it. Clemens (1988, p. 429) recalled that "when I flew a little too high [he would say] that sounds real nice. Any possibility we can test it?" Sachs recalled,

> He supported his students, but he neither coddled us nor allowed overly inflated egos. He would feed us the easy fastball when we needed a hit, but would often fool us with sharp curves and changes of pace when we got cocky. Frank also had the knack for pointing out gaps in a research area or line of thinking, commonly starting out "this is probably a naive question, but. . . ." (Sachs, 1988b, p. 439)

Beach taught his students to publish their research. It was a responsibility, because the work was done at the expense of governmental funds in one way or another. But he also wrote, "I am compulsive about getting something into print before I feel the research is finished. Good, unpublished data make me uncomfortable" (Beach, 1975, p. 73).

On completing research in his laboratory, one remained a member of the Beach family. He sent occasional letters summarizing his doings and inquiring after one's well-being. He visited with students at meetings and, when possible, at their home universities. He shuffled challenging work, such as chapters for contributed books, to the young faculty member in need of the publication and experience. "Frank showed us how the scholarly community is a family in the modern world, how our professional family helps create a sense of community and intimacy despite distance and mobility and almost unbearable social change" (Tiefer, 1988, p. 442).

Great teachers write textbooks and Beach was no exception. He worked hard and completed a fine textbook in comparative psychology. However, it was not up to his standards and he never published it (Dewsbury, 1990).

Having shirked major commitments to classroom teaching most of his life, he repented late in life and began teaching large-enrollment sections. This is a remarkable shift that he did not have to make at a time in life when most psychologists move away from such teaching. In a 1975 addendum distributed privately with copies of his 1974 autobiographical chapter, he described his efforts. He was teaching a course in human sexuality with an enrollment limited to 200, but had plans to make it a campus-wide course and to write his own textbook. Of the large-enrollment comparative psychology class he wrote,

> The course in comparative was too much like a graduate seminar at first, but it is improving, I think; and this Spring Quarter I am confident the results will come nearer to satisfying me than they have previously. . . . As I had anticipated, undergraduate lecturing and the organization of material has proved challenging, stimulating, exhausting, and very rewarding. (Beach, addendum to Beach, 1974)

Because Beach was his own most severe critic, one must imagine the courses to be much better than he would indicate. Terry Christenson (personal communication, September 10, 1998) was a teaching assistant in the course and recalled especially how well Beach fielded questions from the undergraduates.

Beach also taught the graduate proseminar along with Glickman, Irving Zucker, and Marc Breedlove. Although all had similar interests, they had different approaches, and the students often were treated to a show of prominent faculty members locking horns on significant issues of approach.

An indication of the high regard of his former students and others influenced by Beach can be seen in the establishment of the Frank A. Beach Award for an outstanding young investigator in the field of behavioral endocrinology. Annually, at a meetings of the Society for Neuroscience, a young investigator, honored for his or her originality and creativity in research, is first honored at a social event, then presents a brief talk, and finally publishes a brief article in *Hormones and Behavior* (e.g., Rissman, 1991). It is fitting that the award go to a young investigator, as Beach had such influence on the development of those just developing their research careers.

Among the criteria for the American Psychological Foundation's Distinguished Teaching in Psychology Award are that one demonstrate influence as a teacher of students who become outstanding psychologists, develop effective teaching methods or materials, and be an outstanding teacher of advanced research methods and practice in psychology. When he was nominated, former students and nonstudents alike readily wrote letters of support. It is no surprise that he received the award. His methods were not conventional but they worked, and he was an effective and much-loved mentor.

CONCLUSION

As with William James and William Shakespeare, one has to read Beach to appreciate him. The former English teacher had a way with language. This chapter has been deliberately sprinkled with a liberal dusting of quotations to illustrate his style. It will close with more examples of his thought and prose.

Beach was skeptical of the expertise of scientists making pronouncements outside of their fields: "A few scientists, and many more nonscientists, are prey to the misconception that expertise in one area of human knowledge magically endows its possessor with wisdom in other areas" (Beach, 1975, p. 77).

Although Beach wanted to be of service to the field, he placed his other responsibilities first: "It has been my philosophy that the professional scientist owes a certain amount of time and energy to the support and development of his discipline, although the extent of the debt is finite so that it need not be discharged in perpetuity" (Beach, 1974, p. 52).

Beach believed deeply in the value of basic research: "Society must be educated to discriminate between science and technology, and must be willing to support impractical science. A society that cannot do this impoverishes itself in the long run" (Beach, 1975, p. 74).

Beach had a real affection for animals. "The comparative psychologist does not look upon all animals other than man as machines which automatically carry out their life functions without conscious purposes and without any emotional involvement" (Beach, 1945, p. 530). "The most militant and objective 'behaviorist' can not seriously object to the statement that the dog which romps through the snow, barking, leaping, dashing wildly hither and yon, or plays at 'fetch' with his master, is enjoying the experience" (Beach, 1945, p. 530).

"If we remove man from the central point in a comparative science of behavior, this may, in the long run, prove to be the very best way of reaching a better understanding of his place in nature and of the behavioral characteristics which he shares with other animals as well as those which he possesses alone or which are in him developed to a unique degree" (Beach, 1960, p. 17).

"A city dweller lost in the country asked a farmer's child, 'If you wanted to get to Kansas City, which way would you go?' The little boy replied, 'If I wanted to go to Kansas City I wouldn't start from here!' The moral is that selection of an appropriate point of departure constitutes the first step of a successful journey" (Beach, 1979b, p. 127).

"Our journals report an awful lot of experiments not worth doing, but done very well" (Beach, 1975, p. 73).

"Humptydumpyism is endemic during interdisciplinary discourse in which different kinds of specialists use the same words to mean quite different things" (Beach, 1979a, p. 98)

"Surface similitude by itself does not justify theoretical inference" (Beach, 1976b, p. 469).

"Many theorists are so sadly and seriously afflicted with neurophilia (which in its terminal phases inevitably develops into cerebromania) that they are able to seriously entertain only those interpretations of behavior which are couched in the vocabulary of the neurologist" (Beach, 1971, p. 286).

"The degree of assurance with which instincts are attributed to a given species is inversely related to the extent to which that species has been studied, particularly from the developmental point of view" (Beach, 1955, p. 405).

"I may be a dreamer, an incurable optimist, but I believe that if science provides knowledge, society will display wisdom" (Beach, 1966, p. 949).

"No matter what I am, or how I got here, it has been a lot of fun getting here, and the road ahead looks challenging and exciting" (Beach, 1985, p. 16).

"What counts is to have the aims, to be able to work toward them, and to experience the satisfaction of at least believing that progress is being made. I do not want to cross the finish line of this race—not ever—but I do hope I will be able to keep running at my own pace until I drop out still moving in full stride.

It's been one hell of a good race up to this point" (Beach unpublished addendum to Beach, 1984).

REFERENCES

Adler, N. T. (1988). A memorial essay. *Hormones and Behavior, 22,* 427–428.
Aronson, L. R., & Zitrin, A. (1988). At the museum: The formative years. *Hormones and Behavior, 22,* 421–427.
Beach, F. A. (1937). The neural basis of innate behavior. I. Effects of cortical lesions upon the maternal behavior pattern in the rat. *Journal of Comparative Psychology, 24,* 393–436.
Beach, F. A. (1942a). Central nervous mechanisms involved in the reproductive behavior of vertebrates. *Psychological Bulletin, 39,* 200–226.
Beach, F. A. (1942b). Analysis of factors involved in the arousal, maintenance, and manifestation of sexual excitement in male animals. *Psychosomatic Medicine, 4,* 173–198.
Beach, F. A. (1945). Current concepts of play in animals. *American Naturalist, 79,* 523–541.
Beach, F. A. (1947). Evolutionary changes in the physiological control of mating behavior in mammals. *Psychological Review, 54,* 279–315.
Beach, F. A. (1948). *Hormones and behavior.* New York: Hoeber.
Beach, F. A. (1950). The snark was a boojum. *American Psychologist, 5,* 115–124.
Beach, F. A. (1955). The de-scent of instinct. *Psychological Review, 62,* 401–410.
Beach, F. A. (1960). Experimental investigations of species-specific behavior. *American Psychologist, 15,* 1–18.
Beach, F. A. (1961). Karl Spencer Lashley (1890–1958). *Biographical Memoirs of the National Academy of Sciences, USA,* 163–204.
Beach, F. A. (1966). The perpetuation and evolution of biological science. *American Psychologist, 21,* 943–949.
Beach, F. A. (1969). Locks and beagles. *Psychological Review, 24,* 971–989.
Beach, F. A. (1971). Hormonal factors controlling the differentiation, development, and display of copulatory behavior in the ramstergig and related species. In L. Aronson & E. Tobach (Eds.), *The biopsychology of development* (pp. 249–296). New York: Academic Press.
Beach, F. A. (1974). Frank A. Beach. In G. Lindzey (Ed.), *A history of psychology in autobiography* (Vol. 6, pp. 33–58). Englewood Cliffs, NJ: Prentice-Hall.
Beach, F. A. (1975). Pursuit of intellectual orgasm (Interview with J. D. Fleming and D. Maxey). *Psychology Today, 8*(10), 68–77.
Beach, F. A. (1976a). Sexual attractivity, proceptivity, and receptivity in female mammals. *Hormones and Behavior, 7,* 105–138.
Beach, F. A. (1976b). Cross-species comparisons and human heritage. *Archives of Sexual Behavior, 5,* 469–485.
Beach, F. A. (Ed.). (1977). *Human sexuality in four perspectives.* Baltimore: Johns Hopkins University Press.
Beach, F. A. (1978). Confessions of an impostor. In J. Meites, B. T. Donovan, & S. M. McCann (Eds.), *Pioneers in neuroendocrinology II* (pp. 19–35). New York: Plenum Press.
Beach, F. A. (1979a). Animal models and psychological inference. In H. A. Katchadourian (Ed.), *Human sexuality: A comparative and developmental perspective* (pp. 98–112). Berkeley: University of California Press.
Beach, F. A. (1979b). Animal models for human sexuality. In *Sex, hormones, and behavior. Ciba Foundation Symposium 62* (pp. 113–143). Amsterdam: Excerpta Medica.
Beach, F. A. (1984). Let's bury the snark. *Comparative Psychology Newsletter, 4*(2), 1–3.

Beach, F. A. (1985). Conceptual issues in behavioral endocrinology. In R. Gandelman (Ed.), *Autobiographies in experimental psychology* (pp. 1–17). Hillsdale, NJ: Erlbaum.

Clemens, L. G. (1988). Reflections. *Hormones and Behavior, 22,* 428–430.

Davidson, J. M. (1988). A scientist for all seasons. *Hormones and Behavior, 22,* 430–431.

Dewsbury, D. A. (1981). Effects of novelty on copulatory behavior: The Coolidge effect and related phenomena. *Psychological Bulletin, 89,* 464–482.

Dewsbury, D. A. (1988). Reminiscences of Frank Ambrose Beach. *Hormones and Behavior, 22,* 431–433.

Dewsbury, D. A. (1989). Frank Ambrose Beach: 1911–1988. *American Journal of Psychology, 102,* 414–420.

Dewsbury, D. A. (1990). Frank Beach's unpublished textbook on comparative psychology. *Journal of Comparative Psychology, 104,* 219–226.

Dewsbury, D. A. (1997a). Frank Ambrose Beach: April 13, 1911– June 15, 1988. *Biographical Memoirs of the National Academy of Sciences, USA, 73,* 3–22.

Dewsbury, D. A. (1997b). Rhetorical strategies in the presentation of ethology and comparative psychology in magazines after World War II. *Science in Context, 10,* 367–386.

Ford, C. S., & Beach, F. A. (1952). *Patterns of sexual behavior.* New York: Harper.

Glickman, S. E., & Zucker, I. (1989). Frank A. Beach (1911–1988). *American Psychologist, 44,* 1234–1235.

Kimble, G. A., Garmezy, N., & Zigler, E. (1984). *Principles of general psychology* (4th ed.). New York: Ronald Press.

McGill, T. E., Dewsbury, D. A., & Sachs, B. D. (Eds.). (1978). *Sex and behavior: Status and prospectus.* New York: Plenum Press.

Rissman, E. (1991). Behavioral endocrinology of the female musk shrew. *Hormones and Behavior, 25,* 125–127.

Roe, A. (n.d.). Frank A. Beach File. Anne Roe Papers, American Philosophical Society Archives, Philadelphia, PA.

Sachs, B. D. (1988a). In memoriam: Frank Ambrose Beach. *Psychobiology, 16,* 312–314.

Sachs, B. D. (1988b). Reminiscences. *Hormones and Behavior, 22,* 438–440.

Tiefer, L. (1988). In honor of him. *Hormones and Behavior, 22,* 440–442.

Chapter 17

Carl Iver Hovland: Statesman of Psychology, Sterling Human Being

Roger N. Shepard

Yale psychologist Carl Iver Hovland made singularly important contributions to experimental, social, and cognitive psychology (focusing, respectively, on human learning, attitude change, and concept acquisition). In the process, he worked unremittingly "to improve the standards and quality of research in psychology and related fields," earning (in the words of one of his long-time coworkers) universal recognition as a "statesman of the social sciences" (Janis, 1968, p. 530).

Hovland also served as an insightful and trusted consultant to numerous governmental and educational agencies, industrial organizations, and philanthropic foundations. All this he did within a life lasting not quite 49 years. He could hardly have foreseen how limited would be the time available to him; both his

This biography was written for the *Biographical Memoirs* of the National Academy of Sciences and appeared in Volume 73 of the series. It is reproduced here with permission of the National Academy of Sciences.

I thank Hovland's former students and associates for the thoughtful and heart-warming reminiscences they shared with me, including those I have quoted in this memoir (the most extensive supplied by Hovland's former coworkers Harold Kelley and Herbert Kelman) and many others who, though not directly quoted, also contributed helpful information (including Robert Abelson, Irvin Child, Earl Hunt, Kenneth Kurtz, Mark Lepper, Edith Luchins, George Mandler, George Miller, Lloyd Morrisett, John Pierce, Milton Rosenberg, and Burton Rosner). Finally, I thank the members of Hovland's family: Hovland's brother, C. Warren Hovland, his son, David A. Hovland, and, especially, his daughter, Kathie Hovland Walvick, for her expert and painstaking editorial work on the earlier version prepared for the National Academy of Sciences, and his cousin Mary Hovland Jenni, for generously permitting me to include excerpts from the wonderful material she had previously obtained from still other of Hovland's relatives and colleagues—many of whom are no longer living.

*Photo of Carl Hovland courtesy of Kathie Hovland Walvick. Extracts from Jenni 1974 used by permission.

parents lived into their 90s. Yet he compensated, in effect, through his remarkable precocity, quickness of mind, and productive use of every waking moment—along with his extraordinary ability to bring together bright young researchers with widely differing theoretical perspectives, to provide them with support and subtle guidance, and to formulate coherent syntheses of the emerging results. A person of unsurpassed gentleness and moral integrity, Hovland left a deep and permanent mark on everyone who knew him.

MY OWN RECOLLECTIONS

I first met Hovland when I arrived for graduate study in Yale's illustrious Department of Psychology in the fall of 1951. Hovland's title, "Sterling Professor," seemed wonderfully euonymous for this tall, distinguished man, endowed as he was with rare personal qualities and wavy hair turning to silver. Now, some 50 years later, I am astonished to realize that this revered faculty member, who had been serving as chair of the department and director of the Laboratory of Psychology, was at that time only 39 years old.

Particularly striking were the apparent ease and efficiency with which Hovland managed all the many things in which he was always engaged and his constructive use of every moment of time. While showing genuine interest in everyone with whom he had contact, he had a way of keeping administrative interactions brief and to the point. His extraordinary memory enabled him to carry out much of the department's business through chance meetings in the hall or stairway—venues that minimized the risk of someone plunking down in a chair in his office for more than the time needed to resolve whatever issue was at hand. If Hovland did not encounter a graduate student sufficiently soon concerning some matter, the student would find a slip of paper in his or her departmental mailbox with the succinct notation: "See me, CIH." More than once, discussions of my own research were carried out as I tried to keep up with Hovland's rapid stride to the New Haven railway station where he would be catching a train to New York—perhaps to consult with AT&T, the Bell Telephone Laboratories, or the Rockefeller or Russell Sage Foundations.

On those occasions when I did actually sit down in Hovland's office, he would also be reading his mail and talking with someone else on the telephone. When I called him on the telephone, I could hear someone else in his office and the occasional rattle of a letter being opened. And when I sent him a note, I imagined that while he was perusing it, he would also be talking on the telephone with someone in his office. I fantasized having the delivery of my written letter, the playing over the telephone of my recorded voice, and my physical entrance into his office converge on him simultaneously—thus gaining, for once, his undivided attention. In truth, however, I welcomed the brief hiatuses that Hovland's time-sharing entailed as I was striving to marshal my ideas for his assessment.

Another Hovland student, Herbert C. Kelman (now Cabot Professor of Social Ethics at Harvard), described to me how he and Hovland started drafting their 1953 paper (Kelman & Hovland, 1953):

> In consultation with Carl, I designed and carried out an experiment on the sleeper effect [in which the tendency to endorse a proposition from a low credibility source increases as the source is forgotten]. When the data were collected and analyzed, I . . . told him that I would like him to co-author the article reporting the research. In his customary generosity, he told me that this was my experiment and he was not expecting co-authorship. But I insisted—whereupon he pulled out a yellow pad and started writing! Right then and there! (personal communication, March 25, 1997)

Hovland was the most efficient and organized individual I have ever known. But the efficiency and organization was all in his head; it did not depend on external aids. He conducted classes and chaired meetings in his quiet, informal manner without notes, while the desk and side table in his office remained piled with papers in no visible order. When another of my fellow graduate students inquired whether he might retrieve a term paper to correct an error, Hovland briefly rummaged through papers piled on the side table. Then turning to my waiting friend, he remarked, "You may think there is no order here. Actually, there is an order; it's just not an order designed to meet that particular type of request!" And order there evidently was; Hovland's secretary, Jane Olejarczyk, told me: "Quite often he would call and ask me to retrieve some document with instructions like: it's in the third pile from the left on the table by my desk, about a third of the way down, and there's a Russell Sage report, printed on blue paper, just before you get to it. . . . Amazing! He was always on target" (personal communication, May 29, 1997).

Hovland was a master of the Socratic method. Seemingly without a prepared agenda, he would ask the graduate students around the seminar table for their comments on the (always seminal) readings he had assigned, or for their proposals concerning an illustrative problem of experimental design or data analysis he was working through on the chalkboard. At first, this evoked frustration or anxiety in students accustomed to more structured styles of instruction. (A student who had volunteered to calculate—in those days, by means of a slide rule— a number called for by the illustrative problem might find that before he or she was able to come up with the answer, Hovland was already writing it on the board, apparently having arrived at it by his own swifter, purely mental calculation.) Former Yale student Philip Zimbardo (now a professor of social psychology at Stanford) remarked that the combination of Hovland's shyness and intellectual mastery may have prevented him from even suspecting that some students found him intimidating (personal communication, April 3, 1997). Nevertheless, out of our bumbling efforts a coherent picture would gradually crystallize, to be succinctly articulated by Hovland at the end of each class session. It was the goal toward which Hovland evidently had been subtly guiding us all along.

I asked Hovland to serve as my dissertation advisor not only because I valued his quick intellectual grasp but also because he seemed uniquely free of commitment to any particular theoretical position and, hence, supportive of the exploration of promising ideas, wherever they might lead. Because of the great respect everyone had for him, Hovland was also able to give my career a couple of unexpected boosts at its very start. He endorsed the suggestion of a younger member of my dissertation committee, Burton Rosner, to take the unusual step of recruiting a mathematical psychologist from outside Yale to serve on the orals committee of my more-than-usually mathematical dissertation. One consequence was that the up-and-coming outside examiner selected, George A. Miller, invited me to join him a year later as a postdoctoral associate at Harvard. Then, following those two postdoctoral years, both Hovland and Miller recommended my appointment as a member of technical staff in a small basic research group that Hovland had been instrumental in establishing in the Bell Telephone Laboratories, Murray Hill, New Jersey. The research I was able to carry out during my two postdoctoral years at Harvard (where I first learned to program on the Univac 1, just given to Harvard) and during the next eight years at the Bell Labs (where I had access to a major computer facility) undoubtedly contributed to my own ensuing appointment to a professorship at Harvard.

In 1957, I participated—along with both Miller and Hovland—in a Summer Institute on the new computer-simulation approach to modeling human cognitive processes, organized by Alan Newell and Herbert Simon at the RAND Corporation in Santa Monica, California. Simon, who remembers Hovland "with great fondness," mentioned that Hovland and Miller had "co-opted" him to join their small ad hoc committee of the Social Science Research Council, which had some Ford Foundation money for work in cognition. It was this money, Simon said, that made possible their Summer Institute (personal communication, May 27, 1997). Over a lunch with Hovland in Santa Monica that summer, I recalled how my doctoral research at Yale only two years before had necessitated my approximation of the eigen roots and vectors of matrices by hours of tedious computation on mechanical desktop calculators. "When," I wondered, "would Yale obtain a programmable electronic computer?" With a wry smile, Hovland replied that he was on a committee that had just been established at Yale to receive the gift of such a computer—in case one should be offered! Only three years later, the 1960 papers on computer simulation of thinking and concept attainment authored by Hovland, alone and with his student Earl Hunt, were already appearing (Hovland, 1960; Hovland & Hunt, 1960; Hunt & Hovland, 1960).

It was shortly after joining the Bell Labs that I began my one direct research collaboration with Hovland. Herbert Jenkins and I had undertaken a study of classification learning in which human participants learned by trial and error which of two responses was correct for each of the eight possible stimuli having either of two values on each of three binary dimensions (for example, square or triangular, large or small, and black or white). Jenkins and I sought to determine the number of trials required to learn different classifications—in which correct responding required taking account of values on just one, on two, or on all three of the stimulus dimensions.

When we mentioned this study to Hovland, we learned that independently he and two research assistants had just begun presenting research participants with explicit classifications of just such binary-valued stimuli into two groups of four (one displayed on the left, the other on the right). They, however, were measuring speed and accuracy of reconstruction of the two groups from memory, and recording how the participants described the rules they found to govern each classification. We quickly agreed to join forces and, during our ensuing collaboration, Jenkins and I (often together with the Bell Labs learning researcher Ernst Rothkopf) would meet with Hovland—usually at his home in Hamden, outside New Haven.

On these visits, the Hovlands' longtime housekeeper, Elizabeth, would serve us lunch, elegantly presented with fine china, silver, and linens in the Hovlands' formal dining room. I must have been seated in Mrs. Hovland's customary place, because under a slight bump in the rug, there was a button that I sometimes inadvertently hit with my foot, summoning the housekeeper, to my mounting chagrin.

At about this time, a growth in Hovland's neck (in the parotid gland just below his right ear), which had been diagnosed as benign some years earlier, had recurred and was now determined to be malignant. Both the advance of the cancer and the measures undertaken for its treatment (surgery, radiation, and a then-highly experimental chemotherapy) were soon exacting a toll on Hovland's previously inexhaustible energy, entailing a temporary loss of his full head of hair, which had rapidly turned entirely white, and a total deafness in his right ear.

Long before, Hovland's wife, Gertrude, still relatively young and universally regarded with admiration and affection, had been increasingly afflicted with rheumatoid arthritis. Anticipating his own impending death, Hovland became deeply concerned about his wife's growing helplessness. Her neck was at the time so fragile that she had to wear a neck brace whenever she was up and about.

On August 26, 1960, my two colleagues and I made our last scheduled trip from the Bell Labs to the Hovlands' home to discuss the final stage of our collaborative project. We were met at the door by the housekeeper, Elizabeth, who, tearful and barely able to speak, informed us that Mrs. Hovland had had an accident earlier that morning and that Mr. Hovland would not be able to meet with us. We got in the car and headed back to New Jersey.

I later learned that Gertrude, having gotten out of bed without her protective collar, stumbled and fell. Her weakened neck snapped and she died instantly. A few days later, Hovland called me to apologize for not being able to meet with us after our long drive. When I assured him that no apology was necessary and expressed my heartfelt sympathy, he became, for the only time in my experience, choked with emotion and was briefly unable to speak. The loss of his beloved wife was a terrible blow to this most caring and responsible of men—left, as he now was, with two children in their late teens and with less than a year remaining of his own life.

To the end, Hovland continued doing (to the extent that he was physically able) just what he had been doing even before he learned that he was mortally ill. Apparently, Hovland had always proceeded each day with what he regarded as most important—as if that day might be his last. To avoid the stairs, his final weeks were spent in a bed that had been set up in the same dining room where my colleagues and I used to talk with him over lunch. He was cared for by his son, David, then an undergraduate at Yale, and by his daughter, Kathie, who, having just entered Wellesley College, traveled down from Massachusetts to be with her father during the weekends. Hovland died on Sunday night, April 16, 1961, just after Kathie had left for her trip back to Wellesley.

Our monograph on learning and memorization of classifications (Shepard et al., 1961) was published that same year—but not in time for Hovland to see it in print. Along with Hovland's own last published book, *Social Judgment*, completed by his collaborator Muzafer Sherif after Hovland's death (Sherif & Hovland, 1961), and the preceding volume by Rosenberg, Hovland, McGuire, Abelson, and Brehm (1960), our monograph was thus one of the last publications on which Hovland appeared as an author. Some 30 years later, this monograph attracted renewed interest among cognitive scientists, who have used our results to test alternative connectionist or "neural net" models for classification learning, or to elucidate the roles of stimulus dimensions called perceptually "separable" (like size and shape—as in Shepard, Hovland, & Jenkins, 1961, p. 3) versus those called perceptually "integral" (like lightness and saturation of colors—as in Shepard & Chang, 1963, p. 96). And the three students who served as research assistants in this work—Albert Bregman and Earl Hunt (with Hovland) and John Gibbon (with Jenkins and me)—have all gone on to make their own influential contributions at major universities (Bregman in auditory perception at McGill, Hunt in human cognition at the University of Washington, and Gibbon in timing behavior at Columbia).

FAMILY HISTORY

Hovland was born in Chicago on June 12, 1912, to devout parents of Scandinavian descent—Ole C. Hovland (1871–1967), who became a successful electrical engineer and inventor, and Augusta Anderson Hovland (1876–1970), who had no formal education after the age of 12, when she immigrated alone from Sweden. Carl had two long-lived siblings: an older brother, Roger, who also became an engineer, and a younger brother, C. Warren, who became chair of religious studies at Oregon State University, where Hovland Hall is named in his honor.

Carl's own son, David (born 1941), and his daughter, now Katharine Walvick (born 1942), both manifest intellectual aptitudes reminiscent of their father's. David, now a professor at Park College, Texas, earned a PhD in psychology from Harvard where I, having been his father's advisee at Yale, served in turn as David's advisor until I moved to Stanford. Kathie, now senior legal editor in a Washington law firm, received a Wellesley BA in mathematics and became the youngest woman Life Master at bridge, winning bronze medals in two international bridge olympics.

A cousin, Mary Hovland Jenni, though she never met Hovland, developed a keen interest in him and his work while pursuing her own doctoral studies in psychology at the University of Montana in the 1970s. She contacted several of Hovland's family members and former colleagues, asking for their recollections of him. Much of my information about his family and childhood comes from her unpublished report (Jenni, December 1974). Hovland was described, she said, as "a brilliant child, shy, quiet, introverted, unathletic, troubled by illnesses." Hovland's first-grade teacher reportedly said that he "lived in his own dream world and did not relate to the group" (Warren Hovland's letter to Jenni of November 4, 1974). Everyone agreed that Hovland found satisfaction in learning and in scholastic achievement, and many spoke of the early emergence of Hovland's love of music and his impressive proficiency on the piano. During college, Hovland partly supported himself as an organist for the Lutheran Church, though his formal association with the church otherwise ended during this period.

It was a shared love of music that brought together Hovland and Gertrude Raddatz, his wife-to-be. Gertrude was born in Chicago on September 13, 1911, the first of five children. Hovland and Gertrude both attended Chicago's Luther High North, studied piano with the same teacher, and enjoyed playing piano and organ duets. Gertrude went on to study piano at the American Conservatory in Chicago and then to teach piano—until her hands became too crippled by her rheumatoid arthritis.

Manifesting the engineering aptitude of his father and older brother, Hovland experimented with three-dimensional photography and designed and built his own high-fidelity systems. He acquired such expertise in sound reproduction that his advice was reportedly sought by professional audio engineers. (Once, while I was still a graduate student, Hovland took obvious pleasure in inviting me to challenge his new system's capabilities with selections from his extensive collection of classical records. It was my first exposure to the just-perfected stereo reproduction of sound and to the astonishing realism it could achieve.)

PROFESSIONAL HISTORY

As an undergraduate at Northwestern University, Hovland acquired a strong background in mathematics, physics, and biology, as well as in experimental psychology, receiving his AB with highest distinction in 1932 (just before turning 20). On a Catharine White fellowship, he also obtained his master's degree there in 1933 and completed research that appeared in his earliest published papers (the first, coauthored with a stimulating new Northwestern faculty member, G. L. Freeman, on "diurnal variations in performance and related physiological processes" (Freeman & Hovland, 1934).

Concerning a letter recommending Hovland for graduate study, Yale's Walter R. Miles recalled that "the letter's language of so high approval and praise was such as to make [the] Yale professors smile and shake their heads. As events evolved they were using similar language in . . . recommending the same Carl Hovland . . . a very few years later" (Miles, 1961, p. 122). Hovland prepared six papers for publication during his first year and in just two more years he received his 1936 PhD with honors under the prominent Yale learning theorist Clark L. Hull.

Hovland's dissertation provided the first evidence for a law of generalization, in which the tendency to make a response learned to one stimulus falls off exponentially with the distance separating a test stimulus from the original training stimulus along a sensory continuum, such as the continuum of auditory pitch (Hovland, 1937). Beginning with my own dissertation 20 years later, I developed a new approach that provided more definitive evidence for such a law (Shepard, 1958, fig. 2) and, 30 years later, a theoretical justification for the law's possible "universal" character (Shepard, 1987, figs. 1 and 3). Such a law of generalization was also central to the interpretation of the results of our joint study of classification learning (Shepard, Hovland, & Jenkins, 1961, pp. 25–30). I still regard generalization as the most fundamental problem of human, animal, and machine learning—if not, indeed, of education and cognitive science in general.

On completing his dissertation, Hovland was immediately invited to join the Yale faculty, of which he remained a member for the rest of his life. Two 1940 publications illustrate the extraordinary range of his early work at Yale. As part of an interdisciplinary group investigating the connection between frustration and aggression, Hovland and Sears (1940) discovered a substantial (negative) correlation, over a century of U.S. history, between economic indicators (such as the price of cotton) and number of lynchings. At the same time, according to one of his later coworkers, M. Brewster Smith (personal communication, May 15, 1997), Hovland served as the "heavy hitter" on the team of Hull, Hovland, et al. that produced the 1940 monograph *Mathematico-Deductive Theory of Rote Learning* (Hull et al., 1940). This book, though too technically demanding to have been read by many psychologists, has been deemed "as elegant a volume as ever published in psychology" by a later Hovland student, William J. McGuire (now a Yale professor), who decided to pursue a career in psychology after "stumbling upon that volume in [his] undergraduate browsing days" (McGuire, 1996, p. 46). (For other examples of Hovland's early studies of human learning, see Hovland, 1938, 1939, 1951.)

From 1942 to 1945, during America's involvement in World War II, Hovland was on leave from Yale. Recruited by the noted sociologist Samuel Stouffer (himself on leave from the University of Chicago), Hovland headed the experimental section of Stouffer's Research Branch under Maj. Gen. Frederick Osborn's Information and Education Division of the War Department. The primary mission of Hovland's section was to evaluate the training programs and films being prepared by the Information and Education Division for American troops in the United States and Europe. Hovland was responsible for guiding and synthesizing the work of 15 researchers.

Despite his wartime leave, Hovland rose meteorically at Yale through the ranks of instructor (1936), assistant professor (1937), director of Graduate Studies (1941, at the age of 29), associate professor (1943, in absentia), full professor and chair of the Psychology Department and director of the Laboratory of Psychology (1945, at 33), to Sterling Professor (1947, at 36). Indeed, Hovland and *his* 28-year-older mentor Clark Hull were both named to Sterling Professorships in 1947. While I was a graduate student I was told that this made psychology the only department at that time with two Sterling Professors and that this came about because Hovland, in his characteristic generosity and sense of fairness, would not accept the honor in advance of his senior mentor.

Beginning with his research during the war, Hovland brought the methodological talents he had honed in his experimental work on learning and generalization to bear on problems of communication and social psychology. He and a number of those who had worked with him in the research branch prepared a series of volumes, "Studies in Social Psychology in World War II." Hovland was the senior author of Volume 3, the highly influential *Experiments on Mass Communication* (Hovland, Lumsdaine, & Sheffield, 1949).

After returning to Yale, Hovland established the Yale Communication and Attitude Change Program. With the help of the Rockefeller Foundation, this program supported, for more than 15 years (until Hovland's death), research by Hovland and more than 30 coworkers and students. This work established how verbally presented information changes (or renders resistant to change) a recipient's opinions and beliefs as a function of experimentally manipulated variables—such as the recipient's prior position on an issue, the recipient's self-esteem, the credibility of the source, the extremity of the position advocated, the order of presentation of arguments, whether one or both sides of the issue are presented, whether the conclusions of an argument are explicitly stated or are left to the recipient's inference, whether the recipient actively attempts to reproduce the arguments for someone else, whether the recipient is induced to think of counterarguments, whether the presented information is designed to elicit the recipient's emotions (especially fear), the time that has elapsed since the information was presented, and the conditions imposed at the delayed time of assessment of attitude change (for example, whether knowledge of the forgotten high or low credibility source is reinstated, e.g., Hovland, 1948a, 1948b, 1954,

1959; Hovland, Janis, & Kelley, 1953; Hovland et al., 1957; Janis et al., 1959; McGuire, 1996, pp. 42–50, 54–57; Rosenberg et al., 1960; Smith, 1968, pp. 461–462).

Following Hovland's death, his attitude change program was characterized as "the largest single contribution [to the field of social communication] any man has made" (Schramm, 1963, p. 5). More than 30 years later, it was still deemed "the biggest single force within psychology's communication-relevant attitude-change movement" (McGuire, 1996, p. 43), and as "the gold standard for research in social psychology" (Timothy Brock, personal communication, May 20, 1997). Zimbardo has suggested that the secret of the success of this program lay in Hovland's unique conceptual ability to decompose the complex relations between persuasive communications and attitude change in a way that rendered them susceptible to controlled laboratory experiments. Moreover, by "establishing a structural-sequential mode of the input-mediating-output variables and processes involved, Hovland anticipated the later information processing approach that proved so valuable in cognitive psychology" (Zimbardo, personal communication, June 9, 1997).

Hovland also played a crucial role in the formation of what became the Bell Telephone Laboratories' Behavioral Research Center, of which I was a member from 1958 to 1966. It was, I believe, the longest lived of any group whose members were given the freedom to pursue basic psychological research within an industrial setting. According to William O. Baker, former president of the Bell Labs, the establishment of this group came about when Robert Greenleaf of the personnel department of AT&T and Baker (then vice president for research at the labs) decided that in view of the vast number of employees that the Bell System trains every year and the even vaster number of customers that daily interact with the telephone system, a small self-sustaining group of behavioral scientists might be justified within a large laboratory traditionally oriented toward the physical sciences. They turned to Hovland, whose earlier work in industrial psychology had impressed them with its "ingenuity" and "versatility." Baker said, "Carl achieved an extraordinary rapport with our industrial endeavor" (personal communication, May 11, 1995).

Hovland recruited two former students of the brilliant MIT social psychologist Kurt Lewin (chap. 7, *Pioneers III*) to establish strengths in both basic and applied social psychology—Morton Deutsch and Alex Bavelas. But Bavelas (who had been selected to lead the applied effort) did not stay long, at which point a struggle ensued between the Bell Labs and the personnel department of AT&T about whether the new group should be oriented toward basic or applied research. Hovland "played the pivotal role . . . in the decision to support its basic research orientation," said Deutsch, who warmly recalled "Carl's intellectual openness, personal support, and his skills as a mediator of conflict" (personal communication of March 24, 1997).

During the ensuing years, the Bell Labs' Behavioral Research Center attracted a number of creative young psychological researchers. (For more about this center and Hovland's role in it, see the report by Carroll et al., 1984 p. 432). Some time after Hovland's death, when changing circumstances led the Bell Labs (and many other companies) to curtail support for basic research, virtually all of these scientists were able to move to professorships at major universities. Indeed, despite its relatively small size, this center has had as many as five of its members elected to the National Academy of Sciences.

In the last decade of his life, Hovland began to turn his attention to the cognitive processes of concept acquisition, problem solving, and thinking (see Hovland, 1952, 1960; Hovland & Hunt, 1960; Hovland & Weiss, 1953; Hunt & Hovland, 1960; Kurtz & Hovland, 1956; Morrisett & Hovland, 1959; Shepard, Hovland, & Jenkins, 1961). While continuing his collaborations in social psychology, he advised or collaborated with at least 10 researchers in this increasingly active, cognitive area.

The letters his previously mentioned cousin Jenni received in response to her 1974 inquiries to Hovland's former colleagues are remarkably consistent in their expressed admiration of Hovland's intellectual powers, his administrative efficiency, the moral quality of his judgments and actions, and the affection everyone felt for him. Leonard W. Doob, who was a young member of Yale's faculty when Hovland arrived in 1934, wrote, "Clearly he was the outstanding student of the year, coming here with a tremendous recommendation from Northwestern." Even when he had joined the faculty, Doob said, Hovland was "shy and self-contained; you never quite knew what he was thinking. His IQ was incredibly high. He was a very efficient administrator; the details, externally at least, never seemed to bother him because he dealt with them so quickly and apparently painlessly" (Jenni, 1974).

Robert R. Sears, who had been on the Yale faculty with Hovland between 1936 and 1941, in responding to Jenni's 1974 request as David Star Jordan Professor of Social Science at Stanford, wrote,

> Carl was a big man in every respect. He was very gentle and . . . very musical. He was a cheerful, smiling person who came into the office every morning and put his head in my door and said "what's new?" We both had classes over on the main quadrangle . . . at 11:00. . . . He walked so fast that . . . I got to class . . . puffing and panting while Carl went up to a second floor lecture room, bounding two or three steps at a time. . . . He was a wonderful guy. . . . At our house he would sit and play with my son David, who was then about a year old.

Sears's letter concluded, "He was a remarkable man, brilliant in every sense of the word, and a delightful friend and warm companion" (Jenni, 1974; see also the Hovland obituary prepared by Sears, 1961).

Incidentally, Sears's son David later went on for graduate study with Hovland and became a professor at UCLA. About Hovland (who died during David's last year at Yale), David told me: "He took me into his home for several days after I was released from the hospital following an appendectomy. . . . I treasure the memories of the times I [spent] with him, in class and out." An incident that David recalled illustrates Hovland's mixture of warmth, shyness, and propriety: "One year a group of students went to the Hovland house to sing Christmas carols, as a gesture of appreciation; we saw Carl hasten to run upstairs to put on a coat and tie before coming to the door to greet us" (personal communication, May 19, 1997).

Leland DeVinney, one of Hovland's associates in Washington during the war, later became director of Social Science at the Rockefeller Foundation, which provided much of the support for Hovland's attitude change program at Yale. DeVinney wrote,

> In the field of communication and attitude formation . . . [Hovland] is recognized as the leading pioneer." Concerning Hovland and Gertrude, he said, "My wife and I . . . have never known lovelier or finer people," and added, "I also have known many of Carl's associates and students and know that Carl was an extraordinary teacher and research guide. He was highly respected and also loved by all of them. (Jenni, 1974)

Donald R. Young, another of Hovland's associates during the war, who later became director of the Russell Sage Foundation on whose board of directors Hovland served until his death, wrote that he had found it "a joy to work with a man of Carl's qualities. He was among the very best research psychologists, highly skilled, imaginative, and reliable. He always delivered a top product." Recalling his last visit with Hovland, Young said, "He was then so ill that he had to go to bed immediately when the meal was ended, yet he still was the perfect host giving little evidence of either the physical or mental suffering he must have been enduring." Young concluded, "In my seventy-six years I have known few men his equal and none his superior" (Jenni, 1974).

Claude Buxton, who succeeded Hovland as chair of the Psychology Department at Yale, wrote,

> Carl . . . became my dearest friend, . . . a very gentle [and] very moral person, and his code included never taking advantage of anyone or anything . . . . [H]e is one of the two or three people I have ever known who made a moral assessment of his own proposals or ideas . . . he was enormously efficient and organized—one of our colleagues used to say that everything Carl did he did on ballbearings, because it went so smoothly; he was tremendously stimulating to graduate students . . . [who told] me they did more work for [Carl's evening special-interest] no-credit meetings than they ever did in their regular courses. (Jenni, 1974)

Irving L. Janis, who worked with Hovland both in his Experimental Section in Washington and then (as a younger faculty colleague) in his attitude change program at Yale, similarly concluded his letter to Jenni by saying, "You can feel justifiably proud of your cousin. He was a truly great psychologist and a great person" (Jenni, 1974).

Much the same picture emerged from my own more recent inquiries. Jane Olejarczyk, assistant business manager for Academic Affairs and Registrar for Yale's Psychology Department, who began working as Hovland's secretary when she was only 19, said, "Knowing how inexperienced I was with academia he constantly assigned me to projects about which I had no clue and gently insisted that I could do [them]. He didn't lavish praise but I knew I did well when the next task was more difficult than the one before." Olejarczyk spoke of Hovland's "warmth" and said, "There was the feeling when he was about that you were part of a family and that you mattered." She added that "Gertrude Hovland was the epitome of grace" (personal communication, May 29, 1997).

Eleanor E. Maccoby (Browning Professor Emerita of Developmental Psychology at Stanford), who remembers Hovland well and whose late husband, Nathan Maccoby, worked in Hovland's group during the war (see Maccoby, 1963, pp. 43–45, 47–48, 50–52), observed that Hovland was exceptional both in his quick and wide-ranging intelligence and also in his "complete absence of guile" (personal communication, 1996).

Harold H. Kelley (Professor Emeritus of Social Psychology at UCLA), who worked with Hovland in his Yale attitude change program in the 1950s, wrote,

> Of course, the most important thing about Carl was his enormous intellect, his quick understanding of [nearly] everything that was going on, and the ways he let his thought and work roam far and wide. . . . In organizing the personnel of his program, he was deliberately and sympathetically eclectic, grabbing here and there so as to include all possible lines of thought that might bear on the communication/persuasion process. (personal communication, June 24, 1995)

Yale's William J. McGuire noted that "it never bothered Hovland that members of the group . . . were driven by antagonistic theories that made opposite predictions" and remarked that what prevented these decentralized, individualistic projects from "becoming undesirably anarchical was Hovland's particular intellectual excellence as a synthesizer. He could attend a symposium of papers that seemed to have little in common and, if called on to summarize them, seemed able on the spot to abstract out their unifying themes and show that the papers converged in interesting and complex ways to produce a coherent picture" (McGuire, 1996, pp. 48–49).

About Hovland's own research style, Kelley observed that Hovland would "analyze the shortcomings or special conditions of . . . prior work, identify intuitively the as-yet-unstudied factors that would reverse, undo, or clarify the problem." Kelley added, "It always seemed to me that that was his investigative forte—identifying the special conditions surrounding prior work and then expanding the design to pin down the phenomenon more clearly" (personal communication, June 24, 1995).

Following Hovland's death, the New England Psychological Association (of which Hovland was president in 1950) had a memorial session in which Herbert Kelman characterized Hovland as "the world's most non-authoritarian leader" (personal communication). Similarly, Abraham Luchins wrote me, "He was the most efficient and the least officious of people" (personal communication, May 29, 1997). And Hovland's wartime coworker M. Brewster Smith said, "My most vivid memory of Carl . . . was his unique ability to guide the development of appropriate research design by asking just the right questions—always in a tentative way that opened new perspectives or possibilities. . . . I have never since experienced that degree of consultative skill" (personal communication, May 15, 1997). It was in this way that Hovland was, in the words of Timothy Brock, a "visionary founder of subdisciplines" (personal communication, May 20, 1997). Speaking further of Hovland's low-key and indirect style of leadership, Kelley wrote, "I know that left some people (including myself) with a bit of anxiety." (Other letters I received confirmed that Kelley was in fact not alone in this.) "But still," Kelley continued, "he was so warm, interested in your personal life, etc. that one couldn't help feeling great affection for him." "As you can see," Kelley said, "I was very fond of Carl, and also had the utmost respect for him. I regard him as one of the handful of real geniuses in psychology" (personal communication, June 24, 1995).

CONCLUSION

During his short life, Hovland published more than 70 articles, was the editor or coauthor of 7 books, and supervised at least 22 Yale doctoral dissertations. His scientific achievements were recognized by his early election to the American Philosophical Society (1950), the American Academy of Arts and Sciences (1956), and the National Academy of Sciences (1960), as well as by conferral of the Distinguished Scientific Contribution Award by the American Psychological Association (1957) and of the Howard Crosby Warren Medal by the Society of Experimental Psychologists (1961). This last, awarded close to the time of his death, was graciously received for Hovland by his then 19-year-old son, David, in what was recalled by another Hovland admirer, Yale Professor Emeritus Wendell R. Garner, as an unusually "emotional occasion" at the annual meeting of that august society (personal communication, May 17, 1997).

Beyond his earliest research on diverse problems of physiological, perceptual, and industrial psychology, and his subsequent public service and consulting work, Hovland's most influential scientific contributions emerged from the three fields on which he successively focused his principal research efforts: (a) basic processes of human learning and generalization (late 1930s), (b) social communication and attitude change (1940s and 50s), and (c) human concept acquisition and problem solving (1950s until his 1961 death). His work in learning is widely respected and undoubtedly helped shape the quantitative and experimental skills that he later brought to bear on social communication. But it is his work in that second field that has had the most far-reaching impact. One cannot help wondering: If Hovland's life had not been cut short, might not the third line of work he had begun on thinking and concept attainment have had a similarly profound impact on the soon-to-burgeon interdisciplinary field of cognitive science?

For the 10 years I benefited from Hovland's wise and benevolent guidance and, especially, from his example, I—like so many others—feel boundless gratitude. Yet in preparing this memoir some 40 years later, I have gained an aching awareness of how much we and the whole range of the behavioral, social, and cognitive sciences lost back in 1961 as a result of the untimely death of this gifted researcher, statesman of science, and incomparable human being.

REFERENCES

Carroll, J. D., Julesz, B., Mathews, M. V., Rothkopf, E. Z., Sternberg, S., & Wish, M. (1984). Behavioral science. In S. Millman (Ed.), *A history of engineering and science in the Bell System* (pp. 431–471). Indianapolis: AT&T Bell Laboratories.

Freeman, G. L., & Hovland, C. I. (1934). Diurnal variations in performance and related physiological processes. *Psychological Bulletin, 31*, 777–799.

Hovland, C. I. (1937). The generalization of conditioned responses: I. The sensory generalization of conditioned responses with varying frequencies of tone. *Journal of General Psychology, 17*, 125–148.

Hovland, C. I. (1938). Experimental studies in rote-learning theory. I. Reminiscence following learning by massed and by distributed practice. *Journal of Experimental Psychology, 22*, 201–224.

Hovland, C. I. (1939). Experimental studies in rote-learning theory. V. Comparison of distribution of practice in serial and paired-associate learning. *Journal of Experimental Psychology, 25*, 622–633.

Hovland, C. I. (1948a). Psychology of the communicative process. In W. Schramm (Ed.), *Communications in modern society* (pp. 59–65). Urbana: University of Illinois Press.

Hovland, C. I. (1948b). Social communication. *Proceedings of the American Philosophical Society, 92*, 371–375.

Hovland, C. I. (1951). Human learning and retention. In S. S. Stevens (Ed.), *Handbook of experimental psychology* (pp. 613–689). New York: Wiley.

Hovland, C. I. (1952). A "communication analysis" of concept learning. *Psychological Review, 59*, 347–350.

Hovland, C. I. (1954). Effects of the mass media of communication. In G. Lindzey (Ed.), *Handbook of social psychology, Vol. 2* (pp. 1062–1103). Cambridge, MA: Addison-Wesley.

Hovland, C. I. (1959). Reconciling conflicting results derived from experimental and survey studies of attitude change. *American Psychologist, 14*, 8–17.

Hovland, C. I. (1960). Computer simulation of thinking. *American Psychologist, 15*, 687–693.

Hovland, C. I., & Hunt, E. B. (1960). Computer simulation of concept attainment. *Behavioral Science, 5*, 265–267.

Hovland, C. I., Janis, I. L., & Kelley, H. H. (1953). *Communication and persuasion: Psychological studies of opinion change.* New Haven, CT: Yale University Press.

Hovland, C. I., Lumsdaine, A. A., & Sheffield, F. D. (1949). *Experiments on mass communication* (Studies in social psychology in World War II, Vol. 3). Princeton, NJ: Princeton University Press.

Hovland, C. I., Mandell, W., Campbell, E. H., Brock, T., Luchins, A. S., Cohen, A. R., McGuire, W. J., Janis, I. L., Feierabend, R. L., & Anderson, N. H. (1957). *The order of presentation in persuasion* (Yale studies in attitude and communication, Vol. 1). New Haven, CT: Yale University Press.

Hovland, C. I., & Sears, R. R. (1940). Minor studies of aggression: VI. Correlation of lynchings with economic indices. *Journal of Psychology, 9,* 301–310.

Hovland, C. I., & Weiss, W. (1953). Transmission of information concerning concepts through positive and negative instances. *Journal of Experimental Psychology, 45,* 175–182.

Hull, C. L., Hovland, C. I., Ross, R. T., Hall, M., Perkins, D. T., & Fitch, F. B. (1940). *Mathematico-deductive theory of rote learning: A study in scientific methodology.* New Haven, CT: Yale University Press.

Hunt, E. B., & Hovland, C. I. (1960). Order of consideration of different types of concepts. *Journal of Experimental Psychology, 59,* 220–225.

Janis, I. L. (1968). Carl I. Hovland, 1912–1961. In D. L. Sills (Ed.), *International encyclopedia of the social sciences, Vol. 6* (pp. 526–531). New York: Macmillan.

Janis, I. L., Hovland, C. I., Field, P. B., Linton, H., Graham, E., Cohen, A. R., Rife, D., Abelson, R. P., Lesser, G. S., & King, B. T. (1959). *Personality and persuasibility* (Yale studies in attitude and communication, Vol. 2). New Haven, CT: Yale University Press.

Jenni, M. H. (1974). *An inventory and evaluation of source materials on Carl Iver Hovland.* Unpublished manuscript, Missoula, MT.

Kelman, H. C., & Hovland, C. I. (1953). "Reinstatement" of the communicator in delayed measurement of opinion change. *Journal of Abnormal and Social Psychology, 48,* 327–335.

Kurtz, K. H., & Hovland, C. I. (1956). Concept learning with differing sequences of instances. *Journal of Experimental Psychology, 51,* 239–243.

Maccoby, N. (1963). The new "scientific" rhetoric. In W. Schramm (Ed.), *The science of human communication* (pp. 41–53). New York: Basic Books.

McGuire, W. J. (1996). The Yale communication and attitude-change program in the 1950s. In E. E. Dennis & E. Wartella (Eds.), *American communication research: The remembered history* (pp. 39–59). Hillsdale, NJ: Erlbaum.

Miles, W. R. (1961). Carl Iver Hovland. *The American Philosophical Society Yearbook.* Philadelphia: American Philosophy Society.

Morrisett, L. N., & Hovland, C. I. (1959). A comparison of three varieties of training in human problem solving. *Journal of Experimental Psychology, 58,* 52–55.

Rosenberg, M. J., Hovland, C. I., McGuire, W. J., Abelson, R. P., & Brehm, J. W. (1960). *Attitude organization and change: An analysis of consistency among attitude components* (Yale studies in attitude and communication, Vol. 3). New Haven, CT: Yale University Press.

Schramm, W. (1963). Communication research in the United States. In W. Schramm (Ed.), *The science of human communication* (pp. 1–16). New York: Basic Books.

Sears, R. R. (1961). Carl I. Hovland, 1912–1961. *American Journal of Psychology, 74,* 637–639.

Shepard, R. N. (1958). Stimulus and response generalization: Deduction of the generalization gradient from a trace model. *Psychological Review, 65,* 242–256.

Shepard, R. N. (1987). Toward a universal law of generalization for psychological science. *Science, 237,* 1317–1323.

Shepard, R. N., & Chang, J.-J. (1963). Stimulus generalization in the learning of classifications. *Journal of Experimental Psychology, 65,* 94–102.

Shepard, R. N., Hovland, C. I., & Jenkins, H. M. (1961). Learning and memorization of classifications. *Psychological Monographs, 75* (13, Whole No. 517).

Sherif, M., & Hovland, C. I. (1961). *Social judgment: Assimilation and contrast effects in communication and attitude change* (Yale studies in attitude and communication, Vol. 4). New Haven, CT: Yale University Press.

Smith, M. B. (1968). Attitude change. In D. L. Sills (Ed.), *International encyclopedia of the social sciences, Vol. 1* (pp. 458–467). New York: Macmillan and Free Press.

Chapter 18

Stuart W. Cook: A "Complete Psychologist"

John C. Brigham

Creating solid scientific research and theory that could contribute to solving important social problems was the cornerstone of Stuart W. Cook's professional and personal life. Cook's research and writings on prejudice have served as an inspiration to several generations of graduate students and colleagues. His seminal work was recognized in a series of awards from the American Psychological Association (APA), the Society for the Psychological Study of Social Issues (SPSSI), and other organizations. In this chapter I will try to describe the work and the life values of the man who merited these honors.

BIOGRAPHICAL SKETCH

Stuart Wellford Cook was born near Richmond, Virginia, on April 17, 1913, the first child of Arthur B. Cook and Lois (Leonard) Cook. Arthur was from Lima, Ohio, and had moved to the Richmond area in his 20s, where he met his future bride in church. Their second son, Buddy, was born a year after Stuart, and a daughter, Margaret, arrived three years later. Arthur owned several filling stations, where he also sold radios. He also did a little farming on the side. The family lived in Chesterfield County, in the "country" outside of Richmond. Stuart attended a small country grammar school, taking five years to finish the

I am deeply grateful to Stuart Cook's children, Joanna, Steve, and Tim, his grandson Aaron, and his sister Margaret Cook, for their willingness to share with me many personal details about his home life. In addition, I am greatly indebted to Joan Bloom, John Harding, Brewster Smith, Claire Selltiz, Pat Wiser, and Larry Wrightsman for the valuable pieces of information that they provided to me.

*Photo of Stuart W. Cook courtesy of Timothy Cook.

seven grades. As a child he read a lot, according to his sister, "perhaps because there was nothing much else to do" (Margaret Cook, personal communication, 1999).

Later on, the family moved to Westhampton, where Stuart went to high school for one year. His father built a tennis court on their property, perhaps initiating Stuart's lifelong love of the sport. It was then decided to send the boys to military school, so they attended Hargrave Military Academy in Chatham, Virginia. Stuart graduated when he had just turned 16, but decided to take another year of schooling. His sister recalled that the extra year "did wonders for him." He learned to type, was on the debating team, and returned home polished, standing straight and tall, looking "like a shining penny" (Margaret Cook, personal communication, 1999).

Stuart then attended the University of Richmond on a scholarship while living at home. One summer while in college, Stuart, Buddy, and four of their fraternity brothers embarked on a cross-country auto camping trip. It was a great adventure, but Buddy apparently contracted tuberculosis somewhere along the way, as he became ill soon after their return. After undergoing nine surgeries in eight years, Buddy died at the age of 27, a crushing blow to the family. Stuart attained a bachelor's degree in biology in 1934 and a master's in psychology in 1935 from the University of Richmond. He considered medical school, but financial considerations ruled out that option. A professor recommended the psychology program at the University of Minnesota. He applied and was accepted with a teaching assistantship. Cook completed his PhD in 1938, conducting his dissertation research on the production of "experimental neuroses" in rats, with W. T. Heron as his major professor.

Cook first noticed Annabelle Hurley when she was taking an exam that he was helping to proctor. He asked her out after the semester had ended and they were married in 1938, seven months after their first date. After achieving his PhD, Cook was appointed to the clinical staff of the University of Minnesota Hospital and was an instructor in the University of Minnesota psychology department. During this period he was offered a position in the psychology clinic at Harvard, under Henry Murray, but decided to stay in Minnesota. In 1941, while still in his 20s, he became head of the Bureau for Psychological Services for the state of Minnesota. Cook joined the Society for the Psychological Study of Social Issues (SPSSI), an activist group in which he later played a major role, at about the time he received his PhD.

Cook's initial professional publications give no hint of his later career direction. His pre-1940 articles included studies of sex differences in conversation, the learning of nonsense syllables, verbal conditioning of the galvanic skin reflex, judgment of intelligence from photographs, and the experimental neurosis in rats. He also published a study of word associations with none other than B. F. Skinner (chap. 16, *Pioneers III*) as second author (Cook & Skinner, 1939). The only paper that would seem to hint of Cook's later consuming interest in social justice was a study of a measure of attitudes toward fascism (Raskin & Cook, 1938).

Cook's deep concern for human welfare was strongly influenced by his service as a research psychologist with the Army Air Force in the United States and England during World War II. In 1942 he joined the aviation psychology unit at the Santa Ana (California) Army Air Base, in Lt. Col. J. P. Guilford's unit. A captain, Cook, and Lt. Lloyd Humphreys directed a research unit that worked on the development of paper-and-pencil tests to aid in the selection of pilots, bombardiers, and navigators. The unit contained several young social psychologists who would go on to exert major influence on postwar American social psychology, including Harold Kelley and M. Brewster Smith (In Memoriam, 1993, p. 34). From Santa Ana, Cook was sent to England to gather data on bombing proficiency under certain combat conditions. After this, he went to Langley Field, Virginia, where he took command of a research unit studying the selection and training of airborne radar operators.

Cook was profoundly influenced by the emerging awareness of the Jewish Holocaust and the brutality of war, and vowed to his wife that he would focus his postwar efforts on the study of peace or of intergroup relations. His first step in this direction came in 1946 when he was selected by Kurt Lewin (chap. 7, *Pioneers III*) to head the Commission on Community Interrelations of the American Jewish Congress, which directed research on combating anti-Semitism and tested strategies for dealing with anti-Semitic incidents. Here he first explored how involuntary contact on an equal-status basis between individuals and the objects of their prejudice might serve to lessen the prejudice. Cook founded and became director of the Research Center for Human Relations at New York University in 1949, where he expanded his research to include all ethnic groups. In 1950 Cook became head of the psychology department at NYU, a position he held for 13 years. Under his leadership the department underwent a major expansion.

After many years in New York, Cook changed environments dramatically when he became chair of the psychology department at the University of Colorado in 1963. He served as chair for five years, again overseeing significant growth and strengthening of the department and its graduate program. Cook was named Distinguished Professor, one of the university's first, in 1978, the same year that he became director of the university's Institute of Behavioral Science. Though he officially retired in 1980, Cook remained professionally productive, continuing to publish thought-provoking papers through 1990.

Colleagues described Cook as modest, thoughtful, quiet, and unflappable, a remarkably focused listener. He often served as a valued mentor to younger colleagues. One called him "a 'Southern gentleman' in the best sense of the term" (Lawrence Wrightsman, personal communication, 1998). Smith (1994, p. 521) observed that "the many students and colleagues whose lives he touched revered him as the very model of a scientifically and socially responsible psychologist."

Stuart rarely spoke of his work to his children; as a consequence, his son Steve (who later became an attorney) received a jolt in a college class. Steve recalled,

> My father NEVER talked about himself or his work when we were growing up. (He was a devoted parent.) I never asked him why that was. I have come to assume that he felt that we should not grow up in any shadow cast by him. When I was a sophomore in college, if I'd been asked what my father did, I could only have told you that he was a psychology professor. That year, 1968, I was at UC San Diego. I was taking a class called "Sociology and the Law." . . . One of the chapters was about *Brown v. Board of Education.* As was my style, I was reading the chapter while listening to the lecture. You can imagine how stunned I was to read that one of the three drafters of the Social Science Statement cited by the Supreme Court was my Dad! (Steve Cook, personal communication)

The last several years of Cook's life were a painful struggle. He suffered from unrelenting back pain and was unable to play tennis, despite undergoing several surgeries that he hoped would allow him to play again. His beloved wife Annabelle experienced a debilitating stroke. His son Jon, who was the founder and director of a nonprofit organization in Washington, DC, that provided management consulting services to other nonprofit organizations, died of cancer in 1992 at age 50. For five years, Stuart had committed himself to finding out everything he could about Jon's cancer and possible treatment options, and his son's death devastated him. Cook himself died of congestive heart failure at his home in Boulder, Colorado, on March 25, 1993, three weeks before his 80th birthday.

RACE RELATIONS, SEGREGATION, AND THE SUPREME COURT

The hallmark of Cook's career was his never-ending commitment to improving the human condition, especially for socially disenfranchised groups. Most of his research centered on experimental procedures to reduce prejudice and improve relations between Black and White individuals. Thomas Pettigrew, another leading prejudice researcher who had also grown up in Richmond, made an interesting observation about the possible source of Cook's lifelong focus: "Whenever we had occasion to talk at length, our topic was invariably race relations. Somehow, beneath his calm demeanor, Stuart seemed to me to share an inner rage at the racial injustice we had both grown up with in the capital of the Confederacy" (In Memoriam, 1993, p. 37).

Cook's studies of the effects of equal-status interracial contact in naturally occurring situations such as housing developments (Wilner, Walkley, & Cook, 1952, 1955) and in experimentally created small groups are classics in the field. A consistent underlying theme in his work was a basic optimism that people can change, that under the right conditions prejudice and injustice can be reduced and respect between groups enhanced. Toward this end, he repeatedly called for intergroup research that takes a proactive stance, that contributes to better intergroup relations, rather than simply reacting to social events.

In the early 1950s Cook met Thurgood Marshall, who at the time was head counsel for the NAACP and a leader in a series of lawsuits brought to desegregate the nation's schools. Lawyers from the National Association for the Advancement of Colored People's Legal Defense and Education Fund (NAACP-LDF) were working on several segregation cases. Cook served as an expert witness on the psychological impact of segregated schools. Within psychology, the Society for the Psychological Study of Social Issues (SPSSI), Division 9 of the American Psychological Association (APA), was intimately involved in the sequence of events that led up to the landmark decision. In 1951 SPSSI's Committee on Intergroup Relations, formed shortly after World War II, commissioned an "evaluation of the work done in the field of minority personality and adjustment" (Jackson, 1998, p. 148). A subcommittee was formed to prepare a statement on this issue for four school segregation cases that were moving toward the U.S. Supreme Court. Cook was a member of the subcommittee, which developed an outline titled, "Social Scientific Argument Against Segregation in the Schools" (Jackson, 1998).

The Supreme Court agreed to hear the first two of the school segregation cases in 1952. Because there was no longer time for the full subcommittee to meet, Kenneth Clark and Isidor Chein drafted a statement for submission to the Supreme Court. After they had written two drafts, Cook joined them. In 1967, Clark noted that Cook's involvement was "just wonderful because he brought the appearance of white, Anglo-Saxon dispassionateness to our task where I had a tendency to become a little strident" (quoted in Speer, 1968, p. 555). But Cook's participation transcended mere appearances. For example, in the Social Science Statement's original opening paragraph, Clark had written what sounded like a political speech against segregation. Jackson noted that virtually all of this paragraph was struck from the final version, most probably by Cook. Jackson observed, "Perhaps this final version would not stir the blood as the original version did, however, it certainly was more in keeping with the objective tone of a scientific paper" (1998, p. 151).

This appendix to the plaintiffs' legal briefs was titled, "The Effect of Segregation and the Consequences of Integration: A Social Science Statement." The statement did not discuss specific research studies, but referred to the relevant research in 35 footnotes. As Cook was aware, if the Social Science Statement was to have any meaningful authority, it would have to be a dispassionate objective statement concerning social science research and theory. If it were a political tract, in contrast, it would have less force as a scientific statement. The final Social Science Statement made three central arguments: (a) Segregation is psychologically damaging to minority group children. It produces low self-esteem, self-hatred, frustration, and increased chances of delinquency. (b) Segregation is also harmful to majority group children, who experience a "distorted sense of reality," confusion, and "moral cynicism." (c) Desegregation could proceed smoothly if it were done quickly and firmly (Kluger, 1975). The third argument relied heavily on studies of beneficial interracial contact in housing and employment situations, including a landmark study of housing integration conducted by Wilner, Walkley, and Cook (1952). Cook was instrumental in creating a statement that framed the argument strictly in scientific terms, rather than political, legal, or moral ones.

The Statement was subsequently signed by 32 prominent social scientists. Included in the signatures were 14 past or future presidents of SPSSI (Jackson, 1998), and most of the psychologists who had been studying social prejudice since the 1930s. Some had wanted to issue the Statement under SPSSI's name, but Cook, who was SPSSI president at the time, argued that it would be better if SPSSI adopted the role of "arranger and stimulator" (Jackson, 1998, p. 153).

Not everyone was impressed by the Statement. Opposing counsel John Davis wrote a colleague, "I have read the brief and appendix submitted by our opponents and there seems to be nothing in them that requires special comment. I think it perfectly clear from interior evidences that the witness Clark drafted the appendix which is signed by the worthy social scientists. I can only say that if that sort of 'guff' can move any court, 'God save the state'" (quoted in Kluger, 1975, p. 557). Despite misgivings from some of its own lawyers, the NAACP appended the Statement to their brief to the Supreme Court.

During deliberations, the Supreme Court justices asked both sides to prepare new arguments on five questions. The question in which the social scientists were most involved was whether desegregation should be immediate and complete or whether "an effective gradual adjustment" would be better. Clark coordinated the response to this question, reviewing research and consulting colleagues widely. He concluded that immediate desegregation could be effective when imposed swiftly and with firm authority from above. Clark (1953) outlined five conditions that would ensure effective desegregation: (a) a clear and unequivocal statement of policy by prestigious leaders; (b) firm enforcement of the new policy; (c) a willingness to deal strongly with violations; (d) a refusal to allow subterfuge or delay by local authorities; and (e) an appeal to individuals based on their religious principles of brotherhood and the American tradition of fair play and justice.

On May 14, 1954, the Supreme Court ruled unanimously that school segregation was a violation of the 14th Amendment. This was the Court's first decision under its new Chief Justice, Earl Warren. Warren wrote that "modern authority" showed that the assumptions implicit in the 1897 *Plessy v. Ferguson* decision, that had upheld so-called separate but equal facilities, were not valid. All of the seven sources cited in support of this point (in footnote 11) had been discussed in the Social Science Statement.

But the psychologists' job was not yet over. After its *Brown* decision, the Court asked for yet another round of arguments focusing on the issue of immediate versus gradual desegregation. Clark organized a meeting of eminent social scientists (including Cook) to draft a response for the Court. The resulting Social Science memo urged a strict one-year deadline for desegregation. This point was troubling to several group members, including Cook, Gordon Allport, Gardner Murphy, and Arnold Rose, but Clark was adamant that it be included (Jackson, 1998). The memo also pointed out that "there is a considerable body of evidence indicating that where the situation demands that an individual act as if he were not prejudiced, he will do so in spite of his continued prejudice" (quoted in Jackson, 1998, p. 170). The Supreme Court did not make a clear choice between "immediate" and "gradual." Instead, in May 1955 the Court remanded the cases back to the federal district courts, who were ordered to desegregate the public schools "with all deliberate speed" (*Brown v. Board of Education,* 1955).

Although Cook and Kenneth Clark did not always see eye to eye during their struggles to come to a common view on the two social science statements in the early 1950s, they greatly respected each other. Four decades later, Clark wrote,

> Stuart Cook is my friend. He was and is my prototype of a fine human being, a scholar of absolute integrity and a social psychologist who used our science to help our fellow human beings toward equality and toward a functioning democracy. . . . Stuart Cook will remain as my friend and my mentor. I will always think of him as the example of the fact that the science of psychology can best provide the basis for genuine humanity and empathy. (In Memoriam, 1993, p. 31)

EVALUATING THE IMPACT OF THE
SOCIAL SCIENCE STATEMENT

Although the Social Science Statement has been widely lauded as one of psychology's greatest contributions to society, it has remained controversial. Some observers have argued that the Statement really had little or no effect on the Supreme Court. In the 1970s, several psychologists, frustrated by the uneven results of desegregation in the two decades after the *Brown* decisions, questioned whether the points made in the Statement were valid. Cook took it on himself to answer these concerns in a 1979 article titled, "Social Science and School Desegregation: Did We Mislead the Supreme Court?" Cook observed that, although the impact of the Statement on the Justices could never be precisely gauged, "Circumstantial evidence strongly suggests that the information it contained did receive the Justices' attention" (p. 420). He argued persuasively that a careful "reassessment of the 1954 Social Science Statement in the light of subsequent research reveals little to indicate that the Statement misled the Supreme Court either as to the consequences of government-sponsored segregation or the constructive potential of desegregation" (p. 431). Cook went on to point out that the mixed nature of subsequent research results pertaining to the effects of desegregation were not surprising, because "rarely did desegregation occur under what were believed by social scientists to be conditions conducive to favorable outcomes for the children participating. It is surprising that outcomes have been favorable as often as they have" (p. 432). Cook called for future researchers to take an innovative, rather than a reactive, orientation to the study of school desegregation.

Shortly thereafter, Harold Gerard (1983), who had conducted a large-scale study of desegregation in the Riverside, California, schools (Gerard & Miller, 1975), published an article in the *American Psychologist* arguing that the Social Science Statement was "based on well-meaning rhetoric, rather that solid research" (p. 869). He opined further that it was "extraordinarily quixotic" to assume that the conditions specified in the Statement (as outlined previously) could be met in the typical school system. The Statement, he argued, said, in effect, that desegregation would be successful because when "the minority child was now in a classroom with Whites, he or she would no longer have the status of an outcast or a pariah. This knowledge would somehow impart to the child the self-image necessary to do well in school and later enter the mainstream of American society" (p. 869). But Gerard argued that this is not likely to happen. He asserted that research, including studies by Cook and by Clark, have shown that "prejudice is extraordinarily refractory to any attempts to change it. It is a virulent cancer that infects an entire culture from the lowest to the highest rung of the socioeconomic ladder. It is deeply embedded in the fabric of the American character" (p. 870). Gerard concluded that, "At this point, after the heartache and disappointment, I consider myself to be a realist rather than a pessimist. Social scientists were wrong in the belief that change would come easily" (p. 875). Gerard suggested that the Statement was "short-sighted" and that social science had lost credibility as a consequence.

Once again Cook rose to the challenge. In a scholarly reply to Gerard, also published in the *American Psychologist*, Cook (1984a) pointed out that, to some extent, Gerard's derogation of the Social Science Statement followed from a misunderstanding of the context in which the statement was developed. The issue facing the Supreme Court in the early 1950s was de jure government-enforced segregation of Black and White individuals into separate schools that was mandated or permitted by law in 17 states at the time. This was a very different situation than de facto racial segregation resulting from residential patterns, which was the focus of subsequent research, including Gerard's (Gerard & Miller, 1975). Cook asserted that Gerard might have overgeneralized the disappointing results of his own study. Cook wrote,

> In contrast to Gerard's view, this article calls attention to an evident increase in the credibility of the social sciences as reflected by the extraordinary range of policy questions to which social science research is now being applied. This suggests that the social science role in public policy has been steadily growing and will continue to do so in the future. As this applies to the unfinished business of school desegre-

gation, classroom experiments have demonstrated that self-esteem, school achievement, and race relations can be improved by desegregation procedures that are based on established psychological theory. A meaningful role for social scientists in the future would be to conduct research in desegregated schools that might help to maximize the effectiveness of such procedures. In contrast, a meaningful role for social scientists in 1954 was to relate already available knowledge of the consequences of segregation to the policy decisions being made at the time. (1984a, p. 831)

INVESTIGATING THE "CONTACT HYPOTHESIS"

The contact hypothesis, the notion that intergroup contact under certain conditions could reduce prejudice and produce more favorable intergroup attitudes, was a continuing focus of Cook's research career. Cook's interest was stimulated in the late 1940s and early 1950s by the writings of Theodore Newcomb (1947), Goodwin Watson (1947), and Robin Williams (1947), and by discussions with his colleagues at the Commission on Community Interrelations of the American Jewish Congress and the Research Center for Human Relations of New York University. In a 1960 address, Cook declared, "Over the past fifteen years my ideas have developed inseparably from those of my colleagues in these groups; all of my research has been done in collaboration with them" (Cook, 1962, p. 66).

Cook's philosophical approach to the research process, as well as his involvement in creating the Social Science Statement for the *Brown* case, can be seen in an early article that he published with Isidor Chein and John Harding (Chein, Cook, & Harding, 1948). In this paper they described in detail the concept of "action research," as first propounded by Kurt Lewin. They wrote that the field of action research "developed to satisfy the needs of the socio-political individual who recognized that, in science, he can find the most reliable scientist who wants his labors to be for maximal social utility as well as of theoretical significance" (p. 44). They cautioned,

Not only does the action researcher face all of the difficulties which confront the scientist in his laboratory, but an entirely new set of difficulties, extraneous to fact-finding per se, enter the picture. . . . Not only must he make discoveries, but he must see to it that his discoveries are properly applied. It is largely in terms of this job definition that the action researcher differs from the ordinary academic scientist. (1948, p. 44)

They concluded,

We have attempted to describe dispassionately the way in which we see the field of action research. If, occasionally, our enthusiasm has shown through, it is because we do not really see it dispassionately. We see in action research a field of intense theoretical interest as well as tremendous practical and social value. (1948, p. 50)

Many years later in a talk at the APA annual convention, Cook (1984b) expressed some uncertainty about what had happened to action research, whether it had never really gotten underway, or had enjoyed a brief heyday only in the 1940s and 1950s, or whether it had reemerged later under such pseudonyms as program evaluation, experimental social innovations, and social policy research. In contrast to this uncertainty, his early colleague John Harding later commented, "I think Stuart Cook's greatest contribution to psychology was in developing and systematizing the concept of 'action research' first sketched out by Kurt Lewin and Ronald Lippitt" (In Memoriam, 1993, p. 32).

For 35 years, Cook studied the conditions of contact that would produce reductions in prejudice. In his address on receiving the APA's award for Distinguished Contributions to Psychology in the Public Interest, Cook (1985, p. 453) summarized the hypothesis: "The contact hypothesis, as I use it, predicts that a favorable change in attitude and interpersonal attraction will result when there is personal contact with members of a disliked group, provided that five conditions hold." These five conditions are (a) the participants from the two groups must be of equal status in the situation in which the contact occurs; (b) the attributes of the disliked group that become apparent during the contact must disconfirm the prevailing stereotyped beliefs about this group; (c) the contact situation must encourage, or perhaps require, a mutually interdependent relationship—that is, cooperation in the achievement of a joint goal; (d) the contact situation must have a high "acquaintance potential," which allows group members to see each other as individuals rather than as persons with stereotyped group characteristics, and (e) the social norms of the contact situation must favor the concept of group equality and equalitarian intergroup association.

The first large-scale empirical investigation of the effects of contact in which Cook was involved was a study of desegregated housing (Wilner et al., 1952, 1955). They found that desegregated White tenants had more favorable racial attitudes than did segregated ones. (The tenants had no choice about whether they were assigned to segregated or desegregated housing units.) Further, even within desegregated housing, the closer that White tenants lived to Black tenants, the more favorable were their racial attitudes. Cook then turned his attention to creating an experimental situation in which the important aspects of intergroup contact could be studied.

THE "RAILROAD GAME" RESEARCH PROGRAM

The conditions thought critical for improving intergroup attitudes and behaviors were operationalized in Cook's series of "railroad game" studies carried out in

Nashville, Tennessee, in the 1960s (Cook, 1969, 1971). Cook attempted to create a situation that met the optimal conditions for between-group contact that he and others (e.g., Allport, 1954) had so carefully specified. Each iteration of the study involved groups of three female college students—a nonprejudiced Black woman, a nonprejudiced White woman, and a prejudiced White woman—and one Black experimenter and one White experimenter. The first two women were experimental confederates; the prejudiced White woman was the only real research participant (her level of prejudice had been measured previously in an entirely different setting, under different sponsorship). The experiment was described as a study of small group interactions that was sponsored by the military. The scenario consisted of a complex three-person "railroad game," which involved filling shipping orders and keeping track of railroad cars in a system involving 10 stations, 6 railroad lines, and 500 freight cars of six different types. The game was played two hours a day, five days a week, for four weeks. The women were paid for their participation only after they had completed their four-week stint.

Equal status within the contact situation was achieved by assigning the White and Black participants to task roles of equal responsibility. Each woman was trained in one of the three jobs and subsequently trained the other two women in her job. Contact with stereotype-disconfirming Black individuals was ensured by using a Black experimenter who behaved in a stereotype-disconfirming fashion and by selecting Black confederates who had educational backgrounds equivalent to those of the research participants (i.e., they were also college students). Third, a cooperative relationship was encouraged by a task that required interdependence in its execution and provided a reward (a monetary bonus) for group success. It was arranged that the group was always successful in attaining the bonus. Fourth, the contact situation was given a high acquaintance potential by arranging for lunch-break conversations during which the Black confederates brought out individuating information about themselves. Fifth, social norms favoring equalitarian race relations and racial equality were established during the course of the lunch-break conversations. Several of the half-hour conversations were guided by the confederates into topics that gave the White coworker opportunities to express her support for desegregation, nondiscriminatory employment and educational policies, cross-racial social contact, and so forth.

The participants' racial attitudes were remeasured in a group setting several weeks after the "game" had ended, again in an entirely different location under different sponsorship. The results were encouraging in terms of prejudice reduction. About 40% of the research participants changed their racial attitudes significantly on three separate attitude measures when they were given in a completely different setting a month or more after the experiment apparently had ended. By contrast, only 12% of a control group of highly prejudiced women who did not participate in the game showed similar levels of prejudice reduction over the same period (Cook, 1985).

Cook and his colleagues also sought to identify the personality factors that might predict which women changed their attitudes and which did not. They found that a group of measures that assessed attitudes toward people in general and levels of cynicism effectively differentiated "changers" from "nonchangers." Women who became less prejudiced were those who had the most positive and least cynical attitudes toward people. Changers also tended to have lower self-esteem and a higher need for social approval than did nonchangers—two measures that probably indicated general persuasibility (Cook & Wrightsman, 1967).

This research, carried out with colleagues Lawrence Wrightsman and Shirley Watson, was aptly characterized by Smith (1994, p. 521) as "surely the most laborious and realistic laboratory study of attitude change ever attempted." Because each individual participated for approximately a month, no more than nine research participants could be studied in an academic year. Two studies were actually carried out. The initial study involved 23 experimental participants and an equal number of controls and took $2\frac{1}{2}$ years to carry out. After a break of three years, a replication was carried out, using19 experimental participants and 19 controls over a two-year period (Cook, 1985). This time- and labor-intensive study would have been a career-killer if attempted by an untenured faculty member. Cook was more interested in getting it right than in reaping the academic benefits of multiple publications, and the research was described fully only in a presentation for the *Nebraska Symposium on Motivation* (Cook, 1969), in a technical report for the U.S. Department of Health, Education, and Welfare (Cook, 1971), and in much later review papers (Cook, 1984c, 1985).

Armed with the knowledge gained from the "railroad game" studies, Cook decided to focus more closely on one of its components, cooperative interdependence. He and his colleagues organized junior high school students into ethnically mixed "learning teams." For example, Weigel, Wiser, and Cook (1975) found less cross-ethnic conflict and some indications of more cross-ethnic friendships in five-person learning teams (made up of one Black, one Hispanic, and three White children) when compared with comparable classes without such teams. Subsequently, Cook conducted eight studies that investigated the factors that might enhance the positive effect of nonvoluntary intergroup contact. Using a variation of the railroad game setup, they studied young males in the military. Results indicated that more competent groupmates, Black or White, were liked more than were less competent groupmates. If participants were told that their team had succeeded at the task, they also liked their teammates more, regardless of race. These studies are summarized in Cook (1984c, 1985). Cook was aware that although ethnic attitudes may become more positive toward individuals involved in a contact situation, this positive change may not generalize to the group as a whole. Cook (1984c) noted that there may be a need to inject some sort of "cognitive booster" into the cooperative experience to encourage generalization. Such a factor was built into the original railroad game design via "guided conversations" in which the Black confederate discouraged the White participants' attempts to subtype her as an exception, by stressing the many ways in which she was not different from other Black individuals.

THE "COMPLETE PSYCHOLOGIST"

Although Cook's contributions to the study and amelioration of racial prejudice and discrimination were the hallmark of his life and career, it is appropriate to note that, as M. Brewster Smith suggested,

> He was actually the nearest thing to a complete psychologist, whose half-century career included major activity in clinical psychology, experimental psychology, military psychology, research methods, scientific and professional ethics, professional organization, departmental and research administration, and public policy. (1994, p. 521)

Cook played an active role in the infrastructure of psychology. His strong sense of social responsibility manifested itself in the leading role he played in the development of APA's ethical standards for professional practice and for research. He had an abiding concern for the professional and scientific ethics of psychologists, as reflected in his service on the committee that developed APA's general code of ethics, the *Ethical Standards for Psychologists*. In addition, he was the first chair of the APA Ad Hoc Committee on Ethical Standards in Research, which developed APA's research code of ethics, *Ethical Principles in the Conduct of Research with Human Participants*, published in 1973 (American Psychological Association, 1973).

Earlier, as chair of the Joint Council of New York State Psychologists on Legislation, he led the legislative campaign that was responsible for the professional certification of psychologists in New York. The New York Society for Clinical Psychologists voted him their 1956 award for Distinguished Contributions to Clinical Psychology. Cook chaired a national conference on professional training in 1965. He remained active within the APA and attended 50 consecutive annual APA conventions.

Cook also made significant contributions to social science methodology. He coedited the first textbook on procedures for experimental and quasi-experimental research on questions of social significance, *Research Methods in Social Relations* (Jahoda, Deutsch, & Cook, 1951). Subsequently revised by other coauthors in several editions, this book continues to make an important contribution to the training of students, and the royalties continue to benefit SPSSI. Cook and Selltiz (1964) published a widely cited article in the *Psychological Bulletin* that detailed ways to measure socially sensitive attitudes indirectly and covertly. Subsequently, Cook and his colleagues developed a widely used measure of racial attitudes of White individuals, the Multifactor Racial Attitude Inventory

(Brigham, Woodmansee, & Cook, 1976). In later years, Cook also studied ways of increasing energy conservation behaviors; these studies are summarized in Berrenberg and Cook (1981).

CONCLUSION

The term that seems to recur most frequently in descriptions of Cook's career and his life is integrity. He sustained a remarkably high level of concern for others across a 50-year period in his personal life, as well as in his professional one. He was not afraid of controversy, as demonstrated by his publication (with Marie Jahoda) of articles on freedom of thought and "anticipatory ideological compliance," during the height of the repressive McCarthy era in the early 1950s. The most striking finding of the Jahoda and Cook (1952) study of federal employees was the extent to which individuals voluntarily discontinued activities that might seem suspicious, were they to be investigated. These activities included canceling magazine subscriptions, getting rid of certain books, resigning from voluntary organizations, and avoiding conversation about controversial issues. Decades later Cook (1986, p. 70) observed that, "In spite of being familiar with such group mechanisms [responses to threat], the investigators were still not prepared for the extent to which people were adjusting their behavior to avoid exposure to pressure to conform. Individuals did not wait for their behavior to be questioned." Jahoda and Cook (1954) labeled this phenomenon anticipatory ideological compliance. The precise nature of this compliance varied, but individuals'

> knowledge that certain categories of behavior were under surveillance was sufficient to lead them to make anticipatory behavioral changes. The nature of changes differed for different respondents. For some, they were self-conscious, anticipatory precautions, taken sometimes with resignation, sometimes in fear, sometimes with anger. For others, they reflected the growth of uncertainty about their former beliefs in the face of what seemed to be prevalent opinions to the contrary. Still others underwent true belief changes; they now identified some of their former behaviors as being supportive of an unfriendly nation or of an undesirable political philosophy. (Cook, 1986, pp. 70–71)

As Smith (1994) pointed out, in that era, studying the pressures to conform ideologically was a courageous act. Later it became known that Cook was among a distinguished group of social scientists who were black-listed as security risks by the National Institutes of Mental Health and excluded from possible consultative roles.

Two decades later, Cook demonstrated his courage and his commitment to applying social science knowledge to real-world problems in defusing a potentially violent antiwar demonstration at the University of Colorado. In the spring of 1970 American forces invaded Cambodia and the University's Macky Auditorium was filled with angry, rowdy, frightened, and disorganized students who were determined to do something major to protest the government's Vietnam policies. The potential for violence was strong; the possibilities for constructive action seemed slim. Then, as Bernard Bloom later recalled (In Memoriam, 1993, p. 24):

> Enter Stuart Cook on stage in Macky. My memory was that he stood quietly on the left side of the stage while a two-page handout was distributed presenting a list he had prepared of psychological principles that were, in his judgment, important to keep in mind when trying to influence the public to a particular point of view. The list displayed Stuart's unique commitment to social action—the commitment of an absolutely rational man with one foot squarely planted in social reality while the other was planted in the scholarly field of social psychology.
>
> In the 30 minutes or so that Stuart spoke, the audience was transformed from an unruly mob into a quiet community of attentive students—all eager to understand what social science could tell them about how to accomplish what they knew they had to accomplish. I believed then and believe now that Stuart's scholarly lecture saved our university from the threat of uncontrollable chaos and helped make our efforts here in Boulder to influence national policy among the most effective in the nation.

Although Cook could address an unruly crowd or firmly deliver expert testimony about segregation in a hostile courtroom situation, he made his points quietly and carefully, with dignity and integrity. His focus on human welfare can be seen even in his final publication, written when he was in his late 70s, titled, "Toward a Psychology of Improving Justice: Research on Extending the Equity Principle to Victims of Social Injustice" (Cook, 1990). He concluded the article, "in a short period of time we have evolved an impressive account of the psychology of justice. In the years to come, we should undertake an equally vigorous and effective development of the psychology of improving justice" (p. 158). To the end, Cook provided a model of the psychological researcher creating and applying knowledge to help bring about a more humane world.

REFERENCES

Allport, G. W. (1954). *The nature of prejudice*. Reading, MA: Addison-Wesley.

American Psychological Association. (1973). *Ethical principles in the conduct of research with human participants*. Washington, DC: Author.

Berrenberg, J., & Cook, S. W. (1981). Approaches to encouraging conservation behavior: A review and conceptual framework. *Journal of Social Issues, 37*(2), 73–107.

Brigham, J. C., Woodmansee, J. J., & Cook, S. W. (1976). Dimensions of verbal racial attitudes: Interracial marriage and approaches to racial equality. *Journal of Social Issues, 32*(2), 9–21.

Brown v. Board of Education of Topeka, 347 U.S. 483 (1954).

Brown v. Board of Education of Topeka, 149 U.S. 294 (1955).

Chein, I., Cook, S. W., &. Harding, J. (1948). The field of action research. *American Psychologist*, *3*, 43–50.

Clark, K. B. (1953). Desegregation: An appraisal of the evidence. *Journal of Social Issues*, *9*(4), 1–77.

Cook, S. W. (1962). The systematic analysis of socially significant events: A strategy for social research. *Journal of Social Issues*, *18*, 66–84. (The Kurt Lewin Memorial Award Address, September 5, 1960)

Cook, S. W. (1969). Motives in a conceptual analysis of attitude-related behavior. In W. J. Arnold & D. Levine (Eds.), *Nebraska Symposium on Motivation* (pp. 179–235). Lincoln: University of Nebraska Press.

Cook, S. W. (1971). The effect of unintended interracial contact upon racial interaction and attitude change. *Final Report*, U. S. Department of Health, Education and Welfare, Office of Education, Project No. 5-1320. Washington, DC: U.S. Government Printing Office.

Cook, S. W. (1979). Social science and school desegregation: Did we mislead the Supreme Court? *Personality and Social Psychology Bulletin*, *5*, 420–438.

Cook, S. W. (1984a). The 1954 Social Science Statement and school desegregation: A reply to Gerard. *American Psychologist*, *39*, 819–831.

Cook, S. W. (1984b, August). *Action research: Its origins and early application.* Paper presented at the American Psychological Association meeting, Toronto, Ontario, Canada.

Cook, S. W. (1984c). Cooperative interaction in multi-ethnic contexts. In M. Brewer and N. Miller (Eds.), *Groups in contact: The psychology of desegregation* (pp. 155–184). New York: Academic Press.

Cook, S. W. (1985). Experimenting on social issues: The case of school desegregation. *American Psychologist*, *40*, 452–460.

Cook, S. W. (1986). Research on anticipatory ideological compliance: Comment on Sargent and Harris. *Journal of Social Issues*, *42*(1), 69–73.

Cook, S. W. (1990). Toward a psychology of improving justice: Research on extending the equality principle to victims of social injustice. *Journal of Social Issues*, *46*(l), 147–161.

Cook, S. W., & Selltiz, C. (1964). A multiple-indicator approach to attitude measurement. *Psychological Bulletin*, *62*, 35–55.

Cook, S. W., & Skinner, B. F. (1939). Some factors influencing the distribution of associated words. *Psychological Record*, *3*, 178–184.

Cook, S. W., & Wrightsman, L. S. (1967, April). *The factorial structure of "positive attitudes toward people."* Symposium presentation, Southeastern Psychological Association meeting, Atlanta, GA.

Gerard, H. B. (1983). School desegregation: The social science role. *American Psychologist*, *38*, 869–877.

Gerard, H. B., & Miller, N. (1975). *School desegregation.* New York: Plenum Press.

In Memoriam: Stuart W. Cook. (1993). Boulder: University of Colorado.

Jackson, J. P., Jr. (1998). Creating a consensus: Psychologists, the Supreme Court, and school desegregation, 1952–1955. *Journal of Social Issues*, *54*(1), 143–177.

Jahoda, M., & Cook, S. W. (1952). Security measures and freedom of thought. *Yale Law Journal*, *61*, 295–333.

Jahoda, M., & Cook, S. W. (1954). Ideological compliance as a social-psychological process. In C. J. Friedrich (Ed.), *Totalitarianism* (pp. 203–222). Cambridge, MA: Harvard University Press.

Jahoda, M., Deutsch, M., & Cook, S. W. (Eds.). (1951). *Research methods in social relations.* (Two volumes). New York: Dryden Press.

Kluger, R. (1975). *Simple justice: The history of Brown v. Board of Education and black America's struggle for equality.* New York: Vintage Books.

Newcomb, T. M. (1947). Autistic hostility and social reality. *Human Relations*, *1*, 69–86.

Plessy v. Ferguson. (1897). 163 U.S. 537.

Raskin, E., & Cook, S. W. (1938). A further investigation of the measurement of an attitude toward fascism. *Journal of Social Psychology, 9,* 201–206.

Smith, M. B. (1994). Stuart W. Cook (1913–1993). *American Psychologist, 49,* 521–522.

Speer, H. A. (1968). *The case of the century: A historical and social perspective on* Brown v. Board of Education of Topeka *with present and future implications.* Washington, DC: Office of Education, U.S. Department of Health, Education, and Welfare.

Watson, G. (1947). *Action for unity.* New York: Harper.

Weigel, R. H., Wiser, P. L., & Cook, S. W. (1975). The impact of cooperative learning experiences on cross-ethnic relations and attitudes. *Journal of Social Issues, 31,* 219–244.

Williams, R. M., Jr. (1947). *The reduction of intergroup tensions.* New York: Social Science Research Council.

Wilner D. M., Walkley, R. P., & Cook, S. W. (1952). Residential proximity and intergroup relations in public housing projects. *Journal of Social Issues, 8*(1), 45–69.

Wilner, D. M., Walkley, R. P., & Cook, S. W. (1955). *Human relations in interracial housing.* Minneapolis: University of Minnesota Press.

Chapter 19

Roger W. Sperry: Nobel Laureate, Neuroscientist, and Psychologist

Antonio E. Puente

One of the most puzzling experiences one has in teaching courses on the history of psychology is coming to realize that most undergraduate students know little or nothing about Roger W. Sperry's contributions to psychology and many of them do not even recognize the name. What makes this innocence of understanding hard to understand is that these same students usually have some acquaintance with the theories of such giants in the history of clinical psychology as Sigmund Freud (chap. 4, *Pioneers I*) and Carl Rogers (chap. 15, *Pioneers III*), such important experimental psychologists as Gustav Fechner (chap. 1, *Pioneers II*) and Hermann Ebbinghaus (chap. 4, *Pioneers III*), and such system builders as John B. Watson (chap. 12, *Pioneers I*) and Max Wertheimer (chap. 13, *Pioneers I*). One purpose of this chapter is to give readers more knowledge about Sperry, who certainly qualifies as a pioneer in the history of psychology.

As the list of pioneers covered in previous volumes in the *Pioneers* series suggests, students' lack of knowledge about Sperry may result, in part, from a significant gap in the literature of psychology. Except for a book of essays in honor of Roger W. Sperry edited by Trevarthen (1993) and a recent (Hamilton, 1998) memorial edition of the journal *Neuropsychologia*, edited by Charles Hamilton, no useful report of the life, ideas, and research of Sperry exists. This chapter attempts to fill that gap. It presents the life and work of Sperry, relying on the material that is available in his own research and writing as well as that of his students. The chapter contains two major sections: biography and research and theory.

---

*Photo of Antonio E. Puente and Roger W. Sperry courtesy of Antonio E. Puente.

THIS AUTHOR'S RELATIONSHIP TO SPERRY

Even though I did not work with Sperry, readers may understand certain aspects of this chapter better if I present a brief account of my relationship with him. During the early 1980s Cecil Reynolds of Texas A&M University and I developed a series of books on neuropsychology for Plenum Publishing. Several volumes had been published in that series by the late 1980s, and Polly Pechsted, Sperry's last postdoctoral student, had become familiar with them. While Pechsted and I were working together on the executive committee of Division 40 (Clinical Neuropsychology) of the APA—she as program chair and I as member-at-large of the committee—she suggested to Sperry and me that we consider publishing a book about his program of research. So Sperry and I began working together with Pechsted and a student, Heather Griffith, on the development of such a book. The book was never published but, for me, the project evolved into a tutorial and mentoring program. Over the next five years, in correspondence, telephone calls, faxes, and regular visits, Sperry described in detail to me his ideas, his research, and his hopes for psychology and society. Several short published pieces, including an obituary of Sperry in the *American Psychologist* (Puente, 1995), grew out of our relationship. And some of the personal information about Sperry and the opinions that I occasionally express in this chapter derive from the same source.

BIOGRAPHY

By all personal and scholarly accounts, Sperry led an uneventful life until he entered college. He was born in 1913 and was raised in rural Connecticut. Sperry's father, Francis Bushnell Sperry, was a banker; his mother, Florence Kraemer Sperry, was a housewife who later attended business school. Until Francis Sperry's sudden, unexpected death when Roger was 12, the family, including two Sperry sons—Roger (the older) and Russell—was intact, but there was strong sibling rivalry between the brothers.

As a youngster, Sperry enjoyed living in the country. He had special interests in collecting moths and butterflies and dissecting dead wild animals that he found around the family farm. One unusual and significant recollection that Sperry recounted was that, before he went to high school, one of his parents brought home from the public library a book, *Principles of Psychology*, by William James (James, 1890; chap. 2, *Pioneers I*). Thus at the age of 12 Sperry read one of the earliest, longest, and most sophisticated textbooks in the history of American psychology, and his ideas about mind and behavior began to take form while he was still a young teenager.

Francis Sperry's death resulted in a complete change in lifestyle for the family. Florence Sperry moved to West Hartford, Connecticut, where she found work, and the two brothers went to school there. During his high school years, Sperry was a good but not a brilliant student. At that time, he was more interested in sports. He was quarterback of his high school football team and cocaptain of the basketball team. In track and field, he held the state javelin record for a time. Sperry found sports rewarding and, by the end of his junior year in high school, he had decided to pursue a career in athletics. On his application to Oberlin College, he indicated that his number one choice for a career was that of coach for a college athletic team. His second choice was "medical researcher."

Oberlin College

Roger and his brother Russell both enrolled at Oberlin College and graduated from there. Roger attended on a four-year scholarship and earned three varsity letters. He also was captain of the basketball team. Sperry's undergraduate major was English, and it was not until near the end of his college studies that he enrolled in Introduction to Psychology, a course taught by R. H. Stetson, that was to have a significant impact on his career.

For his graduate training in psychology, Stetson had gone to Harvard University, intending to study with William James, but because of James's shift away from psychology toward religion, he went to work with Hugo Münsterberg (chap. 7, this volume) instead. Although Stetson severed direct connections with James, he maintained some contact with him and was indirectly influenced by James's ideas. After graduating from Harvard, he went to Oberlin, where he became a central figure in the department of psychology. His primary focus of research was on phonics and speech.

On his first day of attendance at Stetson's class in 1933, Sperry jotted down two questions on the first page of his notes—questions that Stetson posed as having great importance to psychology: (a) What is consciousness? (b) Where does behavior come from, nature or nurture? The search for answers to these questions was at the heart of Sperry's program of research that spanned more than 50 years. It is interesting to note that when the APA celebrated its 100th anniversary at its annual convention held in Washington, DC, in 1992, Sperry was the author of one of the keynote addresses (Sperry, 1993a)—which was actually delivered by Theodore Voneida, one of his postdoctoral fellows. The speech was a chronicle of Sperry's commitment to the questions initially posed by Stetson in his course at Oberlin. That subject matter was appropriate because the themes for the APA Centennial Convention included the same two questions.

Later on, Sperry often indicated that his own developing ideas about the human mind had matched those of Stetson and that he would have liked to major in psychology. But by the time he entered Stetson's course, it was too late to switch majors. Instead, he completed his English major and took several courses in psychology. After graduation in 1935, Sperry entered a new master's program in psychology at Oberlin that Stetson directed. He obtained an MS in 1937 with a Stetson-directed thesis, describing research on the relationship between the motor system and the nervous system. As he was finishing his master's thesis, Sperry's interests were beginning to focus on the second of Stetson's questions—about the origins of behavior. That focus took Sperry to the University of Chicago.

The University of Chicago

Sperry came into psychology during the heyday of behaviorism, and was exposed to the ideas of Watson and E. L. Thorndike (chap. 10, *Pioneers I*), both of whom emphasized the importance of learning in the development of behavior and stressed its seemingly infinite plasticity. Sperry's ambition as a graduate student was to study this plasticity. In the 1930s one of the most eminent authorities on plasticity was Paul Weiss in the University of Chicago's Department of Zoology. Sperry enrolled in that department in 1937, with a commitment to study under Weiss. He remained at Chicago until 1941—long enough to earn a PhD and, as it turned out, to prove that Weiss's theory of neural plasticity was incorrect.

Weiss and colleagues believed that the basis of plasticity is neurological, as is evidenced by the ability of the nervous system to recover from injury. Sperry's dissertation (Sperry, 1939, 1941) began to cast serious doubts on this aspect of Weiss's theory. More about this later, in the section on Sperry's research and theorizing.

The Yerkes Primate Research Laboratory

Wanting to pursue his work on neural regeneration further, Sperry went from his PhD at Chicago to work with Karl Lashley (chap. 20, *Pioneers I*) as a postdoctoral fellow at Harvard University. Less than a year after Sperry arrived, however, Lashley moved to Florida, as the new director of the Yerkes Laboratories of Primate Biology in Orange Park (see chap. 7, *Pioneers II*), and Sperry went there with him. The Yerkes lab was a research facility supported by Columbia, Harvard, and Yale Universities, and was dedicated to the study of psychological topics with animals. Many of the research subjects there were chimpanzees, some of them made famous by the research of Henry Nissen (chap. 14, *Pioneers III*) and Kenneth Spence (chap. 17, *Pioneers III*).

Along with Lashley, the resident scientists with whom Sperry regularly interacted included Donald Hebb (chap. 16, *Pioneers II*) and Nissen. In addition, numerous visitors, including Frank Beach (chap. 16, this volume) and Karl Pribram, visited the laboratory with some frequency. Regular contacts and luncheon discussions with the scientists at the Yerkes lab had a strong influence on Sperry's theoretical ideas and his experimental methodology. Many of the research paradigms and surgical techniques that came, years later, to be used regularly in his laboratory at the California Institute of Technology were developed during these formative years at Orange Park. During this period, Sperry not only spent long hours in the laboratory, he also enjoyed fishing and sailing on the St. Johns River. In personal conversations, Sperry recalled those Yerkes years with fondness, and I personally believe that they may have had almost as much of an impact on Sperry as Stetson's mentoring at Oberlin.

Transition Years

After finishing his fellowship at Yerkes, Sperry obtained a tenure-track position as assistant professor in the department of anatomy at the University of Chicago (1946–1953). These were difficult years for Sperry. Soon after his return to Chicago, he and his first wife were divorced. In 1949 he was remarried to Norma Deupree, a bacteriologist who had worked on a project at the Yerkes Laboratories. Later on, in 1949, a routine health examination revealed that he had developed tuberculosis and, in 1950, he took a sabbatical leave to go to Saranac Lake in the Adirondacks for treatment. During his time at Saranac Lake, Sperry focused not only on improving his physical condition but also on developing clearer ideas on the relationship between mind and brain. These deliberations resulted in his first publication addressing issues of consciousness (Sperry, 1952).

Returning to Chicago a year later in good health, Sperry resumed his position as assistant professor, but only for a year. At the termination of his contract, he was denied tenure. After some months of job hunting following his failure to obtain tenure at Chicago, Sperry accepted a position with the National Institutes of Health (NIH) as section chief of the Institute of Neurological Diseases and Blindness. He never actually took up physical residence at NIH, however, because in 1952 he accepted an appointment as associate professor of psychology back at the University of Chicago.

In that same year, Sperry was invited to give the annual Hixon lecture at the California Institute of Technology (Caltech) after Norman Horowitz, a well-known geneticist at Caltech, heard Sperry talk at a growth symposium. That institution was looking for a scientist to do behavioral work within the context of its "hard science" curriculum. Largely because of that talk, Sperry was invited to join the faculty at Caltech. He accepted and, in 1954, became the first Hixon Professor of Psychobiology there. He held this position until his retirement in 1984, at which time the institute's board of trustees awarded him the title of Professor of Psychobiology, Emeritus.

The California Institute of Technology

Initially with only a small laboratory in the Division of Biology and essentially no colleagues in similar areas of study—Caltech had begun to switch its focus to the emerging field of microbiology—Sperry initiated a research program that led eventually to the Nobel Prize. During this time the program was staffed by able assistants, graduate students, postdoctoral fellows, and visiting scientists, and he had continuous funding provided by federal and private agencies. At the peak of his research productivity, Sperry occupied a large wing on the top story of Church Hall at Caltech, where he and his students and colleagues worked on several different projects.

In a typical year, Sperry had several graduate students, postdoctoral fellows, and visiting scientists working with him in small teams. He had no particular favorite student. He recognized their individual strengths and weaknesses and was proud of all of their accomplishments. He often talked in very positive terms about the works of Charles Hamilton, Jerre Levy, Colwyn Trevarthen, Eran Zaidel, and others. In Sperry's view Charles Hamilton was the most underrated person who ever worked with him. He considered Hamilton's work to be careful, well-reasoned, and important.

Personal Characteristics

Sperry did not share much of his personal life with others. Although he enjoyed having parties at his home, he kept a low public profile. Sperry enjoyed square dancing, art (including sculpting), and fishing. The Sperrys bought a four-wheel drive camper with large tires and spent most vacation time after 1975 exploring Baja California, where they fished, snorkeled, and used an inflatable boat to visit the off-shore islands. Fossil collecting was another favorite activity. Sperry discovered one of the world's largest ammonite (spiral seashell) fossils.

One of the best-kept secrets about Sperry is the significant role that his wife of 45-plus years, Norma Deupree, played in his career. She was a close intellectual partner, and provided critiques and proofread some of his writings. Toward the end of his career and with the growing discomforts of lateral sclerosis, Sperry relied even more heavily on her for assistance with intellectual and, eventually, personal needs. Sperry died in 1994 in Pasadena, California. Since his death, his widow has dedicated herself to cataloging his illustrations, speeches, films, publications, and correspondence. The volume of material being catalogued is staggering. To date, that project has taken more than seven years and is ongoing.

Sperry's relationships to students and colleagues were relatively reserved and shy. He preferred staying alone in his office, thinking and working. He clearly felt that his time was valuable and that he should devote his energy and attention to activities that were of interest to him and would result in useful information. Students often talked of going to his office and finding him sitting there quietly thinking. He was considered by many to be difficult to talk to, in part because of his personality. (Not only was he shy but he was always preoccupied with the development of his ideas.) But he would often challenge them with penetrating questions. Among these, his favorites included "is it important?" or "what type of impact might this have?"

Throughout his entire career, Sperry was a prodigious researcher. He accomplished this in part by foresight and in part by sheer tenacity. Demonstrating foresight, in the early part of his career, Sperry kept an intellectual diary containing ideas for research and plans for experiments that provided tests of those ideas. Demonstrating tenacity, Sperry's papers went through many drafts and he worked over each of the many drafts carefully. These attributes were combined with experiments that were simple yet comprehensive.

RESEARCH AND THEORY

Recall that Sperry's ideas about the mind and consciousness began to develop when he was a teenager and his parents introduced him to James's *Principles of Psychology* (1890). In chapter 1 of that book, James defined psychology as the "science of mental life" (p. 1). In chapter 2, in his discussion of functions of the brain, James asserted that "man's consciousness is limited to the hemispheres" (p. 65) and later added that the cortex is "the sole organ of consciousness in man" (p. 66). These ideas, rooted in Sperry's thinking at a very early age, were reinforced in Stetson's Introduction to Psychology course at Oberlin. Eventually they became the foundation of his entire program of research.

Sperry believed that if his research program were to shed light on Stetson's two questions, a comprehensive effort would be necessary. In his hands, this effort took shape as a program of systematic investigation that focused on what Sperry called four "turnarounds," because they were phases of his research program that reflected significant shifts in methodology. The following sections present these phases in chronological order.

Nerve Regeneration and Plasticity

Sperry's first phase of research, nerve regeneration and plasticity, spanned the years from 1938–1939 through the mid-1940s. Sperry's approach to the issue of the plasticity of the nervous system was aimed at answering Stetson's question of where behavior originated: in nature (heredity and biology) or in nurture (experience and learning). At bottom, this came down to questions about the causes of individual differences in behavior. Early on, Sperry began to believe that his thesis supervisor, Paul Weiss, as well as most psychologists, attributed too much of the individual variability in behavior to nurture and too little to nature.

Sperry's initial work on this topic was the foundation for his doctoral dissertation, for which he worked on a variety of carefully planned studies, initially with rats and later with other species. Sperry's basic premise was that if the nervous system is as malleable as most psychologists, as well as Weiss, believed, then what an organism learns should be available to the animal even after drastic alterations of its response capabilities. Sperry (1939) first tested this idea by transposing muscles in rats.

The fundamental idea in this research was the following: Movement is controlled by excitatory and inhibitory processes in the brain that inhibit certain muscles and excite others. For example, the operation of a limb requires the inhibition of abductor muscles so that the extensors can be activated. Now suppose that these muscles were switched, so that the excitatory and inhibitory impulses now went, respectively, to the previously inhibited and excited muscles, what should be the behavioral consequences? Weiss had concluded that nerve fibers are interchangeable and that peripheral neural structures could be molded according to the task involved. Organisms should be able to learn to use those muscles in their new arrangement.

Specifically, what Sperry did was to train rats to make a response that required the use of the to-be-transposed muscles. Taking extreme care with both the surgical techniques and the methods of training used to test the effects of his procedures, he cut these muscles and transposed them within the same limb. Then he tried to retrain the animals to make the original response. He found that regardless of the training strategy, the animals were never able to relearn proper use of their limbs.

Sperry then went on to similar studies with sensory nerves and sensory organs. One of the most dramatic results of this research came from work in which he cut the optic nerves of newts and rotated their eyeballs 180 degrees. After the animals had recovered from surgery, they behaved as if their world had been turned upside down. This behavior persisted and was unaffected by experience. Despite the opportunity to obtain food by moving in the direction opposite to that in which it could be seen, the animals never learned to approach it. Sperry proposed that what had happened was that the neural pathways regrew after cutting, but attached themselves back to their original site because each nerve fiber has a chemical marker that leads the cut portion of the fiber to reconnect with the original fiber. This theory, which he called *chemo-affinity*, was the foundation for more recent work on the nerve-growth factor as well as the work of a Nobel Prize winner and Sperry colleague, Rita Levi-Montalcini.

Equipotentiality

The equipotentiality phase of Sperry's research program covered the period from the mid-1940s through the mid-1950s. It was the shortest of the four phases in his career. It involved research that eventually would disprove one the basic theses about the functioning of the nervous system of his postdoctoral supervisor, Karl Lashley.

In a series of experiments, Lashley (1929) began by training rats in mazes. He then damaged different amounts of cortex in different places in the brains of different rats. After the rats had recovered from this surgery, he tested them to determine the effect of the location and amount of brain damage on the rats' retention of the maze habit. He found that the deficits in memory depended much more on the amount of cortex damaged than it did on the location of that damage. Those results led Lashley to his equipotentiality hypothesis: The cortex functions as a whole and the various parts of it contribute almost equally to behavior. Lashley suggested that equipotentiality is a function of neural integration created by the spreading of electrical fields. Electrical activity produced by external stimulation, on arriving at its projection area in the cerebral cortex, spreads horizontally over the entire cortex, giving the whole brain access to any information that is associated with the stimulus producing these effects.

Sperry's experiments on this topic were attempts to block the spread of the hypothetical impulses. At first he used surgery and made longitudinal cuts about 2.4 mm in length in the cortex. But in contrast to what Lashley would predict, the animals' behavior was not affected. Later, he went on to work with visual pattern discrimination, using dielectric plates, mica plates, and tantalum wire implanted in the cortex, to short-circuit the spread of impulses. In some of these experiments, Sperry used cats and simple visual discrimination tasks. These procedures had no greater effect than surgery, and Sperry suspected—and this was later proven—that the spreading of impulses could and did occur but that the spread is vertical rather than horizontal, as Lashley had proposed. This research laid the foundation for the later studies of the two Harvard neuroscientists, David Hubel and Torsten Weisel, who worked on the visual cortex. For their intriguing work, Hubel and Weisel shared the Nobel Prize in Physiology and Medicine with Sperry in 1981.

Split-Brain Research

After working with a variety of species, from simple to complex, and after exploring the issue with a variety of motor and sensory functions, Sperry concluded that, contrary to the opinions of some psychologists, essentially no behavior that is controlled by the peripheral nervous system is malleable or plastic. The question remained, however, about whether this generalization applies to the central nervous system, particularly the cerebral hemispheres. To investigate this question, Sperry had to figure out how to cut fibers in the brain and how to measure the effects of such cutting. This is how the corpus callosum, hemispheric asymmetries, and Sperry's third "turnaround" came into the picture.

Beginning with his interactions with Lashley in the 1940s, Sperry became intrigued with the role of the corpus callosum, the massive fiber bundle that connects the two cerebral hemispheres. Lashley had joked that this structure exists for the sole purpose of keeping the two sides of the brain from sagging together. But Sperry had read reports of investigators who had severed the corpus callosum to control intractable epilepsy. Also, although the publications were not accessible, he had heard about similar nonhuman animal research in Russia. These scraps of information hinted that the corpus callosum did more than that and suggested the possibility of investigating the interhemispheric transfer of information in organisms with the corpus callosum severed. This phase of Sperry's research spanned the longest time-span. It began in 1953 and continued through the 1980s.

Students and Colleagues.   Sperry began his research in interhemispheric transfer of information in organisms with Ronald E. Myers at Chicago, working first with cats. Later, but still during the 1950s, he extended it to research with monkeys. Then, in 1960 at Caltech, he moved on to human patients, working with a host of students and colleagues. This program of research produced the most comprehensive body of information on the functioning of the cerebral hemispheres to date. Sperry is most often recognized for this work (see Sperry, 1981, 1982).

One of Sperry's most important colleagues at Caltech—and throughout his entire career—was Joseph Bogen, a neurosurgical resident who was working under the supervision of Philip Vogel in the early 1960s. He had followed Sperry's work with nonhuman animals and he encouraged Sperry to extend his split-brain (a term coined by Sperry) research to a human patient, a young veteran of the Korean War who suffered from severe and intractable epilepsy. Bogen hypothesized that a split-brain operation might reduce his seizures.

Accepting Bogen's suggestion, Sperry designed a series of tests and experiments that could be carried out on people with split-brain surgery, something that had not been considered in any detail before. After devising the methods of investigation and completing necessary preparation, a graduate student, Michael Gazzaniga, was recruited to administer the psychological tests. A myriad of political problems led to Gazzaniga's becoming senior author of the first publication on this historic line of research. This first study by Gazzaniga, Bogen, and Sperry (1965)was followed later with approximately 70 studies of a total of 16 patients—although only about half of them were tested regularly—ranging in age from adolescence to late adulthood.

A number of students and fellow scientists came to work on this research. Robert Doty, Ronald Myers, Nancy Miner, Mitchell Glickstein, Charles Hamilton, and Ronald Meyer focused on the animal work, whereas others, such as Giovanni Berlucchi, Harold Gordon, Jerre Levy, Richard Mark, Brenda Milner, and Eran Zaidel, did the human studies. Colwyn Trevarthen was unique in that he evenly divided his time between animals and humans. Others such as Donald M. Mackay and Brenda Milner were frequent visitors to the laboratory.

Research Findings.   The two hemispheres of the forebrain are connected by a number of bundles of fibers called commissures, the largest of which is the corpus callosum that connects the cortical parts of the hemispheres. In a normal person, information in one cortex quickly reaches the other through these interhemispheric connections, allowing information from the two halves of the body (and the external world) to be coordinated. As a treatment of last resort, these commissures are sometimes severed in cases of severe epilepsy, a chronic disorder in which an "electrical storm" spreads through the brain, causing convulsions and loss of consciousness. Severing the connections prevents the spread of this massive disturbance to both halves of the brain and often alleviates the symptoms. In his research with these patients, Sperry carefully severed the corpus callosum as well as the other connections, including the optic chiasm, to prevent the crossing of visual information from one hemisphere to the other. In effect, each hemisphere was completely isolated from the other.

When the two hemispheres are separated, the person becomes "two individuals." The right-sided one, connected to the left hemisphere, can talk, read, understand speech, and control the right hand, arm, and leg. The left-sided one, connected to the right hemisphere, is totally without spoken language but can control the left hand, arm, and leg, and perform certain nonverbal perceptual and motor tasks.

Given the extent of damage, what is perplexing about split-brain patients is that, to the untrained observer, they look normal and appear to behave normally. Special tests reveal, however, that the consequences of severing the corpus callosum in these patients are much more serious than appearances suggest. To understand these consequences, it is important to remember several things about the neurological status of split-brain patients.

First, as in people with normal brains, stimulation on the right side of the body continues to be projected to the left side of the brain and stimulation on the left is projected to the right. Also the left and right hemispheres continue to control acts performed by the right and left hands, respectively. The transection of the commissures only separates these connections; it does not change them.

Second, as in most other people, the left hemisphere in split-brain patients contains the language area and usually tends to be more verbal; the right hemisphere tends to be more spatial. Neither hemisphere is totally dominant, however. The left hemisphere is dominant for some things and sometimes can take over but the right hemisphere is intelligent and independent in its own right.

Third, what split-brain patients lose is the ability to integrate the functions of the two halves of the brain. The loss of the coordination between the language abilities of the first individual with the sensorimotor capabilities of the second is the key to understanding many split-brain phenomena.

The right-hemisphere/left-hand individual is better than the left-hemisphere/right-hand one on tasks involving spatial perception, such as copying designs by arranging colored blocks. For this reason, split-brain patients are usually unable to make these copies. Although the right-brain/left-hand individual solves them easily, the left-brain/right-hand person often tries to "help" and undoes the superior accomplishments of the right-brain/left-hand person (Gazzaniga, Bogen, & Sperry, 1965). Such observations led Sperry to realize that two brains are not better than one. In fact, two brains are inferior unless they work together. The integration of the two hemispheres is critically important for purposeful behavior, and for the well-being of the individual—in the case of split-brain patients, two individuals.

In everyday life outside the laboratory, these two individual minds tend to get along well because each of them is attentive to the activities of the other, and each makes use of the other's skills in ways that sometimes become apparent in the laboratory. For example, in one patient, when the investigator asked one of the two minds what the other one had experienced, the left-hemisphere would often make wrong guesses about what the right hemisphere had seen. In those cases when the left hemisphere gave a wrong response about what the right hemisphere had seen, the right-hemisphere individual would shake his head, and the left would then say, "No, I mean. . . . " But as you might anticipate, cohesive behavior is not always present. One morning, one split-brain patient found his left hand casually unzipping the zipper in his pants that his right had just zipped up.

Although both hemispheres in these patients have emotions, there are differences. The left-hemisphere patients can verbally describe their emotions and the reasons for having them; the right-hemisphere patient cannot. Moreover, the quality of the emotions can be different in the two hemispheres. However, this does not imply that the right is incapable of understanding or expressing emotion. Subsequent studies and clinical observations suggests that the right hemisphere is more "emotional" than the left. In his Nobel lecture (1981), Sperry summarized these findings and cautioned against the over-simplified interpretation of complex neurobehavioral phenomena.

The Psychology of Consciousness

When the two hemispheres are connected, as in individuals with normal brains, these two personalities merge and a "unified consciousness" emerges. The fourth and final "turn-around" in Sperry's program of research, which concentrated on consciousness, began with a publication in 1952. It gained formality with a talk on his ideas about consciousness at Caltech in approximately 1962. This phase of his thinking continued through the rest of his career, with some of his articles being published posthumously. Sperry believed this was his greatest insight, an insight that most individuals—starting with his colleagues at Caltech—clearly did not appreciate.

The "Consciousness Revolution"

As early as 1963, Sperry suggested that consciousness is the product of a unified brain. Neural activity gives rise to consciousness when that activity forms a pattern that organizes the complex interactions among individual neurons. Sperry thought of these ideas as a "consciousness revolution" that included the so-called "cognitive revolution." He believed that its importance rivaled that of the Copernican and Newtonian revolutions:

> Reconceived in the new outlook, subjective mental states become functionally interactive and essential for a full explanation of conscious behavior. . . . Reductive microdeterministic views of personhood and the physical world are replaced in favor of a more wholistic, top-down view in which the higher, more evolved entities throughout nature, including mental, vital, social, and other high-order forces, gain their due recognition along with physics and chemistry. (Sperry, 1993a, p. 879)

Moral Values.   In this final phase of his career, Sperry began to consider that consciousness may be the solution to the long-standing problems of humankind and that it may provide the basis for the development of a moral code (Sperry, 1993b). Sperry was a student of Christianity and the other religions that, in all their geographical settings and for several thousand years, have provided moral codes that dictate the qualities of behavior that are good and bad (Sperry, 1988). In the case of Christianity, Sperry believed that its moral code is outdated, especially for Western culture, however useful it may have been for life 2000 years ago. For example, Sperry saw the problem of overpopulation as an unfortunate consequence of Christianity's tenet to "go forth and multiply." To Sperry, such a creed seemed irresponsible and dangerous in light of evidence suggesting that, by the year 2009, the world's population will have exceeded its natural resources.

Sperry's proposed solutions to such problems were simple yet elegant: If individuals were to adopt a value system based on science, problems of this sort would disappear. Sperry argued that contemporary science should help to formulate a viable moral system. Because it is a newer enterprise than religion, until now science has provided little more than facts. It has played a descriptive, not a prescriptive, role. Sperry insisted that science should be able to do more than that. It should replace traditional moral codes by providing them with empirical rather than merely ideological bases. Science has the potential to become the final authority available to humankind for developing beliefs for people to live by (Sperry, 1975). If science replaced religious, nationalistic, and related forms of guidance for human behavior, the ultimate goals of human existence would be more efficiently realized (Sperry, 1988). Sperry believed these goals to be the preservation of the biosphere and the species.

PRODUCTIVITY, RECOGNITION, AND IMPACT

As a youngster, Sperry was a good but not brilliant student and an unassuming athlete who hoped to become a college coach or perhaps a "medical researcher."

After a chance reading of James's (1890) *Principles of Psychology* and subsequent exposure to psychology at Oberlin, he settled on something like his second choice and began a career in neuropsychology that spanned half a century. The experiments he designed and performed were simple, elegant, and directly aimed at answering the seemingly unanswerable philosophical questions that lie at the foundation of psychology: the nature of consciousness and the origins of the mind. He always interpreted his results systematically, integrating previous concepts and advancing the field toward issues never previously considered.

Productivity

Sperry's output was enormous. On average he published about 10 articles a year—approximately 300 publications, of which he was usually the sole author. In addition he served as a mentor for about 100 graduate students, postdoctoral fellows, and visiting scientists. What may be unique about this contribution is that Sperry made it despite a reserved, shy personality, and significant self-doubt. As I reported in my obituary of Sperry (Puente, 1995), he questioned his impact on the world, possibly because of his incessant questioning and his impatience with less than excellence and his irreverence for traditional views of the world.

Some of Sperry's output was triggered by his discontent with the lack of applicability of science. He looked at the quagmire of problems bedeviling the modern world and concluded that science rather than religion is their solution—society's "way out." He fervently believed that humanity could and should preserve the future and that psychology could and should lead the way for other disciplines to follow. He believed that psychology, with its roots in the study of the mind, provided an exceptional and robust paradigm. Specifically the cognitive revolution, which he thought of as the "consciousness revolution," provides insight into probable solutions to age-old philosophical questions of the mind and practical solutions to problems that could affect the future of humankind (e.g., overpopulation).

Recognition

Psychology, science generally, and even western culture all recognized the importance of Sperry's scientific work. He was a member of the American Psychological Association, the National Academy of Sciences, the Pontifical Academy of Sciences, the British Royal Society, and the USSR Academy of Sciences. He received honorary degrees from Cambridge University (1972), the University of Chicago (1976), Rockefeller University (1980), and Oberlin College (1982).

Sperry also received numerous awards (18 major ones) honoring his contributions, among them the Howard Crosby Warren Medal (1969) from the Society of Experimental Psychologists, the Passano Award (1973) from the Passano

Foundation, the Karl Lashley Award (1976) from the American Philosophical Association, the Wolf Prize in Medicine (1979) from the Wolf Foundation, the Lasker Medical Research Award (1979) from the Albert and Mary Lasker Foundation, the National Medal of Science (1989), and the Lifetime Achievement Award (1993) from the American Psychological Association. Most notable of this type of recognition was the Nobel Prize for Physiology and Medicine (1981). Sperry is the only person to have won a Nobel Prize who has received a degree in psychology (his master's degree from Oberlin). Others, such as Ivan Pavlov, Niko Tinbergen, Konrad Lorenz, and more recently Herbert Simon, were trained, worked, and published in other fields.

Impact

As can happen, Sperry's impact on psychology has been less than might be expected from the honors he received. Psychology has accepted Sperry's work, but only in a circumscribed way. Almost all psychologists know about Sperry's split-brain studies and the resulting understanding of hemispheric asymmetries. But, as a field, psychology has not fully assimilated either his nerve regeneration work, his ideas about consciousness, or his neurophilosophy with the moral implications it implies.

When Sperry (1952) first proposed his studies of mind and brain, his ideas were well-received. In his presentation at the Caltech Division of Biology Seminar in 1962, however, in which he provided greater detail on several aspects of his theory, including his notions about consciousness, those ideas were met with skepticism. To Sperry this was a personal and intellectual disappointment. To him, the cognitive or consciousness revolution seemed to rival the Copernican and Newtonian revolutions in importance and potential impact and he was puzzled when his thoughts were neglected, rejected, and ignored. Probably the most important reason for this reaction resides in psychology's half-century focus on behaviorism with its emphasis on the environment and learning. Such a psychology would tend to underestimate the importance of Sperry's findings on the role of nature and consciousness.

CONCLUSION

Sperry's program of research focused on four ideas that he called "turnarounds": nerve regeneration and plasticity, equipotentiality, split-brain studies, and the psychology of consciousness. Superficially, these four areas appear distinctly different. Indeed, the research in each phase was conducted for the purpose of answering very different questions. In a broader sense, however, there were connections. Sperry believed that the first two to three phases of his program indicated, especially with nonhuman animals, that behavior is not very malleable and that, contrary to modal psychological opinion, behavior comes much more from heredity than environment—the answer to R. H. Stetson's second question. And all of his research laid the foundation to ask Stetson's first question, What is consciousness, and to the answer, "Consciousness" is an expression of the integrated functioning of the brain which has the power to organize behavior for the betterment of humankind.

REFERENCES

Gazzaniga, M. S., Bogen, J. E., & Sperry, R. W. (1965). Observations on visual perception after disconnection of the cerebral hemispheres in man. *Brain, 88,* 231–236.

Hamilton, C. R. (1998). Preface—Special issue in honor of Roger W. Sperry. *Neuropsychologist, 36,* 953–954.

James, W. (1890). *Principles of psychology.* New York: Holt.

Lashley, K. S. (1929). *Brain mechanisms and intelligence.* Chicago: University of Chicago Press.

Puente, A. E. (1995). Roger Wolcott Sperry (1913–1994). *American Psychologist, 50,* 940–941.

Sperry, R. W. (1939). Functional results of muscle transplantation in the hind limb of the albino rat. *The Anatomical Record, 75,* 51.

Sperry, R. W. (1941). *Functional results of crossing nerves and transposing muscles in the fore and hind limbs of the rat: A dissertation submitted to the faculty of the Division of Biological Sciences in candidacy for the degree of Doctor of Philosophy.* Chicago: University of Chicago Libraries.

Sperry, R. W. (1952). Neurology and the mind–brain problem. *American Scientist, 40,* 281–312.

Sperry, R. W. (1975). In search of the psyche. In F. G. Worden, J. P. Swazey, & G. Adelman (Eds.). *The neurosciences: Paths of discovery.* Cambridge: MIT Press.

Sperry, R. W. (1981). Some effects of disconnecting the cerebral hemispheres. Nobel Lecture. *Les Prix Nobel.* Stockholm, Sweden: Almqvist and Wiksell.

Sperry, R. W. (1982). Some effects of disconnecting the cerebral hemispheres (Nobel Lecture). *Science, 217,* 1223–1226.

Sperry, R. W. (1988). Psychology's mentalist paradigm and the religion/science tension. *American Psychologist, 43,* 607–613.

Sperry, R. W. (1993a). The impact and promise of the cognitive revolution. *American Psychologist, 48,* 878–885.

Sperry, R. W. (1993b). *Science and moral priority.* New York: Columbia University Press.

Trevarthen, C. (Ed.). (1993). *Brain circuits and functions of the mind: Essays in honor of Roger W. Sperry.* Cambridge: Cambridge University Press.

Chapter 20

Hans Eysenck: Apostle of the London School

Arthur R. Jensen

Hans Jurgen Eysenck (1916–1997) was probably the world's most famous psychologist of his period, rivaled in renown only by Jean Piaget (chap. 9, *Pioneers III*) and B. F. Skinner (chap. 16, *Pioneers III*). In Britain he became a well-known public figure because of his many popular books, interviews in the mass media, and appearances on radio and television. Almost from the beginning of his brilliant career, spanning 55 years, he was a popular and controversial subject of conversation in British psychological circles. He was one of those rare individuals who become the subject of anecdotes—some apocryphal, many true—that express a gamut of emotions ranging from extravagant vituperation, to wonderment, to veneration. In this respect, with the possible exception of Sigmund Freud (chap. 4, *Pioneers I*) there probably has been no other psychologist like him. Eysenck himself would have hated any other kind of comparison with Freud, because he was a leading critic of Freudian psychoanalytic theory and practice in the second half of the 20th century.

CHARACTER AND REPUTATION

One of his colleagues at the University of London's Institute of Psychiatry, where Eysenck spent his career, once remarked that he never thought of Eysenck as a real person but rather as some kind of phenomenon or institution. I thought it a perceptive insight. But why would anyone say this about a person who, to all appearances, was perfectly normal, steady, reasonable, decent, and kindly?

---

*Photo of Hans Eysenck courtesy of Arthur R. Jensen.

The answer undoubtedly has to do with Eysenck's incredible level of activity and productivity, emanating continuously from a seemingly quiet, introverted (but not in the least shy), even-tempered, unhurried man. The amount of work he accomplished day after day was incredible. Eysenck usually gave the impression of not being busy. Somehow it appeared that everything he did was exceedingly easy for him to do. Colleagues who might take a week or two to write a journal article, a book chapter, or a research proposal would see him routinely perform such tasks in a single morning's session of dictation to his secretary or a dictating machine. He dictated at the speed with which one normally reads aloud—without back-tracking, interrupting, or correcting. When I was in his department he dictated a complete book during his two weeks summer vacation—one complete chapter every morning! Once, when I asked how it was possible for him to do all this, he said it was a gift for which he was most grateful. He said that each chapter was already thought out before he left for work, and rehearsed while he walked to the office. There, it was simply a matter of "reading out" what was already in his head. His expository prose was notably clear and highly readable—a "natural style," he called it. Remarkably, English was not his native language, but his third, after German and French.

During his career, Eysenck wrote 61 books, edited 10 more, and published more than 1000 journal articles, reviews, and book chapters. One of the recognized measures of scientists' influence is the frequency of citations of their publications in the professional literature. According to the Institute for Scientific Information, which publishes the *Social Science Citation Index* (SSCI), Eysenck's SSCI citation count is exceeded by only three individuals: Freud, Karl Marx, and Jean Piaget, in that order. After Piaget died in 1980, Eysenck was the most frequently cited living psychologist.

In spite of his prodigious output, Eysenck's writing took only about half his daily working time. He founded the graduate Department of Psychology, with both a research division and a clinical training division, in the Institute of Psychiatry at the old Maudsley Hospital, Britain's leading psychiatric center; he was its head for 30 years, until his official retirement at age 65. Eysenck was also chief psychologist at the Royal Bethlehem (from which the word, "bedlam," came) Hospital, England's oldest and largest psychiatric facility. He founded and edited two psychological journals, *Behaviour Research and Therapy* and *Personality and Individual Differences*. He regularly taught courses for the resident physicians in psychiatric training at Maudsley and held seminars for graduate students and the many postdoctoral fellows who spent a year or two in his department.

Eysenck and his wife Sybil also held "at homes" every Wednesday evening for his faculty and postdocs to discuss their own research and the related literature. He gave countless invited addresses at psychological conferences and lectured at numerous universities, not only in Europe and North America but in such far-flung places as Australia, Egypt, Hong Kong, India, Israel, Mexico, Singapore, South Africa, and South America. He was an excellent and memorable lecturer, a model of organization and lucidity, typically with a bit of showmanship thrown in that made his appearances events that audiences talked about long afterward. Although he was invariably polite, Eysenck was impatient with those who rejected the idea that personality could be studied objectively and quantitatively in the manner of the natural sciences. The calm, polished, and sharp manner in which he routed opponents who challenged him was legendary; it left some spectators in awe while others were amused or angered.

While working for three years (1956–1958 and 1964–1965) in Eysenck's department, I observed his daily routine. He walked to his office every day, arriving regularly at 8:30 a.m. He had a large correspondence, and as a "warm-up" dictated answers to all the letters in each day's mail, reading each one and answering it almost simultaneously. His desk was always perfectly clean; secretaries brought things in, he acted on them then and there, and then they took them out. I never saw work pile up on him. Even after returning from two weeks abroad, he would clean up a huge pile of mail in just a morning's session of dictation. If his correspondence was not enough warm-up, he would dictate a letter to the editor of one of the London dailies or a popular magazine, but not necessarily about anything psychological. One day his secretary told me he had dictated such a letter explaining his ideas for solving the traffic and parking problems in central London. A member of his staff once remarked that Eysenck had more opinions about more different things than anyone since George Bernard Shaw. After these warm-up exercises, he dictated materials for a book, a journal article, a research proposal, or a progress report to one of the granting agencies that supported him. While dictating, he seldom sat down at his desk, but paced around in his office. I asked him once if so much continuous dictation ever tired him. He gave a typical Eysenckian answer. Pointing to his jaw, he said, "Yes, I suppose this gets a little tired sometimes" (never his brain, of course!).

At the midmorning coffee break, when everyone went to the cafeteria, Eysenck never drank coffee or tea. He used this time to permit students or staff to discuss technical or research problems with him. He usually skipped lunch and, during the lunch hour, played tennis or squash. A lifelong sportsman, he was a serious and intensely competitive player. Afternoons were usually devoted to receiving his many professional visitors, giving lectures, conducting seminars, editing journals, and conferring with doctoral students on their dissertation projects. For a busy man, he was amazingly accessible. He avoided faculty meetings, which he considered a waste of everyone's time, and always had an excuse to absent himself from routine academic affairs. As a benevolent autocrat, he simply ran the department in an unobtrusive and somewhat *laissez-faire* manner, once saying that he confined all his administrative chores to the last hour of every Friday afternoon. He always walked home from work between about 4:30 and 5:00 P.M.

Eysenck seldom took work home with him but spent his after-dinner hours reading. He was a voracious and speedy reader, and read widely in psychology and the other sciences (particularly physics), as well as the philosophy of science and detective novels. His lifelong habit of omnivorous reading showed in his conversation and in his writing. He was immensely erudite. His quick grasp and ready memory for everything he read were amazing, as one would discover in discussing one's own publications with him. Some colleagues have called him a genius, but he insisted that he was not. He generally applied that exalted term to the likes of Shakespeare, Newton, Beethoven, and Einstein. Genius or not, his exceptional ability, quickness of mind, and intellectual grasp were striking to all who knew him.

BIOGRAPHY

The story of Eysenck's life is detailed in his autobiography (1997) and in a biography by Gibson (1981). Eysenck was born on March 4, 1916, in Berlin when Germany was engaged in World War I and headed for a catastrophic defeat just two years later. Hans grew up during the turmoil of postwar Germany. Both of his parents were talented theatrical performers, his father a popular stage actor, his mother a beautiful film star. At the age of 8, Hans himself appeared as an actor in a movie in which he played the part of a boy who reconciled his estranged parents. In real life, however, Hans's own parents were estranged. Because their professional engagements required frequent travel, they left Hans in Berlin with his maternal grandmother, who cared for him throughout most of his childhood and adolescence.

Despite the generally hard conditions that prevailed in postwar Germany, Hans's parents and grandmother provided a comfortable environment that was rich in German literary and musical culture. Although Hans was amply exposed to classical and operatic music, he never took a real interest in it. I noticed in my several attempts to have conversations with him about music that he had a surprising amount of knowledge about music for a person who did not listen to it but that this knowledge was purely verbal and factual, not really musical. As far as I could tell, he neither possessed classical recordings nor attended concerts, which abounded in London, one of the musical capitals of the world. In discussing this with him in his later years, he explained that he once volunteered to take an experimental test of basic musical aptitudes, which revealed that his pitch discrimination was exceedingly poor—he could not discriminate even half-tones. It is known that individuals with poor pitch discrimination rarely become classical music lovers and, of course, never become professional musicians. Eysenck was not lacking in aesthetic sense, however. He derived much pleasure from literature, particularly the great German and English poets, whose works he began reading in his youth.

What is known of Eysenck's schooling in Berlin reveals nothing remark-able, although evidently he was a bright pupil. He skipped one grade and grad-uated at age 17 from Berlin's top academic high school, the all-boys Prinz Heinrich Wilhelm Realgymnasium. As a student, he excelled in sports, par-ticularly boxing and tennis—he remained an avid tennis player and played al-most daily until he was past 80. In the academic sphere, he was attracted to the "new physics" of relativity and quantum theory and considered a career in physics. Though Eysenck was apparently an all-round excellent student, there is no evidence that he was conspicuously gifted in mathematics, as were so many of the eminent physicists, particularly the Nobel Prize winners. Hav-ing discussed many issues in statistics, psychometrics, and quantitative ge-netics with Eysenck, however, it is my impression that he was probably near the 99th percentile among psychologists in quantitative ability, but this math-ematical expertise seemed to reflect high general ability rather than a special talent.

Eysenck's famous predecessors in the London School, Charles Spearman (chap. 6, this volume) and Cyril Burt, probably possessed a special talent in math-ematics, as did America's greatest psychometrician, L. L. Thurstone (chap. 6, *Pi-oneers III*). These three were the great pioneers of psychometric science and sta-tistical psychology. Along with the British statistician Karl Pearson (1857–1936), they enlarged on the highly creative but embryonic ideas about mental mea-surement originated by Sir Francis Galton (chap. 1, *Pioneers I*).

When the Nazi party came to power and Hitler was declared chancellor in 1933, Eysenck was in his senior year in the Gymnasium. He had applied for admission to the University of Berlin to major in physics, but he seemed al-ready to have developed a contempt for the racist doctrines and totalitarian politics of the Nazi party. When he discovered that a condition for admission to the university was joining Hitler's SS and wearing its black military uni-form, he refused, certain that he could not in good conscience consent to that condition.

Eysenck's mother, who had divorced Eysenck's father and married a movie producer who was Jewish, emigrated to France when Hitler came to power. Sens-ing the unhappy prospects of living under the political conditions in Nazi Ger-many, Eysenck soon followed. There he entered the University of Dijon, where he studied French literature. Because of his defection from Hitler's Germany, many have mistakenly believed that Eysenck himself was Jewish. Actually, his parents were Lutheran Christians and he never adopted any religion. His only Jewish relatives were his stepfather and his second wife, Sybil, the daughter of a noted Austrian concert violinist Max Rostal.

In 1934, at age 18, Eysenck left France for England, where he spent a se-mester at the University of Exeter to improve his English in preparation for the entrance exam for the University of London. On gaining admission to Univer-sity College, London, intending to study physics, he was dismayed to discover that his high school transcript lacked certain prerequisites for enrollment in the physics department and that enrollment quotas were already filled in all the other sciences except psychology. Hence it was entirely by accident and default that Eysenck got into psychology, a field that he did not even know existed until entering University College.

The head of the Psychology Department at University College was Sir Cyril Burt, one of Britain's most noted psychologists and one of only three who were ever knighted—the other two were Sir Frederick Bartlett (chap. 9, this volume) and Sir Godfrey Thomson. The psychology that Burt taught immediately captivated Eysenck's interest and enthusiasm. In his 88th year, Burt told me that, during his long tenure, of all his students Eysenck was "the brightest and most industrious" (personal communication, July 1970). He encouraged Eysenck to study for a PhD. Eysenck did so, and also worked as Burt's research assistant. He received the PhD in 1942 at age 26. His dissertation was an experimental study of the objective measurement of the aesthetic properties of visual figures.

While Eysenck was a student, Britain went to war with Germany, and horrific times, including the Luftwaffe's nightly air raids on London, lay ahead. Because of his German background and his official war-time status as an "enemy alien," Eysenck had difficulty securing employment commensurate with his qualifications. His outstanding performance as a graduate student, however, had come to the attention of the distinguished educational psychologist Philip E. Vernon, who was employed by the armed forces personnel research department during the war. Vernon recommended Eysenck for a position as research psychologist at the Mill Hill Emergency Hospital, a large psychiatric facility serving the British armed forces during the war. Eysenck obtained a grant from the Rockefeller Foundation, which provided funds to hire three clinical psychologists as research assistants. During his four years at Mill Hill (1942–1946), he published approximately 30 research papers in areas related to its psychiatric mission—clinical assessment and psychiatric diagnosis, hypnosis, neuroses, personality differences, and social attitudes.

The chief at Mill Hill was one of Britain's leading psychiatrists, Sir Aubrey Lewis, who at the end of the war became head of the Maudsley Hospital and was appointed professor of psychiatry. Having been impressed by Eysenck's work at Mill Hill, Lewis invited him to the Maudsley as director of its psychology department which, under Eysenck's instigation and with Lewis's backing, was granted full status as a graduate department of psychology in the University of London in 1950, with Eysenck appointed as Reader (equivalent to associate professor). He was elevated to full professor in 1955, at age 38, the youngest person ever to occupy a professorial chair of psychology in a British university. With the exception of the years 1950 and 1954, when he was a visiting professor at the University of Pennsylvania and the University of California, Berkeley, Eysenck spent his entire postwar career as professor and head of the psychology department in the Institute of Psychiatry. In number of journal publications and their frequency of citation, Eysenck's department became by far the most productive in Britain and ranked among the world's top psychology departments. To everyone who observed the inner workings of Eysenck's department, it was obvious that its unique character, ferment, air of excitement, and unusual productivity and fame were attributable in large part to Eysenck's own diligence and the powerful influence that stemmed from what can only be called his phenomenal and unflagging mental energy.

Although British universities require faculty to retire at age 65, Eysenck's retirement activities, except for teaching and administration, continued as usual. Because he needed more work space for his research, his personal secretary, his library, and his extensive reprint files than the Institute could provide after his retirement, he bought a flat near the Institute, which served as his workplace for the last 16 years of his life.

When I saw Eysenck in 1996, four months after his 80th birthday, he appeared in excellent health. He had just finished another book (his last published work, as it turned out) and was beginning another on health and personality. He was full of plans and enthusiasm for his future projects. That summer, I attended the talk he gave at the Eighth International Congress on Personality in Ghent, Belgium, in which he explained his theory of individual differences in achievement as a multiplicative interaction of cognitive abilities and personality factors. I was struck by how masterfully it was delivered—with all the clarity of thought and organization I had witnessed in his lectures some 40 years earlier. He was still the same Eysenck. But then, only two months later, while playing tennis with his son, he was troubled by double vision. A battery of diagnostic tests revealed a brain tumor, calling for immediate surgery. It proved to be malignant, and the ensuing brain operations to control the growing cancer took a terrible toll, rendering the last year of his life an absolute hell. A partial paralysis confined him to a wheelchair. He was unable to read or write and barely able to speak. Yet he fully understood everything that went on around him and was amazingly brave and dignified. In my visit to him, just two months before he died, I explained a rather complicated study I had recently completed and showed him the graphs for the article I had written about it. He studied them for a minute or so, then asked some very pointed and insightful questions about the study, albeit with some difficulty in speaking. His critical faculty was still sharp.

Less than a year before Eysenck's misfortune, the organization he was instrumental in founding—and of which he was the first president—the International Society for the Study of Personality and Individual Differences, planned a special dinner to honor him at its convention in July 1997 in Aarhus, Denmark. Eysenck's condition made it seem impossible for him to travel. But, defying all the challenges, and against his family's wishes, Eysenck insisted on going. And of course he did go. He appeared at the convention's dinner in his honor with characteristic dignity and attentive presence. The after-dinner ceremony included encomiums by colleagues and the presentation of a handsome 800-page Festschrift of substantive commentaries summarizing his lifetime contributions to the field (Nyborg, 1997). It was an intensely moving occasion. And it was the last time I saw the great man. In less than two months, on September 4, 1997, he died at home in Herne Hill, where he had lived for 42 years, just one mile away from the Institute of Psychiatry.

SCIENTIFIC CONTRIBUTIONS

Before summarizing Eysenck's contributions to the various fields that interested him, something should be said about why was he was so controversial, both in the psychological community and in the popular media. This reaction stems from several factors.

First, Eysenck typically took skeptical or contrary positions on psychological topics in which there were strong vested interests in some particular viewpoint—for example, on the nature–nurture issue. He was a doubter and iconoclast about beliefs that were held most dearly by many psychologists and the general public. His views were not rigid or dogmatic, but at any given time he would take a strong stand on an issue. He was clear, unambiguous, and did not mince words or pull his punches. He refused to straddle fences or walk fine lines on any subject. He explicated his own views cogently and with a relentless logic that frustrated those who opposed him.

Second, although Eysenck published hundreds of articles in academic journals and many technical and professional books, some of his academic contemporaries looked askance at his publicizing his views of psychology so successfully in the popular media—in paperback books, articles in newspapers and magazines, and on the radio and television. In Britain he was a celebrity. No other psychologist, and few academics in any other field, had as wide a public audience for so many decades.

Third, Eysenck's critics say that he took on too many different subjects, and in each of them stirred things up, proposed provocative theories, tested many clever hypotheses, and wrote prolifically, but too often failed to pursue a phenomenon long enough to establish a solid empirical basis for the further scientific advancement of the topic. I do not believe that this claim can be justified in the case of Eysenck's most original and most important research on the dimensions of personality.

The actual keys to Eysenck's controversial reputation are probably to be found in his totally uncompromising application to everything in psychology of five principles discussed in his autobiography: (a) Human beings are *biosocial* organisms whose behavior is conditioned by biological and genetic as well as experiential and social factors. (b) Dualism, the notion that mind and body are fundamentally distinct and separate entities, must be rejected. Instead body and mind must be viewed as a continuum, just as space and time are viewed as a continuum in modern physics. (c) Psychology must be a unified science, reconciling the two major disciplines of scientific psychology—the correlational study of individual differences in behavior (*differential* psychology) and the nomothetic study of the general laws of behavior (*experimental* psychology). (d) The distinction between applied and pure science, borrowed from physics, is inapplicable to psychology, which deals with the behavior of organisms. If it is to understand such phenomena psychology must be more applied than physics. It must study phenomena at their own level of complexity rather than deducing usefully precise understandings from atomistic laws like those of physics. (e) For any assertion in psychology there should be an attempted empirical proof, preferably experimental, and no assertion should be accepted without adequate proof. Theories or hypotheses are worthless unless they are formulated in such a way as to be empirically testable, and theories must be clearly distinguished from demonstrated facts. Eysenck's outspoken adherence to these principles—which most psychologists today would take for granted but were not generally accepted in the 1950s—probably contributed to his reputation as the psychologist that most psychologists love to hate.

The London School

Eysenck's thinking and research stemmed from a particular influence in his educational background—the "London School," of which he was both a product and the leading apostle during the latter half of the 20th century. The name "London School" refers to the kind of psychology that dominated research and teaching in the first half of this century in the Department of Psychology of the University of London, under the leadership of the two most eminent professors in its history, Charles Spearman (from 1906 to 1931) and Sir Cyril Burt (from 1932 to 1950), and carried on by Eysenck at the University of London's Institute of Psychiatry.

The London School viewed psychology essentially as a branch of natural science. Its intellectual progenitors were Charles Darwin (chap. 2, *Pioneers III*) and his half-cousin, Francis Galton (chap. 1, *Pioneers I*). It emphasized the evolutionary, genetic, and biological basis of behavior, and developed the objective measurement of individual differences, or psychometrics. This field became known later as *differential psychology*, which measures and studies individual differences, to distinguish it from experimental psychology, founded by Wilhelm Wundt (chap. 3, *Pioneers III*) in Leipzig, Germany, which sought to discover general laws of sensation, perception, and behavior through controlled experiments. In this view individual differences "average out" in the behavior under investigation.

These two branches of psychology, founded respectively by Galton and Wundt, are what Lee Cronbach (1957) referred to in his presidential address to the American Psychological Association in 1957 as the "two disciplines of scientific psychology." Cronbach deplored the fact that throughout the history of psychology these two disciplines had taken such separate paths with so little interaction between them. Eysenck's scientific aim can be viewed as a mission to coordinate the correlational and experimental scientific disciplines in the study of behavior. In line with his responsibility at Mill Hill and later as a research professor in the Institute of Psychiatry, his studies naturally focused mainly on individual differences in personality.

Personality Research

Eysenck's most important contribution is unquestionably his work on personality, which nicely illustrates his attempt to amalgamate Cronbach's two scientific disciplines. It is the field in which he is most truly a great pioneer.

Eysenck's work on personality began at the Mill Hill Hospital, where he had access to exceptionally large samples that provided the data for his research program in the early years of his career. During his four years at Mill Hill, he gathered a wide variety of information related to personality (questionnaires, objective behavior tests and ratings, and psychiatrists' diagnoses of each patient's mental condition). Eysenck referred to this phase of his work as the *taxonomic* problem. He noted that in the history of the natural sciences the quantification or measurement of phenomena and the creation of a systematic classification of their attributes were the first steps in their development. He insisted that the science of personality should follow the same path. His approach, considered radical at the time, stood in marked contrast to the then-prevailing study of personality, which held that each individual's personality was a unique configuration of characteristics, describable only in literary terms, much as a biographer or a novelist would portray an individual.

Eysenck brought his training in the London School to bear on the problems of measurement and classification of personality by applying the psychometric methods, particularly *factor analysis*, invented by Spearman and further developed by Burt, who had used the method to develop a taxonomy of cognitive abilities. If this approach should prove successful in the domain of personality, it meant that an individual's personality could be described (nomothetically) in terms of quantitative positions on a limited number of uncorrelated dimensions instead of idiographically in terms of the individual's unique characteristics. Eysenck's aim was not to describe particular people in detail but to discover the main independent dimensions along which they differ in personality—dimensions that account for a large proportion of the total variance in a great number of descriptive characteristics (assessed by questionnaires and ratings) and behavioral tendencies (measured by laboratory tests).

In three dozen studies based on more than 10,000 research participants, sampled from both psychiatric and nonpsychiatric populations, Eysenck and his assistants applied factor analysis to extensive batteries of diverse measures of behavior. These analyses clearly revealed two large orthogonal (uncorrelated) factors, one that ranged continuously from extreme extroversion to extreme introversion, a dimension that Eysenck labeled *extroversion* (E), and another that ranged from extreme emotional instability and proneness to anxiety to extreme emotional stability and absence of anxiety, labeled *neuroticism* (N). These studies were described in Eysenck's first book, *Dimensions of Personality* (1947). Another dimension, *psychoticism* (P), which is orthogonal to E and N but not clearly latent in the set of variables included in the earlier factor analyses at Mill Hill, was a later addition to Eysenck's taxonomy of personality dimensions. It came into focus when he began studying the personalities of psychopathic prisoners and recidivists. The term *psychoticism* refers to a trait that is not limited to describing clinical psychosis. It also includes characteristics in the nonpsychiatric population, which may predispose people to psychosis and, in an exaggerated form, become the symptoms of a full-blown clinically diagnosed psychosis—but also has a relationship to such nonmalignant traits as creativity.

The three dimensions in Eysenck's theory of personality are actually superfactors, or higher order factors in a hierarchical factor analysis. Each higher order factor dominates a number of less general, or lower order, traits that characterize the three superfactors, as shown in Table 20.1. Eysenck described himself as extremely low on E, at absolute zero on N, and middling on P.

Conventional psychiatric diagnoses of neurotic patients were found to represent particular interactions of the E and N dimensions; that is, certain diagnostic groups fell into different quadrants of the space created by the intersection of these dimensions. For example, patients diagnosed as hysteric occupied the quadrant described by high E, high N. Anxiety and depressive

TABLE 20.1
The Super-Factors Extroversion, Neuroticism, and Psychoticism and Their
Manifest Traits in Eysenck's Theory of the Structure of Personality

Extraversion	Neuroticism	Psychoticism
Sociable	Anxious	Aggressive
Lively	Depressed	Cold
Active	Guilt feelings	Egocentric
Assertive	Low self-esteem	Impersonal
Sensation seeking	Tense	Impulsive
Carefree	Irrational	Antisocial
Dominant	Moody	Unempathic
Surgent	Emotional	Creative
Venturesome	Worrisome	Tough-minded

disorders were low E, high N. Psychopaths (particularly criminals and recidi-vists) were high E, high P.

Neurophysiological Bases of Extroversion, Neuroticism, and Psychoticism

After Eysenck's first book, several more quickly followed [*The Scientific Study of Personality* (1952b), *The Structure of Human Personality* (1953), *The Dynamics of Anxiety and Hysteria* (1957), *The Biological Basis of Personality* (1967)], each one breaking new ground and, assuming that the taxonomic stage was sufficiently complete, developing the second, explanatory stage of a theory of personality. These books described the formulation and experimental tests of hypotheses about the neurophysiology of E, N, and P. The hypotheses relating personality factors to their neural or physiological causes were suggested by the behavioral characteristics that showed the highest loadings on a given factor.

Eysenck focused first on extroversion. His hypothesis for E was not based on direct observation of the neurophysiology of the central nervous system but on what has been termed a "conceptual nervous system," consisting of hypo-thetical constructs derived from the analysis of behavior rather than from the direct study of brain physiology. The theoretical constructs most relevant to E were neural excitation and inhibition as formulated by Ivan Pavlov (chap. 3, *Pioneers I*) to explain the phenomena of classical conditioning, as modified by Clark L. Hull (chap. 14, *Pioneers I*) in his theory of learning. In Hull's the-ory, the Pavlovian construct, excitation, became *excitatory strength*, and inhi-bition became *reactive inhibition*, which tends to block the immediate repeti-tion of the response that produces it and to reduce its magnitude to a degree that depends on the amount of work involved in that response and the length of time since it occurred. Reactive inhibition builds up with the repeated elic-itation of responses and decays during periods of inactivity. Eysenck's theory postulated that there are individual differences in the rates of accumulation and dissipation of reactive inhibition: Individuals in whom it builds up more rapidly and dissipates more slowly than average are behaviorally more extroverted; those in whom it builds up more slowly and dissipates more rapidly are be-haviorally more introverted.

Eysenck was dedicated to the hypothetico–deductive method of investigation, exemplified in Hull's research on learning, in which specific hypotheses are de-rived from theory and are tested in experiments. The methods used in studies of Hullian learning theory to test the predicted effects of reactive inhibition pro-vided the model that Eysenck used to test his theory of E, as measured by the Maudsley Personality Inventory (in its later revision, the Eysenck Personality In-ventory; Eysenck & Eysenck, 1963). Eysenck's specific predictions were that high- and low-scoring groups on the E scale should differ in the indices of re-active inhibition obtained in experiments on the conditioning and extinction of the eye-blink response, on reminiscence in motor learning, on the serial position effect in rote learning, the gradual deterioration of performance in prolonged vigilance tasks, and the like. Many such experiments performed in Eysenck's lab substantiated his theory, but some decidedly did not.

Eysenck consistently rejected any theory, including his own, that was contradicted by empirical evidence. The failures in these tests of the hypothesis relating extroversion to reactive inhibition happened often enough for that hypothesis eventually to be discarded. Eysenck replaced it with a theory that invoked individual differences in cortical excitation, or activation, via the brain's ascending reticular formation, which influence the rate of consolidation of neural traces laid down by experience. This cortical activation theory of E proved to be more consistent with the experimental evidence, particularly that from studies of the behavioral effects of stimulant and depressant drugs, which have opposite effects on cortical activity and simulate the behavioral effects of low and high E, respectively. Extroverts had lower levels of activation than introverts, and numerous differences in their responses to drugs known to affect the reticular activating system and other forms of stimulation showed the neural activation theory to be more often consistent with the experimental evidence than were predictions from reactive inhibition theory.

Neuroticism (N) was explained as individual differences in the lability of the autonomic nervous system and the balance between its sympathetic and parasympathetic components, the sympathetic system activating emotional responses such as fear or anxiety and aggression or hostility (the so-called fight or flight reaction to threat), the parasympathetic system activating relaxation and pleasurable feelings associated with bodily functions. High N results from overreactivity of the sympathetic nervous system, as reflected by individual differences in the galvanic skin response, the pupillary response, and other indices of sympathetic activation, as well as by well-established behavioral effects of anxiety on learning and performance under varying conditions of stress.

Psychoticism (P) was a relative latecomer to Eysenck's personality theory and there was less empirical research on its causal basis than on E and N. It is also both more complex and more tentative in Eysenck's theorizing, which connects P mainly with the brain's biochemistry, particularly certain neurotransmitters such as dopamine, serotonin, and the enzyme monoamine oxidase.

Behavioral Genetics

The London School, with its roots in the Darwinian and Galtonian views of human nature, was interested in the genetic basis of individual differences, and Eysenck considered this an essential pillar in his theory of personality. Using the method of comparing monozygotic (identical) and dizygotic (fraternal) twins originally suggested by Galton to determine the proportion of genetic variance in a given trait—termed its *heritability*—Eysenck investigated the genetics, first of N and E and later P. He found that genetic factors contributed about 50 percent of the individual differences variance in each of these personality factors. Over the years, Eysenck built up a registry of hundreds of pairs of twins who could be called on for participation in behavioral genetic studies. Heritability studies were also performed in Eysenck's lab on other traits that were of interest because of their interactions with the main dimensions of personality. These traits included authoritarianism, prejudice, conservatism, religion, sexuality, and criminality, all of which turned out to have a substantial genetic component. Virtually all of Eysenck's findings in behavioral genetics have been substantiated by other investigators in this field.

The animal laboratory of the Institute of Psychiatry, founded by Eysenck in the early 1950s, performed genetic studies involving the behavioral testing and selective breeding of rats for traits resembling some of the features of both N and E, such as anxiety and behavior reflecting reactive inhibition. The rats' response to genetic selection, creating distinct strains with respect to the selected traits, proved the inheritance of behavioral traits in rats that in some ways could be likened to "personality" differences, such as emotionality.

Intelligence

Eysenck claimed that his first interest in psychology was in intelligence, because it was the first mental trait that was actually susceptible to measurement. Because he was employed at the Institute of Psychiatry, however, research on personality, abnormal psychology, and therapy had to take precedence. His contributions to intelligence research did not surface importantly until the late 1960s. Eysenck's position on intelligence was entirely consistent with the London School's view of intelligence as a biologically based, genetically conditioned, general ability. Although giving due credit to the role of factor analysis in the study of mental abilities and to Spearman's discovery of the g factor, Eysenck emphasized the importance of focusing on the physiological basis of individual differences in g. He suggested methodologies for advancing the field in this direction. He offered the hypothesis that mental speed, measured by reaction time and the latency of evoked brain potentials, is the probable causal basis of individual differences in general ability, or Spearman's g factor. His lab took up studies of the average evoked potential (AEP) and found that not only the speed and latency of the AEP but also the complexity of its wave form are correlated with IQ. Moreover, statistical analysis showed that the AEP is correlated specifically and exclusively with the general factor (g) of the battery of eleven diverse subtests used to measure IQ. This is especially interesting because the g factor accounts for only about 50 percent of the total variance in the 11 subtests. Eysenck later concluded that mental speed is a function of a phenomenon that is more basic than g—namely, errors in the transmission of neural impulses in the CNS, which are reflected not only by the person's average reaction time (RT) but also by its trial-to-trial consistency, which is correlated even more highly with IQ than is the median RT.

Although Eysenck himself did comparatively little original work in the field of intelligence, he wrote numerous articles and several comprehensive books about it that were highly influential and are still among the best expositions of the subject. His last book, written for a general audience and published posthumously in 1998, provides a highly readable summary of his views on intelligence, creativity, and genius.

Behavior Therapy

In 1952, Eysenck became psychology's *enfant terrible* when he reviewed all of the existing evidence on the therapeutic efficacy of psychotherapy and psychoanalysis and concluded, in an article published in the *Journal of Consulting Psychology*, that existing evidence failed to prove that these therapies had any beneficial effect that was greater than the recovery rate of control groups who had received no treatment. This claim immediately aroused great antagonism toward Eysenck from clinical psychologists and psychotherapists the world over. Although Eysenck's conclusion has since been disputed by comprehensive meta-analyses performed years later, after more and better evidence on the effects of psychotherapy had accumulated, Eysenck never abandoned his original conclusion and even used the meta-analyses that claimed to contradict him to bolster his original claim. Eysenck is now in a minority, but he is not alone in this position. The issue is still open. It may well be unanswerable in any general sense.

In place of psychotherapy, Eysenck advocated what became known as *behavior therapy*, and he was among the pioneers of its theory and practice. Conventional psychotherapy—commonly called "talk therapy"—is based on the theory that neurotic symptoms reflect complexes hidden in the unconscious that can be brought to awareness and dealt with through some form of verbal interaction with a therapist. In contrast, behavior therapy rejects the notion of unconscious complexes, claiming that the symptoms themselves constitute the neurosis. It treats the symptoms directly and changes the patient's behavior and attitudes by methods derived from such behavioristic learning theories as those of John B. Watson (chap. 12, *Pioneers I*), Ivan Pavlov (chap. 3, *Pioneers I*), Hull, and Skinner with the aid of such processes as experimental extinction, reciprocal inhibition, desensitization, and reinforcement. Behavior therapy was widely used with patients at the Institute of Psychiatry and was also studied with experimental methods, about which Eysenck wrote six books and countless articles. In 1960, he founded and for 18 years edited the journal *Behaviour Research and Therapy*.

Glimpses of Other Topics

Eysenck did research on a number of other subjects that can be classified under seven headings, about which he wrote innumerable articles and 13 books, 7 of them with coauthors. If all his work were judiciously divided among a dozen academic psychologists, each of them could claim a distinguished career. In the space available, it will be possible to say just a few words about each of these contributions. Pro and con discussions of Eysenck's main contributions are given in a volume edited by Mogdil and Mogdil (1986).

Reminiscence.   The phenomenon of reminiscence, which occurs most clearly in motor learning, denotes a gain in level of performance after a period of rest that follows a practice session. Theorists in the Hullian tradition attribute it to the dissipation of reactive inhibition during the rest period. Eysenck did much research on reminiscence and explained it as the result of the consolidation of neural traces during rest, a theory that better accorded with the experimental evidence than the theory of reactive inhibition.

Crime and Personality.   Eysenck hypothesized that many types of delinquency and criminality result from undersocialization and that individuals differ in personality factors that determine susceptibility to the socializing influences of the family and society. Because personality factors all reflect genetic components, delinquency and criminality are also influenced in part by genetic factors. Laboratory and behavior–genetic studies of prisoners and recidivists have generally borne out predictions from Eysenck's theory.

The Psychology of Politics.   Eysenck showed that social and political attitudes and party affiliation are associated with personality traits that can be mapped in the quadrants of two dimensions: (a) tender-minded versus tough-minded and (b) radical versus conservative. Eysenck's controversial finding that communists and fascists have certain predisposing traits in common (both are extreme on the tough-minded dimension) but fall at opposite positions on the radical versus conservative dimension (communists are radical; fascists are conservative) provoked attacks from both extremes of the political spectrum.

Creativity and Genius.   In his last major book and one of his best, *Genius: The Natural History of Creativity* (1996), Eysenck summarized his theory and research on creativity and genius. He argued that the kinds of achievement that society recognizes as creative genius depend not only on high general ability or exceptional special talent but also on certain personality traits: unusual zeal and persistence through thick and thin, as first suggested by Galton. But, according to Eysenck, the unique creativity that characterizes works of genius also reflects a higher than average level of the P factor, trait psychoticism. He cites examples of high P among some of the greatest geniuses in history and explains the psychological nature of the causal connection between P and socially significant creativity. It is a fascinating theory.

Smoking and Health.   Eysenck's research on smoking examined the hypotheses that a tendency to smoke is related to high E (borne out by his studies) and that the same individuals are more predisposed to developing lung cancer. After reviewing the entire scientific literature on the effects of smoking, Eysenck challenged the prevailing belief in a direct *causal* connection between smoking and cancer. Because the vast majority of smokers never develop lung cancer, and because lung cancer also occurs in nonsmokers, he concluded that the evidence did not prove that the correlation between smoking and lung cancer is the result of direct causation. Instead, he suggested that it might reflect genetic predisposing factors, some of which are traits of personality (particularly high E), that caused people to smoke. Many investigators in the area considered this theory not only highly controversial but also detrimental to the efforts of public health workers to persuade people to quit smoking. But at the time, the evidence was equivocal and, strictly speaking, was in fact inadequate to reject the null hypothesis regarding direct causality.

Some people have wondered whether Eysenck himself was a smoker who was trying to rationalize his habit. Actually Eysenck was a nonsmoker; he even said he hated smoking. On two occasions when I was in his company and someone asked if anyone minded if they smoked, Eysenck emphatically said, "Yes, I hate it. Please don't smoke!" He also advocated and did studies on the use of behavior therapy to help people give up smoking.

Toward the end of his life, Eysenck collaborated with medical researchers on the relationship of personality factors to health and risk for cardiovascular disease and cancer and found evidence that E is positively correlated with the former and negatively with the latter. He suggested that the modification of predisposing personality traits by means of behavior therapy might prove prophylactic against these forms of disease.

Parapsychology and Astrology.   Consistent with his conviction that scientists should be skeptical of all explanatory theories yet remain completely open-minded about any phenomena for which there was objective evidence, Eysenck took an interest in the claims of parapsychology and astrology, subjects generally considered beyond the pale by the majority of scientists. He believed some data purporting to show extrasensory perception and psychokinesis actually met the same standards of experimental and statistical acceptability as would be required to establish the reality of any other kind of phenomena in science. He insisted on making a clear and essential distinction between data (or phenomena), on the one hand, and their theoretical explanation, on the other. He believed that when the data of parapsychology gave no reason to be suspect, they should not be dismissed out of hand. Rather, they should somehow be explained in naturalistic terms, even if that might mean fundamentally revamping our conception of the nature of the physical universe.

As for astrology, Eysenck's investigations found that its theoretical predictions regarding personality traits were no better than chance. But he also came across correlations between birth dates (related to certain astrological signs) and occupational choice that were statistically significant and were replicated on different samples. These data remain unexplained, by Eysenck or anyone else. But Eysenck believed that such phenomena are worth pursuing. He of course would have sought a naturalistic explanation, which he believed might open new vistas in science.

CONCLUSION

A succinct summing up of Eysenck's long and remarkable career is provided by the citation accompanying Eysenck's election, in 1994, as a William James Fellow, the highest honor bestowed by the American Psychological Society, "In Recognition of a Lifetime of Distinguished Contribution to Psychological Science":

> For more than fifty years, he has led the struggle to bring science to bear on the most significant psychological issues of our times. A skeptic who insists that human aspirations conform to fact and not vice-versa, he brings phenomena from the penumbra into the light. At the age of fifteen [Eysenck actually emigrated from Germany in 1934, at age 18] he fled Hitler's Germany and within twenty years he became one of England's most prominent scientists. His seminal early work on individual differences focused on extroversion, neuroticism, and psychoticism as the underlying dimensions of personality. He led and won the battle to put therapy on a scientific behavioral footing. With a version of human nature as biosocial, he breathed life into the study of the genetics of personality. He has allied himself with unpopular positions, such as the attack on psychoanalytic therapy, the selective contribution of cigarettes to cancer based on personality, the genetics of intelligence, the benefits of behavior therapy for physical health, and the puzzling but strong predictive power of planetary position at birth on career choice. He is an articulate, moderate, and stable voice raised to defend positions in need of a defender. Time and again, the accumulation of facts has vindicated him.

> For the reach of his visionary intellect, for the grasp of his scholarly achievements, for his students who have fanned across the globe to lead the next generation, for his good sense, for his vigorous voice, for his devotion to fact, and above all for his unflagging courage, we recognize Hans Eysenck as a leader in psychological science.

REFERENCES

Cronbach, L. J. (1957). The two disciplines of scientific psychology. *American Psychologist, 12,* 671–684.

Eysenck, H. J. (1947). *Dimensions of personality.* London and Boston: Routledge and Kegan Paul.

Eysenck, H. J. (1952a). The effects of psychotherapy: An evaluation. *Journal of Consulting Psychology, 16,* 319–324.

Eysenck, H. J. (1952b). *The scientific study of personality.* London: Routledge and Kegan Paul.

Eysenck, H. J. (1953). *The structure of human personality.* London: Methuen.

Eysenck, H. J. (1957). *The dynamics of anxiety and hysteria.* London: Routledge and Kegan Paul.

Eysenck, H. J. (1967). *The biological basis of personality.* Springfield, MA: C. C. Thomas.

Eysenck, H. J. (1996). *Genius: The natural history of creativity.* Cambridge: Cambridge University Press.

Eysenck, H. J. (1997). *Rebel with a cause: The autobiography of Hans Eysenck.* (Revised and expanded edition). Brunswick, NJ: Transaction Books.

Eysenck, H. J. (1998). *Intelligence: A new look.* New Brunswick, NJ: Transaction Books.

Eysenck, H. J., & Eysenck, S. B. G. (1963). *The Eysenck Personality Inventory.* San Diego, CA: Educational and Industrial Testing Service, and University Press of London.

Gibson, H. B. (1981). *Hans Eysenck: The man and his work.* London: Peter Owen.

Mogdil, S., & Mogdil, C. (Eds.). (1986). *Hans Eysenck: Searching for a scientific basis for human behavior.* London: Falmer Press.

Nyborg, H. (Ed.). (1997). (Ed.). *The scientific study of human nature: A tribute to Hans J. Eysenck at eighty.* New York: Elsevier.

Chapter 21

Sigmund Koch: Human Agency and the Psychological Studies

David Finkelman and Frank Kessel

Sigmund Koch devoted a professional career of more than a half a century to exploring the prospects and conditions for a significant psychology. His analyses and assessments were frequently disturbing, both to other psychologists and to himself. But although he was a critic—often a vigorous one—of much of the psychological enterprise, his message was ultimately hopeful. He urged a psychology that was at once more ambitious and more modest—more ambitious in its tackling of problems of genuine human significance, more modest in its expectations of the increments in genuine knowledge that could be anticipated. He hoped and believed that the result would be a more meaningful psychology, one that could make an authentic contribution to human knowledge.[1]

---

[1]Three other preliminary points: First, given that Koch's "voice" was such an integral part of his message, and because of the color and power of his prose, we have used more of Koch's own words than is typical for a chapter of this sort. Second, because many of Koch's ideas and concepts are difficult to convey in a brief presentation, interested readers are urged to consult the cited original sources, not only for greater depth on the ideas discussed but also for others we have not mentioned—for example, the significance of "disciplined connoisseurs" of human experience. Finally, simply for lack of space, we must allow these brief reflections from William Bevan to speak of, and for, Sigmund Koch the person and connoisseur of lived experience:

> I remember one afternoon in the fall of 1943, soon after he'd got his Ph.D. and begun as an instructor at Duke, Sig leading a frightened 18-year-old [Bevan himself] through the litany of the oral preliminary examination—with incredible patience and kindness. . . . I've talked to a number of friends who remember Sig from their student days. What has emerged is, first, a splendid teacher; also a lover of fast sports cars; a host who always served the best in liquor, a preference for Tanqueray gin; the owner of a small hi-fi and record business; a heavy cigarette smoker; a person who appreciated the presence of a pretty woman. (quoted in Kessel & Bevan, 1995)

*Photo of Sigmund Koch courtesy of Patricia Mathis.

Excerpts from Koch, Finkelman, & Kessel (1999) reprinted with permission of University of Chicago Press. Excerpts from Koch (1992) reprinted with permission. Copyright 1992 by the American Psychological Association.

BIOGRAPHY

Koch was born in New York City on April 18, 1917, into a family of high scholarly achievement. His sister Adrienne became a well-known scholar in the field of early American history; his sister Vivienne a literary scholar (Leary, Kessel, & Bevan, 1998). Koch's own earliest interests were in the arts, and literature in particular; he edited the literary section of his high school newspaper, won a national competition among high school poets for inclusion in an anthology of modern poetry, and won his graduating-class literary award with an essay in criticism (Koch, 1977/1999n, p. 29). When Koch began his undergraduate studies at New York University in the fall of 1934, it was as an English major. There he met and became friends with poet and writer Delmore Schwartz, who published his first pieces in a magazine he and Koch edited; Koch had founded the magazine himself the summer before.

Early in his college career Koch found his interests turning to philosophy, particularly to logical positivism, the movement that rejected much of traditional philosophy as lacking an empirical basis and therefore as being technical nonsense ("non-sense"). By 1934, positivism had become the dominant force in philosophical thinking worldwide (Koch, 1977/1999n, p. 29), and it proved seductive to young Koch as well. Later, he was to describe his rapid conversion this way:

> In no time at all, I was a confirmed positivist, with confident answers to the conveniently narrow range of questions that the position accredited as "meaningful." . . . From among the range of philosophical positions thrown up by a twenty-five-hundred year history, I was able to arrive at a rational and mature choice in approximately two weeks. I fear that in all fields of scholarship such celerity of commitment is the rule: young persons enthusiastically plunge into their conceptual beds of Procrustes at the moment the sheet is turned down by someone they find admirable; often they do not emerge for the rest of their lives. (Koch, 1977/1999n, p. 30)

Koch further narrowed his focus to the philosophy of science, and the science on which he chose to concentrate was psychology. ("What field in the panoply of scholarship seemed more desperately to *need* help?" he was to ask later; Koch, 1977/1999n, p. 30). As a result, he decided to supplement his major in philosophy with the equivalent of a second major in psychology, earning his undergraduate degree from NYU in 1938.

His dual interests in philosophy and psychology led Koch to graduate study at the University of Iowa with Herbert Feigl, who shared these interests. Kurt Lewin's presence on the faculty also influenced his decision to go to Iowa, and Kenneth Spence (chap. 17, *Pioneers III*) joined the faculty the same year Koch arrived. All three were significant influences on Koch's early thinking.

Koch's master's thesis applied the tools of logical positivist analysis to the topic of motivation. The thesis was published in 1941 as two articles in *Psy-*

chological Review (Koch, 1941a, 1941b). Their impact on the field was immediate and strong, and they remained among his most influential and widely cited publications. His own ultimate assessment of them was quite different, however. Years later, he would describe them as "the silliest and most superficial documents I have ever written" (Koch, 1977/1999n, p. 32).

After receiving his MA from Iowa in 1939, Koch entered the Duke University PhD program in psychology. He was impressed with the exceptional quality of several members of the Duke department, including Donald K. Adams, who served as his thesis advisor, and especially Karl Zener, who had a profound impact on him. After receiving his PhD in 1942, he remained at Duke University as a faculty member (ultimately as professor) until 1964.

In the early 1940s, Koch's logical positivist sympathies led him to a similarly favorable view of behaviorism, which he expressed in a highly enthusiastic review of Clark Hull's *Principles of Behavior* (Koch, 1944). Over the next few years, however, his views about both positivism and behaviorism underwent a slow but ultimately profound shift. By 1950, when he participated in the Dartmouth summer symposium on learning theory, his views on Hull (chap. 14, *Pioneers I*) had become overwhelmingly negative (Koch, 1954). Perhaps Koch's most spirited criticism of behaviorism is in his contribution to the 1963 Rice Symposium on behaviorism and phenomenology (Koch, 1964/1999h). And several years later, he would define behaviorism as "the strongest possible wish that the organism and the person not exist—a vast, many-voiced, poignant lament that anything so refractory to the assumptions and methods of 18th-century science should clutter up the worldscape" (Koch, 1969, p. 252).

In 1952, Koch was chosen to direct and edit the large "self-study" of psychology, sponsored by the American Psychological Association (APA) and funded by the National Science Foundation, that resulted in the six volumes of *Psychology: A Study of a Science*, published between 1959 and 1963. It was also in the 1950s that Koch developed what he later judged to be his most important theoretical contributions: his theory of definition and his concept of "value properties." (These contributions, along with others, are discussed in greater detail later in the chapter.)

Koch became director of the Ford Foundation's Program in the Humanities and the Arts in 1964. Working closely with W. McNeil Lowry,[2] he administered a multimillion dollar endowment program for symphony orchestras; he also played an instrumental role in supporting the growth of regional theaters, including the Arena Stage in Washington, DC, and the Guthrie Theater in Minneapolis. More directly related to his own scholarly interests, Koch initiated an international Study Group on the Unity of Knowledge aimed at establishing com-

---

[2]We are grateful to Marcia Thompson, a colleague of Koch and Lowry at the Ford Foundation, for delving into the Foundation's archives to unearth some of this information.

mon theoretical ground among various currents of scientific and humanistic thought. Collaborating with Michael Polanyi, who chaired the group, Koch organized a series of interdisciplinary conferences focused on emerging intellectual trends (e.g., structuralism); these gatherings helped shape some of Koch's subsequent ideas and writings (e.g. Koch, 1967/1999c).

In 1967, Koch returned to the academy as Stiles Professor in Comparative Studies at the University of Texas, a university-wide position that involved him in the areas of philosophy, psychology, and the arts. He remained there until 1971. It was during this period that the humanistic psychology movement became prominent in American psychology; one of its most visible manifestations was the encounter group phenomenon. Koch's appalled reaction to encounter groups, first expressed in an address at Albion College in Ohio in 1969, was subsequently published in several sources (Koch, 1971a, 1972, 1973), and became widely known.

In 1971, Koch moved from Texas to Boston University, where he served a two-year term as vice president for academic affairs, before returning full-time to the faculty as University Professor of psychology and philosophy. While there, he edited (with David Leary) *A Century of Psychology as Science* (Koch & Leary, 1985/1992), which could be described as a "mini-follow-up," 20 years later, to *Psychology: A Study of a Science*. In his last major project, he was able to realize his long-held dream of establishing an "aesthetics research center," in which summit-level artists were invited to discuss their own work and the creative process.

Koch died in Brookline, Massachusetts, on August 10, 1996.

MAJOR THEORETICAL CONTRIBUTIONS

Koch's theoretical work encompassed a number of different areas, but all his work was "animated by a coherent set of attitudes towards the nature of inquiry, creative effort, and knowledge" (Koch, 1999j, p. 1). The key to that world view was his emphasis on the absolute centrality of the human element in all forms of inquiry—scientific, humanistic, or other. For much of Koch's career, the reigning approaches to the nature of knowledge prevalent in psychology and philosophy tended to minimize, ignore, or even deny the importance of this element, particularly in regard to scientific endeavor, placing emphasis instead on the power of one or another set of *rules* that were often claimed to be self-correcting and even to *guarantee* progress. These approaches conformed to "the stereotype of science as some kind of inexorable bulldozer which carves out great, linear, ever-lengthening highways of truth" (Koch, 1956, p. 45). Koch protested vigorously against such a conception. It was his emphasis on "the human context and agency of science" (Koch, 1977/1999n, p. 45), as well as other forms of inquiry, that marked all of his work. As Koch himself acknowledged, this perspective closely corresponded with the views of the scientist–philosopher Polanyi (1958).

The Nature of Psychology

Questions regarding the fundamental nature of psychology concerned Koch throughout his career. Among the most important questions were the following two: Is psychology a unified (or unifiable) discipline, and is it a science? In Koch's more extended analyses, this question took more differentiated forms: Is it, *can it*, or *should* it be a science? And, in either case, "science" in what senses? After having quite different opinions earlier in his career, Koch came to the view that psychology is not a unitary discipline but a collectivity of disciplines, and that although "some few of [the disciplines] may qualify as science . . . most do not" (Koch 1979/1999g, p. 414). His views on both issues are captured in his suggestion that the term "psychology" be replaced by a term more revealing of reality, "the psychological studies."

In regard to the unitary nature of psychology, Koch wrote that "nothing so awesome as the total domain comprised by the functioning of all organisms (not to mention persons) could possibly be the *subject matter* of a coherent discipline" (Koch, 1977/1999n, p. 23). Moreover, he argued, even a casual perusal of psychology's history reveals a clear tendency toward fractionation rather than integration.

Koch's opinion that psychology is a splintered discipline is supported by the proliferation of specialized journals and professional organizations in psychology, which continues apace. But Koch most assuredly did not advocate that the psychological studies be pursued in isolation, either from each other or from broader contexts of scholarship or application. On the contrary, he emphasized that charting the relations between and among the various psychological studies, as well as their relations with other disciplines and the broader social world, was a vital task.

Koch acknowledged that some of the psychological studies had legitimate claims to scientific status, but asserted that most were more akin to the humanities:

> Fields like sensory and biological psychology may certainly be regarded as solidly within the family of the biological, and, in some reaches, natural sciences. But psychologists must finally accept the circumstance that extensive and important sectors of psychological study require modes of inquiry rather more like those of the humanities than the sciences. And among these I would include areas traditionally considered "fundamental"—like perception, cognition, motivation, and learning, *as well as* such more obviously rarified fields as social psychology, psychopathology, personology, aesthetics, and the analysis of "creativity." (Koch, 1977/1999n, p. 25)

It is important to note that Koch believed that psychology should be empirical, rational, and analytic, and that he saw a place for mathematical and statistical methods. He was as supportive of tough-minded, differentiated analysis of psychological events, and as critical of sloppy, fuzzy, or superficial thinking, as anyone. But in his view science is not the only avenue to rigorous analysis and clear understanding, as the work of any competent philosopher, historian, or literary critic reveals. In most of the psychological studies, therefore,

> continued application of this misleading metaphor [i.e., science] can only vitiate, distort or pervert research effort. . . . Such concepts as "law," "experiment," "measurement," "variable," "control," "theory," do not behave sufficiently like their homonyms in the established sciences to justify the extension to them of the term "science." To persist in the use of this highly charged metaphor is to shackle these fields of study with exceedingly unrealistic expectations concerning generality limits of the anticipated findings, predictive specificity and confidence levels, feasible research and data processing strategies, and modes of conceptual ordering. The inevitable heuristic effect is the enaction of imitation science rather than the generation of significant knowledge. Pursuit of imitation science, though a highly sophisticated skill, can only lead to the evasion and demeaning of subject matter and to a constriction of problematic interests. It is a deadly form of role-playing if one acknowledges that the psychological universe has something to do with persons. This kind of spurious knowledge can result in a corrupt human technology and spew forth upon man a stream of ever more degrading images of himself. (Koch, 1971/1999k, pp. 133–134)

Although Koch believed psychology should be more closely aligned with the humanities, he was no advocate—or even friend—of the humanistic psychology movement that came to prominence in psychology, and the culture at large, in the late 1960s. Indeed, his diatribe against one of the most visible manifestations of humanistic psychology—encounter groups—is one of the most forceful criticisms of that social phenomenon ever penned. Koch saw that many of the criticisms of behaviorism (and mainstream psychology more generally) he had raised were shared by the humanistic psychologists; this made it all the more ironic that "the 'humanist' wing of psychology . . . had embraced a conception of man which, if anything, was *more* reductive, demeaning, and callow than that of behaviorism" (Koch, 1999j, p. 312). He characterized the encounter group movement this way:

> It is my assessment that the group movement is the most extreme excursion thus far of man's talent for reducing, distorting, evading, and vulgarizing his own reality. It is also the most poignant exercise of that talent, for it seeks and promises to do the very reverse. It is adept at the image-making maneuver of evading human reality in the very process of seeking to discover and enhance it. It seeks to court spontaneity and authenticity by artifice; to combat instrumentalism instrumentally; to provide access to experience by reducing it to a packaged commodity; to engi-

neer autonomy by group pressure; to liberate individuality by group shaping. . . .
It can provide only a grotesque simulacrum of every noble quality it courts. (Koch,
1973/1999e, pp. 315–316)

Koch's assessment of a more recent set of ideas emanating from the humanities and influencing psychology, particularly social psychology, was less negative but still marked by serious qualification. He was leery of the tendency of
postmodern, "social constructionists" to dissolve the self in a sea of social "discourse." As he put it, "I think it more important to be deeply conversant with a
few great texts than to proclaim that human beings can be read as texts. Or that
they *are* texts!" (Koch, 1992b, p. 965).

Theory of Definition

Psychology has long been dominated by approaches to definition—originally borrowed from logical positivism and cognate views—that are phrased in terms of
"simple observables" or "operations." After considering the issue of definition
for many years, Koch came to regard such approaches as positively pernicious.
"Such reductive definitional schemata confound symptom and meaning," he
wrote; "if taken seriously they denude the universe of everything worth talking,
or indeed thinking, about" (Koch, 1977/1999n, p. 25). As a way of showing the
misleading character of these approaches, Koch provided an analysis of the word
"dignity," a term with psychological relevance and of a complexity comparable
to the trait-names used by personality psychologists.

Suppose, he said, we were to begin with a superficial symptomatic definition of "dignity," involving such indicators as "erect bearing" or "quiet voice."
Even at this general level, such a definition is not susceptible to precise "operational" specification, unless we thought we could specify "an angular criterion for 'erect bearing,' and a decibel cutoff point for 'quiet voice'" (Koch,
1976/1999m, p. 154). But even if we could, sensitive users of the word would
be far from satisfied with such a coarse-grained definition. They might say,
"'Erect bearing, yes, but not stiff or haughty.' 'Quiet voice, probably, but not
always—there are times when the essence of dignity is passionate, even ex-
plosive utterance'" (p. 154). Refining the concept of "quiet voice" further, one
might say, "'Not quiet but, rather, a tone adjusted to a balanced, fitting, yet
self-contained assessment of a situation'" (p. 155). But this still fails to capture some of the most important subtleties of the word. "Thus, dignity may involve fittingness or appropriateness, but certainly not in the sense of observing, or conforming to, *propriety*. Rather, what seems involved is a flexible
appropriateness 'above' propriety, in which individuality is consistently defined, yet subtly, rather than conspicuously or flamboyantly" (p. 155). And
even *this* analysis, Koch argued, does not begin to exhaust the full ramifications and intricacies of the word and concept.

Among other things, Koch's analysis shows that if we wish to define with precision and delicacy any reasonably complex or subtle word, we must frequently use words and concepts that are *just as* complex or subtle as the word to be defined. A definition cannot be phrased in terms of a simplified observation base or any set of straightforward operations.

Based on this kind of analysis, Koch rejected all reductive approaches to definition of the sort mentioned earlier. In their stead, he proposed a "perceptual" theory of definition. When a definition is understood, it involves a process of perceptual learning, so that definition, at bottom, is a perceptual training process. Using the example given previously, the best way to teach someone what "dignity" is would be to isolate examples of dignity that were particularly vivid, salient, or conspicuous, and identify them as prototypical instances of the concept. The fact that such examples might be difficult to find shows why we frequently must resort to verbal definitions of the sort given. But a verbal definition is in fact a form of "surrogate pointing" (Koch, 1976/1999m, p. 162), in which we try to guide the person to those contexts in which the property we are trying to identify can be seen most clearly. Moreover, the subtle and complex character of many psychological concepts means that definition is "sensibility—dependent and probabilistic: nothing says that the intended property or relation will be noted—or brought into comparable resolution—by all addressees" (Koch, 1977/1999n, p. 26).

Among the "reductive definitional schemata" that Koch criticized and rejected, one that has been highly influential in psychology is that of "operational definition," still very much a part of contemporary psychological thinking. In this regard, Koch was particularly exercised over how the views of Percy Bridgman, the physicist who coined the term, had been distorted by psychologists. In his last major publication (1992/1999l), Koch discussed this process in detail, arguing persuasively that Bridgman's impact "proved to move psychology in a direction diametrically opposed to his deepest commitments. And his occasional efforts to correct or mitigate the situation were characteristically met by therapeutic efforts to bring him into line with the therapists' own misconstruals of the earliest and crudest version of his position" (p. 377). Indeed, in many ways Bridgman's mature position on the nature of definition bore a closer resemblance to Koch's than to the stereotype that is to this day widely prevalent in psychology.

There is a meaningful relationship between Koch's theory of definition and his view of most of the psychological studies as akin to the humanities; because the perceptual theory of definition emphasizes that meaning is sensibility-dependent, different inquirers will "see" the world differently, and, in an important sense, will "speak" different languages. The complexity of psychological events means that to some extent, these languages are likely to prove incommensurable:

> If psychological events had a kind of logical layer-cake structure, or some kind of orderly crystal-like faceting (and if the human mind were something like a cam-

era), we could perhaps conclude that the languages might be ultimately summable, combinable into some kind of logical structure or fusible into some more general "containing" language. But psychological events tend not to be like that. Characteristically, they are multiply determined, ambiguous in their human meaning, polymorphous, contextually "environed" or embedded in complex and vaguely bounded ways, evanescent and labile in the extreme. Relative to their different analytical purposes, predictive aims, practical ends in view, metaphor-forming capacities, perceptual sensitivities, preexisting discrimination repertoires, different *theorists* . . . will make asystematically different perceptual cuts upon the same domain. They will identify "variables" of markedly different grain and meaning-contour, selected and linked on different principles of grouping. The cuts, variables, concepts, that is, will in all likelihood establish different universes of discourse, even if loose ones. (Koch, 1976/1999m, p. 180)

For Koch, such a perspective implied a scholarly enterprise that—to become and remain vital—has to be positively plural, where a variety of conceptual frameworks and modes of inquiry are cultivated. Why such a perspective seemed so foreign to psychology for so much of Koch's professional life was a source of both deep disquiet and analysis.

Cognitive Pathology and Ameaningful Thinking

Koch's view of psychology was of a field that had gone badly awry. He thought this traceable in large part to the dubious gift we all have "for the mismanagement of our own minds" (Koch, 1979/1999g, p. 397). His observations of these errant thought processes—his own as well as those of others—led him to "found" the discipline he called "cognitive pathology," devoted to "the study of misfirings of the scholarly and creative impulse" (Koch, 1979/1999g, p. 396). Semi-tongue-in-cheek, he described its "metatheory" as "epistemopathologistics," and his own theoretical analyses, in which he tried to excise various forms of cognitive pathology from the tissue of psychological thinking, as a series of "epistemopathectomies."

Koch cited the following as ways of thinking—widely prevalent in psychology and elsewhere—as some of those that bear the marks of cognitive pathology: (a) jargon and "word magic"; (b) single-principle imperialism; (c) substitution of *program* for *performance*; (d) the tendency to make so restrictive a definition of the field of study as to render the study beside the point or, indeed, finished before begun; (e) facilitation of progress by making arbitrary and strong simplifying assumptions (e.g., imaginary "boundary conditions," counterfactual assumptions about the mathematical properties of data); (f) proposing "as if" models that observe the restrictions just mentioned, and then forgetting those restrictions; (g) the tendency to select a "simple case" and then to assume that it will be merely a matter of time and energy until the "complex case" can be handled by application of easy composition rules; (h) the tendency to accept on authority or to invent a sacred, inviolable "self-corrective" epistemology that renders all inquiry in the field a matter of application of rules that preguarantee success; (i) corollary to the preceding, viewing all aspects of the cognitive enterprise as so thoroughly rule-regulated that they make the role of the cognizer superfluous; (j) the tendency to persist so rigidly, blindly, patiently, in the application of these rules—despite extensive indications of their disutility—that the behavior would be characterized as schizophrenic in any other context; (k) the tendency to accept any "finding" conformable to some treasured methodology in preference to "traditional" wisdom *or* individual experience, no matter how frequently confirmed the nonscientistic knowledge may be; (l) a remarkable and telling disproportion between the attention given to the foundation commitments of one's work and that given to superficial or pedantic details of implemental character—one dwells happily within the "superstructure," however shoddy or worm-eaten the "substructure" (Koch, 1979/1999g, pp. 397–398).

One particular form or type of cognitive pathology became a focus of Koch's interest and analytic effort, what he termed *ameaningful thinking:*

> Ameaningful thought or inquiry (the prefix has the same force as the *a-* in words like *amoral*) regards knowledge as the result of "processing" rather than of discovery. It presumes that knowledge is an almost automatic result of a gimmickry, an assembly line, a methodology. It assumes that inquiring behavior is so rigidly and fully regulated by rule that in its conception of inquiry it sometimes allows the rules totally to displace their human users. (Koch, 1977/1999n, p. 28)

Ameaningful thinking is contrasted with the (unfortunately) much rarer phenomenon of *meaningful* thinking:

> In meaningful thinking, the mind "caresses," flows joyously into, over, around, the relational matrix defined by the problem, the object. . . . There is a merging of person and object, problem, task; one is *inside* the problem or object; better, one *is* the problem; better still, *"one"* is not—only the problem or object, its terms and relations, exist, and *these* are real in the fullest, most vivid, electric, irrefragable way. (Koch, 1965/1999b, p. 240)

Koch asserted that cognitive pathology in general and ameaningful thinking in particular were widespread, not only in psychology but also in the sciences, humanities, and the arts, and particularly in the recent history of these fields. Moreover, he said that their presence could be seen in the problematic impact of psychology on the culture at large. Analyzing George Miller's (1969) influential APA presidential address urging psychologists to "give psychology away" (that is, to make psychological knowledge freely available for the solution of real-world problems), Koch criticized both the idea that psychology indeed had profound resources to give away and the notion that applying such resources as psychology will prove beneficial. In a memorable phrase, he wrote, "I believe that the most charitable thing we can do is not to give psychology away, but to take it back" (Koch, 1980/1999i, p. 306). This critique of Miller relates to an important feature of Koch's distinctive voice and sometimes misunderstood style. The idea of taking psychology back was offered "as a figure of speech known as hyperbole. . . . I think my position has been misinterpreted in a number of ways, possibly as a result of my tendency to make somewhat large, dashing generalities in a quasi-humorous way" (Koch, 1980, p. 60).

In later years, Koch plumbed the deeper ramifications of the "ameaning" syndrome: "The ultimate 'meaning' of ameaning is indeed that it is a fear-driven species of cognitive constriction, a reduction of uncertainty by denial, by a form of phony certainty achieved by the covert annihilation of the problematic, the complex, and the subtle" (Koch, 1979/1999g, p. 407). He saw it as

> at the basis of the endemic human need for crawling into cozy conceptual boxes—any box, so long as it gives promise of relieving the pains of cognitive uncertainty or easing problematic tension. This poignant human need, at any cost, for a frame, an abacus, a system, map, or set of rules that can seem to offer a wisp of hope for resolving uncertainty makes all of us vulnerable—in one degree or another—to the claims of simplistic, reductive, hypergeneral, or in other ways ontology-distorting frames, so long as they have the appearance of "systematicity." Moreover, having climbed into our conceptual box, on one adventitious basis or another, we are prepared to defend our happy domicile to the death—meaning, in the typical instance, *your* death. It is not that we don't want you to join us inside (we would be delighted to accommodate the whole human race); it's just that we don't want you tampering with our box or suggesting—by your location in another one—that there are other places in which to live. (Koch, 1979/1999g, pp. 407–408)

Value Properties

Koch (1969/1999d) introduced the concept of "value properties" in part as an attempt to correct what he perceived to be a gross imbalance in the dominant theories of motivation in psychology. Most such theories, he observed, phrase motivational phenomena primarily in "extrinsic" and "deficit" terms; they view behavior as directed toward goals that restore some lack or deficiency in the organism. But, Koch asserted, such an approach badly distorts, or overlooks entirely, some of the most important human activities. Many such activities do *not* fit this pattern; rather, they are undertaken "in and for themselves," and although they can be described in extrinsic terms, doing so seriously misrepresents their essential nature. Koch provided the example of a person looking at a painting:

> X looks at a painting for five minutes, and we ask, "Why?" The grammar of extrinsic determination will generate a lush supply of answers. X looks in order to satisfy a need for "aesthetic experience." X looks in order to derive pleasure. X looks because the picture happens to contain Napoleon and because he has a strong

drive to dominate. X looks because "paintings" are learned reducers of anxiety. X looks in order to satisfy a need based on the association of the color of his mother's dress with the ground-color of the painting. Answers of this order have only two common properties: They all refer the behavior to an extrinsic, end-determining system, *and* they contain very little, if any, information. Anyone who has looked at paintings as paintings knows that if X is *really* responding to the painting, then any of the above statements which may happen to be true are trivial.

A psychologically naive person who *can* respond to paintings would say that an important part of the story—the essential part—has been omitted. There is a sense in which X could be looking at the painting only because of something intrinsic in the act of looking at this particular painting. Such a person would say that *if* the conditions of our example presuppose that X is really looking at the painting *as* a painting, the painting will produce a differentiated process in X which is correlated with the act of viewing. The fact that X continues to view the painting or shows "adience" towards it in other ways, is equivalent to the fact that this process occurs. X may report on this process only in very general terms ("interesting," "lovely," "pleasurable"), or he *may* be able to specify certain qualities of the experience by virtue of which he is "held" by the painting. (Koch, 1969/1999d, pp. 203–204)

The properties of the painting that produce this experience in the viewer are what Koch termed "value properties." As this example shows, value properties are of particular importance in regard to aesthetics, a topic Koch (1969/1999d) explored in some detail.

Koch's views on this topic foreshadowed the later interest in "intrinsic motivation." Indeed, Koch's contribution to the 1956 *Nebraska Symposium on Motivation*, where he introduced the earliest version of these ideas, was titled "Behavior as 'Intrinsically' Regulated." Whether or not his ideas directly influenced later generations of thinking on motivation, there can be little doubt that Koch anticipated this kind of seismic shift in psychological theory. The similarity between his views in a variety of areas and others that emerged far later led Koch to this typically tart observation: "Though at one time I was seen (if seen at all) as a candidate for incarceration in a rubber room, I am probably now more likely to be thought a somewhat inhibited libertarian" (Koch, 1999j, p. 41).

The State A–State B Distinction

Another of Koch's contributions to the study of motivation was his distinction between two states of human functioning that he termed "State A" and "State B" (Koch, 1956). His descriptions of these states were drawn in the first instance from his own experience, which in itself was a bold act, given the atmosphere in psychology prevalent in the 1950s when Koch first introduced the analysis. Koch described State A as "the rather flaccid, routine, anxiety- and guilt-laden, extrinsic pressure-driven, end-gaining condition in which most of us subsist most of the time" (Koch, 1965, p. 58). While in State A, any complex or creative intellectual activity is extremely difficult. The motivating force for working on the problem is experienced as external in origin. It is difficult to summon the mental energy needed to do justice to an issue of any complexity, and all cognitive activities (e.g., reading, writing, memory, the apprehension of complex or subtle relationships) function at levels far below optimal. Thus an authentic encounter with the problem at hand—as well as any significant progress—is unlikely.

This is contrasted with "State B," which Koch described as "a lamentably infrequent condition which was characterized as representative of human motivation at its most energized levels" (Koch, 1965, p. 58):

> The central and decisive "mark" of State B is domination of the person by the problem context, or, better, by a certain direction defined by the problem context—a "diffuse" but absolutely compelling direction. All systems of personality seem "polarized" into the behavior; thus the personality is either integrated or, in a special sense, simplified, as you will. In State B, you do not merely "work at" or "on" the task; you have *committed yourself* to the task, and in some sense you *are* the task or vice versa.

> Perhaps one of the most remarkable properties of B is that thoughts relevant to the problem context seem to well up with no apparent effort. They merely present themselves. The spontaneity and fluency of ideation and the freedom from customary blockages seem similar to certain characteristics of a dream or certain states of near-dissociation. As in these latter conditions, it is often difficult to "fix," hold in mind, the thoughts which occur. In fact, in State B, most of the "effortfulness" or "strain" encountered has to do not with the generation of ideas relevant to the problem context but with their decoding, fixing, or verbalization, and their selection and assemblage with respect to socially standardized requirements of communication. Effortful as such operations may be, verbalization, writing, reading, and all functionally significant breakdowns thereof are at a qualitatively different level from the A state of affairs. (Koch, 1956, pp. 67–68)

The description of State B is of obvious relevance and importance to the issue of creativity; indeed, some might refer to State B as "the creative state" (Koch, 1999j, p. 47). As noted later in the context of Koch's research, his description of State B bears a distinct resemblance to many descriptions provided by artists and others of their mental activity during periods of creative work. There is also some similarity between State B and Maslow's (1968) concept of a "peak experience," as well as more recent notions of experiential "flow" as developed by Csikszentmihalyi (1990) and others.

As should be evident, there are coherent connections among the concepts discussed in this and the preceding two sections: meaningful and ameaningful thinking; value properties; and State A and State B. "The type of intellectual activity described as characteristic of State A would be roughly illustrative of what we are calling *ameaningful* thinking, while the State B activity syndrome would be illustrative of *meaningful* thinking" (Koch, 1965/1999b, p. 239). Moreover, the "intrinsic" quality attributed to State B—where the motivation is experienced as *intrinsic* to the problem context, rather than coming from external forces—bears a close affinity to the "intrinsic" quality of value properties—where certain activities or objects are prized and attractive because of certain intrinsic properties they possess in other words, their value properties. Moreover, these ideas are all expressions of Koch's deeper commitment to the central role of agency in human inquiry.

OTHER FACETS OF KOCH'S WORK

Although Koch is viewed primarily as a psychological theorist, his intellectual and professional activities spanned a range of other areas. Among such contributions are writings on historical issues in psychology, his editorial work, and later research on artists and the creative process.

Koch as Historian

Koch did not think of himself as a historian, but his work was informed by an acute historical sensibility and an appreciation for the historical forces that have shaped psychology. Most of his publications contain at least some discussion of historical issues. Probably most of his *explicitly* historical writing concentrated on psychology's recent history or "near history," part of which he himself had lived through. Of particular interest and importance is his analysis of what he called the "Age of Theory," which lasted from roughly 1930 to 1960. This was the period that was dominated by the major learning theorists of the day (Hull, chap. 14, *Pioneers I;* Tolman, chap. 15, *Pioneers I*; Lewin, chap. 7, *Pioneers III*; Skinner, chap. 16, *Pioneers III*; Guthrie, chap. 10, *Pioneers II*). According to Koch:

> The mark of the Age of Theory, especially in its classic phase (circa 1930–1950), was that all activities were to be subordinated to production of a "commodity" called "theory" *in a quite special sense defined by the Age.* It is as if something called "theory" became an end in itself—a bauble, a trinket—of which it was neither appropriate nor fair, certainly most naive, to inquire into its human relevance. (Koch, 1979/1999g, p. 400)

The guiding principles for the Age of Theory came primarily from the logical positivism of the early 1930s. The *effect* of the Age of Theory "code" on psychology was, in Koch's view, highly detrimental—it had a restrictive and trivializing impact on the selection of problems to be studied and the methods used to study them, as he described in detail in a number of publications (e.g., 1959b,

1964/1999h, 1965/1999b, 1979/1999g). Moreover, he saw that "code" still subtly at work through to the end of his life.

In many important ways, Koch believed that psychology's difficulties could be traced back considerably earlier than the Age of Theory—at least as far back as its founding as an independent discipline. Koch argued that the difference between the conditions under which psychology was founded, as compared to the established sciences, were of great long-term consequence and bode ill for the fledgling "science":

> The institutionalization of each new field of science in the early modern period was a *fait accompli* of an emerging substructure in the tissue of scientific knowledge. Sciences won their way to independence, and ultimately institutional status, by achieving enough knowledge to become sciences. But at the time of *its* inception, *psychology was unique in the extent to which its institutionalization preceded its content and its methods preceded its problems.* If there are keys to history, this statement is surely a key to the brief history of [psychology]. Never had a group of thinkers been given so sharply specified an invitation to create. Never had inquirers been so harried by social need, cultural optimism, extrinsic prescription, the advance scheduling of ways and means, the shining success story of the older sciences. . . . From the earliest days of the experimental pioneers, man's stipulation that psychology be adequate to *science* outweighed his commitment that it be adequate to man. (Koch, 1959b, pp. 783–784)

Koch explored this theme in more detail in his incisive analysis of the role of Wilhelm Wundt (chap. 3, *Pioneers III*) and his 19th-century contemporaries in the emergence of psychology as an independent discipline (Koch, 1985/1992a). That work, in turn, contributed to the emergence of a new generation of critical scholarship on the history of psychology.

Koch's Study of Art and Artists

As mentioned earlier, Koch had a long-standing interest in the arts. His early commitment to literature and poetry, and his service as director of the Ford Foundation's Program in the Humanities and the Arts, are two manifestations of this. While at Duke, Koch conceived of the idea of forming an institute to support a program of research in the arts (Koch, 1999j, p. 43). Years later, he was able to fulfill this long-time dream by establishing an Aesthetics Research Center at Boston University. Koch brought to the center some of the best-known artists in a variety of fields. The project was inaugurated in early 1983; by 1988 he had completed 16 in-depth, eight-hour, investigative conversations with such major artists as Edward Albee, Edward Larabee Barnes, Saul Bellow, Phyllis Curtin, Eric Hawkins, Arthur Miller, Toni Morrison, Virgil Thomson, Violette Verdi, and Richard Wilbur. (Koch, 1999j, pp. 43–48, provided a more detailed, though still brief, description of the project.) The conversations were recorded and contain a treasure trove of information—still mostly unmined—both about the individual artists and about artistic and creative processes in general. In his conversations with these artists, Koch found support for his ideas concerning the importance of State B episodes for creative work; he reported that "the detailed characteristics of this mode have been spelled out with remarkable unanimity by our artists" (Koch, 1999j, p. 47). Koch's work with artists can be seen as falling into the tradition of "qualitative analysis," which has gained considerable currency in recent years.

Koch as Editor

It was in his role as editor of the six-volume *Psychology: A Study of a Science* that Koch first became widely known. The *Study* was the most extensive and ambitious project of its kind ever attempted in psychology; it involved nearly 90 contributors, including many of the stellar names in the field. Koch brought a painstaking, exacting, and thorough approach to all phases of the project, from its inception in 1952 until the publication of the final volume in 1963. A comment by Fred Attneave, one of the contributors to the study, provides some sense of this:

> I can assert with some fervor that the demands Editor Koch made of his authors were, at least verbally, formidable indeed. On first reading his remarkable document with the innocent title *Suggested Discussion Topics* [Koch, 1959a], I was seized with a paralysis that made it impossible for me to write anything for months, quite analogous to the paralysis of a golfer induced to study the . . . anatomical diagram showing all the muscles that must be coordinated in hitting a ball. (Attneave, 1959, p. 350)

In the course of the editorial process, the contributors frequently found themselves the recipients of numerous multiple-page single-spaced letters, engaging them on matters of both content and form. Another of the contributors, Carl Rogers (chap. 15, *Pioneers III*), said that he never worked as hard on any piece of writing in his professional career as he did on his chapter for the study.

Koch's efforts did not go unrecognized, as can be seen in E. G. Boring's (1959) review of the first volume of the *Study*. In the review, titled "L'encyclopédie au Koch," Boring said, "Really this is a stupendous undertaking that Koch is engineering and has already brought well along since its planning began away back in 1952. . . . Perhaps we have here psychology's great encyclopedia" (pp. 345–346).

Koch was a contributor to the *Study* as well as its editor; his most notable contribution was the 50-page "epilogue" which appeared at the end of volume 3 (Koch, 1959b). However, what was to have been his most important contribution—the seventh, "postscript" volume, to be titled *Psychology and the Human Agent*— never appeared. The volume was described as "in preparation" in each of the six published volumes, and Koch referred to it several times in his volume 3 epilogue. The prospect of its publication generated considerable interest. Boring, for example, closed his review of volume 1 with the words, "the final volume will be a grander review than any encyclopedia ever had" (Boring, 1959, p. 346).

Many years later, in explaining why it was never published, Koch wrote, "The manuscript for the projected volume 7 of that *Study* was on the verge of completion more times than I care to remember; a succession of career changes created so long a delay between the Study proper and its postscript that I ultimately decided not to carry it through" (Koch, 1999j, p. 1). However, much of the material that would have been contained in volume 7 can be found in the posthumously published collection of Koch's papers (Koch, 1999j); for him this long-planned collection served as a surrogate volume 7.

Koch was ambivalent about his long service as editor of the *Study*. The tremendous burden it imposed on him—and that he imposed on himself—meant that he had little time to work on projects more directly his own. But the respectability conferred by his association with the *Study* may have given him the freedom, in later years, to develop ideas that were at considerable variance from the mainstream. In assessing the *Study's* impact on the field, Koch expressed satisfaction that it had helped promote a more tolerant and open-minded attitude in psychology, encouraging both a greater flexibility in regard to theoretical formulations and a broader range of substantive research interests (Koch, 1977/1999n).

Koch assumed the editorial mantle once more in his career. In 1979, when psychology's centennial as an "independent, experimental science" was being celebrated by the APA, Koch was serving as president of two of its divisions: General Psychology (Division 1) and Philosophical Psychology (Division 24). In that dual role, he invited well-known representatives of the major fields in psychology to address the APA convention on how their fields had fared over the century. With the assistance of David Leary, the papers were published in a volume titled *A Century of Psychology as Science* (Koch & Leary, 1985/1992), which Koch described as "a miniature—and editorially less interventionistic—successor to the six-volume *Psychology: A Study of a Science*, which enables a second fix upon the status of the discipline two decades after the original one" (Koch, 1999j, p. 42.)

Koch offered a mixed assessment of the changes that had occurred over that period: "At surface levels, the 'Age of Theory' attitude complex is a thing of the past. At sub-surface levels, the reading must be more ambiguous" (p. 42).

KOCH THE PERSON AS REFLECTED
IN HIS VIEWS OF OTHERS

Although we have already mentioned some of Koch's most salient qualities as a scholar, several others of importance are worth commenting on. It is interesting to note that many of these can be seen in the descriptions he provided of people who had touched his life, either directly or through their writing.

In describing Delmore Schwartz, Koch remarked on "the unattainable altitude of his standards" (Koch, 1977/1999n, p. 29). That Koch had extremely high standards for his own work is beyond question. Virtually everything he wrote went through multiple drafts; even then, he was rarely satisfied. Indeed, many of his papers were never submitted for publication because they did not meet his high standards. His perfectionism extended to his editorial contributions, as well as to his work with the Aesthetics Research Center: In preparation for his conversations with each artist, he immersed himself in the artist's life and work, as well as the available critical and biographical literature bearing on each. Because of the extensive output of the artists he interviewed, as well as the diversity of the fields represented (the participants included visual artists, novelists, playwrights, choreographers, composers, and architects), the amount of preparation he undertook was formidable, but no less than what he considered the essential minimum.

In a review of Ludwig von Bertalanffy's book *Robots, Men, and Minds*, Koch described the founder of general systems theory as "a member of that tiny but irreplaceable society of thinkers who will not take 'yes' for an answer merely because it carries a majority-sanction in official scholarship" (Koch, 1971c, p. 310). Koch was clearly a member of that same group. Especially during the early years of his dissidence in the 1940s and 1950s, Koch's views placed him in a very small minority, and he described himself as "lonely" (Koch, 1971b, p. 674). In later years, at least some of his ideas gained greater currency. But his judgment that cognitive pathology was a well-nigh universal phenomenon, and that its manifestations "are as characteristic of 'cognitive science' theorists, developmental 'stage theorists,' humanistic psychologists, psycholinguists, and reality therapists as they are of the most stolidly unregenerate, positivistically-buttressed behaviorists" (Koch, 1999j, p. 3) ensured that his position would not win the endorsement of a majority of his psychologist colleagues.

In his paper on Bridgman, Koch (1992/1999l) identified a number of Bridgman's emphases that appear in Koch's own work, including "a persistent and instructive effort to curb the overgeneralizing tendencies of the human mind" (p. 384) and "an ardent effort to restore science to its human agency—to subvert the recently prevailing tendency in philosophy and elsewhere to analyze and represent science as if it were a disembodied rule structure" (p. 385). Worth underlining is his assertion that in Bridgman's work one finds "an ardent championship of 'integrity'" (p. 389). Koch quoted Bridgman:

> For me, integrity in the individual implies intellectual honesty, but it is more than this. It is a frame of mind. Integrity demands that I *want* to know what the facts are and that I *want* to analyze and to understand my mental tools and know what happens when I apply these tools to the facts. . . . [T]here is one thing which I may

not do and retain my integrity—if I have a new vision of something which I did not appreciate before, I may not try to put the vision back and pretend that I did not have it and refuse to admit that there may be consequences. (Bridgman, 1959, quoted in Koch, 1992/1999l, p. 389)

In a similar way, Koch had a clear-eyed view of psychology as a discipline with serious defects and deficiencies. Koch was temperamentally incapable of overlooking or minimizing the problems and difficulties that he identified; he was compelled by his own sense of intellectual integrity to report them. In his view, such honest diagnosis was an absolute prerequisite to any improvement in the state of the field.

Finally, his description of Karl Zener (Koch, 1969/1999f) provided, not surprisingly, a host of similarities with Koch himself. These include his portrayal of Zener as a keen observer of humans and their artifacts, with particular emphasis on their artistic creations. Another similarity concerns the nature of Zener's writing and his attitude toward it. Koch described that writing as "thoroughly lucid but not easy" (Koch, 1969/1999f, p. 357), a description that applies equally to Koch's writings. And in trying to explain the small size of Zener's published corpus, he said, "For him, writing was more than a torture; at some level he must have seen it as the ultimate dishonesty—rendered the more grievous by its permanence" (p. 357). Although Koch's published writings are more extensive than Zener's, they are also less extensive than one would expect, given the breadth of Koch's interests and the abundance of his abilities. This can be partially explained by the fact that his own attitude toward writing bore similarities to Zener's. In particular, the fact that volume 7 of the *Study of a Science* was never published probably can be attributed in part to this similarity, as well as to Koch's imposingly high standards.

CONCLUSION

After a brief flirtation with logical positivism and behaviorism, Koch spent most of his professional career critical of much of psychology. But he was a critic "from within"—intimately familiar with the theories he criticized and the research associated with them, as well as their philosophical underpinnings. His broad and deep knowledge of the field, his intellectual honesty and courage, and the sheer power and force of his writing combined to make his one of the most telling critiques of contemporary psychology that has been offered. In his *positive* proposals—most notably his theory of definition and his concept of value properties, as well as his exploration of the work of creative artists—he sought to help psychology reconnect with its human subject matter, in part by making it more responsive to scholarship and insights in the humanities and the arts. His scholarship will stand as a perennial challenge to the presuppositions and "business-as-usual" mentality of mainstream psychology and as an inspiration to those who would challenge those presuppositions and who share his commitment to creating a more significant psychology.

It is appropriate to end this chapter with three quotations from Koch himself. The first is from Koch's intellectual autobiography presented at the APA convention in 1977, where he described himself as an "anti-hero." It contains a characteristically harsh assessment of both psychology and of himself, in the context of a hope that others might learn from his mistakes and failings:

> I have concentrated on the story of my professional "origin point" because I think it as much an account of an archetype as it is of an interval in the life of one anti-hero. Psychology can be nothing save a malign and deceitful joke if its scholars do not bring their full human resources to the process of inquiry. Yet its atmosphere— educational, cognitive, valuational—works towards attenuation and denial of the very qualities in its inquirers which could render their inquiry worthwhile. In each fumbling pilgrimage towards dignity, there is the chance of discovering—perhaps enlarging—the dignity of the field. I know that my own anti-heroic pilgrimage has been largely a failure. Whether it has been an utter one, I mercifully cannot know. But it is possible to hope that younger and more courageous pilgrims will find the initiation-archetype I have sought to convey instructive. Time, I fear, has not invalidated the applicability of that archetype. (Koch, 1977/1999n, pp. 37–38)

But Koch's pilgrimage was assuredly *not* a failure, even by his own standards as enunciated several years before. In a discussion of the attempts to "unify" psychology—which he believed were doomed to failure—he had said,

> The one-hundred-year search for a principle of coherence (whether theoretical, paradigmatic, or, indeed, metaphysical) adequate to all psychology is, in effect, the restless search of psychologists for *morale*. In some degree, every psychologist has suspected that his career may be addressed to a discipline that does not exist: that he has embarked upon a hollow commitment which will render his effort expendable, even ludicrous, in the eyes of history. I am an old dog, but have not yet had a colleague or professional acquaintance who has not manifested such a concern during those quiet evenings, parties or bar tête-à-têtes that conduce towards honest loquacity. And some, like William James, have publicly celebrated an inner hell of such doubts in every third paragraph.

> But these anxious qualms spring from a thin nineteenth-century conception of the "disciplines"—especially those of scientific cast—from which psychologists seem somehow unable to detach themselves. If a man sees some part of human or organismic reality in a fresh and revealing way, and can communicate some part of that vision to one other person, *he* is no failure. That other person need not assimilate (or even apprehend) the vision (system, theory, paradigm) in full and literal detail, or even be able to specify precisely or localize what precisely he has learned. The criterion of significant influence need only be that the "donor's" vision enable the recipient to glimpse aspects of reality which he otherwise would not have noted.

And the taker, in turn, will build *his* vision, at least in part, upon the ladder of the donor's vision.

Perspectives *cascade*, one from the other, but unlike the cascading of water, they may rise as well as fall. Such a relation guarantees that the cumulation of knowledge—in psychology as in other forms of inquiry—will be as inevitable as the certainty that no two inquirers will bring the same sensibility to their viewing of the world.

The calling of psychologist may seem a lonelier one than that of natural scientist, but a man is not cut off from his fellows by the absence of a *lingua franca*. Indeed, the absence of a *lingua franca* may move him towards richer and more subtle modes of communication. It is perhaps true that the practice of psychology calls for greater heart and independence in its inquirers than does that of many other disciplines. By this token, the psychologist may find his morale through the belated recognition of his own courage. (Koch, 1974/1999a, pp. 113–114).

Perhaps the most balanced assessment that Koch rendered is contained in the final paragraph of his 1979 APA address, the last time he addressed *in extenso* the fundamental issues with which he had grappled throughout his career:

And so—ponderous scholar and unrelenting epistemopathectomist though I be—I find I have written a sermon. But a moral analysis of the past, by inviting a change of heart, is a surer bridge to a tolerable future than any confident methodological manifesto. I have been inviting a psychology that might show the imprint of a capacity to accept the inevitable ambiguity and mystery of our situation. The false hubris with which we have contained our existential anguish in a terrifying age has led us to prefer easy yet grandiose pseudoknowledge to the hard and spare fruit that is knowledge. To admit intellectual finitude, and to accept with courage our antinomal condition, is to go a long way toward curing our characteristic epistemopathies. To attain such an attitude is to be free. (Koch, 1979/1999g, p. 416)

REFERENCES

Attneave, F. (1959). Perception [Review of the book *Psychology: A study of a science* (Vol. 1)]. *Contemporary Psychology, 4,* 350–351.

Boring, E. G. (1959). L'encyclopédie au Koch [Review of the book *Psychology: A study of a science* (Vol. 1)]. *Contemporary Psychology, 4,* 345–346.

Bridgman, P. W. (1959). *The way things are*. Cambridge, MA: Harvard University Press.

Csikszentmihalyi, M. (1990). *Flow: The psychology of optimal experience*. New York: Harper and Row.

Kessel, F., & Bevan, W. (1995, August). Sigmund Koch as anti-hero. In F. Kessel (Chair), *On dissidence and reconstruction: Honoring Sigmund Koch*. Symposium conducted at the annual meeting of the American Psychological Association, New York City.

Koch, S. (1941a). The logical character of the motivation concept. I. *Psychological Review, 48,* 15–38.

Koch, S. (1941b). The logical character of the motivation concept. II. *Psychological Review, 48,* 127–154.

Koch, S. (1944). Hull's *Principles of behavior*: A special review. *Psychological Bulletin, 41,* 269–286.

Koch, S. (1954). *Clark L. Hull. Modern learning theory* (pp. 1–176). New York: Appleton-Century-Crofts.

Koch, S. (1956). Behavior as "intrinsically" regulated: Work notes towards a pre-theory of phenomena called "motivational." In M. R. Jones (Ed.), *Nebraska Symposium on Motivation, 1956* (Vol. 4, pp. 42–87). Lincoln: University of Nebraska Press.

Koch, S. (1959a). Appendix: Suggested discussion topics for contributors of systematic analyses. In S. Koch (Ed.), *Psychology: A study of a science* (Vol. 1, pp. 713–723).

Koch, S. (1959b). Epilogue. In S. Koch (Ed.), *Psychology: A study of a science* (Vol. 3, pp. 729–788). New York: McGraw-Hill.

Koch, S. (Ed.). (1959–1963). *Psychology: A study of a science* (Vols. 1–6). New York: McGraw-Hill.

Koch, S. (1965). The allures of ameaning in modern psychology. In R. Farson (Ed.), *Science and human affairs* (pp. 55–82). Palo Alto, CA: Science and Behavior Books.

Koch, S. (1969). Value properties: Their significance for psychology, axiology, and science. *Psychological Issues, 6,* 251–279.

Koch, S. (1971a). The image of man implicit in encounter group theory. *Journal of Humanistic Psychology, 11,* 109–127.

Koch, S. (1971b). Reflections on the state of psychology. *Social Research, 38,* 669–709.

Koch, S. (1971c). [Review of the book *Robots, men and minds*]. *Philosophy Forum, 10,* 310–320.

Koch, S. (1972). An implicit image of man. In L. N. Solomon & B. Berzon (Eds.), *New perspectives on encounter groups* (pp. 30–52). San Francisco: Jossey-Bass.

Koch, S. (1973). The image of man in encounter groups. *American Scholar, 42,* 636–652.

Koch, S. (1980). Psychology and its human clientele: Beneficiaries or victims? In R. S. Kasschau & F. S. Kessel (Eds.), *Psychology and society: In search of symbiosis* (pp. 27–60). New York: Holt, Rinehart and Winston.

Koch, S. (1992a). Foreword: Wundt's creature at age zero—and as centenarian: Some aspects of the institutionalization of the "new psychology." In S. Koch & D. E. Leary (Eds.), *A century of psychology as science* (pp. 7–35). Washington, DC: American Psychological Association. (Original work published 1985)

Koch, S. (1992b). Postscript. In S. Koch & D. E. Leary (Eds.), *A century of psychology as science* (pp. 951–968). Washington, DC: American Psychological Association.

Koch, S. (1999a). The age of the "paradigm." In S. Koch, D. Finkelman, & F. Kessel (Eds.), *Psychology in human context: Essays in dissidence and reconstruction* (pp. 91–114). Chicago: University of Chicago Press. (Original work presented 1974)

Koch, S. (1999b). The allures of ameaning in modern psychology. In S. Koch, D. Finkelman, & F. Kessel (Eds.), *Psychology in human context: Essays in dissidence and reconstruction* (pp. 233–266). Chicago: University of Chicago Press. (Original work published 1965)

Koch, S. (1999c). Ameaning in the humanities. In S. Koch, D. Finkelman, & F. Kessel (Eds.), *Psychology in human context: Essays in dissidence and reconstruction* (pp. 267–290). Chicago: University of Chicago Press. (Original work presented 1967)

Koch, S. (1999d). The concept of "value properties" in relation to motivation, perception, and the axiological disciplines. In S. Koch, D. Finkelman, & F. Kessel (Eds.), *Psychology in human context: Essays in dissidence and reconstruction* (pp. 192–230). Chicago: University of Chicago Press. (Original work published 1969)

Koch, S. (1999e). The image of man in encounter groups. In S. Koch, D. Finkelman, & F. Kessel (Eds.), *Psychology in human context: Essays in dissidence and reconstruction* (pp. 312–416). Chicago: University of Chicago Press. (Original work published 1973)

Koch, S. (1999f). Karl Edward Zener: A contrast case. In S. Koch, D. Finkelman, & F. Kessel (Eds.), *Psychology in human context: Essays in dissidence and reconstruction* (pp. 350–365). Chicago: University of Chicago Press. (Original work published 1969)

Koch, S. (1999g). The limits of psychological knowledge: Lessons of a century qua "science." In S. Koch, D. Finkelman, & F. Kessel (Eds.), *Psychology in human context: Essays in dissidence and reconstruction* (pp. 395–416). Chicago: University of Chicago Press. (Original work presented 1979)

Koch, S. (1999h). Psychology and emerging conceptions of knowledge as unitary. In S. Koch, D. Finkelman, & F. Kessel (Eds.), *Psychology in human context: Essays in dissidence and reconstruction* (pp. 51–90). Chicago: University of Chicago Press. (Original work published 1964)

Koch, S. (1999i). Psychology and its human clientele: Beneficiaries or victims? In S. Koch, D. Finkelman, & F. Kessel (Eds.), *Psychology in human context: Essays in dissidence and reconstruction* (pp. 291–311). Chicago: University of Chicago Press. (Original work published 1980)

Koch, S. (1999j). *Psychology in human context: Essays in dissidence and reconstruction* (D. Finkelman & F. Kessel, Eds.). Chicago: University of Chicago Press.

Koch, S. (1999k). Psychology versus the psychological studies. In S. Koch, D. Finkelman, & F. Kessel (Eds.), *Psychology in human context: Essays in dissidence and reconstruction* (pp. 115–143). Chicago: University of Chicago Press. (Original work published 1971)

Koch, S. (1999l). Psychology's Bridgman versus Bridgman's Bridgman: A study in cognitive pathology. In S. Koch, D. Finkelman, & F. Kessel (Eds.), *Psychology in human context: Essays in dissidence and reconstruction* (pp. 366–392). Chicago: University of Chicago Press. (Original work published 1992)

Koch, S. (1999m). A theory of definition: Implications for psychology, science, and the humanities. In S. Koch, D. Finkelman, & F. Kessel (Eds.), *Psychology in human context: Essays in dissidence and reconstruction* (pp. 147–191). Chicago: University of Chicago Press. (Original work published 1976)

Koch, S. (1999n). Vagrant confessions of an asystematic psychologist: An intellectual autobiography. In S. Koch, D. Finkelman, & F. Kessel (Eds.), *Psychology in human context: Essays in dissidence and reconstruction* (pp. 21–48). Chicago: University of Chicago Press. (Original work presented 1977)

Koch, S., & Leary, D. E. (Eds.). (1992). *A century of psychology as science.* Washington, DC: American Psychological Association. (Original work published 1985)

Leary, D. E., Kessel, F., & Bevan, W. (1998). Sigmund Koch (1917–1996). *American Psychologist, 53,* 316–317.

Maslow, A. (1968). *Toward a psychology of being.* (2nd ed.). New York: Van Nostrand.

Miller, G. A. (1969). Psychology as a means of promoting human welfare. *American Psychologist, 24,* 1063–1075.

Polanyi, M. (1958). *Personal knowledge: Towards a post-critical philosophy.* Chicago: University of Chicago Press.

Index

Numbers in italics refer to listings in reference sections.

383